CHARMED CIRCLE

This book is dedicated
to my son, Charles

CHARMED CIRCLE

*Twenty-Game–Winning Pitchers
in Baseball's 20th Century*

by MEL R. FREESE

McFarland & Company, Inc., Publishers
Jefferson, North Carolina, and London

British Library Cataloguing-in-Publication data are available

Library of Congress Cataloguing-in-Publication Data

Freese, Mel R., 1933–
    Charmed circle : twenty-game-winning pitchers in baseball's 20th
century / by Mel R. Freese.
        p.   cm.
    Includes index.
    ISBN 0-7864-0297-0 (sewn softcover : 50# alkaline paper) ∞
    1. Pitchers (Baseball)—United States—Biography.   2. Pitchers
(Baseball)—Rating of—United States.   3. Baseball—United States—
Records.   I. Title.
GV865.A1F74   1997
796.357'22'0922—dc21
[B]   97-7448
                                                                  CIP

Manufactured in the United States of America

McFarland & Company, Inc., Publishers
    Box 611, Jefferson, North Carolina 28640

Acknowledgments

Without the valuable aid of the books and authors listed below it would have been extremely difficult, if not impossible, to finish this book. Therefore to all of you a heartfelt thanks is given.

We thank David S. Neft and Richard M. Cohen for their 1995 edition of *The Sports Encyclopedia: Baseball*; *Total Baseball*, edited by John Thorn and Pete Palmer; *When the Grass Was Real*, by Donald Honig; *The Glory of Their Times*, by Lawrence S. Ritter; *Baseball America's 1996 Almanac*, distributed by Simon and Schuster; *The Image of Their Greatness*, by Lawrence S. Ritter and Donald Honig; and last but not least, *Cooperstown*, by *The Sporting News*. Once again, my sincere thanks to all those involved in the foregoing works.

I thank my wife, Martha, for her patience, indulgence and understanding during the hundreds of hours spent researching, writing and rewriting this book. Without her support I would have had great difficulty finishing this book.

Finally, I owe a great debt of thanks and appreciation to my son, Charles, who not only helped with the editing of this book, but was my inspiration, the one who supported me all the way through the difficult days of writing. I sincerely appreciate and thank him for all his efforts.

My wish now is that my final work proves worthy of those from whom I have drawn information and who have given me support.

Table of Contents

Introduction
20-Game Winners in the 20th Century

In all sports there are levels that separate the good from the great, the star from the all-star. In basketball it is averaging 20 points per game, in hockey scoring 50 goals, in football it is the 1000-yard rusher, in baseball it is the .300 hitter, and on the pitching side it is the 20-game winner.

Since 1901 there have been over 5600 pitchers to toe the rubber in the major leagues, and of this number only 372 have ever won 20 or more games in a season. Thus only 6.5 percent of all pitchers have ever achieved that elusive goal. To carry it further, 204 did it just one time, which means only 168 have ever achieved 20 wins or more in two separate campaigns, or approximately three out of every 100 pitchers.

When we review multiple 20-win seasons, we find that only 94 pitchers ever turned the trick three times or more. Of that group only 51 have ever won 20 or more in four different seasons, or less than 1 percent of all pitchers who have toiled in the 20th century.

Some pitchers who won 20 games are in the Hall of Fame, while others, such as Lou Fette and Jim Turner of Boston, each won 20 for the Boston Braves, and after that were journeyman pitchers at best. Others, like Harry Brecheen of the St. Louis Cardinals, who won 20 only once, pitched winning ball from 1943 to 1949, and never won fewer than 14 during 1944–49.

Jim Bunning won 224 games, had four seasons of 19 and three of 17, and finally was admitted to the Hall of Fame in 1996, 25 years after he retired. While most 20-game winners were good or even great pitchers, there were exceptions. Some got injured and were never the same. Bill James won 26 games as a 22-year-old in 1914 to help put Boston into the World Series. Then he injured his arm and was out of baseball within two years. There are many more I could mention, but I believe you have the idea. I have tried to detail them in this book.

Entering the 1995 season, there were four pitchers who had won 20 or more games three times: Dave Stewart (four), Roger Clemens, Tommy Glavine and Jack Morris (three each). Stewart's last 20-win season was 1991, while Morris last won 20 in 1992. It was questionable how long each could pitch effectively, and both retired in the early part of the 1995 season.

Clemens has a 20–21 record for the past two years and previously won 20 in 1990; at age 33, he could still possibly do it a couple more times. The best candidates are Glavine and Greg Maddux, as they are both 31 entering the 1997 season and would seemingly have several good seasons ahead of them. Maddux ranks as one of the top pitchers in the game, although he has only two 20-win campaigns. Both pitchers were hurt during the 1994 and 1995 campaigns by strike-shortened seasons, causing Maddux to lose a chance at two 20-plus win seasons and Glavine at least one, if not two. In 1996, Maddux finished at 15–11, 2.72 ERA and Glavine at 15–10, 2.98 ERA. With a few breaks each could have won 20. Clemens was 10–13 with a 3.63 ERA, one of the best in the league, and led the league with 257 strikeouts.

By now the reader should be getting some idea of how difficult it is to achieve 20 wins in a season, and then to do it more than once, or on a consistent basis. In the history of the game (during the 20th century), only nine pitchers have ever turned the trick seven seasons or more, which is like saying one pitcher in every 600 has accomplished that goal, or one every decade for the 20th century.

If you figure a pitcher will start 35 times and have six to eight no decisions, that means he must win 70 to 75 percent of his decisions to make the charmed circle. It becomes increasingly difficult in today's pitching environment, where the starter is rarely expected to go nine innings. There are a lot of games where he could possibly have been the winner, but that decision goes to another pitcher.

This book provides a reference, season by season, as well as by individual pitcher, for every 20-game winner during the 20th century. In each season the pitchers are listed in chronological order by wins, with a separate listing for the American and National League. I have also included the two seasons of the Federal League (1914–15), as all those records are considered part of the official major league statistics.

I have provided a brief synopsis of each season's pennant race, the World Series for that year, and outstanding or special events that occurred in some seasons. Examples of the latter are Babe Ruth's 60 home runs, Joe DiMaggio's 56-game hitting streak, Ted Williams hitting .406, and Roger Maris' 61 home runs in a season.

At the end of the publication is a listing, alphabetically, of all pitchers who have had at least one 20-game victory season, with their career won–lost record, winning percentage, ERA and number of times in the charmed circle.

There is a separate listing for all pitchers based on the number of times they achieved 20 or more wins in a season. For example, for those achieving 20 wins three or more times, the pitchers are ranked by the number of average wins per season. When there is a tie, they are ranked alphabetically. There are seven categories for number of times from one to six, plus a special category for the nine pitchers who achieved it seven or more times.

Of the 204 pitchers who achieved 20 wins one time, 100 of them made 20 on the button. One victory difference and the number would be greatly reduced. There are ten pitchers who did it twice, hitting 20 exactly each season, and one pitcher who turned the trick three times.

The reader will see how the game has changed, as in the first two decades when pitching dominated, and in the 1920s and 1930s when hitting led the way, although a number of pitchers still had outstanding seasons and careers. The 1940s and 1950s saw a blend of the two. By the 1960s, there was a trend toward the lower-scoring game. However, the 1980s and 1990s again saw a marked increase in hitting; part of this is undoubtedly traced to expansion.

For the first couple of decades or so it was commonplace for many teams, if not all, to complete 100 games or more. On several occasions, teams went with five or six pitchers. Contrast this to today's strategy where a starter goes five to seven innings, then in comes a setup man for one or two, followed by the closer. Relief pitching is critical today, whereas in the first half of this century few teams had good relievers. At that time a relief pitcher was considered on his way out or just a rookie. If a game needed to be saved, the manager called on one of his starters, often his ace.

One last point for consideration: winning 20 or more games in a season does not necessarily ensure a successful career, as there are 53 pitchers who won 20 or more in a season, but finished their careers with losing records. This means one of every seven pitchers who had at least one 20-win season finished his career with a losing record. In some cases, consistency was more important in establishing winning careers than one or two big seasons.

This reference should help settle many arguments about who won the most games in a given season, or how many times a given pitcher led the league in victories or achieved 20 or more wins in a season. Most of the time the main sources used for determining the 20-game winners agreed, but occasionally there was a difference. In those instances I used the reference most favorable to the pitching. As the reader follows the book, he or she will see a history of the game unfolding, and the changes that take place. Enjoy it in good health.

To assist the reader, an asterisk is placed by a statistic to indicate that the pitcher led in that particular category.

1901–1909

1901

THE FIRST SEASON FOR THE AMERICAN LEAGUE

Pitching staffs were completing better than 80 percent of their games, while Philadelphia led the way with 124 complete games out of 137 games started. Washington used only five pitchers, while Milwaukee (forerunner of the St. Louis Browns) used six and Detroit seven. Most teams relied on five or six pitchers to do 90 to 100 percent of the pitching. Milwaukee was not only last in the league (48–89), but also had the fewest complete games—107.

The 20-game winners were led by Cy Young, who won 33 for Boston, but his team finished second, four games behind Chicago, led by Clark Griffith's 24 wins and Roy Patterson's 20 victories. In all, six pitchers won 20 or more, and three (Young, Griffith, and Joe McGinnity) would enter the Hall of Fame.

Pitcher/Team	G	GS	CG	W	L	Pct	ERA	SO	W	IP
Cy Young, Boston	43	41	38	33*	10	.767	1.63*	158*	37	371
Joe McGinnity, Balt	48*	43*	39*	26	19	.573	3.56	75	96	382*
Clark Griffith, Chgo	35	30	26	24	7	.774*	2.66	67	50	267
Roscoe Miller, Det	38	36	35	23	13	.639	2.95	79	98	332
Chick Fraser, Phila	40	37	35	20	15	.571	3.81	110	132*	331
Roy Patterson, Chgo	41	35	30	20	16	.556	3.88	127	62	312

Ironically, while Chicago had two 20-game winners, the only stats in which their pitchers led were winning percentage and shutouts, as Griffith and Young tied with five each. The leaders in other categories were from also-rans. Remember, it is winning percentage that determines who is number one; thus Chicago led in that most critical category.

This was before the era of the relief specialists; it was typical for the starters to also perform double duty by relieving, especially in critical games. This practice would continue at least until the late 1950s, and on some teams until the early 1960s. By that time, each team would have its own relief ace.

During the season 22 pitchers had 20 or more complete games, with seven exceeding 30. Roscoe Miller started 36 games and completed 35 while posting a 23–13 mark for Detroit. Miller lasted only three more seasons and never had a winning year again, finishing with Philadelphia in the National League in 1904. His final career mark was 39–45.

Chick Fraser, pitching for Philadelphia, had a 20–15 mark as he completed 35 of his 37 starts. Fraser had been pitching since 1896 with Louisville and would remain in the majors through 1909, but would never win 20 again. Five times during his career he lost 20 or more, three times in the 20th century.

Patterson would have one more 20-win season in the majors, but after 1903 would not win over nine games in a season; 1907 would be his final year, as he closed out with a 81–73 mark.

This was Griffith's only 20-win season in the 20th century, although he had six in the 19th century and for his career won 237 games. He was a regular starter for a couple more seasons and then a spot starter and reliever through 1906. From 1909 through 1914 he appeared in eight games with a mark of 0–1. Later an owner of the Washington Senators, he is in the Hall of Fame.

Starting in 1899, McGinnity won 20 or more for eight straight years, but for our purposes we count only the period 1901–1906. The fewest seasonal innings he pitched during that stretch were the 320 in 1905.

If we were including the 19th century, Young would have the most 20-win seasons, as he did it six times in the 20th century and ten times in the nineteenth century.

Starting pitchers were expected to go nine innings. This may help explain why some careers were curtailed due to overwork. However, the likes of Walter Johnson, Grover Alexander and Young seem to refute that theory. Saves were virtually unheard of, and when a relief pitcher was needed to save a game, the manager called on the ace of his staff. A case in point is Baltimore's "Iron Man" McGinnity. He appeared in a league high 48 games, started 43 and completed a league best 39. His three saves equalled or exceeded six teams in the league. Through most of the first 50 years of this century, the leading pitcher in appearances would be a starter. Relief pitching as a separate category didn't come into prominence until the second half of this century.

While the 1901–19 era is considered the "dead-ball era" and the time of low-scoring games, during the first couple of seasons this pattern didn't hold true. It wasn't until the dust had settled in the baseball wars following the turn of the century that we saw the beginning of the low-scoring games, which lasted until after World War I. Pitching was the dominant factor in the game.

THE NATIONAL LEAGUE LOSES ITS MONOPOLY ON BASEBALL

Prior to this year, the National League was the only recognized major league. With the advent of this season they lost that monopoly, although it wouldn't be for another year or so that the courts ruled in favor of the American League. Many of the teams were hurt by the defection of players to the American League. Most severely hurt were the Eastern ball clubs.

Although the Chicago Cubs finished fifth with a 53–86 mark, they led with 131 complete games in 140 starts. Brooklyn, which came in third with a 79–57 mark, had the fewest at 111. Pitching staffs were not deep in this era. The Boston Braves used only five pitchers, while second-place Philadelphia and the Cubs each used seven. A review of all teams shows that over 90 percent of all games were pitched by five-men staffs.

Pittsburgh (with a 90–49 mark) was led to a seven-and-one-half game margin over Philadelphia by Deacon Phillippe (22 wins) and Jack Chesbro (21 wins). The Pirates' Chesbro, who also led in percentage, was tied with Al Orth of Philadelphia for the most shutouts at six. Pittsburgh also had the ERA leader (Jesse Tannehill), although he did not win 20 games.

The National League boasted nine 20-game winners. Pittsburgh and Brooklyn each had two, and only the Chicago team failed to have a 20-game winner.

Pitcher/Team	G	GS	CG	W	L	Pct	ERA	SO	W	IP
Bill Donovan, Bklyn	45*	38	36	25*	15	.625	2.77	226	152*	351
Jack Harper, St. Louis	39	37	28	23	13	.639	3.61	128	99	309
Deacon Phillippe, Pgh	37	32	30	22	12	.647	2.22	103	38	296
Noodles Hahn, Cinn	42	42*	41*	22	19	.537	2.71	239*	69	375*
Jack Chesbro, Pgh	36	28	26	21	10	.677	2.37	129	52	288
Red Donahue, Phil	35	34	34	21	13	.618	2.61	89	60	304
Al Orth, Phil	35	33	30	20	12	.625	2.27	92	32	282
Kid Nichols, Boston	38	34	33	20	15	.571	3.22	143	90	321
C. Mathewson, NY	40	38	36	20	17	.541	2.41	221	97	336
Vic Willis, Bos	38	35	33	20	17	.541	2.36	133	78	305

Donovan, who tied for the league lead in games (45) with Dummy Taylor (18–27) of New York and Jack Powell (19–19) of St. Louis, was a starting pitcher.

To illustrate how pitching dominated the league, seventh-place New York and last-place Cincinnati each had a 20-game winner. Christy Mathewson won 20 games for New York, as he had 36 complete games in 38 starts while posting a 2.41 ERA, far below the league average. Noodles Hahn won 22 for Cincinnati with a 2.71 ERA while completing 41 of 42 games. This was the first of three straight 20-win seasons for Hahn.

For Phillippe this was the first of three straight 20-plus win seasons, although he already had won 20 or more during 1899–1900. Meanwhile, this was the first of six consecutive 20-win seasons for Chesbro, four with the Yankees in the American League.

Nichols is only credited with two 20-win seasons in the 20th century, but had ten in the 19th century, when he did the majority of his pitching. Al Orth is another pitcher who split time between the two centuries, but had his two 20-plus win seasons in the 20th century. Donahue was 69–95 in the last century and 96–80 in this century, including both his 20-win seasons.

Harper had a career 80–64 record, but if we remove his two 20-win seasons he is only 34–42. Donovan twice won 25 games in his career for his only 20-plus win seasons, but also had one season of 18 and four at 17.

An example of the high percentage of complete games can be seen in the Boston pitching staff, where Kid Nichols, Vic Willis and Bill Dineen completed 97 of 103 starts. In Philadelphia we find Al Orth and Red Donahue winning 41 games between them, while completing 64 of 67 starts and posting a composite 2.45 ERA. There were 25 pitchers to have 20 or more complete games, with 13 exceeding 30 and one (Hahn) with 41.

There was no World Series this first season with two major leagues. We would not see a World Series until 1903. There are generally two reasons given: First, the National League considered the American League inferior; secondly, there was bitterness on their part toward the new league.

1902

THE AMERICAN LEAGUE BEGINS TO COME OF AGE

When the Milwaukee franchise gave up the ghost and moved to St. Louis, they took on the former name of the St. Louis Cardinals, which in the late 19th century had been called the Browns. The Browns fared quite well, as they stole several players from their city rivals (the St. Louis Cardinals) and came in second, five games behind Philadelphia. The previous season, Red Donahue had won 21 games for the Chicago Cubs, while Jack Powell and Jack Harper won 42 games total for the St. Louis Cardinals. Their presence on the St. Louis Browns accounted for 61 of the team's 76 wins.

The Philadelphia team was paced by Daffy Rube Waddell, with 24 wins, and Eddie Plank, in at 20 for his first season at that plateau. There would be many more. Waddell missed over a month of the season as he jumped the team, but still managed 26 complete games in 27 starts with a 2.08 ERA and a 24–7 mark. Once again Boston's Cy Young led the way with 32 wins, but they could only finish third. Seven pitchers won 20 games, with six of them from the first three teams.

Donahue and Powell were standouts for the Browns, as they each won 22 games while completing 69 of 73 starts. Powell also topped the loop with three saves, more than all but two clubs. Harper rounded out the St. Louis trio with 17 victories.

Bill Dinneen became the first modern pitcher to win and lose at least 20 games in the same season, as he was 21–21. This feat would be duplicated many times over the next several seasons. Dinneen deserved a better fate, as he posted a fine 2.94 ERA with 39 complete games in 42 starts. It seems Boston just couldn't score enough when he was on the mound.

Joe McGinnity would achieve 21 wins, splitting his time between Baltimore, where he was 13–10, and New York in the National League, where he was 8–8. More on that later.

Twenty-one pitchers had over 20 complete games, with seven exceeding 30, including a high of 41 by Cy Young. Some critics have questioned Young's career mark of 511 wins because he pitched part of his career in the 19th century. If one reviews his achievements during the 20th century, I believe that should put to rest any question about his ability. This year he was 32–11 with a 2.15 ERA and 41 complete games in 43 starts.

From 1901 through the finish of his career in 1911, Young posted a 225–146 mark. During this period his age ranged from 34 to 44, a time when most pitchers have long since quit the league. Young would have been a winner in any era.

Roy Patterson achieved his second consecutive and last 20-win season, as he was 20–12 for the White Sox. He would remain in the league for five more seasons, but never win over 15, three times falling below ten.

Pitcher/Team	G	GS	CG	W	L	Pct	ERA	SO	W	IP
Cy Young, Boston	45*	43*	41*	32	11	.744	2.15	160	53	385*
Rube Waddell, Phila	33	27	26	24	7	.774	2.05	210*	64	276
Red Donahue, STL	35	34	33	22	11	.667	2.76	83	65	316
Jack Powell, STL	42	38	36	22	17	.564	3.21	137	93	328
Bill Dinneen, Boston	42	42	39	21	21*	.500	2.94	136	99	371
Roy Patterson, Chgo	34	30	26	20	12	.625	3.06	61	67	268
Eddie Plank, Phila	36	32	31	20	15	.571	3.30	107	61	300

The shutout leader was Addie Joss (5) of Cleveland, but he had to settle for a 16–13 mark. We will hear more of him later.

Washington, although they led the league with 130 complete games in 138 starts, could only finish sixth on a 61–75 mark. Ironically, Philadelphia had the fewest with 114.

This would mark the last season for Baltimore until 1954, as they finished last with a 50–89 mark. The franchise would be transferred to New York. Although it would be 20 years before they would rise to power, when they did the Yankees would dominate the American League for over 40 years.

For Plank this was the first of four straight 20-win seasons in a career that spanned 17 years, during which he won 20 or more eight times.

THE NATIONAL LEAGUE CONTINUES TO FRET AND STEW

National League teams continued to suffer losses through raids by the American League. It wouldn't be until the end of the season that war would be ended, peace would reign, and the business of playing baseball would be the main concern.

Pittsburgh won for the second successive season with a 103–36 mark, placing them 27½ games ahead of runner-up Brooklyn. This is the widest margin in the history of the game.

Pittsburgh was paced by Jack Chesbro (28–6), Deacon Phillippe (20–9), and Jesse Tannehill (20–6). Although they dominated the pitching stats, their 131 complete games only tied with Brooklyn for second, as the Chicago Cubs led with 132 in 141 starts.

The league boasted six 20-game winners, and Pittsburgh had three of them. This was the second of four straight years that Chesbro exceeded 20 wins, and marked his high-water mark in victories in the National League. This was the second consecutive season for Phillippe to be at or over the 20-win mark. He actually exceeded the mark from 1899 through 1903, but only three of the years qualify for our study, as the first two were in the 19th century.

This was Tannehill's first 20-win season in the 20th century, although he would shortly add two more. From 1901 through 1905 he won 96 games. He had also won 20 or more from 1898 through 1900, with a total of 69 wins for the three seasons.

Noodles Hahn turned in another brilliant season with 35 complete games in 36 starts, as he was 23–12 with a lofty 1.77 ERA. It is a wonder that he didn't win even more with that ERA, even in this era of low-scoring games. Another standout was Jack Taylor, who was in the midst of his 186 consecutive complete games (a record that will probably stand forever). Taylor had a minuscule 1.33 ERA and a 23–11 mark with 33 complete games in 33 starts. Again, one might wonder why he didn't win 30, until one reviews the scores of the games he lost. He should have sued the Cubs for non-support.

Doc White won 16 for seventh-place Philadelphia, but lost 20 despite a 2.53 ERA and 34 complete games in 35 starts. Christy Mathewson had a sub-par 14–17 season for last-place New York, although he had 29 complete games in 32 starts with a 2.11 ERA. Joe McGinnity joined the team after midseason and was 8–8 with 16 complete games in 16 starts and a 2.06 ERA. This gave McGinnity an overall record of 21–18, as he had been 13–10 in the American League. Since he finished his season in the National League, he will be listed here as a 20-game winner. Both could have sued their team for lack of support. Shortly things would change.

The league had 24 pitchers with 20 or more complete games and nine exceeding 30, including a high of 45 by Vic Willis, as he won 27 games with a 2.20 ERA. Teammate Togie Pittinger also won 27 games and had 36 complete out of 40 starts. What a duo—with 54 wins and a composite 2.35 ERA, including 11 shutouts!

Pitcher/Team	G	GS	CG	W	L	Pct	ERA	SO	W	IP
Jack Chesbro, Pgh	35	33	31	28*	6	.824*	2.17	136	62	286
Togie Pittinger, Bos	46	40	36	27	15	.643	2.52	174	128*	389
Vic Willis, Boston	51*	46*	45*	27	19	.587	2.20	225*	101	410*
Jack Taylor, Chgo	36	33	33	23	11	.676	1.33*	53	43	325
Noodles Hahn, Cinn	36	36	35	23	12	.657	1.77	142	58	321
Joe McGinnity, NY	44	39	35	21	18	.538	2.85	106	78	352
Jesse Tannehill, Pgh	26	24	23	20	6	.769	1.95	100	25	231
Deac Phillippe, Pgh	31	30	29	20	9	.690	2.05	122	26	272

Chesbro, in addition to his league-leading 28 wins and .824 winning percentage, was the leader with eight shutouts. All other categories were led by pitchers from also-ran teams. Although Pittinger and Willis won 54 games for Boston, the rest of the team could only post a dismal 19–30 mark, and thus they finished 29 games out of first place.

For the second consecutive year, there was no World Series, as the National League still considered the American inferior.

However, in the off-season peace was made, and baseball would have no more turmoil until the Black Sox Scandal of 1919.

1903

THE AMERICAN LEAGUE TRIUMPHS

This would mark the first season of the league format that would prevail for the next 51 seasons, ending only when the St. Louis Browns moved to Baltimore for the 1954 season. New York had now replaced Baltimore and improved to a 72–62 mark for a fourth-place finish.

Cy Young led the league for the third straight year in victories, this time with 28, but was finally able to pitch his team to a first-place finish as Boston, with a 91–47 mark, won over Philadelphia by 14 games. Cleveland, which finished third, led with 125 complete games, while New York was last with 111.

Boston operated with a five-man pitching staff, while Washington tried a six-man staff but finished last with a 43–94 mark. Over 90 percent of the pitching was done by five or six men on every team.

There were eight pitchers to fashion 20 or more wins, with Boston having three and runner-up Philadelphia two. With his 28 wins, Young completed a three-year record of 93–28. Teammate Tom Hughes had his only 20-win season and career best mark at 20–7. The rest of his career he was just 111–168. Bill Dinneen was the third member of the trio to win 20 games, with a 21–11 mark for his second of three consecutive 20-plus win seasons.

Eddie Plank, with 23 wins, and Rube Waddell, with 22, paced the Philadelphia club. The two also had 67 complete games in 78 starts and a composite 2.41 ERA. Cleveland's Earl Moore completed every one of his 26 starts as he fashioned a 20–8 mark with a 1.77 ERA, an excellent number even for this low-scoring era.

Jack Chesbro, in his maiden American League season, won 21 games for the New York Highlanders (soon to be called the Yankees), as he joined the charmed circle for the third straight year and was only one season away from his all-time career mark for victories. Willie Sudhoff turned in his best season for the St. Louis Browns with 21 wins and a 2.27 ERA. For the rest of his career, he was only 82–120.

While no other pitcher won 20, a couple do deserve honorable mention. George Mullin had 19 wins for Detroit and also tied for the lead in saves with three. His 2.24 ERA shows he could have won a few more with a break here or there. He also had 31 complete games in 36 starts. Chicago's Doc White was only 17-15, but had a 2.13 ERA, while playing for a team with only a .247 batting average.

There were 23 pitchers with 20 or more complete games, and 12 exceeded the 30 mark.

This is simply further evidence of the heavy reliance of all managers on their starting pitchers. The creed of the era was simple: "Finish what you start."

Pitcher/Team	G	GS	CG	W	L	Pct	ERA	SO	W	IP
Cy Young, Boston	40	35	34	28*	9	.757*	2.08	176	37	342*
Eddie Plank, Phila	43*	40*	33	23	16	.590	2.38	176	65	336
Rube Waddell, Phila	39	38	34*	22	16	.579	2.44	302*	85	324
Bill Dinneen, Boston	37	35	32	21	11	.656	2.23	148	66	299
Jack Chesbro, NY	40	36	33	21	15	.583	2.77	147	74	325
Willie Sudhoff, STL	38	35	30	21	16	.569	2.27	104	56	294
Long Tom Hughes, B	33	31	25	20	7	.741	2.57	112	60	245
Earl Moore, Cleve	28	26	26	20	8	.714	1.77*	142	56	239

Waddell struck out 302 batters to set a new major league record. The next season he would better this mark, and it would remain unchallenged until 1946 and unbroken until the early 1960s. The shutout leader was Cy Young.

Two tragedies occurred. The first was in January when Detroit pitcher Win Mercer committed suicide by gas inhalation. The second remains a mystery today. Ed Delahanty (who is in the Hall of Fame with the fourth-highest lifetime average of .346) left his team in Detroit and returned East. Somewhere around Buffalo he got off the train. His body was found at the bottom of Niagara Falls two days later. He either fell in a drunken stupor, or was pushed or thrown off, or committed suicide. To this day the truth is not known.

THE NATIONAL LEAGUE IS EMBARRASSED

Peace had finally come to the National League, but at a price. Many of its stars had defected to the American League, and under the court ruling were allowed to remain there. Thus, the new league was soon able to compete on an even keel.

Pittsburgh won again, but this time its margin of victory was only 6½ games, as New York and Chicago (eight back) gave a spirited chase. New York had two 30-game winners: Joe McGinnity with 31 and Christy Mathewson with 30. Unfortunately, the rest of the staff was only 23–22. Altogether, nine pitchers won 20 or more games.

Sam Leever led in ERA (2.08), shutouts (7), winning percentage (.781) and he had a career high 25 wins as he combined with Deacon Phillippe (24–9) to pace the Pittsburgh team. Leever was a stalwart of the Pirate staff from 1899–

1908, averaging 18 wins per season. Phillippe completed his fifth straight 20-win season (his third this century), and averaged over 18 wins from 1899–1907. The two formed a dynamic duo for the Pittsburgh club. They also had 61 complete games in 67 starts and a composite 2.25 ERA.

However, the real pitching story had to be in New York, as McGinnity and Mathewson combined for 61 wins, 81 complete games in 90 starts and a composite 2.35 ERA. McGinnity also appeared ten times in relief and had the distinction of exceeding 30 wins, while also losing 20 games.

Chicago had a trio of 20-game winners with Jack Taylor (21), Jake Weimer (20) and Bob Wicker (20). This would be Wicker's high-water mark; he was 17–9 and 13–6 the next two years, faded fast, and was out of baseball by 1907. Weimer was a 30-year-old rookie who would win 58 games the next three seasons, then fade and be through by 1909. For Taylor this was the middle year of three consecutive 20-plus win seasons. His career was somewhat checkered; he was a consistent loser until he broke the barrier with 23 wins in 1902. He would pitch until 1907, twice more exceeding 20 wins.

Noodles Hahn again found his way into the charmed circle, this time with a 22–12 mark, but it would be his last big season. He would be finished by 1907. The other 20-game winner is Henry Schmidt, who was a 30-year-old rookie and went 22–13 in what would be his only big league season.

For the season, 24 pitchers had 20 or more complete games, with nine having 30 or more, McGinnity's 44 being tops. In a reversal of form, Togie Pittinger and Vic Willis went from a combined 54–34 to 30–39, with the former leading the loop with 22 losses.

Pitcher/Team	G	GS	CG	W	L	Pct	ERA	SO	W	IP
Joe McGinnity, NY	55*	48*	44*	31*	20	.608	2.43	171	109	434*
C. Mathewson, NY	45	42	37	30	13	.698	2.26	267*	100	366
Sam Leveer, Pgh	36	34	30	25	7	.781	2.06	90	60	284
Deac Phillippe, Pgh	36	33	31	24	9	.727	2.43	123	29	289
Noodles Hahn, Cinn	34	34	34	22	12	.647	2.52	127	17	296
Henry Schmidt, Bkyn	40	36	29	22	13	.629	3.83	96	120	301
Jack Taylor, Chgo	37	33	33	21	14	.600	2.45	83	57	312
Jake Weimer, Chgo	35	33	27	20	8	.714	2.30	128	104	282
Bob Wicker, Chgo	33	27	24	20	9	.690	3.02	110	74	247

In addition to leading in winning percentage and ERA, Leveer also led in shutouts. All other categories were led by McGinnity. Cincinnati and Philadelphia led with 126 complete games, while last-place St. Louis had the fewest—111.

In the first year of the World Series, the National League was embarrassed, as powerhouse Pittsburgh was defeated by Boston five games to three. Any doubt that the American League was a major league was now removed.

1904

THE AMERICAN LEAGUE AND NEW YORK ALMOST MAKE IT

Jack Chesbro pitched his heart out for New York by winning a 20th-century record 41 games, but unfortunately in the next-to-last game of the season, he uncorked a wild pitch in a 3–2 defeat to Boston that gave the Red Sox the pennant. This is the closest New York would come until the 1920s. Chesbro had a season that seems out of the pages of a Hollywood script, as he led in wins (41), winning percentage (.774), games (55), games started (51), complete games (48) and innings pitched (455). The victory, games started and complete games are still modern-day records. Despite his 41–12 mark and Jack Powell's 23–19, New York fell 1½ games short, as the rest of the staff was only 28–28.

Once again Cy Young paced Boston, this time with 26 wins (including a perfect no-hit game), as their five-man pitching staff set a modern record of 148 complete games in 157 games. Bill Dinneen with 23 wins and Jesse Tannehill with 21 gave the big three 70 victories. This was Dinneen's third straight 20-win season, but his last big season. Although he pitched five more seasons, he would only have one more winning year. Meanwhile, this would be the first of two consecutive 20-plus-win seasons for Tannehill in a Red Sox uniform. The trio completed 107 of 109 starts.

Ten pitchers posted 20 or more wins this season. Nick Altrock and Frank Owen each won 21 for Chicago, the first of three consecutive 20-win seasons for both pitchers. Bill Bernhard had the winningest season of his career with 21 wins for Cleveland. Teammate Red Donahue chipped in with 19. Donahue would pitch two more years with a combined 19–26 mark to finish his career at 165–175.

Donahue's career can be looked at in three phases. From 1895 to 1898 he was 33–77. From 1899 to 1904 he was 113–72. He finished his last two seasons at 19–26.

Eddie Plank and Rube Waddell were like twins for the Philadelphia Athletics, as they each were 26–17. Plank had 37 complete games in 43 starts and a 2.14 ERA, while Waddell had 39 complete games in 46 starts and a 1.62 ERA. Plank, despite winning over 20 on eight occasions for a career 326 wins, never led the league in wins. Someone was always having a better year.

The top award for pitching frustration would have to go a trio of pitchers for Detroit. The three all had excellent ERAs, but were victims of little offensive support. Wild Bill Donovan had the only winning record at 17–16, despite his 2.46 ERA. The other two didn't fare as well. George Mullin had a 2.40 ERA with 42 complete games in 44 starts, but was only 16–24. Ed Killian had a 2.44 ERA and 32 complete games in 34 starts but was just 15–20.

It was a year marked by real iron-man performances. Twenty-seven pitchers exceeded 20 complete games, 20 of them went over the 30 mark, and three exceeded 40.

Pitcher/Team	G	GS	CG	W	L	Pct	ERA	SO	W	IP
Jack Chesbro, NY	55*	51*	48*	41*	12	.774*	1.82	239	88	455*
Cy Young, Boston	43	41	40	26	16	.619	1.97	200	29	380
Eddie Plank, Phila	43	43	37	26	17	.605	2.14	201	86	357
Rube Waddell, Phila	46	46	39	26	17	.605	1.62	349	91	383
Bill Dinneen, Boston	37	37	37	23	14	.622	2.20	153	63	336
Jack Powell, NY	47	45	38	23	19	.548	2.44	202	92	390
Jesse Tannehill, Bos	33	31	30	21	11	.656	2.04	116	33	282
Nick Altrock, Chgo	38	36	31	21	13	.618	2.96	87	48	307
Bill Bernhard, Cleve	38	37	25	21	13	.618	2.13	137	55	321
Frank Owen, Chgo	37	36	34	21	15	.583	1.94	103	61	315

The three categories which Chesbro didn't lead were won by Young, who had 10 shutouts; Addie Joss, with a 1.59 ERA; and Waddell, who broke his own strikeout record with 349. No one would come close to Waddell's mark until Bob Feller's 348 in 1946. At that time there would be a dispute about Waddell's record. Finally, 61 years later Sandy Koufax would break the record with 382, and in 1973 Nolan Ryan would best that with 383.

NATIONAL LEAGUE PACED BY
MCGRAW, MATHEWSON AND MCGINNITY

The title says it all as John McGraw cajoled, insulted, berated and taunted his players to a 13-game pennant win over the Chicago Cubs. Of course, Joe McGinnity's 35–8 and Christy Mathewson's 33–12 marks didn't hurt either.

Eight pitchers notched 20 wins or more, including Patsy Flaherty of Pittsburgh, who was 19–9 with them after a 1–2 log with the White Sox. Deacon Phillippe of Pittsburgh was only 10–10 after three straight 20-win seasons.

If there had been an MVP award, McGinnity would have won it this year, as he led with 35 wins, six saves (more than six other teams), a .814 winning percentage, 51 games, nine shutouts, 408 innings pitched and a brilliant 1.61 ERA. Teammate Christy Mathewson was no slouch, with his 33 wins and 2.03 ERA. They also combined for 71 complete games.

Jake Weimer got his second consecutive 20-win season for Chicago, and with a little more batting support could have had a higher win total, since his ERA was 1.91. After a two-year absence where he was only 23–20, Jack Harper returned to the charmed circle with a 23–8 mark and 2.37 ERA for Cincinnati. However, their long-time pitching ace, Noodles Hahn, slipped to 16–18 and in two years would be out of baseball.

St. Louis had two 21-game winners in Jack Taylor and Kid Nichols. Taylor was in the midst of his 186 consecutive complete games, but could have fared better with more batting support. Despite a 2.22 ERA, he lost 19 times.

Frustration seemed to be the way of the day for several pitchers. Brooklyn's Oscar Jones lost a league high 25 games despite a 2.75 ERA, while teammate Jack Cronin lost 23 even though he had a 2.70 ERA. Boston's Vic Willis tied for the league loss lead with 25, although he sported a 2.85 ERA and 39 complete games. Teammate Togie Pittinger posted a 2.66 ERA and 35 complete games, but still lost 21, giving him 43 for two years. Kaiser Wilhelm also lost 21 for Boston. Philadelphia's Chick Fraser completed the 20-loss club (which numbered six for the season) with a 14–24 mark.

For the year, 27 pitchers had 20 or more complete games, with 12 of them breaking the 30 barrier. Chicago and Cincinnati each had five pitchers with 20 or more complete games, while St. Louis had four.

The St. Louis Cardinals set the National League complete game record with 146 in 157 games, but could only manage a fourth-place finish. McGraw's New York Giants, despite being the pennant winner, had the league "low" of 127 complete games. Meanwhile, the Chicago Cubs, Cincinnati Reds and Boston Braves each primarily used five or six pitchers.

Pitcher/Team	G	GS	CG	W	L	Pct	ERA	SO	W	IP
Joe McGinnity, NY	51*	44	38	35*	8	.814*	1.61*	144	86	408*
C. Mathewson, NY	48	46*	33	33	12	.733	2.03	212*	78	368
Jack Harper, Cinn	35	35	31	23	8	.742	2.37	125	85	285
Kid Nichols, STL	36	35	35	21	13	.618	2.02	134	50	317
Dummy Taylor, NY	37	36	29	21	15	.583	2.34	138	75	296
Jack Taylor, STL	41	39	39*	21	19	.525	2.22	103	82	352
Patsy Flaherty, Pgh	34	33	32	20	13	.606	2.05	68	69	285
Jake Weimer, Chgo	37	37	31	20	14	.588	1.91	177	97	307

McGinnity took the shutout title with nine, and although saves were not an official category, he led the league with six. Every individual pitching honor went to the Giants with the exception of complete games, as Taylor (St. Louis) copped that with 39, in the midst of his 186 consecutive complete games.

This is the last season there would be no World Series until the strike ending the 1994 season. McGraw was still angered at Ban Johnson, president of the American League, dating back to their troubles in 1902. President John T. Brush (New York Giants) supported McGraw, but then proposed that in the future there be a compulsory series between the winners of each league. Both leagues agreed, and until today the rules governing playing and financial matters of the series date from what is known as the "Brush Rules."

—————— 1905 ——————

AMERICAN LEAGUE: THE ELEPHANTS ARE TAMED BY THE GIANTS

Ten pitchers again won 20 or more, paced by Rube Waddell with 26, who was one of three hurlers to turn the trick for Connie Mack's A's and guide them to a pennant by a two-game margin over the White Sox. Cleveland led the league with 139 complete games, and for the first time a team fell below the 100 mark, as the New York Club "only" had 88. Times have certainly changed!

This was Ty Cobb's rookie year, and while he batted only .240, he would never again hit less than .324 (which would be his mark in his last season—1928). Cy Young posted the worst mark of his career to date, as he was only 18–19.

Waddell won 26 games despite a shoulder injury that sidelined him for over a month of the season, which undoubtedly cost him a chance for 30 or more wins. The other question is, with a 1.48 ERA, how did he lose 11 times? It was evidently lack of support. Eddie Plank had another great season with 25–12, 2.26 ERA and 35 complete games, but finished second to teammate Waddell. Andy Coakley rounded out the Philadelphia trio with a 20–7 mark, his only 20-win season. In fact, he was only 38–53 for the balance of his career.

Frank Owen and Nick Altrock won 22 and 21 respectively, to make it two years in a row for the duo to reach the coveted plateau. Frank Smith, with 19, and Doc White with 18 could have also reached the magic mark, given a little more run support, as they had ERAs of 2.13 and 1.77 respectively.

Detroit got hitting support and this time supported their trio of pitchers. Ed Killian and George Mullin each benefited by winning 22 games apiece. Wild Bill Donovan was able to garner 18. This was the first of two times Killian would reach the 20-win plateau, while Mullin would make it five times and be close several others.

Jesse Tannehill won 22 games for Boston to complete a five-year run of 96 wins. The last three seasons of the 19th century he had won 69, giving him a total of 165 for the eight years, or almost 21 wins a season. He would slip to 13 wins next season and then hang on as a part-timer through 1911. Young's season was an enigma as he was only 18–19, but had a super 1.61 ERA and 32 complete games in 34 starts. No doubt a lack of batting support cost him a victory total in the mid-20s.

Addie Joss and Jack Chesbro rounded out the 20-win corps by each winning that number exactly for their teams. For Chesbro it was quite a comedown from his 41 victories the prior year. For Joss it was the first of four consecutive 20-win seasons in a career that would be prematurely ended by his untimely death at age 31 in 1911. In eight full seasons he won 155 games. Certainly a much higher total would have been achieved had Joss not died and been able to pitch into his late 30s or even early 40s, as did many other pitchers of the time.

Every season has tough-luck or heartbreak pitchers, and this year was no exception. We have already pointed out a few, even though they had winning seasons, with the exception of Young. But there had to be real frustration on the St. Louis staff, as the team finished last and lost 99 games. Henry Howell had 36 complete games in 37 starts, a 1.98 ERA, but was only 14–21. Willie Sudhoff had 23 complete games, 2.99 ERA and only a 10–20 record. The last of the frustrated trio was Fred Glade with a 2.81 ERA, 28 complete games, but a dismal 7–24 mark.

There were 26 pitchers with over 20 complete games and eight over the 30 mark. Five teams had four pitchers each to have 20 or more complete games.

Pitcher/Team	G	GS	CG	W	L	Pct	ERA	SO	W	IP
Rube Waddell, Phila	46*	34	27	26*	11	.703	1.48*	287*	90	329
Eddie Plank, Phila	41	41*	35*	25	12	.676	2.26	210	75	347
Jesse Tannehill, Bos	36	31	27	22	10	.688	2.48	113	59	272
Frank Owen, Chgo	42	38	32	22	14	.611	2.10	125	56	334
Ed Killian, Detroit	39	37	33	22	15	.595	2.27	110	102	313
George Mullin, Det	44	41*	35*	22	18	.550	2.51	168	138*	348*
Nick Altrock, Chgo	38	34	31	21	11	.656	1.88	97	63	316
Andy Coakley, Phila	35	31	21	20	7	.741*	1.84	145	73	255
Addie Joss, Cleve	33	32	31	20	11	.645	2.01	132	46	286
Jack Chesbro, NY	41	38	24	20	15	.571	2.20	156	71	303

Philadelphia pitchers led or tied in every category except shutouts, which was won with eight by Killian, and innings pitched, which was captured by Detroit's Mullin. He also tied Plank for games started and completed, besides leading in issuing bases on balls.

Chicago used six pitchers while Philadelphia relied on five, with a sixth pitcher appearing in six games and a seventh in one game.

NATIONAL LEAGUE: REVENGE FOR 1903

Once again it was John McGraw, Christy Mathewson and Joe McGinnity leading the New York Giants to the pennant, this time assisted by Red Ames, who won 22 games. However, pitching laurels went to Mathewson with his 32–8, 1.27 mark. To say that Mathewson's season was outstanding would simply be an understatement. The 32 wins are remarkable, as are the eight shutouts and 206 strikeouts (especially for this time), but what is the most astounding is the 1.27 ERA. When you look at that you have to wonder how he lost eight games—much like you question Bob Gibson's nine losses over 60 years later when he posted a 1.12 ERA. It becomes even more amazing when you realize the Giants averaged five runs a game, especially high for that time, when most teams would score only three or four per game.

Almost lost in the shadow of Mathewson are the other members of that Giant staff. McGinnity won 22 games with a 2.87 ERA and a league high 46 appearances. Red Ames had his finest season with a 22–8, 2.74 log. Ames pitched through 1919 but never again approached these heights, as his biggest victory total was 15, a number he achieved three times.

There were eight 20-game winners, with only the Giants and Pittsburgh Pirates having more than one. Deacon Phillippe won 22 games and Sam Leever 20 for the Pirates. For Phillippe it marked his last 20-plus-win season, while Leever would crack the circle the following year.

Togie Pittinger bounced back from successive 20-loss seasons to win 23 games for Philadelphia. En route he would rack up 29 complete games, tie for league appearances at 46, and log 337 innings. Bob Ewing checked in with his only 20-win season for Cincinnati.

Boston and Brooklyn battled all year for the champion of futility, and Brooklyn edged out Boston 104 losses to 103. Harry McIntire was 8–25 and Mel Eason 5–21 for the hapless Dodgers.

Meanwhile Boston set a record for futility as they had four pitchers who lost 21 or more. Irv Young won 20 but lost 21, despite a 2.90 ERA and a league high 41 complete games in 42 starts. This was his only 20-win season, as he had a career mark of 63–95. Chick Fraser was 14–21 with a 3.21 ERA, while Vic Willis set the modern-day loss mark with 29 as he won 11 while posting a respectable 3.21 ERA. The fourth member of the quartet was Kaiser Wilhelm, who was 4–23 with a 4.34 ERA. This gave him a two-year mark of 18–43. He would follow this with another 20-plus-loss season, making him one of two pitchers in modern-day baseball to lose 20 or more in three straight seasons.

Boston captured the complete game title with 139, while the second-place Pirates were last with 113. Strangely, the Giants were next to last with 117. There were 25 pitchers to exceed 20 complete games, with 11 going over the 30 mark. Ironically, Boston and Brooklyn were the only two teams to have four pitchers to complete 20 or more games each. Boston had three to exceed 35, but still lost 103 games.

Pitcher/Team	G	GS	CG	W	L	Pct	ERA	SO	W	IP
C Mathewson, NY	43	37	32	32*	8	.800*	1.27*	206*	64	339
Togie Pittinger, Phil	46*	37	29	23	15	.605	3.10	136	104	337
Red Ames, NY	34	31	21	22	8	.733	2.74	198	105	263
Deac Phillippe, Pgh	38	33	25	22	13	.629	2.19	133	48	279
Joe McGinnity, NY	46*	38	26	22	16	.579	2.87	125	71	320
Bob Ewing, Cinn	40	34	30	20	11	.645	2.51	164	79	312
Sam Leever, Pgh	33	29	20	20	5	.800*	2.70	230	54	81
Irv Young, Boston	43	42*	41*	20	21	.488	2.90	156	71	378*

The World Series lasted five games, with the Giants taking the title. All five games were decided by shutouts, with Mathewson pitching three complete-game shutout victories. McGinnity tossed the other for the Giants, and he also was the victim of a shutout by Chief Bender. Mathewson had also led the National League in shutouts with eight.

1906

THE AMERICAN LEAGUE GETS EVEN

Although the Chicago White Sox hurlers garnered few individual honors, collectively they were good enough to edge out the New York and Cleveland teams in a close three-team dogfight. The A's stumbled, partly because Eddie Plank was limited to 26 games, although he did post a 19–5 mark. However, Rube Waddell slipped to 16–16, while Andy Coakley was ill and came in at 7–8.

Cleveland and St. Louis tied for team honors with 133 complete games, while New York was last with 99. Eight pitchers posted 20 or more wins; New York's Al Orth led the way with 27. Frank Owen and Nick Altrock each posted 20 wins for the third consecutive season for Chicago, but it would be the last winning season for each pitcher. Altrock would pitch spasmodically for another 15 years, but after 1908 he would be primarily a pitching coach for the Washington Senators. His record for the balance of his career was only 15–31. Meanwhile, Owen came up with injuries and only appeared in 39 games over the next three seasons as he fashioned a 9–11 mark and retired in 1909.

Orth had his second 20-win season and the biggest year of his career with 27 wins and a league-leading 36 complete games. This was also Orth's last winning year as he went 16–34 for the next two years, and then was out of baseball by 1909. Teammate Jack Chesbro had his last big season with 24 wins, as he also led in appearances (49) and games started (42). Evidently the many innings he pitched took their toll as Chesbro was 20–30 for the next two seasons, and then finished at 0–5 in 20 games in 1909. Many baseball historians have held that the repeated pitching of 300 innings or greater per season eventually takes its toll on a pitcher's arm. The accuracy of this may be hard to determine, except to cite a number of pitchers during the 19th and 20th centuries to whom this analysis might apply.

Cleveland had a trio of 20-game winners in Bob Rhoades (22), Addie Joss (21), and Otto Hess (20). Although this was Rhoades' only 20-plus-win season, there were three other years where he won between 15 and 18 games. This was the second of four consecutive 20-win seasons for Joss. Hess had an erratic career, as in ten seasons he exceeded .500 only twice and was in double-digit wins three times.

Waddell's 16–16 seasons can be blamed more on weak hitting (the A's were fifth in runs scored) than on inept pitching, as he fashioned a 2.21 ERA, excellent even in this era of low ERAs. Casey Patten had a modicum of success for Washington with a 19–16 mark and a 2.16 ERA, playing for the second-weakest hitting team in the league. The previous three seasons, Patten lost 67 games while winning 39.

George Mullin won 21 games for Detroit, his second consecutive season at that level. Altogether, Mullin would win 20 or more on five occasions. From 1903 through 1911, the fewest number of victories he would have in any season was 17. Jess Tannehill fell to 13–11 in his last winning season, as Boston fell to last place. Tannehill had averaged almost 21 wins per season over the eight previous years. At age 39, Cy Young posted the worst season of his career with a 13–21 log and a 3.19 ERA. The end was near for the great right-hander.

The honor for king of futility had to go to Boston's Joe Harris, as he fashioned a 2–21 mark and 3.52 ERA with 20 complete games in 24 starts. There were 26 pitchers with over 20 complete games, while six exceeded 30. Four teams had four pitchers to post 20 or more complete games.

Pitcher/Team	G	GS	CG	W	L	Pct	ERA	SO	W	IP
Al Orth, NY	45	39	36*	27*	17	.614	2.34	133	66	339*
Jack Chesbro, NY	49*	42*	24	24	16	.600	2.96	152	75	325
Bob Rhoades, Cleve	38	34	31	22	10	.688	1.80	89	92	315
Frank Owen, Chgo	42	36	27	22	13	.629	2.33	66	54	293
Addie Joss, Cleve	34	31	28	21	9	.700	1.72	106	43	282
George Mullin, Det	40	40	35	21	18	.538	2.78	123	108*	330
Nick Altrock, Chgo	38	30	25	20	13	.606	2.06	99	42	288
Otto Hess, Cleve	43	36	33	20	17	.541	1.83	167	85	334

Strikeout honors again went to Waddell (287), while the ERA crown was won by Doc White (Chicago) with 1.52. Teammate Ed Walsh led in shutouts with 10. Cleveland, Chicago and St. Louis each relied primarily on six pitchers.

NATIONAL LEAGUE: UPSET OF THE CENTURY

The Chicago Cubs set the modern major league record of team victories with 116, while suffering only 36 losses for a .763 winning percentage. They finished 20 games ahead of the New York Giants as they posted a team ERA of 1.76.

The Cubs were led by Mordecai "Three-finger" Brown (26–6) and Jack Pfiester (20–8). They had several other pitchers with fine records, but no other 20-game winners, although Ed Reulbach finished at 19–4. Brown had lost the top two joints of his index finger and the little finger on his right hand was paralyzed at age seven when he accidentally stuck it in his uncle's corn-shredding machine. The accident gave him a natural knuckleball and probably helped put him in the Hall of Fame.

Brown's 26 wins marked the first of six consecutive seasons in which he would win 20 or more games. During the period 1904–10 his highest ERA was 1.86, quite an enviable record. Although a good pitcher, Pfiester was not in Brown's class—but few were. This was Pfiester's only 20-win season. While Reulbach only exceeded 20 wins one time during his career with Chicago, he was consistently a winner, finishing well above .500 every season from 1905 to 1912, while leading the league in winning percentage three straight years (1906–08).

The league boasted seven 20-game winners, the Giants' Joe McGinnity leading the way with 27. This marked the eighth straight year McGinnity had won 20 or more games dating back to 1898, and it would be his last at that level. McGinnity would pitch two more seasons before retiring after the 1908 campaign. Mathewson did what would become for him an annual event—winning 20 or more games—as he logged a 22–12 mark. For 12 consecutive seasons (a National League record), Mathewson would win 20 or more games. Dependability became his trademark.

After several years of frustration, including 54 losses for the last two seasons, Vic Willis escaped from Boston, landed with the Pirates, and won 22 games for the first of four straight 20-plus-win years. He would eventually win

247 games, but it would take until 1995 to elect him to the Hall of Fame. Team-mate Sam Leever had his last 20-plus-win year with 22 wins, although he continued to pitch winning ball for the remainder of his career, which ended with the 1910 season.

Jake Weimer won 20 or more for the third time in four years, but after two more seasons he would be out of baseball. This proved to be his last big year, as he was 19–21 over the next two years.

Ironically, there were six pitchers to lose 20 games, four on the Boston Staff, who had a composite 49–95. This marked the second consecutive season Boston had four pitchers to lose 20 or more. No other team in the history of the game ever duplicated this inglorious feat. They were Irv Young (16–25), Big Jeff Pfeffer (13–22), Vive Lindeman (12–23) and Gus Dorner (8–26). Dorner's mark included a 0–1 stint with Cincinnati.

Twenty-two pitchers had 20 or more complete games with seven exceeding 30, of which four were on Boston's staff. Boston did have some consolation as they led with 137 complete games. Perhaps they should have gone to their bullpen a little more often. The Giants were last with 105.

Pitcher/Team	G	GS	CG	W	L	Pct	ERA	SO	W	IP
Joe McGinnity, NY	45*	37	32	27*	12	.692	2.25	105	71	340
M Brown, Chgo	36	32	27	26	6	.813*	1.04*	144	61	277
Sam Leever, Pgh	36	31	25	22	7	.759	2.32	76	48	260
C Mathewson, NY	38	35	22	22	12	.647	2.97	128	77	267
Vic Willis, Pgh	41	36	32	22	13	.629	1.73	124	76	322
Jake Weimer, Cinn	41	39	31	20	14	.588	2.21	141	99	305
Jack Pfiester, Chgo	31	29	20	20	8	.714	1.56	153	63	242
Jack Taylor, Chgo	34	33	32	20	12	.625	2.00	61	86	302

Several individual honors went to a pitcher who lost 25 games: Irv Young of the Boston Braves (he also won 16). He led with games started (41), complete games (37) and innings pitched (358). Brown captured the shutout title with nine. Jack Taylor's streak of 186 consecutive complete games was broken on August 19th when he was relieved. This is a record that will undoubtedly stand forever, especially with today's pitching philosophy.

The Cubs were heavy favorites in the World Series, but were stunned by the normally light hitting White Sox, who had only two regulars that batted over .260 for the season. Walsh led the way with a 2–0 mark for the White Sox, who upended the Cubs in six games. Brown lost two of three decisions and Pfiester also lost twice. It would be a long winter for Cub fans.

——————— 1907 ———————

AMERICAN LEAGUE: A QUARTET OF TEAMS

Four teams battled through most of the season for the pennant, and at the end only eight games separated first-place Detroit from fourth-place Cleveland.

Each team posted strong pitching, with the Tigers having three 20-game winners and a fourth at 19. Philadelphia checked in with two while the White Sox had three. Although Cleveland had only one, they boasted a strong staff headed by Addie Joss' league-leading 27 wins. After two consecutive losing years, Cy Young bounced back with 22 wins.

Wild Bill Donovan had a career best year with a 25–4 log, 2.17 ERA, 27 complete games in 28 starts and a league-high .862 winning percentage to pace the Detroit team. From 1901 through 1910, Donovan won 25 twice, 18 twice, and 17 four times. He experienced only one losing season, going 9–15 in 1906. For his career he won 186 games with a .572 winning percentage, but is not in the Hall of Fame. Perhaps his case should be reviewed.

Teammate Ed Killian also won 25 games, as he reached the charmed circle for the second time in his career. While his career was not the caliber of Donovan's, he did have a winning record for his lifetime at 102–78, a .567 winning percentage. George Mullin was the third member of the team to win 20 games, but unfortunately he also lost 20. This marked the second time in the last three seasons he had both won and lost 20 or more in the same year.

Eddie Plank had another big season winning 24, but again was the bridesmaid as other pitchers had higher win totals. This would be his fate throughout his career. Some pitchers have one big season in their career and never come close again. Such was the situation with Jimmy Dygert as he was 21–8 for Philadelphia this season. His next highest total was 11, achieved the years before and after this season, but he lost 13 and 15 respectively each year.

Chicago also had a trio of 20-game winners, headed by Doc White (27–13) who tied Joss for the lead in wins. From 1901 through 1911, White won at least 10 games each year and amassed 179 wins, but this would be his only 20-win season. However, he certainly made it a big one. Teammate Ed Walsh won 24 games and led in appearances, games started, complete games, innings pitched and ERA. His may well be a situation of overuse, as five times he pitched 369 innings or more, twice exceeding 400. Walsh had several great years ahead of him, but by age 31 in 1912 he was flamed out and would be a hanger-on for a few years after that.

The third member of the trio was Frank Smith, who won 23 games for his first season at that level. Smith would slip to 16 wins next year, but bounce back to win 25 in 1909. After that he was just a journeyman pitcher and finished out his career with Baltimore and Brooklyn of the Federal League in 1915.

Joss continued flashing the brilliance that eventually put him in the Hall of Fame, as he had a 27–11 mark with a 1.83 ERA. Young, toiling for a seventh-place Boston team, won 22 games at age 40 with a 1.99 ERA. Many of his 15 losses can be attributed to the weak hitting of his teammates, who sported the lowest average in the league and the fewest runs scored.

Barney Pelty of the St. Louis Browns posted a fine 2.67 ERA, and 29 complete games in 31 starts, but was only 12–21, due mainly to lack of batting support. Washington unveiled a rookie by the name of Walter Johnson, who appeared in 14 games, starting 12 and completing 11. Johnson sported a 1.86 ERA, but was only 5–9. This was to be his bane throughout his career. Although he won 417 games (second only to Cy Young's 511), he undoubtedly could have won many more with a better team behind him. For his career, the Senators played less than .500 ball, although he pitched at almost .600.

St. Louis, although sixth in the standings, led in complete games. New York was last for the third straight year with a mark below 100 at 93. Although the number of pitchers with 20 or more complete games would remain high for many years to come, slowly the total was falling. This year 21 pitchers exceeded that mark, with five in the 30-or-above range.

Pitcher/Team	G	GS	CG	W	L	PCT	ERA	SO	W	IP
Addie Joss, Cleve	42	38	34	27*	11	.711	1.83	127	54	339
Doc White, Chgo	46	35	24	27	13	.675	2.26	141	38	291
Bill Donovan, Det	32	28	27	25	4	.862*	2.19	123	82	271
Ed Killian, Det	41	34	29	25	13	.658	1.78	96	91	314
Eddie Plank, Phila	43	40	33	24	16	.600	2.20	183	85	344
Ed Walsh, Chgo	56*	46*	37*	24	18	.571	1.60*	206	87	432*
Frank Smith, Chgo	41	37	29	22	11	.667	2.47	139	111*	310
Cy Young, Bos	43	37	33	22	15	.595	1.99	147	51	343
Jimmy Dygert, Phila	42	28	18	20	9	.690	2.34	151	85	262
George Mullin, Det	46	42	35	20	20	.500	2.60	146	106	357

Other than Donovan's leading winning percentage, individual honors went to pitchers on also-rans, but it was Detroit's pitching depth and the hitting of Ty Cobb and Sam Crawford that spelled the eventual difference. Plank also led in shutouts with eight. Chicago captured the team ERA with 2.22.

NATIONAL LEAGUE: CUBS LIVE UP TO THEIR PRESS CLIPPINGS

Still smarting from their upset defeat in the World Series at the hands of their crosstown rival White Sox, the Cubs took out their revenge on the National League. Chicago finished at 107–45 for a 17-game margin over second-place Pittsburgh. Once again it was pitching that dominated, as the Cubs had five dependable starters, with two of them exceeding 20 wins.

Orval Overall was a 23-game winner for the Cubs, while Mordecai Brown won 20 for the second straight season. Ed Reulbach turned in another fine performance at 17–4, while the staff had an ERA of 1.73, exceptional even in this era of low-scoring games.

Vic Willis, with 22 wins, made the charmed circle for the second consecutive season, while teammate Lefty Leifield reached it for the first and only time with exactly 20 wins. While this was Leifield's only 20-win season, he did win 103 games from 1906 through 1911, as he gave the Pittsburgh Pirates consistently winning pitching.

With a 22–8 mark, Tully Sparks had his best season while pitching for Philadelphia. From 1905 through 1908 Sparks won 71 games, and although he

pitched from 1897 through 1910, he won only 50 other games. Christy Mathewson continued rolling along, as he chalked up a league-high 24 wins, but
teammate Joe McGinnity could only win 18, while losing the same number. In
one more season McGinnity's career would be finished.

Boston broke the spell as they only had one pitcher to lose 20 games—Irv
Young who dropped 23, giving him three consecutive seasons of 20 or more
losses for a total of 69 over the three seasons. The league's top loser was Stony
McGlynn for the St. Louis Cardinals with a 14–25 record. McGlynn pitched
for three seasons (1906–08), and after he was 1–6 next year, he would be out of
the majors, never to return.

St. Louis, although last in the standings, was first with 127 complete games
while Pittsburgh was last with 111. Like their counterpart, the American League,
the number of pitchers with over 20 complete games was slowly declining.
Twenty-three made the mark, with three going over 30. One bit of tragedy
occurred in spring training when Boston's 24-year-old playing manager Chick
Stahl took his life by drinking carbolic acid. No one ever discovered the reason
for the suicide.

Pitcher/Team	G	GS	CG	W	L	Pct	ERA	SO	W	IP
C Mathewson, NY	41	36	31	24	13	.649	2.00	178*	53	315
Orval Overall, Chgo	36	31	26	23	8	.742	1.68	141	69	268
Tully Sparks, Phila	33	31	24	22	8	.733	2.00	90	51	260
Vic Willis, Pgh	39	37	27	22	11	.667	2.33	109	69	293
M Brown, Chgo	34	27	20	20	6	.769	1.39	107	40	233
Lefty Leifield, Pgh	40	33	24	20	16	.556	2.33	112	100	286

Team ERA honors went to Chicago with their 1.73 mark. Most of the individual stats were garnered by non-20-game winners. The Cubs' Ed Reulbach,
with a 17–4 mark, had a league-high .810 percent, while teammate Jack Pfiester
(15–9) led with a 1.15 ERA. Overall led in shutouts with eight.

The Cubs took out their revenge on Detroit by sweeping the Tigers four
straight in the World Series, with each victory a complete game. Detroit scored
only six runs, with Cobb batting .200 and Crawford .238.

1908

AMERICAN LEAGUE: A BITTERLY
FOUGHT, SEASON-LONG BATTLE

When the dust had settled, only 1½ games separated Detroit, Cleveland
and Chicago, in that order. St. Louis—in fourth—was only 6½ games out, as
they now had Rube Waddell, who gave them a 19-win season. The league had
its fewest 20-game winners, with only four, topped by Ed Walsh's 40 wins, as
he copped most of the individual honors.

Although Walsh would win 195 games during his career, have a .607 winning percentage, and exceed 20 wins four times, it is this season for which he will always be remembered and probably the main factor for his entrance in the Hall of Fame. Walsh is one of only two pitchers who won 40 or more games in a season during the 20th century. Ironically, both are in the American League.

With 40 wins, Walsh ranks second behind Jack Chesbro for most victories in a single season. If the awards had existed, he would have won the MVP and Cy Young and anything else they could have given him. His final record was 40–15, and he also led in winning percentage (.727), appearances (66), games started (49), games completed (42), innings pitched (464), strikeouts (260), shutouts (12), saves (7), and ERA (1.43). This was a truly outstanding and remarkable pitching feat. His win total was greater by five than the next two men combined on the Chicago pitching staff.

It is conceivable that Walsh could have won close to 50 that season given better hitting support, as the Chicago team was next to last in hitting with a .224 mark (low even for the dead-ball era). While Walsh would have several more good seasons, including two of 27 wins, he never again approached the heights of this year.

Ed Summers was a rookie and broke in with 24 wins, which would be his only season at or above the 20-win plateau. After a sophomore season of 19 wins, he would quickly fade and by 1912 be out of baseball—an example of another flower that bloomed and quickly faded. However, he did enjoy this one moment of glory.

Addie Joss had his last big season for Cleveland at age 28 as he won 24 games. The illness that was to claim his life in less than three years would soon begin taking control of his body. Joss' great year was overshadowed by Walsh. Joss had nine shutouts to go with his league-low 1.16 ERA. The question that remains is how he lost 11 games. With a few breaks, he could have broken the 30-win barrier.

Cy Young showed that he could still fog them past the hitters at age 41, as he turned in a 21–11 record on a 1.26 ERA, with 30 complete games in 33 starts. His record also was hurt by lack of adequate batting support. Rube Waddell turned in his last big year as he won 19 games for the St. Louis Browns. He would pitch one more full season and part of 1910 before calling it quits.

Jack Chesbro had fallen on hard times, as his New York team finished last and he was only 14–20. When the season ended, little did he realize, he had won his last major league game. The next year Chesbro would be 0–5 and then call it a career. Teammate Joe Lake was the league's other 20-game loser as he posted a 9-22 log.

Walter Johnson missed over a month of the season due to illness, but posted a 14–14 mark in his second season. His 1.65 ERA attests to how effectively he pitched, but lack of adequate support deprived him of a much better record. As we will see, this was the course his career would take.

Detroit led with 120 complete games, and New York was again last (in standings also) with 91. They now had the distinction of being the only team in either league to have less than 100 complete games in a season, and they accomplished it four straight years.

Pitcher/Team	G	GS	CG	W	L	Pct	ERA	SO	W	IP
Ed Walsh, Chgo	66*	49*	42*	40*	15	.727*	1.42	269*	56	464*
Addie Joss, Cleve	42	35	29	24	11	.686	1.16*	130	30	325
Ed Summers, Detroit	40	32	24	24	12	.667	1.64	103	55	301
Cy Young, Bos	36	33	30	21	11	.656	1.26	150	37	299

Walsh lost in one of the greatest pitching duels ever, under pressure on October 2nd, when he allowed only four hits in a 1–0 loss to Joss, who hurled a perfect game.

This season saw the lowest number of pitchers with 20 or more complete games to date, at 17, with two exceeding 30 (Young and Walsh). A brief comment on Young: At age 41 he had a 1.26 ERA, hurled 30 complete games and won 21. No wonder the annual pitching award is named for him.

Detroit was no match for Chicago in the World Series, losing in five games as Summers and Wild Bill Donovan each lost twice. Only George Mullin could win a game for Detroit.

NATIONAL LEAGUE: THE MERKLE BONER

The National League race was just as hotly contested as the American League this year, with only one game separating Chicago from Pittsburgh and New York. However, it was the failure of 19-year-old Fred Merkle to touch second base as the supposed winning run scored for the Giants against the Cubs in the bottom of the ninth that caused the furor.

There were two out in the bottom of the ninth, score tied 1–1, with Moose McCormick on third and Merkle on first, when Al Birdwell singled to center to score McCormick. However, Merkle failed to touch second and was then tagged out, nullifying the winning run and causing a postponement because of darkness.

The game was rescheduled and Mordecai Brown beat Christy Mathewson 4–2 for the championship. The Cubs three-year record was 322–136, for a .703 winning percentage. Brooklyn led the way with 118 complete games, and for the first time the National League had teams with less than 100, as St. Louis, New York and Boston tied for the fewest with 92.

Seven pitchers won 20 games, with Mathewson the biggest winner at 37. Brown came in second with 29. Mathewson set the modern-day (20th-century) record for wins by a pitcher in the National League. His ERA of 1.43 was the best in the league, and with a little better support he could have joined the charmed circle of 40-win pitchers.

Mathewson's season was almost as outstanding as Walsh's. He led in saves (5), appearances (54), games started (44), complete games (34), innings pitched

(391), strikeouts (250), shutouts (11), as well as the ERA and win totals. What a pitching matchup there could have been had their respective teams made it to the World Series! However, unlike Walsh, Mathewson would win 20 or more for the next six seasons to become one of the greatest pitchers in the history of the game.

Hooks Wiltse had pitched winning ball for four years, but broke through this year to win 23 games for the Giants. His record in any other season would have been very good, but in 1908 it paled in comparison to teammate Mathewson. Iron Man Joe McGinnity spent his last season in the big time, and posted an 11–7 mark with just seven complete games in 20 tries—a far cry from his big winning days of just a few years earlier.

While Mordecai Brown had to take second place to Mathewson, he did have some consolation, as his team went to the World Series and he would win two games. Brown's nine shutouts and 1.47 ERA were bettered only by Mathewson. He too was used heavily in relief, and tied Mathewson for the league lead with five saves. With a few breaks, Brown could have broken the 30-win barrier, but at times his teammates didn't provide enough firepower.

Ed Reulbach helped Brown pitch the Cubs to a pennant and World Series with a 24–7 mark. While this was his only 20-win season for Chicago (he would win 21 for Newark of the Federal League in 1915), he was completing a three-year run of leading the league in winning percentage, while compiling a composite 60–15 mark. Although he never again won 20 for the Cubs, he continued to pitch effective winning ball for the next several seasons.

In his first full season, Pittsburgh's 22-year-old Nick Maddux posted a 23–8, 2.22 ERA record, but could never come close to those stats again. In fact, Nick lasted only two more seasons and by 1911 would be gone from the majors. He was another of the pitchers who had one shining moment in the glory spotlight.

For teammate Vic Willis, it was another story as he captured his third consecutive 20-plus-win season, sixth overall and fifth in this century. Willis eventually would be selected to the Hall of Fame in 1995. It was overdue, but he finally made it.

Twenty-three-year-old George McQuillian, working in his first full season, broke the 20-win barrier as he won 23 games. This would be his only time at that level, and although he pitched for ten more seasons in the majors, he never again came close to his 1908 performance. When McQuillian retired he left behind a career mark of 85–89, distinguished only by this rookie season.

Boston's pitching staff was replaced by Brooklyn's for futility, as they almost tied Boston's record of four 20-game losers. Brooklyn had three at that level and a fourth that lost 19. The unhappy, unfortunate and undistinguished quartet was Kaiser Wilhelm (16–22), Henry McIntire (11–20), Jim Pastorius (4–20), and Nap Rucker (17–19). Wilhelm had pitched for Boston the two previous seasons and was part of their infamous quartet. His losses this year gave him a three-year total of 67, while winning 33.

Rucker won 116 while losing 123 from 1907 through 1913. Thus, while he was on the short end of many games, he did manage to put up a decent total of victories. Despite the 81 losses by Brooklyn's quartet, they escaped the basement, as St. Louis lost four more games and had the league's top loser in Bugs Raymond at 15–25.

Pitcher/Team	G	GS	CG	W	L	Pct	ERA	SO	W	IP
C Mathewson, NY	56*	44*	34*	37*	11	.771	1.43*	259*	42	391*
M Brown, Chgo	44	31	27	29	9	.763	1.47	123	49	312
Ed Reulbach, Chgo	46	35	25	24	7	.774*	2.02	133	106	298
Nick Maddox, Pgh	36	32	22	23	8	.742	2.28	70	90	261
Vic Willis, Pgh	41	38	25	23	11	.676	2.07	97	69	305
Hooks Wiltse, NY	44	38	30	23	14	.622	2.24	118	73	330
Geo McQuillan, Phila	48	42	32	23	17	.575	1.52	114	91	360

The National League also saw a drop in the number of pitchers with 20 or more complete games, as only 17 made the magic number, with five of them exceeding 30. The Cubs were victorious in World Series play, again defeating Detroit, this time in five games with Brown and Orval Overall each winning two games. This would mark the last time the Cubs would win a World Series through the current season. While they have won seven more pennants, they would never gain another world championship.

1909

AMERICAN LEAGUE: THREE IN A ROW, BUT NO CIGAR

The Detroit Tigers won their third straight pennant with a 3½-game margin over the surprising Philadelphia Athletics, as Connie Mack was building his first dynasty of pennant and World Series winners. George Mullin with 29 and Ed Willet with 22 paced the Tigers. The only other pitcher to win 20 games was Frank Smith of Chicago, with 25.

When Mullin won a career high 29, it marked the fourth time in his career that he exceeded 20 wins. Mullin turned in a fine season, but didn't dominate the statistics the way Walsh had the prior season. The only other category he led was winning percentage (.763). Teammate Ed Willet had his lone 20-win season as he won 22. The rest of his career he was a sub-.500 pitcher. Although he remained in the big leagues through 1915, the closest he came to 20 wins was 16 in 1910 and 17 in 1912.

Willett's career record of 102–99 is a little misleading. For 1906–07 he was 1–8 and for 1914–15 he was 6–19. Between these years, Willett posted a respectable 95–72, averaging 16 wins per season.

This seemed to be the season that pitchers had their career best years, as Chicago's Frank Smith won 25 games to mark the second time he broke the

20-win barrier. Smith picked up several of the categories vacated by Ed Walsh as he led in appearances (51), games started (41), games completed (37) and innings pitched (365).

Teammate Walsh took a precipitous drop from 1908, as his victory total slid from 40 to 15. He appeared in less than half the games (31), while also starting 20 fewer. Undoubtedly the work of 1908 had taken its toll. However, he was still an effective pitcher as he posted a 1.41 ERA and a league high eight shutouts. He just couldn't answer the bell as often as in prior seasons. Walsh had hurled 886 innings the past two years.

Even though he missed 20 wins, Young just kept rolling along, as he had 30 complete games and a 2.26 ERA to go with his 19 wins. He seemed unstoppable, even though he was now 42. Addie Joss posted a 1.70 ERA, but only a 14–13 record, as he was limited to 28 starts. Lack of hitting support and the onset of the illness that would claim his life took their toll.

Walter Johnson was a year away from starting his string of ten consecutive 20-or-more-win seasons. However, this year he was only 13–25, by far his poorest record. It should be noted that he had a 2.21 ERA (the same as Mullin and better than Willett) and 27 complete games. He had the misfortune to pitch for a team that averaged only 2.5 runs per game. It was teammate Bob Groom who was the big loser, with a 7–26 mark in his maiden season despite a respectable 2.86 ERA.

Detroit led the league in complete games, while Boston posted the lowest total of the decade with 75, making them the first team to complete less than 50 percent of their starts. The trend toward fewer complete games, more relief and larger pitching staffs was starting to take shape. The role of the relief specialist was several decades away, but the seeds were slowly being planted.

Pitcher/Team	G	GS	CG	W	L	Pct	ERA	SO	W	IP
George Mullin, Det	40	35	29	29*	9	.763*	2.22	124	78	304
Frank Smith, Chgo	51*	41*	37*	25	17	.595	1.80	177*	70	365*
Ed Willett, Det	41	34	25	22	9	.710	2.33	89	76	293

The decline in complete games could be seen, as only 12 pitchers had more than 20 and only Smith exceeded 30. For the first time, a team failed to have at least one pitcher with 20 complete games, as neither Boston nor St. Louis had a pitcher to reach that level.

Mullin and Smith led in all major categories except shutouts and ERA. The shutout crown went to Ed Walsh (Chicago), with eight, while Harry Kraus posted a 1.39 ERA for Philadelphia. Shibe Park opened its doors and would be home to baseball for the next 60 years.

The Tigers fared no better in World Series play, losing to Pittsburgh in seven games as Ty Cobb had another bad series, hitting only .231 with just two stolen bases.

NATIONAL LEAGUE: A NEW
BALLPARK AND NEW WORLD CHAMPION

Although Chicago posted a 104–49 log, their three-year reign came to an end as Pittsburgh won a club record 110 games, while losing only 42. Little did Cub fans realize at the time that 88 years later they would still be looking for another world title.

Pittsburgh had a balanced pitching staff, although Howie Camnitz won 25 and Vic Willis added 22. Mordecai Brown gave the Cubs another big year with 27, and Christy Mathewson chalked up 25 for the Giants, who won 92 but were 18 games out of first place. There was a total of six 20-game winners, all on the first three clubs.

A new name shot to the forefront in pitching as Camnitz posted a 25–6 mark, and tied for a league-best winning percentage at .806 and a 1.62 ERA. Camnitz had pitched winning ball the prior two seasons, but this was his first time in the 20-win club. Although he would dip to 12-13 the next season, he would bounce back to make it twice more into the charmed circle.

Vic Willis, with a 22–11 record, marked his fourth consecutive 20-plus-win season. It was the eighth of his career and the sixth of this century. For my analysis I do not include 19th-century statistics. Willis' 22 wins showed his consistency, as he had won 23, 21, and 23 the three prior years. He averaged 22 wins for the four seasons.

Mordecai Brown topped the loop in victories as he posted a 27–9 log, with 32 complete games in 34 starts and a 1.31 ERA. He also had seven saves (more than four other teams) and eight shutouts. In shutouts, he tied Mathewson for second, as teammate Orval Overall led with nine. Overall also won 20 games as he posted a 1.40 ERA. This was his second time at the 20-win level.

Overall's career lasted only seven seasons, for a combined 108–71. While a member of the Cincinnati team he was 22–28, but 86–43 with the Cubs. Ed Reulbach turned in another fine pitching performance for the Chicago team as he was 19–10 with a 1.76 ERA, which was the team's ERA and the best in the league.

Like his counterpart Walsh in the American League, Mathewson was used considerably less this season, as he appeared in 19 fewer games and started 11 fewer. However, his fall was only from 37 to 25, as he tied for the best winning percentage in the league (.806) based on his 25–6 mark, while leading with a scintillating 1.14 ERA. The last 20-game winner was teammate Hooks Wiltse, with an even 20, as he made the mark for his second consecutive year. Although he would not win 20 again, he continued pitching winning ball for the next few years.

Run production was slowly rising, as several team ERAs were creeping up, but it would still be several seasons before the real lively ball was introduced. St. Louis escaped the cellar, but had another 20-game loser, this time in the person of Fred Beebe, who was 15–21. During his 3½ years with St. Louis, he was 36–62. Beebe would play for three different teams over the next three seasons before leaving the big time.

Boston recaptured last place and had two more 20-game losers, as Al Mattern was 16–20, which during his five-year stint with the Braves would give him a composite 36–58 mark. Teammate Cecil Ferguson was 5–23 to top the loop in defeats.

Brooklyn paced the loop with 126 complete games, with only Chicago and New York also exceeding the century mark. St. Louis had the fewest complete games at 84 as the trend continued toward fewer complete games, more relief pitching and larger pitching staffs.

Pitcher/Team	G	GS	CG	W	L	Pct	ERA	SO	W	IP
M Brown, Chgo	50*	34	32*	27*	9	.750	1.31	172	53	343*
C Mathewson, NY	37	33	26	25	6	.806*	1.14*	149	36	275
Howie Camnitz, Pgh	41	30	20	25	6	.806*	1.62	133	68	283
Vic Willis, Pgh	39	35*	24	22	11	.667	2.23	95	83	290
Orval Overall, Chgo	38	32	23	20	11	.645	1.42	205*	80	285
Hooks Wiltse, NY	37	30	22	20	11	.645	2.01	119	51	269

A further decline in complete games could be seen as the number of pitchers with 20 or more slipped to 15, while only Brown exceeded 30.

In the World Series, Pirate rookie Babe Adams stole the show as he pitched three complete-game victories. During the regular season he was a spot starter and reliever with a 12–3 mark.

Forbes Field would be used for over 60 years and is the only ballpark in baseball where a no-hitter was never pitched. On a sad note, President Harry C. Pulliam's reign as head of the National League ended with a nervous breakdown and his suicide by pistol on July 29 in New York.

2

1910–1919

———————— 1910 ————————

AMERICAN LEAGUE: CONNIE MACK'S FIRST CHAMPIONSHIP

The Philadelphia Athletics became the first American League team to win 100 games or more as they posted a 102–48 mark to finish 14½ games in front of New York. Once again, pitching was the dominant factor, as Jack Coombs had a league high 31 wins and Chief Bender another 23 to pace the A's. Their combined win-loss mark was 54–14.

This year baseball became the "official" national pastime when President Howard Taft threw out the first ball on opening day in Washington, then Walter Johnson pitched a one-hit 1–0 shutout over the A's. The rest of the season was downhill for Washington as they finished seventh, despite Johnson winning 25 games with a scintillating 1.35 ERA. The practice of the president throwing out the opening game ball has continued to this day.

Johnson led the league in every major category except ERA, wins and winning percentage. Given a better team, he would undoubtedly have accomplished more.

There were five pitchers to win 20 or more games. Former big winners such as Ed Walsh, Doc White, Rube Waddell and Frank Smith were missing from the list. However, Walsh did lead the league with a 1.27 ERA, tied for game appearances with 45, and won 18 games despite having a weak hitting team behind him, which was a key factor in his 20 defeats.

Prior to this season, Jack Coombs had a four-year career mark of 35–35. There was nothing in these four seasons to distinguish him or lead one to expect what would happen in 1910. Coombs won 31 games, or only four less than he had managed in his first four years. He also tied Walsh for appearances at 45, had 35 complete games in 38 starts, a league-high 13 shutouts and a sparkling 1.30 ERA.

Coombs would follow this with two more big winning seasons, then become seriously ill and miss most of the 1913 and 1914 campaigns. Following the 1914 campaign, he would become the property of the Brooklyn Dodgers and pitch through 1918 with mixed results. He was 28–18 the first two years, but only 15–25 the last two.

Chief Bender had been with Philadelphia for seven years, pitched winning ball, and won at least 15 games in five of those years, but had never reached the 20-win plateau until this season. His 23–5 mark gave him the winning percentage title, while he sported a 1.58 ERA and 25 complete games in 28 starts. For the next four years, Bender was one of the keystones of the A's team, as he compiled a 68–24 record.

Then he made the mistake in 1915 of jumping to Baltimore in the Federal League and was only 4–16. He came back to pitch two years with Philadelphia in the National League and was 15–9, closing out his career with a 212–128 mark and a .624 winning percentage, which landed him in the Hall of Fame.

Russ Ford, a 27-year-old Canadian in his first full season, was 26–6 for the New York Yankees. He posted a brilliant 1.65 ERA and 29 complete games in 33 starts. Ford would pitch three more years for the New York team, winning 22 in 1911, but losing 39 games the following two years. Then he would jump to Buffalo of the Federal League in 1914 and finish his career with that team through the 1915 season.

George Mullin won 20 or more games for the fifth time in his career as he logged a 21–12 record. From 1903 through 1911, the fewest games Mullin won was 17. For his career he had 228 wins, but is not in the Hall of Fame. Perhaps the veterans committee should take a further look at him.

Walter Johnson had his first of ten consecutive 20-plus-win seasons as he was 25–17 for the lowly Washington Senators. Without Johnson they were 41–68. Johnson tied for the lead in appearances with 45, led in games started (42), complete games (38), innings pitched (374), strikeouts (313) and ERA (1.35). Certainly a team with better support would have earned him six to ten more wins. Again, this was to be his albatross throughout his career.

The A's led in complete games with 123, while Cleveland supplanted New York as the last-place finisher in this category with 92. There were 14 pitchers to hurl 20 or more complete games, with three exceeding 30. Slowly the number of hurlers in this category was declining.

Pitcher/Team	G	GS	CG	W	L	Pct	ERA	SO	W	IP
Jack Coombs, Phila	45*	38	35	31*	9	.775	1.30	224	115	353
Russ Ford, NY	36	33	29	26	6	.813	1.65	209	70	300
Walt Johnson, Wash	45*	42*	38*	25	17	.595	1.35	313*	76	374*
Chief Bender, Phila	30	28	25	23	5	.821	1.58	155	47	250
George Mullin, Det	38	32	27	21	12	.636	2.87	98	102	289

Ty Cobb lost the batting crown by a .001 edge to Nap Lajoie. Hitting was on the increase as a "livelier" ball was introduced, and the league saw a significant increase in runs scored. This was just a harbinger of things to come. Cy Young was nearing the end of a brilliant career and posted only a 7–10 mark with

Cleveland; however, he did achieve his 500th win during the season, finishing with 504 to become the only pitcher in the history of the game to win over 500.

Coombs also won three games in the World Series triumph over Chicago. The fourth win was a complete-game victory by Chief Bender.

NATIONAL LEAGUE: THE CUBS RETURN TO THE TOP

After failing to win in 1909, the Chicago Cubs won in big style by posting a 104–50 mark and a 13-game margin over the New York Giants. Although signs of increased hitting abounded, pitching still dominated the game. Mordecai Brown with 25 and rookie King Cole with 20 wins paced the Cubs.

For Brown this marked his fifth consecutive season with 20 or more wins as he was 25–14, while tying Christy Mathewson for the complete game lead with 27, leading in shutouts with seven and posting a 1.80 ERA. Brown also tied Henry Gaspar for the lead in saves with seven.

Rookie teammate King Cole broke in with a 20–4 mark and led with a .833 winning percentage. This would be his only 20-win season, and after a follow-up year at 18–7 he would quickly fade and be out of baseball by 1916. However, for this one season he was outstanding.

Brown and Cole had to be at their best, as injuries slowed down two of the Cubs, prior big winners, Orval Overall and Ed Reulbach; each was limited to 12 wins. A sore arm sidelined Overall and in another year his career would be over, while Reulbach would continue to pitch effectively for several more seasons.

Christy Mathewson led the loop with 27 wins. The next closest on his team was Doc Crandall with 17. For Mathewson this marked the eighth straight year he had won 20 or more games. In fact, the fewest victories he totaled from 1903 through 1914 was 22 in 1906. The only other pitcher to win 20 or more was Earl Moore of Philadelphia, who posted a 22–15 log. Moore had pitched in the American League from 1901 through 1907, mostly with Cleveland. Although he never won 20, four times he notched between 15 and 19 wins.

Moore joined the Philadelphia team in 1908, but saw action in only three games. In 1909 he was 18–12 and it looked like he would have several more big winning seasons. Such was not to happen, as he never had another winning season, although he pitched through 1914. His composite mark for the last four years was 37–52, which pulled his career mark down to 162–154.

Deacon Phillippe, after much inactivity for the two previous seasons, sparkled for the Pirates—primarily in a relief role. He appeared in 31 games, only eight as a starter, while compiling a 14–2 mark with a 2.29 ERA. This would be the 38-year-old's last fling, as after pitching three games in 1911 Phillippe retired with a 188–109 mark. Phillippe had five seasons with over 20 wins, three of which were in the 20th century, but he's still not in the Hall of Fame.

Brooklyn had the biggest loser in George Bell as he posted a 10–27 mark, despite a respectable 2.65 ERA. Brooklyn had the weakest hitting attack in the league and this undoubtedly contributed to many of Bell's defeats.

Boston almost duplicated its feat of four 20-game losers. Cliff Curtis was 6–24, Buster Brown came in at 9–23, while Sammy Frock was 9–20 (although one loss was with Cincinnati), and Al Mattern was 16–19.

Brooklyn was the only team to complete over 100 games, as they led with 103, while Pittsburgh was last with 73, becoming the third team to complete fewer than 50 percent of their games. The St. Louis Cardinals were right behind Pittsburgh with 74. This was the lowest complete game totals to date, only eight pitchers had 20 or more, and for the first time in league history no pitcher had 30 complete games.

Pitcher/Team	G	GS	CG	W	L	Pct	ERA	SO	W	IP
C Mathewson, NY	38	35	27*	27*	9	.750	1.90	184	60	318
M Brown, Chgo	46	31	27*	25	13	.658	1.86	143	64	295
Earl Moore, Phila	46	35	19	22	15	.595	2.58	185*	121	283
King Cole, Chgo	33	29	21	20	4	.833*	1.80	114	130	240
George Suggs, Cinn	35	30	23	20	11	.645	2.40	91	48	266

Brown led the league in shutouts with seven, but lost the magic in the World Series. He was 1–2 with a 5.50 ERA while the Cubs lost to the A's four games to one.

1911

AMERICAN LEAGUE: THE WHITE ELEPHANT CONTINUES TO TRAMPLE THE OPPOSITION

The Philadelphia Athletics started slowly but righted themselves in May. By early August, they caught the Detroit Tigers and eventually won the pennant by 13½ games. They were paced again by Jack Coombs (28–12) and Eddie Plank (22–8). The Tigers, although possessing a fine hitting attack, had weak pitching as their team ERA was second highest in the league.

For the second straight year, Coombs was the winningest pitcher in the league; his 28–12 record gave him a two-year composite of 59–21. He also led in games started with 40. Teammate Plank had another fine year; while also leading with six shutouts, he posted an excellent 2.10 ERA.

Plank was a victim of circumstances throughout his career when it came to winning titles or leading in a category. Although he won 20 or more eight times, and won 326 games, he never led in that category. He had a career 2.35 ERA, but never led the league. Despite having 410 complete games in 529 starts, he only led once—with 35 in 1905. Plank had a career winning percentage of .628, but could only lead one time in this category, in 1906 with .760 based on a 19–6 record.

Five other pitchers won 20 games or more, with Ed Walsh posting 27 for Chicago and Walter Johnson 25 for the seventh-place Washington team.

Walsh's ERA climbed almost a run a game over the prior year from 1.27 to 2.22, but he went from 18–20 to 27–18. The main factor was the hitting support he received. In 1910 the team behind him batted .211 and scored 456 runs, while this year's club batted .269 and scored 717 runs. He could have used some of that support the prior season.

Johnson had another superlative season as he won 25 for the second straight year, enroute to his ten consecutive 20-plus-win seasons. He had another brilliant ERA, this time 1.89. He did relinquish the strikeout title to Walsh at 255 to 207. Starting in 1912 he would lead the league in strikeouts for eight straight years. For his career, he led 12 times. Johnson also completed 36 of his 37 starts for the year.

Vean Gregg broke in with Cleveland and took the league by storm as he was 23–7, while leading in winning percentage (.767) and ERA (1.81). This was the first of three consecutive 20-win-seasons for the Cleveland lefty. Vean appeared in 34 games, starting 26 and completing 22.

Smokey Joe Wood had been around the league for a few years, but he was barely over .500 until he burst on the scene with a 23–17 mark for Boston this year. He did double duty as a starter and reliever, appearing in 44 games, starting 33, completing 25, saving five games and posting a 2.02 ERA. This season was just a warm-up for one of the finest years ever compiled by any pitcher, but we have to save that for next season.

Russ Ford had his second consecutive 20 plus win season as he was 22–11 with a 2.28 ERA. This was his last winning season with New York, as he was 13–21 and 12–18 the next two years before jumping to Buffalo in 1914, where he won 21 games.

There was a tragic note to the season; Addie Joss died of tubercular meningitis on April 14, 1911, prematurely ending a brilliant career. Joss had 160 career wins in less than nine full seasons and died one day short of his 31st birthday. Certainly he would have won at least 250 games—perhaps even 300—had he not been struck down in his prime by this tragic illness.

Ironically, Detroit led the league with 109 complete games, despite having a relatively weak pitching staff. Washington was the only other team to break the 100 barrier, with 106, bolstered by Johnson's league-leading 36. Chicago, despite 33 complete games by Walsh, was last with 86.

Not only was the number of complete games declining, so was the number of hurlers with over 20 complete games. This season there were only nine to complete 20 or more and just two to reach the 30 level. Soon we would see 30 complete games all but disappear as a seasonal event.

Pitcher/Team	G	GS	CG	W	L	Pct	ERA	SO	W	IP
Jack Coombs, A's	47	40*	26	28*	12	.700	3.53	185	119	337
Ed Walsh, Chgo	56*	37	33	27	18	.600	2.22	255*	72	369*
Walt Johnson, Wash	40	37	36*	25	13	.658	1.89	207	70	323
Vean Gregg, Cleve	34	26	22	23	7	.787*	1.81*	125	86	244
Joe Wood, Boston	44	33	25	23	17	.575	2.02	231	76	277

Pitcher/Team	G	GS	CG	W	L	Pct	ERA	SO	W	IP
Eddie Plank, A's	40	30	24	22	8	.733	2.10	149	77	257
Russ Ford, NY	37	33	26	22	11	.667	2.28	158	76	281

Ty Cobb and Sam Crawford formed the most fearsome batting tandem in the league, as Cobb hit .420 and Crawford batted .378. Unfortunately, Detroit's pitching wasn't equal to the challenge and they finished a distant second behind Philadelphia. Cobb won his fifth batting title, but was given hot pursuit by Cleveland rookie outfielder Shoeless Joe Jackson, who batted .408—the highest runner-up average ever in baseball.

The A's pitching continued to dominate in the World Series. They had a composite 1.29 ERA, with Chief Bender winning two games and Coombs and Plank one each. Fenway Park opened in Boston, and almost nine decades later, baseball is still played there.

NATIONAL LEAGUE: BACK TO THE TOP, BUT NO CHAMPIONSHIP

Fire ravaged the Polo Grounds, and the New York Giants had to play their games in the same park with the New York Highlanders (who shortly would be called the Yankees). It wasn't until September that they could return to the rebuilt Polo Grounds, and when they did, the Giants won 20 out of 24 to win by 7½ games over the Chicago Cubs.

Christy Mathewson with 26 and Rube Marquard with 24 won just over half the Giants' 99 victories. The Cubs, well-balanced staff was paced by Mordecai Brown's 21 wins. However, league honors went to Philadelphia rookie Grover Cleveland (Pete) Alexander, who posted a 28–13 mark, still the highest win total by a rookie pitcher. Without Alexander, Philadelphia was 51–60.

This was Mathewson's ninth straight 20-plus-win season, and the seventh time he had exceeded 25. His 1.99 ERA was the best in the league, while his five shutouts tied him with Nap Rucker for third place. His 27 complete games marked the eleventh straight season of 20 or more, with 22 being the fewest. For his career he would have 20 or more complete games 14 times, 13 exceeding 25, and six in the 30s.

Marquard had broken in with the Giants at the end of the 1908 season, and through his first two full years had only a 9–18 record. There was certainly nothing to indicate the success he would soon enjoy that would make him an eventual Hall of Famer. Marquard led the league with a .774 winning percentage as he was 24–7 for the first of three consecutive 20-win seasons. He led the league in strikeouts with 237, the only time he would achieve this goal.

New York's Doc Crandall proved to be an effective swing man, as he started 15 games while relieving 26 times and posting a 15–5 mark with five saves. This would be his function for several years on the teams for which he pitched.

Brown had his sixth straight 20-plus-win season, which was also his last.

He too was a double-duty pitcher, relieving 26 times, starting 27 games and completing 21. His double duty gave him what was then a major league high of 13 saves to go with his 21 victories. Brown would pitch five more years in the majors, but the closest he would come would be 17 wins in 1915.

Pittsburgh unveiled two 20-game winners: Babe Adams won 22 and Howie Camnitz had 20. For Adams it was a fine follow-up to his 18-win season the previous year. While he would win 20 or more only one more time, he would turn in six other seasons between 13 and 17 wins. His final career mark of 194–140 has not placed him in the Hall of Fame. Pitchers with lesser credentials are there. But that's a story for another day.

Camnitz had his second consecutive 20-win season, and the third in the last four years. However, it would also prove to be his last winning season. The next year he would split time between Pittsburgh and Philadelphia and be only 9-20. In 1914 he would play for Pittsburgh in the Federal League and be 14–19 before calling it quits after appearing in four games in 1915. Camnitz finished with a career 133–106 record.

Alexander's initial season was superlative to say the least. He not only led in victories, but complete games (31), innings pitched (367) and shutouts (7). With a little more batting support, Alexander could have undoubtedly passed the 30 mark. In a reversal of form, teammate Earl Moore went from a 22-game winner to a 19-game loser (he did win 15).

Bob Harmon helped St. Louis to some degree of respectability with his only winning season in nine, as he posted a 23–16 mark. During his career with St. Louis and Pittsburgh, the next best he could achieve was an 18–18 mark for the Cardinals the next year. Harmon did perform yeoman work as he appeared in 51 games, started a league-high 41, completed 28 and had four saves.

Another pitcher who saved his best year for this campaign was Nap Rucker; he was 22–18 for seventh-place Brooklyn. In the three prior seasons Rucker had lost 19, 19 and 18, respectively. He would revert to form the next two years as he lost 21 and 15. Rucker is another example of a pitcher used very heavily in double duty: he started 33 times, completed 23 and relieved 15 times, while saving four games.

There was a total of eight 20-game winners for the season, with only Cincinnati and Boston not producing a 20-game winner. In fact, Boston's "best" pitcher was Buster Brown with an 8–18 mark, as the team struggled to a 44–107 season.

No team had 100 complete games. This was first time that had happened in either league. New York led the way with 95, while hapless Boston was last with 73. Cincinnati also failed to complete at least 50 percent of their starts: they finished only 77 in 159 games.

Pitcher/Team	G	GS	CG	W	L	Pct	ERA	SO	W	IP
Pete Alexander, Phil	48	37	31*	28*	13	.683	2.57	227	129	367*
C Mathewson, NY	45	37	29	26	13	.667	1.99*	141	39	303

Pitcher/Team	G	GS	CG	W	L	Pct	ERA	SO	W	IP
Rube Marquard, NY	45	33	22	24	7	.774*	2.49	237*	106	278
Bob Harmon, STL	51	41*	28	23	16	.590	3.13	144	181*	348
Babe Adams, Pgh	40	37	24	22	12	.647	2.34	133	42	293
Nap Rucker, Bklyn	48	33	23	22	18	.550	2.72	190	110	316
M Brown, Chgo	53*	27	21	21	11	.656	2.80	129	55	270
Howie Camnitz, Pgh	40	33	18	20	15	.571	3.14	139	84	268

Brown continued to perform double duty for Chicago, starting and relieving, as shown by his 27 starts and 26 relief appearances. In addition to his 21 wins, he led the league with 13 saves, although it was still not an official statistic. Alexander captured most of the individual titles, including shutouts with seven.

The Giants dominated team batting statistics, but Pittsburgh's Honus Wagner won his eighth and final batting title with a .334 mark.

——————— 1912 ———————

AMERICAN LEAGUE: SMOKEY JOE AND HOT TY COBB

Ty Cobb attacked a heckler on May 15th and was suspended, but the entire Detroit club supported him and refused to play. Therefore, Detroit made up a team of sandlotters, collegians and aging coaches, and lost to Philadelphia 23–2. They were scheduled the next day, but Connie Mack graciously agreed not to play. The regulars returned on May 21, and Cobb was reinstated on the 26th, but poor morale and weak pitching doomed them to a sixth-place finish.

Philadelphia got off to its usual poor start, and although they won 90 games came in third 15 games out, despite 26 wins from Eddie Plank and 21 from Jack Coombs. This would be Coombs' last big season.

Boston put it all together to win 105 games, a team record that still stands. Smokey Joe Wood led the way with a 34–5 mark and ten shutouts, and only Walter Johnson fanned more batters. Ironically, this would be Wood's last big year; the most he would win again would be 15.

Wood had one of the greatest seasons of any pitcher in the 20th century, only matched by Jack Chesbro's 41 wins, Ed Walsh's 40, Christy Mathewson's 37 or Walter Johnson's 36. It was truly an outstanding year for Wood as he hurled 35 complete games in 38 starts, in addition to relieving five times. Unfortunately, he broke his hand the next season and lasted only three more years.

Injuries limited Wood over the next three campaigns; his record would be a fine 35–13, but the most starts in any one season would be 18. Here was another brilliant career prematurely ended, as Wood was only 25 when he called it quits with the Red Sox after the 1915 season. Although he tried a couple of comebacks with the Cleveland Indians in the latter part of this decade, they were abortive and he appeared in only a few games. After winning 34 games, Wood had 80 wins by the time he was 22 and seemed headed for an easy 300-plus wins, but fate stepped in and derailed his career.

Teammate Hugh Bedient picked his rookie season to win 20 games, a feat he would never duplicate. Bedient saw considerable action for the Red Sox as he appeared in 41 games, while starting 28 of them. Bedient pitched two more years with the Red Sox before jumping to Buffalo in the Federal League in 1915, which proved to be his last year in the majors. His record for those three years was only 39–44, after such a promising start.

Washington was a surprising second, mainly on the arms of Johnson (33–12) and Bob Groom (24–13). In almost any other season 33 wins would lead the league, but this year Johnson had to settle for second place. He continued double duty for the Senators as he started 37 times, completing 34 while relieving 13 times. His 1.39 ERA and 303 strikeouts were the league's best. The strikeouts were the first of eight straight years he led the league, while his 1.39 ERA was the third of seven straight years below 2.00. Eleven times during his career, Johnson had an ERA below 2.00.

For Groom this marked the first winning year of his career, and although he pitched for ten seasons he enjoyed only one more year above the .500 mark. Groom's mark for his first three seasons was 32–60; thus his 24 wins in 1912 represented a complete reversal of form. While his ERA was only slightly lower than in 1909–10, the league scored considerably more runs in 1912. In 1909 and 1910 the teams averaged slightly over 3.6 runs per game, while they averaged almost a run per game more in 1912. Thus his 2.62 ERA is far more meaningful than his 2.86 and 2.76 of earlier seasons.

Eddie Plank, although enjoying the finest season of his career, was once again a bridesmaid, despite his brilliant 26–6 mark with a 2.21 ERA. As stated earlier, it was his misfortune to always find someone having a better season. This marked the seventh year that Plank won 20 or more games. He would achieve that goal one more time before he retired. In 17 seasons, in addition to his 20-win campaigns, he had another eight years in which he won between 14 and 19. Only in his final season did he fail to post a winning mark, finishing with a 5–6 record in 20 games for the 1917 campaign when he was 42.

Teammate Jack Coombs notched his third straight 20-plus-win season with a 21–10 mark, giving him an 80–31 record for the three years 1910–1912. Coombs was also called on for double duty: in addition to his 32 starts he also relieved eight times and saved three games. This was his last big season as illness sidelined him for most of the next two years. His career with Philadelphia was effectively ended, although he pitched for Brooklyn from 1915 to 1919 with mixed results.

Ed Walsh enjoyed another great season, winning 27 games for the White Sox while posting a 2.15 ERA. He led the league in appearances (62), games started (41), saves (10) and innings pitched (393). Walsh also fanned 254—third in the league and an unusually high total for that era. Only the St. Louis Browns had a lower team batting average; thus Walsh was once again deprived of several wins because of weak hitting.

Vean Gregg notched his second consecutive 20-win season for Cleveland as he finished 20-13. Gregg would have one more 20-win season before fading. After winning 63 games in his first three seasons, Gregg won only 29 in his final five.

Russ Ford had almost a reversal of his previous season; he was 13–21 for what would be the first of two big, successive losing seasons. Ford was a real anomaly. In his first five full seasons, he won 20 or more three times, compiling a composite 69–23, while in the other two he was 25–39. After he jumped to Buffalo in 1914, Ford lasted only one more season, finishing at 5–6 for a career 99–71 mark.

For the Red Sox, Buck O'Brien had his only 20-win season. He broke in with Boston in 1911 and was 5–1. Then came his big season in 1912, when he was 20–13, with a 2.58 ERA. The next season he was 4–9 with a 3.70 ERA (relatively high for the era), when he was traded to Chicago. He was 0–2 there and that finished his career at age 31.

Boston took the team complete-game title with 110, one more than last-place New York, while Chicago was last with 84, despite 32 by Ed Walsh. For the season, 14 pitchers exceeded 20 complete games, with four breaking the 30 barrier.

Pitcher/Team	G	GS	CG	W	L	Pct	ERA	SO	W	IP
Joe Wood, Boston	43	38	35*	34*	5	.872*	1.91	258	82	344
Walt Johnson, Wash	50	37	34	32	12	.727	1.39*	303*	76	368
Ed Walsh, Chgo	62*	41*	32	27	17	.614	2.15	254	94	393*
Eddie Plank, Phila	37	30	24	26	6	.813	2.21	110	83	260
Bob Groom, Wash	43	40	29	24	13	.649	2.82	179	94	316
Jack Coombs, Phila	40	32	23	21	10	.677	3.29	120	94	262
Hugh Bedient, Boston	41	28	19	20	9	.690	2.92	122	55	231
Vean Gregg, Cleve	37	34	26	20	13	.606	2.59	184	90	271
Buck O'Brien, Bos	37	34	25	20	13	.606	2.58	276	90	115

While Tris Speaker paced Boston with a .383 mark, he finished third behind Joe Jackson (.395) and Ty Cobb (.410). Many hitters had great seasons, but with Cobb on the field they usually finished second best.

NATIONAL LEAGUE: REPEAT CHAMPS, BUT SAME STORY IN OCTOBER

The New York Giants got off to a hot start, and even a slump in July and August couldn't slow them down. They won 103 games to beat Pittsburgh by 10 games. En route to the title, Rube Marquard won 26 games, with a record 19 in a row. Christy Mathewson contributed 23 wins.

Marquard was never better than in this his career-best season; his 26 wins paced the loop. This was the middle year of three consecutive 20-plus-win seasons during which he was 73–28. After the 1913 campaign, Marquard would pitch 12 more years, but never again crack the charmed 20-win circle, although he came close in 1917 with 19. Marquard had only a lackluster 119–131 for his last 12 seasons, including 22 losses in 1914. But in 1912, he was the king of the hill.

Mathewson was winning 20 or more for the tenth straight season, and his 23 wins marked the second-lowest total during that streak. During this same three-year period, he posted a 74–36 mark to give the Giants a dynamic duo that averaged 24 wins each during the 1911–1913 seasons. Rookie teammate Jeff Tesreau led the league with a 1.96 ERA while posting a 17–7 record. More would be heard from him later.

The Pirates got 24 wins from Claude Hendrix and a 22–12 mark from Howie Camnitz, but this would be his last winning season. Over the next two seasons he would win 23 while losing 39. Hendrix seemed to follow a pattern of good year, bad year, or at best, fair year. In 1911, Hendrix was only 4–6, and following this campaign he would be 14-15 in 1913, only to bounce back the next season and be a big winner again.

Larry Cheney of Chicago also won 26 to tie Marquard for the league lead. This was Cheney's first full season and the first of three consecutive 20-plus-win years. His seems to be another instance of overuse. During the 1912–14 seasons, Cheney appeared in 148 games, starting 113 and completing 74. Cheney led the loop with 28 complete games this year.

Pete Alexander slipped to a 19–17 mark, while Mordecai Brown was on his way out, as his overworked arm could only make it for 15 games and a 5–6 mark. Alexander appeared in 46 games, starting 34 and completing 26 while compiling a 2.55 ERA. His was another example of a light-hitting team behind him; only Cincinnati had a lower team batting average. This 19-win total was the lowest number Alexander fashioned in his first seven seasons.

George Suggs almost made it two seasons in three with 20 wins, but fell one short as he posted a 19–16 mark to go with his 2.94 ERA. Suggs would be another of the players that would jump to the Federal League, and in 1914 would enjoy his greatest season when he won 24, but he would never return to the National or American League.

Nap Rucker virtually reversed his 1911 record as he was 18–21, making the fifth straight season in which he lost at least 18 games. Only in 1911 did he win more than he lost, as he posted a 22–18 mark. Boston's Lefty Tyler was the league's big loser as he posted a 12–22 record for the last-place Braves. Shortly Tyler would right himself and pitch winning baseball for five consecutive seasons.

No team had 100 complete games. The Pirates led with 94, while St. Louis set a new low with only 62. In a few decades this number would lead the league, but that's another story. Another sign of the declining number of complete games was that no pitcher had more than 28, and only 13 exceeded the 20 mark.

Pitcher/Team	G	GS	CG	W	L	Pct	ERA	SO	W	IP
Larry Cheney, Chgo	42	37	28*	26*	10	.722	2.85	140	111	303
Rube Marquard, NY	43	38	22	26*	11	.703	2.57	175	80	295
Claude Hendrix, Pgh	39	32	25	24	9	.727*	2.58	176	105	289
C Mathewson, NY	43	34	27	23	12	.657	2.12	134	34	310*
Howie Camnitz, Pgh	41	32	22	22	12	.647	2.83	121	82	277

Several of the key statistics were won by non-20-game winners. The season opened without Cy Young, winner of 511 games, who announced his retirement in spring. Chicago's Heinie Zimmerman replaced Honus Wagner as batting champion with a resounding .372 mark. Wagner hit .324.

In the World Series, it was the same old story for New York as they lost in seven games, with Mathewson being 0–2 despite a 1.57 ERA, while Smokey Joe Wood was 3–1 with a 3.68 ERA. Marquad tried his best with a 2–0 mark and .50 ERA, but the Giants came up a little short.

—————— 1913 ——————

AMERICAN LEAGUE: THE WHITE ELEPHANT RETURNS

Although the final margin was only 6½ games, the issue was never really in doubt, as the Philadelphia Athletics took over first place in late April and never relinquished the lead. For once Philadelphia was paced more by its offense than pitching, as only Chief Bender won over 20. Eddie Plank had 18; Jack Coombs was ill and appeared in only two games.

Washington tried to make a race of it, mainly on the arm of Walter Johnson, who clocked in with a 36–7, 1.09 ERA season that included 30 complete games and 12 shutouts. Cleveland fashioned two 20-game winners, as did Chicago. However, Cleveland's third-place finish could be traced to the .373 hitting of Joe Jackson and a .335 mark by Nap Lajoie as much as their pitching.

Bender's 21-win season was his second and last at that level, although he had a total of 11 seasons in double digits, with nine of them exceeding 15. His career total of 212 wins was built on consistency rather than a few big years. This is what eventually got him elected to the Hall of Fame.

Johnson had the greatest season of his career. He exceeded 25 wins for the fifth straight year when he posted the third-highest win total in modern American League history. The real question is how Johnson lost seven games during the season with a 1.09 ERA. He led the league in victories, complete games, ERA, innings pitched (346), shutouts and strikeouts (243). Without Johnson, Washington was a lackluster 54–57, while with him they finished second. It is interesting to fantasize what his career mark might have been if he had played for a consistently winning or contending team.

Boston slipped to fourth as Smokey Joe Wood broke his hand and was 11–5.

Wood's situation is one of baseball's real tragedies. Here was a pitcher who looked like a certain 300- or even 400-game winner and by age 25 was through. Whether he started pitching too soon is not certain, but he put a strain on his shoulder and was never the same pitcher again—hero with 34 wins at 22, and out of baseball as a pitcher before his 26th birthday. Wood could always hit and became an outfielder with the Cleveland Indians. Between 1918 and 1922 he played five years in their outfield averaging around .285, then called it quits and coached baseball at Yale for 20 years.

Meanwhile, Ed Walsh developed a sore arm and was 8–3 for Chicago. No doubt the years of heavy pitching had finally taken their toll on the big right-hander. From 1906 to 1912, he averaged 360 innings and 51 appearances per year. Eventually the price had to be paid. Walsh would hang around until 1917, but appear in only 17 games with a 5–4 record over the next four years. Walsh later served as a coach, manager and umpire and was eventually elected to the Hall of Fame.

Cy Falkenberg had been in the big leagues for eight seasons and compiled only a 68–77 mark. What happened this year surprised everyone, as he blossomed into a 23-game winner with a fine 2.22 ERA. He would jump to the Federal League in 1914, where he enjoyed his greatest season. His career was finished after the 1916 season with the Philadelphia Athletics.

His teammate, Vean Gregg, fashioned his third straight 20-win season, giving him 63 wins for his first three years in the big leagues. However, this was the end of his success. The most games he would win after this year was 12. He would leave the big leagues after the 1916 campaign, only to return in 1918 and then surface after a seven-year absence with the Washington Senators in 1925.

Rookie Reb Russell broke in with a bang, winning 22 games for Chicago, while leading the league in appearances with 51 and posting a 1.91 ERA. It appears that he was destined to take over Walsh's place in the category. However, his success would not equal the big right-hander's, as the most he ever won again was 18. After one game in the 1919 season, he was out of the majors.

Teammate Jim Scott won 20, but also lost 20 despite a 1.91 ERA, as he too was a workhorse appearing in 48 games, starting a league-high 38. Another Chicago pitcher, Ed Cicotte, of whom we will hear more later, had an 18–12 record while posting a 1.56 ERA. Chicago pitchers deserved a better fate, but a league low of 486 runs scored didn't help their cause.

St. Louis, although finishing last, led with 101 complete games. However, a new trend was developing. Although Philadelphia won the title, they were last with 69 complete games. Relief pitching was slowly making its way into the league, although the true era of the relief pitcher was decades away. Only nine pitchers bettered the 20 complete game level, with only Johnson attaining 30—another sign of the changing times.

Pitcher/Team	G	GS	CG	W	L	Pct	ERA	SO	W	IP
Walt Johnson, Wash	47	36	30*	36*	7	.837*	1.09*	243*	38	346*

Pitcher/Team	G	GS	CG	W	L	Pct	ERA	SO	W	IP
Cy Falkenberg, Cleve	39	36	23	23	10	.700	2.22	166	68	276
Reb Russell, Chgo	51*	36	25	22	16	.578	1.91	122	79	316
Vean Gregg, Cleve	44	34	23	20	13	.606	2.23	166	124*	286
Chief Bender, Phila	48	22	16	21	10	.677	2.21	135	59	237
Jim Scott, Chgo	48	38*	27	20	20*	.500	1.91	158	86	312

Stuffy McInnis, Eddie Collins and Frank Baker all hit better than .320 to pace Philadelphia.

Those three, along with shortstop Jack Barry, formed the fabled $100,000 infield of that era. While a paltry amount today, that was a magnificent sum in those days. Baker also led the league with 12 home runs, his third straight title.

Tris Speaker batted .365 and Joe Jackson .373, but both trailed Ty Cobb, who won another title with a .390 mark.

The A's won another World Series, primarily on pitching, as Chief Bender was 2–0 despite a 4.00 ERA, and Plank had .50 ERA but could only go 1–1. The other victory was picked up by Joe Bush.

NATIONAL LEAGUE: THREE-TIME WINNER AND THREE-TIME LOSER

The story of the New York Giants is summed up in the title caption, as they won their third straight pennant but lost for the third consecutive season in the World Series. The Giants broke out early and won by 12½ games over a surprising Philadelphia team. The New York club was paced by Christy Mathewson (25–11), Rube Marquard (23–10), and Jeff Tesreau (22–13).

Philadelphia got a 27–12 mark from Tom Seaton, who would jump to the Federal League next year, and when he returned in 1916 could win only six games. Pete Alexander was 22–8. Larry Cheney and Babe Adams were also in the 20-win group.

This was another great season for "The Big Six," as Mathewson had been nicknamed, a moniker that Sam Crane of the *New York Journal* had hung on him because of his punctuality and efficiency, likening him to the city's number-one fire engine company. He also led the league with a sparkling 2.06 ERA.

Marquard reeled off 23 wins as he completed three years with 72 wins to complement Mathewson's 74 for the same campaigns. However, this was Marquard's last big season, although he did have several winning years ahead of him. He also had some big losing seasons on the horizon, but for now he was still a prince to go with the king of pitchers.

Tesreau rounded out the trio with 22 wins in only his second season. He also had a fine 2.17 ERA, while leading the league with 38 starts. Tesreau enjoyed two more big seasons, but was through by age 30—a fate that seemed to strike many of the pitchers of this era. It has often been traced to the overwork, a combination of starting and relieving, or the high number of complete games. It certainly wasn't true of all pitchers, such as Walter Johnson, Alexander or Mathewson, but it did seem to fit the mold for many pitchers in this era.

An unheralded pitcher stole the limelight from the big names: Seaton led the league with 27 wins, but he too would be finished at age 30 in 1917. However, this year he was sensational, winning 27, appearing in 52 games, with 21 complete games in 35 starts, 2.60 ERA, league-high 322 innings pitched and 168 strikeouts, also tops in the circuit.

Alexander bounced back with 22 wins for the first of five consecutive 20-plus-win seasons, and the second-lowest total of his first seven years. Alexander was also a workhorse, appearing in 47 games and hurling 305 innings. In fact, this was the fewest innings he pitched in any of his first seven years.

Cheney led the league in appearances with 54 while winning 21 games, the second straight season at 20 or more. He also pitched 305 innings, marking his second consecutive year above the 300 level. He was a durable pitcher, starting and relieving as needed by his team.

Adams won 21 games, making his second trip to the charmed circle. Although he never won 20 or more again, he did enjoy several fine years; eight times he won between 11 and 17 games. When Adams retired he had a career 194–140 mark and 2.76 ERA, but he is not in the Hall of Fame. Perhaps a good case could be made for him, but that is a story for another day.

Boston paced the league with 105 complete games, while Brooklyn was last with 70. Only New York, Chicago and Boston completed over 50 percent of their starts, as managers were relying on their bullpens more frequently. Only seven pitchers topped the 20-complete-game level, with Lefty Tyler (16–17) the best at 28. Times were changing and would continue to do so.

Pitcher/Team	G	GS	CG	W	L	Pct	ERA	SO	W	IP
Tom Seaton, Phila	52	35	21	27*	12	.692	2.60	168*	136*	322*
C Mathewson, NY	40	35	25	25	11	.694	2.05*	93	21	306
Rube Marquard, NY	42	33	20	23	10	.697	2.50	151	49	288
Pete Alexander, Phila	47	35	23	22	8	.733	2.79	159	75	306
Jeff Tesreau, NY	42	33	20	22	13	.629	2.50	151	49	288
Babe Adams, Pgh	43	37	24	21	10	.677	2.15	144	49	314
Larry Cheney, Chgo	54*	36	25	21	14	.600	2.57	136	98	305

Chicago had found itself a new workhorse in Cheney, who also led with 11 saves, but after one more good year he would pitch his arm out. It would be many years before managers came to realize that you can't start and relieve someone 45–50–55 times a year, season after season.

Gavvy Cravath (Philadelphia) led the league with a .341 mark and 19 home runs (a phenomenal amount for that time). This marked the initial season for Ebbets Field in Brooklyn, which would remain the home of the Dodgers until their surprise move to Los Angeles in 1957. Ebbets Field became a unique fixture in baseball annals, with their favorite "Bums," a nickname given the Dodgers by their fans. It was sometimes also called the "peoples' cherce."

The major event of the year was the announcement that the Federal League was going to become a major league, and baseball wars began as they raided the National and American Leagues. This was to last for two years.

1914

AMERICAN LEAGUE: WAR ON THE HOME FRONT

While war raged in Europe, baseball experienced its own war, which would last through the 1915 season: the Federal League was formed by raiding players from both American and National League teams.

Philadelphia captured the title handily, winning by 8½ games over Boston, although their biggest winners were Chief Bender and Bullet Joe Bush with 17 wins each. Eddie Plank had a 15–7 mark; Jack Coombs was ill again and appeared in only two games. It marked the first time a team had won the pennant without a 20-game winner.

Only three pitchers would crack the charmed circle, with Walter Johnson winning 28 for the third-place Senators. Ray Collins (Boston) and Harry Coveleski (Detroit) were the other 20-game winners.

Johnson turned in another superlative effort as he led in virtually every important pitching category. He was tops with 28 wins, 51 appearances, 40 starts, 33 complete games, 372 innings pitched, 225 strikeouts, 9 shutouts and a 1.72 ERA. He was saddled with 18 losses, but many of those can be attributed to poor batting support.

From 1910 through 1918, Johnson never pitched fewer than 300 innings, while leading in strikeouts from 1912 through 1919. To illustrate his importance to Washington, subtract his record and they were sub-.500 again. This time the team was 53–55.

Collins finally cracked the 20-win circle by winning exactly that number. He had a near miss the previous year when he won 19. However, he would last only one more season and be gone by 1916 at only 29, another career shortened or stopped at a young age.

Coveleski had bounced around the National League from 1907 to 1910 with little success, compiling only a 12–12 mark. Finally he resurfaced with Detroit in 1914 and won 20 or better for the first of three seasons. His initial mark was 22–12 with a 2.50 ERA. Coveleski was also used in double duty. In a few seasons his younger brother, Stan, would be a star pitcher for Cleveland, four times winning 20 or more for them, and later adding a fifth 20-win season for Washington. But for now our focus is on Harry.

To add a side note about a couple of former big winners, Joe Wood was 9–3 as he appeared in only 18 games, and Ed Walsh was limited to eight games and a 2–3 mark.

Again no team had 100 complete games, as New York, although finishing seventh, led the way with 97, while last-place Cleveland had the fewest with 69. The fewest number of pitchers to complete 20 games was recorded, as only six turned the trick, with only Johnson's 33 breaking the 30 mark.

Pitcher/Team	G	GS	CG	W	L	Pct	ERA	SO	W	IP
Walt Johnson, Wash	51*	40*	33*	28*	18	.635	1.71	225*	74	372*
Harry Coveleski, Det	44	36	23	22	12	.647	2.49	124	100	303
Ray Collins, Boston	39	30	16	20	13	.606	2.51	72	56	272

Johnson captured nearly all the pitching titles, including shutouts with ten. Only the ERA and winning percentage eluded him. The former went to Dutch Leonard (19–5) of Boston with a 1.01, while Bender with a 17–3 mark led in percentage with .850.

Philadelphia was heavily favored to win in the World Series, but in one of the greatest sports upsets of all time lost to Boston in four straight. It would be 15 years before Connie Mack's team returned to the top. With increased pressure from the Federal League, and suspicion that some players laid down in the Series, Mack began selling off his stars and breaking up the team, leading to a decline during which the A's would be the league doormat for many years to come.

This season saw the introduction of a player who in later years would have the most significant impact of anyone on the game. That player was 19-year-old Babe Ruth, who in four games posted a 2–1 record. While he would win 94 games in a five-year pitching career, his real fame would be as the greatest home run hitter and fan attraction in the game.

NATIONAL LEAGUE: A CHAMPION RISES OUT OF THE ASHES OF PHOENIX

Just as the mythological Phoenix would rise out of the ashes, the Braves came from last place on July 18 to win the pennant by 10½ games over New York. They hit first place on September 1 and stayed there for good, as they capped a drive that produced a 34–10 record.

Dick Rudolph (27–10) and Bill James (26–7) formed the core of the Boston pitching staff. James won only 11 other games in his big league career, while Rudolph had more success, winning 22 and 19 the next two seasons.

This was Rudolph's stellar campaign. His 27 wins tied him with Alexander for the league lead. While he would never again reach these heights, he did enjoy some degree of success, for all intents finishing his career in 1920, although he was back in 1922–23 and 1927 for eight games and a 1–4 record. However, this year was all Rudolph's: he appeared in 42 games, starting 36 and completing 31, while hurling six shutouts and posting a 2.36 ERA.

Teammate Bill James posted one less win, but had a brilliant 26–7 mark with an excellent 1.90 ERA with four shutouts. James saw double duty with 46 appearances, including 37 starts and 30 complete games. Unfortunately, James injured his shoulder the next season and was never the same pitcher again. He was finished at age 23 with the 1915 season—another potentially brilliant career lost to injuries.

Jeff Tesreau and Christy Mathewson won 50 games between them, but Rube Marquard could post only a 12–22, a major cause for the Giants' demise. Five other pitchers won 20 or more, highlighted by Pete Alexander's 27 wins, which tied him with Rudolph for the league lead. This was Tesreau's greatest season as he led the league in starts (40) and shutouts (8). Tesreau never won 20 again, although he did have 19 the next season and never pitched losing ball in a seven-season career that closed at the end of the 1918 campaign.

No one knew it at the time, but this was Mathewson's last big season, as well as his last winning campaign. In two years he would retire from the game at the age of 36 and be dead by age 45 of pulmonary tuberculosis brought on by a gas attack in World War I. However, this was another typical Mathewson season with 24 wins, 41 appearances and 29 complete games in 35 starts.

The Giants' failure to win the pennant can be traced to Marquad's reversal of form as he posted his poorest year with a 12–22 mark. Late in 1915 he was traded to Brooklyn where he had mixed success. Marquad would pitch until 1925, finishing with the Boston Braves.

Although he fell one win short at 19–6, this was perhaps Bill Doak's finest season as he led the league with a 1.72 ERA. Doak would win 20 games in 1920, but his overall performance this year stands out as the best. Doak had 14 full seasons in the big leagues (most with St. Louis) and had mixed success, enjoying six winning seasons and eight losing ones, although twice he did lead in ERA.

A new big winner burst onto the scene in the person of Hippo Vaughn, who was a big man at 6' 4" and 215 lbs. Vaughn had been with New York and Washington in the American League from 1910 through 1912, recording a lackluster 27–32 mark. The Cubs acquired him in 1913 and he turned in a 5–1 mark in seven games, but it was this year he came into his own. Vaughn won 21 games with a 2.05 ERA, had 23 complete games in 35 starts and a total of 42 appearances. This was his first of three successive 20-win seasons, which would eventually become five in six years.

From 1914 through 1920, Vaughn won 143 games while losing 93; he finished his career with a 178–137 record and 2.48 ERA. To date he has not had a nibble for the Hall of Fame.

Meanwhile, teammate Larry Cheney posted his third straight 20-win season with a 20–18 mark. Cheney led the loop in games (50), starts (40) and posted an excellent 2.55 ERA. He deserved to have several more victories. After this season Cheney faded and was traded to Brooklyn in late 1915. He had one more good season, winning 18 for the Dodgers in 1916, finishing his career with the 1919 campaign.

In his first full season, Jeff Pfeffer was 23–12 with a minuscule 1.97 ERA as he hurled 27 complete games in 34 starts, while also making nine relief appearances. From 1914 through 1916, Pfeffer won 67 games for Brooklyn. He had an off season in 1917 and spent 1918 in the service, and although he didn't win 20 games again he posted several winning seasons for Brooklyn and St. Louis after the war.

Pete Alexander tied Rudolph for the league lead in wins with 27. He also led in complete games (32), innings pitched (355), and strikeouts (214). Alexander was a real workhorse for the Philadelphia club; teammate Erskine Mayer also toiled in 315 innings while winning 21 but dropping 19. Their ERAs were very similar: 2.38 for Alexander and 2.56 for Mayer. Both could have won more games with a few breaks.

Red Ames posted a 15–23 mark for last-place Cincinnati, despite a fine 2.64 ERA. Ames was in 47 games, starting 36, and also led the league with six saves. His career spanned 17 seasons with four teams, mostly New York and St. Louis, and included 12 years with ten or more victories, but ten with ten or more defeats.

Boston led the loop with 104 complete games, while Chicago, finishing fourth, was last with 70. A total of ten pitchers had 20 or more complete games, with three topping 30.

Pitcher/Team	G	GS	CG	W	L	Pct	ERA	SO	W	IP
Dick Rudolph, Bos	42	36	31	27*	10	.730	2.36	138	61	336
Pete Alexander, Phil	46	39	32*	27*	15	.643	2.38	214*	76	355*
Bill James, Bos	46	37	30	26	7	.788*	1.90	156	118	332
Jeff Tesreau, NY	42	40*	26	26	10	.722	2.38	189	128	322
C Mathewson, NY	41	35	29	24	13	.649	3.00	80	25	312
Jeff Pfeffer, Bklyn	43	34	27	23	12	.657	1.97	135	91	315
Hippo Vaughn, Chgo	42	35	23	21	13	.618	2.05	165	109	294
Erskine Mayer, Phil	48	39	24	21	19	.525	2.58	116	91	321
Larry Cheney, Chgo	50*	40*	21	20	18	.526	2.55	157	140*	311

Tesreau was the shutout king with eight as the Giants led the league with 20. Rudolph and James each won two games in the series, as Boston held Philadelphia to a .172 batting average.

The National League suffered greater losses to the upstart Federal League and the league war would continue through the 1915 season before peace would be established. Peace would then reign in baseball until the labor strife of the 1970s through the 1990s.

FEDERAL LEAGUE: DEEP POCKETS ARE PANACEA FOR HUNGRY BALLPLAYERS

Chicago businessman James A. Gilmore became president of the Federal League and induced millionaires Phil Ball, Charles Weeghman and Robert Ward, among others, to field teams. The players were the beneficiaries, as they received salaries heretofore unknown.

There were eight pitchers to win 20 or more games. Some were familiar names, while for others these two seasons would be their fleeting moment of glory. All records achieved in the Federal League seasons of 1914–15 are counted in major league totals, although some baseball purists question the judgment of such decisions.

In a three-team race, Indianapolis with an 88–65 record edged out 87–67 Chicago and 84–70 Baltimore. Cy Falkenberg was the big winner for Indianapolis, while Claude Hendrix (Chicago) paced the league with 29 wins. Indianapolis had the most complete games (104) and Kansas City the fewest (82).

Falkenberg had his biggest season with 25 wins, while leading in appearances (49), starts (43), innings pitched (377), strikeouts (236) and shutouts (9). He also posted a 2.22 ERA. Without a doubt, this was his finest hour. However, the wear and tear of this year proved too much and he was through by the end of the 1916 season, recording only a 14–20 record for his last two years.

Claude Hendrix had won 24 games for Pittsburgh in 1912 and led the league in winning percentage with .727; thus he was no stranger to the 20-win circle. However, 1914 with Chicago proved his finest hour as he posted a 29–10 mark for the best season of his career. He tied Falkenberg for appearances with 49, while posting a league-high 34 complete games in 37 starts. Hendrix also had six shutouts and five saves, further examples of his versatility.

Jack Quinn broke in with the New York Yankees in 1909 and finished with Cincinnati in 1933, missing only the 1916–17 campaigns. When he broke into the big leagues the emphasis was on pitching, but by the time he retired it had become a hitters' game, especially with the dramatic increase in home runs. However, for 1914 Quinn posted his career best as he won 26 games. The closest he would ever come again was 18, a feat he accomplished three times.

Some baseball purists question Quinn's season as it occurred in the Federal League. Two points should be remembered. If we dispute his record, then all others should stand the same test. Secondly, he did win 247 games during his career. Maybe he wasn't a *great* pitcher, but a pretty decent one for most of his career; he was in double-digit wins 12 times and posted 14 winning seasons.

Teammate George Suggs was no stranger to the 20-win club, having posted that number for Cincinnati in 1910 and 54 during the 1910–12 seasons before slumping to 8–15 in 1913.

This was Suggs' last big season and his best as he won 24 games with 26 complete games in 38 starts, while making 46 appearances. He and Quinn accounted for 50 of Baltimore's 84 wins, pitched 662 innings and had a combined 2.75 ERA.

Another former American Leaguer, Russ Ford, posted a 21–6 mark for Buffalo. Ford had won 48 games for the Yankees during 1910–11, then slumped to a 25–39 mark the next two seasons; but he had one moment of glory left— this 1914 year with Buffalo. His .778 winning percentage was the league's best, as were his six saves. Ford made 35 appearances, with 26 of them starts.

Tom Seaton was coming off his big season (27–12) with the Philadelphia Phillies when he jumped to Brooklyn and was 25–14. Although only 27, this was his last big year. Seaton would pitch three more seasons but win only 25 games, while losing 27 during that stretch. By age 30 his major league career was over.

Elmer Knetzer is another example of a pitcher whose greatest season was in the Federal League. For his six non-Federal years he was 31–43, while during his two campaigns here he was 38–26, including a 20–12 mark for Pittsburgh this year. In his six seasons in the National League he posted only one winning year.

Gene Packard is yet another pitcher whose best years were in the Federal League. For his career he had a winning record, 85–69, but in his six National League seasons he was barely over .500 at 45–43, while he won 20 games in each of his two Federal League years. Pitchers such as Packard and Knetzer lend some credence to the claim that Federal League records and statistics should not be counted in major league totals. However, there are other pitchers, such as Hendrix and Ford, who were successful in both leagues. The debate will undoubtedly continue as long as baseball is played.

Pitcher/Team	G	GS	CG	W	L	Pct	ERA	SO	W	IP
C Hendrix, Chgo	49*	37	34*	29*	10	.744	1.69	189	77	362
Jack Quinn, Balt	46	42	27	26	14	.650	2.60	164	65	343
Tom Seaton, Bklyn	44	38	26	25	14	.641	3.03	172	102	303
Cy Falkenberg, Ind	49*	43*	33	25	16	.610	2.22	236*	89	377*
George Suggs, Balt	46	38	26	24	14	.632	2.91	132	57	319
Russ Ford, Buffalo	35	26	19	21	6	.778*	1.82	123	41	247
Elmer Knetzer, Pgh	37	30	20	20	12	.625	2.88	146	88	272
Gene Packard, KC	42	34	24	20	14	.588	2.89	154	88	302

Rankin Johnson (Chicago), with a 9–5 record (after posting only a 4–9 mark for the Boston Red Sox of the American League) was credited with the best ERA (1.58), while Falkenberg led in shutouts with nine. There would be no postseason play for Indianapolis. All the teams would begin the next season with high hopes.

1915

FEDERAL LEAGUE: A QUICK BIRTH AND A SHORT LIFE

This season would prove to be the swan song for the Federal League. By year-end, peace would be made when Judge Kenesaw M. Landis handed down his decision. Several owners were given chances to purchase a National or American League Franchise. The other teams were left to become part of a new minor league. Baltimore was left out in the cold. Finally, in 1922, Justice Oliver

Wendell Holmes ruled that baseball was exempt from suit under antitrust laws, giving it protection that has lasted until today.

This was another hot race, with 1½ games separating Chicago, St. Louis and Pittsburgh, in that order. George McConnell paced Chicago with a 25–10 mark. He would win a total of 16 other games in the big leagues. There were eight other pitchers to win 20 or more, some for the only time in their career, while others such as Eddie Plank and Ed Reulbach, former stars in the National or American Leagues, were winding down their careers.

In four seasons prior to this year, McConnell was 12–29. He played one more year (1916) in which he was 4–12 for the Chicago Cubs. His record certainly supports the contention that Federal League records shouldn't count as major league statistics. However, for this one season he was superb, posting a 2.20 ERA in 303 innings in addition to his league-high 25 wins and best winning percentage (.714).

Dave Davenport led the league in appearances (55), starts (46), complete games (30), strikeouts (229) and shutouts (10), while compiling a 22–18 mark, as one of three St. Louis pitchers to win 20 or more. This, too, was Davenport's only 20-win season, as he posted a 51–65 mark for the balance of his career.

The next pitcher didn't need the Federal League to inflate his career numbers. Eddie Plank was a proven 20-game winner, having broken that barrier seven times with the Philadelphia Athletics, as well as seven other years between 14 and 19 wins per season. Plank was winding down his career, but was still good enough to have a 21–11 mark, 2.08 ERA and appear in 42 games, with 23 complete in 31 starts.

Doc Crandall was the third member of that trio. While this was his only 20-win season, he had never posted a losing mark up to this point in his career. His 21 wins this year proved to be his career best, but prior to this year he had posted a fine 80–45 mark, mostly with the New York Yankees. In his situation it is hard to say whether he greatly benefited from the Federal League.

Frank Allen pitched for the Brooklyn Dodgers from 1911–14 and was 15–41. He joined Pittsburgh of the Federal League late in 1914 and went 1–0. Then in 1915 he had his career-best year, as he was 23–13 with a 2.51 ERA and a league-high six shutouts. Following this season he spent two years with the Boston Braves and was 11–13—another example of a pitcher who benefited from the outlaw league.

Nick Cullop, with his 22–11 record, enjoyed his best major league season. The prior year he was 14–20, with 19 of those losses coming with Kansas City of the Federal league. Ironically, Cullop's record was almost identical for the two years, except for his win-loss mark. He made 44 appearances, had 36 starts and 22 complete games both years, while posting a 2.34 ERA in 1914 and 2.44 in 1915.

Cullop had a 21–25 record for the balance of his career, posting his only other winning season with the Yankees at 13–6 in 1916. His record was 14–19 in 1914 and 22–11 in 1915. Did he benefit from the scaled-down major league?

Let the reader be the judge. Teammate Gene Packard, whom we have already discussed, had his second consecutive 20-win season.

Ed Reulbach certainly didn't need the Federal League to bolster his career marks, although he did enjoy his second 20-win season this year with a 21–10 mark for Newark. Previously, in eight seasons with the Chicago Cubs, Reulbach was 135–62. Then with Chicago and Brooklyn for 1913–14 he was only 19–27 before his one last moment in the spotlight with this campaign. Reulbach pitched one more full season with the Boston Braves in 1916 and was 7–6 before retiring with a 182–106, .632 winning percentage, but he is not in the Hall of Fame.

Al Schulz had a career mark of 47–62, but when we subtract his 21–14 mark for 1915, he was only 26–48 for his other four years, including 9–12 with Buffalo of the Federal League in 1914. He was certainly another pitcher who benefited from the reduced level of competency in the Federal League.

Three pitchers who fell on hard times were Russ Ford (he dropped to 5–9), George Suggs and Jack Quinn. Suggs slipped to 11–17 with a 4.13 ERA, while Quinn was 9–22. However, Quinn would stick around until 1933 and have several good if not outstanding seasons, including pitching for the 1929 and 1930 pennant-winning Philadelphia Athletics.

Did the Federal League benefit these pitchers and bolster their records? There were 17 20-game winners during the two years of its existence, and for 13 of those it was the pitcher's best year. Even if we exclude pitchers such as Jack Quinn and Claude Hendrix, at least 11 of these pitchers benefited immensely from the scaled-down league. However, long ago the decision was made to count these records as part of major league stats. Rather than comment further, I repeat: let the reader be the judge.

Newark (Indianapolis in 1914) led with 100 complete games, while seventh-place Brooklyn was last with 78.

Pitcher/Team	G	GS	CG	W	L	Pct	ERA	SO	W	IP
G McConnell, Chgo	44	35	23	25*	10	.714*	2.20	151	89	303
Frank Allen, Pgh	41	37	24	23	13	.639	2.51	127	100	283
Nick Cullop, KC	44	36	22	22	11	.667	2.44	111	67	302
Dave Davenport, STL	55*	46*	30*	22	18	.550	2.20	229*	96	393*
Ed Reulbach, Newark	33	30	23	21	10	.677	2.23	117	69	270
Eddie Plank, STL	42	31	23	21	11	.656	2.08	147	54	258
Al Schulz, Buffalo	42	38	25	21	14	.600	3.08	160	149*	310
Doc Crandall, STL	51	33	22	21	15	.583	2.59	117	77	313
Gene Packard, KC	42	31	21	20	12	.625	2.68	108	714	282

Davenport, who garnered most of the individual statistics, also led in shutouts with ten. Again there was no postseason play, and a league that had started with a bang ended with a whimper. Baseball would remain calm for another three generations, until free agency in the early 1970s.

AMERICAN LEAGUE: END OF AN ERA AND START OF ANOTHER

The Philadelphia A's went from league champs to cellar dwellers, as Connie Mack had sold off much of the team and they finished at 43–109. Meanwhile, the Boston Red Sox gained the crown by one game over Detroit on the basis of strong pitching depth. Rube Foster led the way with a 20–8 mark, and Babe Ruth, in his first full season, was 18–8, while leading the team with four home runs in only 92 at bats. Ruth had more homers than 45 players who batted over 300 times each.

Foster pitched only five years in the big leagues, all with the Red Sox, and except for a rookie 3–4 mark, had a winning season each year. The 1915 year was his peak as he posted a fine 20–8 mark with a 2.12 ERA. Foster finished his career with a 58–34 record after the 1917 season. Teammate Ruth was 18–8 with a 2.44 ERA and showed the brilliance that would soon make him the premier lefthander in the league, if not in baseball. However, as great as he was as a pitcher, his real and lasting fame came from his hitting prowess.

Another Red Sox pitcher, Smokey Joe Wood, whom we have already discussed, was able to appear in 26 games and have a 14–5 mark while posting the league-low ERA at 1.49. Although there were abortive attempts, arm trouble basically forced him to call his career quits with this season. Wood appeared in seven games in 1917, 1919 and 1920, but with only a 0–1 mark.

Harry Coveleski and Hooks Dauss posted identical 23–13 marks for the Tigers. This marked the second straight 20-plus-win season for Coveleski, who would also reach that mark the next season. Coveleski showed his durability and versatility by tying Faber in games with 50, of which 36 were starts. He logged a 2.44 ERA while pitching 313 innings.

This was Dauss' first trip to the charmed circle, but not his last, as he twice more won 20 or more. Dauss was also a workhorse, appearing in 46 games of which 35 were starts, while posting a 2.50 ERA and hurling 310 innings. During his career, which lasted until 1926, Dauss won 222 games, with 14 of his 15 years in double-digit victories, and only three losing seasons. However, as of this writing he is not in the Hall of Fame.

Jim Scott and Red Faber each won 24 for third-place Chicago. For Scott this was his premier season. It marked his second 20-win campaign and his last winning season. Scott was only 13–21 for the next two years and was out of baseball after 1917. For his career Scott was only 107–113, but this year he was superb. He made 48 appearances, had 35 starts with 27 complete games, and a gaudy 2.04 ERA.

This was Faber's second year in the big leagues and his first 20-plus-win season, but he would crash the barrier three more times. Faber pitched winning ball for his first ten seasons and 12 of the first 13. From 1921 on, he had the misfortune to pitch for one of the weakest teams in the league. He and Ted Lyons would form a pitching twosome that was at the mercy of an inept team behind them, as both spent their entire careers with the Chicago White Sox.

Walter Johnson was again the league's big winner at 27–13, as the "Big Train" just kept rolling along. This marked the sixth straight year he won 25 or more games, as well as the third straight season he led in complete games, shutouts and innings pitched, while the fourth straight year he was strikeout king. Despite a 1.55 ERA, he lost that title to Wood's 1.49.

Honorable mention goes to several pitchers on second division teams. Ray Caldwell won 19 games with 31 complete in 35 starts for the Yankees, while teammate Ray Fisher had 18 wins and a 2.11 ERA. This season gave Caldwell 36 wins in two years, but it would be several seasons before he again tasted the rarefied air of a big winner. This season represented the peak of Fisher's career.

Carl Weilman won 18 games for a weak St. Louis team while posting a 2.34 ERA and appearing in 47 games, of which 31 were starts. During the 1914–16 campaigns, he won 54 games but lost 49, many due to weak support. Weldon Wyckoff of the Philadelphia Athletics was the big loser with 22, and shortly would be out of the league.

Only fifth-place New York posted 100 complete games to lead the league, while seventh-place Cleveland was last with 62. As complete games were slowly falling, the use of relief pitchers was on the rise, although most managers still used their starters quite frequently in relief.

A total of nine pitchers had 20 or more complete games, with three over the 30 mark.

Pitcher/Team	G	GS	CG	W	L	Pct	ERA	SO	W	IP
Walt Johnson, Wash	47	39*	35*	27*	13	.675	1.55	203*	56	337*
Jim Scott, Chicago	48	35	23	24	11	.686	2.04	120	78	296
Red Faber, Chicago	50*	32	22	24	13	.649	2.56	182	99	300
Harry Coveleski, Det	50*	38	20	23	13	.639	2.44	150	87	313
Hooks Dauss, Det	46	35	27	23	13	.639	2.50	132	112	310
Rube Foster, Boston	37	33	22	20	8	.714	2.12	82	86	255

Ruth's 18–6 mark gave him a league-high .750 percentage. This season Ty Cobb won the batting title with a .369 mark that included a league-high 144 runs, a record 96 stolen bases and 99 RBIs.

Boston won the World Series in five games, with Foster winning twice. Ruth didn't pitch in the Series.

NATIONAL LEAGUE: A NEW CHAMPION AS AN OLD HERO FADES

The league featured a first-time winner in Philadelphia, led by Pete Alexander's 31–10 mark and assisted by Erskine Mayer with 21 wins. At the other extreme, the once-powerful Giants fell to last place, with Christy Mathewson falling to 8–14 as his arm went dead. Although only 36, his career would last only one more season, and he would be dead at 45 of tuberculosis.

Alexander led the league in virtually every major category, as he pitched

Philadelphia to their first-ever pennant. This marked his second successive season leading in wins, complete games, innings pitched and strikeouts. He also led with 12 shutouts, a .756 winning percentage and a league-low 1.22 ERA. This also marked the first of three successive 30-win campaigns. Mathewson is the only other pitcher to accomplish that feat in the 20th century. Certainly the war had a negative affect on Alexander's career; although he posted many fine seasons after 1918, they were not of the caliber of the 1911–17 vintage.

This marked Mayer's second straight season at 21 wins, but it was also his last. Although he continued to pitch winning ball for several years, the most he ever won again was 16 in 1918. This season he was a fine compliment to Alexander, as the two accounted for almost 60 percent of the team's victories.

The great Mathewson finally was stopped. At age 34 he was a subpar 8–14 with his highest full season ERA, 3.58, and only the second losing record in his career. Mathewson pitched one more year and then retired. He was 36 when he served in the army during World War I, in which he was gassed. He could no longer pitch when he returned and in a few years was dead from tuberculosis, which has been attributed to the gassing he suffered during the war.

Boston finished second as Dick Rudolph won 22, but Bill James finished at 5–4 after suffering a shoulder injury that ended his career. This was Rudolph's last 20-plus-win season, although he did win 19 the next year. After that he faded; although he lasted several more seasons, he was never again one of the league's top pitchers.

James is even more tragic, for after winning 26 games the previous year he seemed headed for a brilliant career. However, a shoulder injury limited him to 13 games this season and ended his career the following year. A potentially great pitcher was lost, and his career ended at age 24.

Hippo Vaughn and Al Mamaux were the league's other 20-game winners. With 20 wins, this marked Vaughn's second consecutive 20-plus-win season, and he would achieve that mark in five different years. In only his second full season, Mamaux turned in a brilliant year with 21–8, 2.03 ERA in 36 games, of which 31 were starts. He followed this with another 21-win season in 1916, but then was only 29–42 for the balance of his career, which lasted until the early 1920s.

Honorable mention goes to Jeff Tesreau, who toiled for the last-place New York Giants, as he appeared in 43 games, 36 starts and won 19 while pitching 306 innings and posting a 2.29 ERA. Certainly better support would have provided him with his third straight 20-plus-win season.

On the strength of Alexander's 36 complete games, Philadelphia led the way with 98, while fourth-place Chicago was last with 71. Only seven pitchers had 20 or more complete games, with two breaking the 30 mark.

Pitcher/Team	G	GS	CG	W	L	Pct	ERA	SO	W	IP
Pete Alexander, Phil	49	42	36*	31*	10	.756*	1.22*	241*	64	376*
Dick Rudolph, Bos	44	43*	30	22	19	.537	2.38	147	64	341

Pitcher/Team	G	GS	CG	W	L	Pct	ERA	SO	W	IP
Al Mamaux, Pgh	38	31	17	21	8	.724	2.03	152	96	252
Erskine Mayer, Phil	43	33	20	21	15	.583	2.36	114	59	275
Hippo Vaughn, Chgo	41	34	18	20	12	.625	2.87	148	77	270

Philadelphia was paced into the Series by Alexander and home run-hitting champ Gavvy Cravath, who led the majors with what was then a record 24. In the Series, despite a 1.53 ERA, Alexander was only 1-1. It would be 35 years before Philadelphia would play in another World Series and 30 years after that before they would be crowned World Champions.

1916

AMERICAN LEAGUE: TWO IN A ROW

Only four games separated the first three teams, but once again depth in pitching proved the difference and Boston edged out Chicago by two and Detroit by four games. Boston was led by Babe Ruth, 23–12, who also played in the outfield in addition to pinch-hitting.

This was Ruth's first of two successive 20-plus-win seasons and for his abbreviated pitching career he was an outstanding 94-46 with a career 2.28 ERA. Had he not switched to the outfield he probably would have approached 400 career wins—certainly 300–350. However, as great a pitcher as he was, his legendary impact on the game would be as a hitter.

Ruth made 44 appearances, had 40 starts and pitched 324 innings while leading with nine shutouts and a league-low 1.75 ERA. Ruth certainly demonstrated his ability as a moundsman. This gave him a 43-21 record for his brief career to this point.

Harry Coveleski won 21 for Detroit. This was Coveleski's third straight but last 20-plus-win season. However, brother Stan was emerging as a big winner; he won 15 this season and soon would be one of the league's most dominating pitchers. Harry had another fine season as he amassed 324 innings in 44 games while compiling a 1.97 ERA. After this year he would appear in 19 games and post a 4–7 mark over the next two years before retiring. Although he and brother Stan were in the big leagues together for four seasons, they never pitched against each other as a matter of principle.

Bob Shawkey pitched the New York club into fourth place with his 24 victories. This marked Shawkey's first 20-plus-win season and also the largest victory total of his career. Following World War I, three times he would win 20 games, and from 1919–24 he won 110 games. For his career he has 196 career wins, but no consideration for the Hall of Fame. His durability and versatility shone at this season. He led in saves with eight, appeared in 53 games, of which only 27 were starts, and he completed 21 while posting a fine 2.21 ERA. He certainly was a real asset to his team.

Eddie Plank had returned to the American League. He was winding his career down with the St. Louis Browns and was 16–15, but had an excellent 2.33 ERA.

Walter Johnson again topped the league with 25 wins, but lost 20 as Washington finished seventh at 76–77. Philadelphia was the only other team under .500, but they were last with a horrible 36–117 mark, a record for losses in a single season. Without Johnson, Washington was 51–57. The team ranked seventh in scoring and tied for last in hitting. Thus Johnson, despite leading in starts (38), complete games (36), innings pitched (371), strikeouts (228) and posting a brilliant 1.89 ERA, lost 20 games. With any support at all his record could have been 30 to 35 victories. Still, this marked the seventh straight season he won 25 or more games. It also was the fourth straight season he led in complete games, innings pitched and strikeouts.

Ironically, Philadelphia led with 94 complete games, as Bullet Joe Bush was 15–24 and Elmer Myers 14–23. The rest of the staff were an unbelievable 7–70, including 1–16 by Tom Sheehan and 1–18 by Jack Nabors. Cleveland was last with 65 complete games, as four teams completed less than 50 percent of their starts. Only six pitchers had 20 or more complete games, with just Johnson and Myers exceeding 30.

Pitcher/Team	G	GS	CG	W	L	Pct	ERA	SO	W	IP
Walt Johnson, Wash	48	38	36*	25*	20	.556	1.89	228*	132	371*
Bob Shawkey, NY	53	27	21	24	14	.632	2.21	122	81	277
Babe Ruth, Boston	44	40*	23	23	12	.657	1.75*	170	118*	324
Harry Coveleski, Det	44	39	22	21	11	.656	1.97	108	63	324

Although relief pitching was on the increase, much of it still was done by starting pitchers. A couple to illustrate: Shawkey was in 53 games, starting 27, while the leader in appearances was St. Louis' Dave Davenport with 59 games, 31 of them starts. Ruth was shutout king with nine, while Eddie Cicotte of Chicago led in percentage with .696 on his 16–7 mark.

The Red Sox repeated in the Series, winning in five games as Ernie Shore won twice and Ruth was 1–0 with a .64 ERA. Ty Cobb batted .371, but lost his batting title to Cleveland's Tris Speaker with a .386 mark.

NATIONAL LEAGUE: ANOTHER FIRST-TIME WINNER

For the fourth consecutive season there was a different winner, and for the third straight season, a team winning their first title. This time it was the Brooklyn Dodgers, who would go on to become one of the most successful franchises in the game. Although quite adept at winning pennants, they didn't fare very well in World Series play.

The league had a four-team race, with only six games separating Brooklyn, Philadelphia, Boston and New York, in that order. Jeff Pfeffer had his career-best year with 25 wins. This gave him 67 wins for 1914–16. Although he pitched until the 1920s, Pfeffer never again won 20 games, but did have several good winning seasons. This year he was outstanding, as he posted a 1.91 ERA while pitching 329 innings and completing 30 of 37 starts.

Pete Alexander, in the middle of his three consecutive 30-plus-win seasons, almost pitched Philadelphia to the title with his 33–12 mark, 1.55 ERA, 16 shutouts and league-high 167 strikeouts. This was the third consecutive year he led in victories, complete games, innings pitched and strikeouts, and the second straight he led in shutouts and ERA. The 16 shutouts he posted this year still hold the single-season modern record for any pitcher.

Eppa Rixey and Al Mamaux were the other 20-game winners in the league. Rixey had been in the league for four seasons and posted only a 32–38 mark, although pitching effectively. The bane of his career was that most of the time he pitched for losing teams. Therefore he has the lowest winning percentage of any pitcher in the Hall of Fame. He won 20 or more on four occasions, while losing 20 or more in two different seasons.

This year Rixey was outstanding, as he ably assisted Alexander in pitching the Phillies into second place. His 1.85 ERA was second only to Alexander. The two were 55–22, while the rest of the team was only 36–40, which kept them out of first place.

Although Mamaux would pitch for another eight years, he would have only one more winning season. However, this year he showed what a workhorse he could be as he hurled 310 innings, appeared in 45 games, completing 26 of 38 starts and posting a 2.53 ERA.

Christy Mathewson was only 3–4 for the Giants when he was traded to Cincinnati, where he was 1–0 in his only start. He then retired and managed the club for the balance of the season. Mathewson left behind a remarkable 372–187 mark (some historians credit him with 373 victories), 80 shutouts (third on the all-time list, behind Walter Johnson and Alexander) and a career 2.13 ERA. He won 20 or more games 13 times, including 12 in a row. He also won 30 or more four times, including three years in a row (1903–05), and holds the National League single-season record of 37 wins (1908). It's unfortunate that he did not pitch as long as Johnson or Alexander. Surely he would have won 450, and perhaps even approached 500.

Hippo Vaughn failed to win 20 games (he was 17–15), but would bounce back for the next three years in a row giving him five of six seasons with 20 or more wins. Vaughn still turned in an admirable season, appearing in 44 games, starting 35, logging 294 innings and posting a fine 2.20 ERA.

Boston and Philadelphia tied for the lead in complete games with 97, with Brooklyn one back, while St. Louis was last in the league in victories and complete games with 58. Ten pitchers completed 20 or more games, with only Alexander and Pfeffer achieving 30 or more.

Pitcher/Team	G	GS	CG	W	L	Pct	ERA	SO	W	IP
Pete Alexander, Phila	48	45*	38*	33*	12	.733	1.55*	167*	50	389*
Jeff Pfeffer, Bklyn	41	37	30	25	11	.694	1.91	128	63	329
Eppa Rixey, Phil	38	33	20	22	10	.688	1.85	134	74	287
Al Maumax, Pgh	45	38	26	21	15	.583	2.53	163	136*	310

Boston's Tom Hughes captured the winning percentage title with an .842, based on his 16–3 mark. Brooklyn's only victory in the Series was by the old Philadelphia ace, Jack Coombs, who was 13–8 in the regular season.

1917

AMERICAN LEAGUE: A NEW CHAMPION IS CROWNED

Boston won one game less than the previous year, but finished nine games behind the front-running Chicago White Sox, despite 24 wins from Babe Ruth and 22 from Carl Mays. Ruth also saw occasional duty as an outfielder and pinch hitter, batting .325. Meanwhile, Eddie Cicotte copped pitching honors with 28 wins and a 1.53 ERA while leading Chicago to the pennant.

Cicotte achieved his greatest season to date. In addition to his 28 wins, he led the league with 347 innings pitched and a sparkling 1.53 ERA. He also did much double duty, appearing in 49 games, completing 29 of 35 starts, hurling seven shutouts and gaining four saves. Cicotte would later be a prominent figure in the infamous Black Sox Scandal, but for now these were his halcyon days.

This was Cicotte's tenth year in the big leagues, but his first time to win 20 or more. Prior to this time he had pitched .500 ball or better in six of his nine campaigns, but his highest victory total had been 18 in 1913. He was 118–101 coming into this season. When he was suspended from baseball, he was 208–149. With a few years still to pitch, he could have won 275 games and made the Hall of Fame instead of the Hall of Shame.

Ruth had his second straight 20 plus-win season. He had 35 complete games in 38 starts and a 2.02 ERA while pitching 326 innings. This was his last full season as a pitcher. From here on out the concentration was on his hitting, although he did help pitch Boston to their last World Series title the next season; more on that later.

This was Mays' third season and his first time to win 20 or more, a feat he would accomplish five times during his career. Mays was not a very popular player, in fact one of the most disliked, which wasn't helped by the fact that he killed the only player—Cleveland shortstop Ray Chapman—ever to die from an injury received in a baseball game. Chapman died when he was beaned by Mays. These factors have probably helped keep him out of the Hall, despite impressive credentials including the five aforementioned 20-plus-win seasons, 207 career wins and a .622 career winning percentage.

In this his maiden 20-win season, Mays was brilliant. He had shown what he could do by winning 18 the previous year; this year he blossomed fully. His final mark was 22–9, 1.74 ERA, 35 games, 33 starts, 27 complete games and 289 innings pitched. Whatever personality quirks he may have had, Mays was one terrific pitcher.

Jim Bagby of Cleveland and Walter Johnson of Washington won 23 each. This marked Bagby's first entry into the 20–win class, but from 1916 through 1921 he never won fewer than 14 nor had a losing record, while winning 118 games. He was a workhorse, performing double duty; five of the six years he was in 40 or more games and twice led the league in appearances. This season he was in 49 games; 37 were starts and he completed 26. To go with his 1.94 ERA, he had seven shutouts and six saves. These stats attest not only to his durability and versatility, but effectiveness as well.

Stan Coveleski almost made the charmed circle, but fell one short with his 19–14 record. He had a minuscule 1.81 ERA with a league-high nine shutouts. Only two teams in the league had a lower team batting average than Cleveland and this undoubtedly attributed to a number of Coveleski's and Bagby's losses. Coveleski was also a well-used pitcher, appearing in 45 games with 25 complete out of 36 starts.

Johnson's victory total could have been higher with a better team behind him. Without Johnson, the Senators were 51–63. Although he had 30 complete games in 34 starts, he lost out in leading the league to Ruth. He also finished second in innings pitched and victories, but maintained his strikeout crown. Once again he was used often by Washington, appearing in 47 games and posting a 2.21 ERA. Only the New York Yankees had a lower team batting average; thus we can see the major reason for many of Johnson's defeats.

Hooks Dauss, although he didn't win 20, turned in another fine season for Detroit with 17 wins, giving him 78 over the past four seasons. He was in 37 games, with 22 complete of 31 starts while posting a 2.42 ERA.

Boston led the loop with 115 complete games, 28 more than their nearest rival, New York, while seventh-place St. Louis had the fewest at 65. Nine pitchers had 20 or more complete games, with only Ruth and Johnson posting 30 or better.

Pitcher/Team	G	GS	CG	W	L	Pct	ERA	SO	W	IP
Eddie Cicotte, Chgo	49	35	29	28*	12	.700	1.53*	150	70	347*
Babe Ruth, Boston	41	38	35*	24	13	.649	2.02	128	108	326
Jim Bagby, Cleve	49	37	26	23	13	.639	1.96	83	73	321
Walt Johnson, Wash	47	34	30	23	16	.590	2.30	188*	67	328
Carl Mays, Boston	35	33	27	22	9	.710	1.74	91	74	289

Chicago's Reb Russell had a .750 winning percentage based on his 15–5 record. Two future Hall of Famers retired. Eddie Plank, winner of 326 career games (third highest for a left-hander), finished at St. Louis with a 5-6 season. Sam Crawford called it a career at Detroit as a pinch hitter in his final year.

The White Sox won the World Series in six games. The pitching hero was Red Faber, who was 3–1. Cicotte was 1–1.

NATIONAL LEAGUE: A RETURN TO THE TOP

For the fifth consecutive year, a new champion was crowned. This time it was a former winner, the New York Giants. The team was led by Ferdie Schupp (21–7), who had the best season of his career. Once again Philadelphia was second, basically on the strength of Pete Alexander's third straight 30-win season.

Although Schupp is credited with ten seasons in the big leagues, he won only 61 games, as many of his years he had limited game appearances. His next closest win total was 16 in 1920. For his career he had a fine winning mark of 61–39. Schupp fashioned 25 complete games in 32 starts, six shutouts and a 1.95 ERA.

Without Alexander, Philadelphia was only 57–52, showing once again the reliance of this franchise on the hard-throwing right-hander. This marked the third consecutive season he won 30 or more games. It also was the fourth straight year he led the league in victories, complete games, innings pitched and strikeouts. He also led in shutouts for the third consecutive year, but lost in his bid to be ERA king for the third consecutive year.

Twenty-game losers permeated first-division staffs as Eppa Rixey, despite a fine 2.27 ERA, was only 16–21 for Philadelphia. St. Louis' Bill Doak won 16, but also lost 20. This was a very unusual situation, as the second and third-place clubs each had 20 game losers.

Christy Mathewson, now retired, but full-time manager of the Cincinnati Reds, brought them home fourth as Fred Toney won 24 and Pete Schneider 20, although the latter lost 19. Ironically, it was the third straight season Schneider lost 19 but the first time he had a winning mark. This also proved to be Schneider's only winning season as he finished his career with the Yankees in 1919 and a 59–86 mark.

Toney was a different story. He won 139 games during his 12 season career and posted a .500 or better record in eight of the 12 years. This season was his high-water mark as he had 31 complete games in 42 starts, pitched 340 innings, had seven shutouts and a 2.20 ERA.

Hippo Vaughn returned to the 20-win circle with a 23–13 mark. This marked the third year in the last four that he won 20 or more and was the start of a string of three consecutive 20-win years, stopped only in 1920 for four straight when he fell one victory short at 19. Vaughn was a workhorse: from 1914 through 1920, he never worked fewer than 270 innings, twice exceeding 300, as well as leading the league on two separate occasions. Mathewson's old pitching buddy, Rube Marquard, was in his third season with Brooklyn and emerged with a 19–12 record. While never again a big winner, he continued pitching until the 1925 season.

Finally, a pitcher we will be hearing more about was emerging: Wilbur

Cooper of the Pittsburgh Pirates. Although the Pirates were last, he posted a fine 17–11 record. This was the start of an eight-year string in which he won 161 games, four times over 20 and never winning less than 17. For his career, he totaled 216 wins with only four losing seasons in 15, but is not in the Hall of Fame.

Sixth-place Boston topped the circuit with 105 complete games, while St. Louis was last with 66. There was a jump in the number of pitchers posting over 20 complete games as the league had 13, of which two exceeded 30.

Pitcher/Team	G	GS	CG	W	L	Pct	ERA	SO	W	IP
Pete Alexander, Phil	45	44*	35*	30*	13	.698	1.86	201*	58	388*
Fred Toney, Cinn	43	42	31	24	16	.600	2.20	123	77	340
Hippo Vaughn, Chgo	41	39	27	24	13	.639	2.01	195	91	296
Ferdie Schupp, NY	36	32	25	21	7	.750*	1.95	147	70	272
Pete Schneider, Cinn	46	42	25	20	19	.513	1.97	142	119*	334

St. Louis finished third based on their hitting, as they had Rogers Hornsby at .327, the second-best hitter in the league. This season saw the retirement of two Hall of Famers when Johnny Evers and Honus Wagner both hung up their spikes.

1918

AMERICAN LEAGUE: REPEAT WINNERS IN A "NON-ESSENTIAL" SEASON

Baseball was ruled "non-essential" to the war effort and the season ended on September 2nd. Teams played between 122 and 128 games, depending on rainouts. Boston regained the top spot from Chicago with Carl Mays winning 21. Babe Ruth contributed 13 wins, but more importantly was playing part-time in the outfield, and led the league with 11 home runs.

Three other pitchers won 20 or more games in the war-shortened season. They were Cleveland's Stan Coveleski, Washington's Walter Johnson and Philadelphia's Scott Perry. The latter was a unique accomplishment as Philadelphia finished last for the fourth straight year, en route to what would be seven consecutive last-place seasons.

This marked Mays' second straight 20-plus-win season, and his 30 complete games in 33 starts were the league's top. Mays would be traded in mid-season the following year and in 1920 and 1921 would enjoy his two biggest years, both with the New York Yankees. This is also when the ill-fated beaning of Ray Chapman would happen.

Coveleski broke the 20-win barrier for the first of four consecutive seasons. His 22 wins almost put Cleveland into the World Series for the first time. Between 1918 and 1921, Coveleski won 93 games. From 1916 through 1926 he never won fewer than 13 games, breaking the 20 mark five times. His final mark of 215–142 earned him his place in the Hall of Fame.

Johnson had another big season, winning 23 games in an abbreviated year. Once again, without Johnson the ballclub was barely over .500. This marked Johnson's ninth straight 20-plus-win campaign and his fifth time to lead in victories. While he led in strikeouts for the seventh straight season, he was second in complete games at 29, but that was all the starts he made, in addition to ten relief appearances. His eight shutouts also topped the league. No wonder many consider him the greatest pitcher of all time.

Perry was only a journeyman pitcher with a career 40–68 mark, but he shone brightly this one season for last-place Philadelphia as he won 21 while losing 19 and posting a gaudy 1.98 ERA. He tied Mays for the complete-game lead at 30, while logging a league-high 332 innings.

Despite a shortened season, the Boston Red Sox were tops with 105 complete games, while New York was last with 59. The league averaged better than a 60 percent completion factor. In this shortened year, eight pitchers had 20 or more complete games, with two at the 30 level.

Pitcher/Team	G	GS	CG	W	L	Pct	ERA	SO	W	IP
Walt Johnson, Wash	39	29	29	23*	13	.639	1.27*	162*	70	325
Stan Coveleski, Cleve	38	33	25	22	13	.629	1.82	87	78	311
Carl Mays, Boston	35	33	30*	21	13	.618	2.21	114	81	293
Scott Perry, Phila	44	36*	30*	21	19	.525	1.98	81	111	332*

Johnson and Mays tied for the lead in shutouts, while Boston's Sad Sam Jones copped the percent title at .762 with his 16–5 mark. The Red Sox won the Series in six games, with Mays and Ruth each winning two games. Ruth extended his scoreless string to 29⅔ innings, a record that lasted until 1961 when broken by the Yankees' Whitey Ford. This was the last time the Red Sox won the World Series, although they have made four more trips since then.

NATIONAL LEAGUE: ANOTHER NEW CHAMPION

War played havoc with both leagues, as players were drafted, some enlisted and others went into war industries for the duration. The Chicago Cubs thought they had a lock on the pennant when they bought Pete Alexander from Philadelphia over the previous winter. Unfortunately, he got into just three games before he was drafted.

The Cubs, however, had enough pitching with Hippo Vaughn and Claude Hendrix both cracking the 20-win barrier in the shortened season to win by 10½ games over the New York Giants. No other team had a 20-game winner. Chicago's Lefty Tyler, Brooklyn's Burleigh Grimes and Pittsburgh's Wilbur Cooper each won 19. Undoubtedly the shortened season deprived them of 20 or more wins.

Vaughn grabbed most of the pitching honors as he led in wins (22), shutouts (eight), innings pitched (290), strikeouts (148) and ERA (1.74). This marked his fourth 20-plus-win season in five years and he would repeat in 1919, but he has never had a look in for the Hall of Fame.

Hendrix had not been much help to his team the prior two years; he posted a combined 18–28 mark, with both years being below .500. However, he responded brilliantly in 1918 with a 20–7 mark to help pace the Cubs to a pennant. This would be his last winning season as he was 10–14 and 9–12 in his final two campaigns. Although Hendrix had a winning career mark of 144–116, he posted winning seasons only in four of his ten years. Without a doubt, his record benefits from three 20-win seasons in which he was 73–26, while being only 71–88 for the other seven years.

Seventh-place Boston led with 98 complete games, while last-place St. Louis had only 72. This would be the last time St. Louis would finish last until 1990, the longest streak of any team in major league history. No pitcher recorded 30 complete games. Art Nehf was high with 28 as six pitchers reached the 20 plateau.

Pitcher/Team	G	GS	CG	W	L	Pct	ERA	SO	W	IP
Hippo Vaughn, Chgo	35	33*	27	22*	10	.668	1.74*	148*	76	290*
Claude Hendrix, Chgo	32	27	21	20	7	.741*	2.78	86	54	233

Vaughn and teammate Tyler (19–8) tied for the leadership in shutouts with eight. Vaughn was only 1–2 in the World Series despite having a 1.00 ERA. This was the lowest-scoring Series since 1905; only 19 runs were scored by the two teams in the six games.

1919

AMERICAN LEAGUE: THE BEGINNING OF THE END

Chicago for the last two decades had been one of the most consistently winning teams, several times winning the pennant. When they won in 1919 but lost the World Series, most people just chalked it up to a tired team losing in the showdown. It wouldn't be until a year later that the facts came out and eight players were banished from the game forever. But we are getting ahead of our story.

The season was limited to 140 games, but Eddie Cicotte was 29–7 to pace Chicago and become only the second pitcher in eight years to unseat Walter Johnson as the league's biggest winner. Lefty Williams also won 23 for the White Sox.

Stan Coveleski won 24 for runner-up Cleveland, and Bob Shawkey's 20 wins helped put the Yankees in third place. Other 20-game winners included Detroit's Hooks Dauss, St. Louis' Allan Sothoron, and, of course, Johnson.

When Cicotte was banished after the 1920 season he had won 208 games, including 50 during the 1919 and 1920 campaigns. Even though he was 37, most baseball people believed he had enough left in his arm to give several more good seasons and if not reach 300, certainly make the Hall of Fame.

In 1919 he was simply unbelievable, leading the league with 29 wins and the same number of complete games while posting a brilliant 1.82 ERA. His .806 winning percentage was tops as were his 307 innings pitched. Cicotte also made five relief appearances.

Teammate Williams, who was also barred after the 1920 season, had his first of two 20-win seasons with a 23–11 mark. He followed that with 22 wins, and then banishment at the age of 27. His chance for fame and greatness were gone. He missed much of the 1918 season due to wartime commitments, but during the 1917, 1919 and 1920 years, he won 62 games.

Coveleski got his second of four straight 20-win seasons as Cleveland was a bridesmaid for the second straight year. Coveleski was a hard worker, appearing in 43 games, starting 34, completing 24 and posting the same number of wins.

Shawkey had moved over from Philadelphia to the Yankees in 1915 and had proven to be a winning pitcher. The war interrupted his career, but he returned in 1919 to win 20 games for the second time and the first of two straight seasons. Altogether he would have four 20-plus-win campaigns and four others at 16 or better. However, that and his 198–150 mark have not qualified him for the Hall to date.

This marked Dauss' second time to win 20 or more as he posted a 21–9 record for fourth-place Detroit. For his career he won 222 games but has not made it to the Hall, and only a vote by the veterans committee could now place him there.

In 11 seasons, some for only a few games, Sothoron had only two winning years. This was one as he posted a 20–13 mark, with a 2.20 ERA. His second highest victory total had been in 1917, when he won 14 games but lost 19. He finished with a career 91–100 record.

For an American League record tenth straight year, Johnson posted 20 wins or more. Only Christy Mathewson with 12 straight is ahead of him. Johnson just made it, as he won an even 20 games, but posted the top ERA at 1.49, led for the eighth straight year in strikeouts and was first with seven shutouts. Without Johnson the Senators were a hapless 36–70.

Boston fell into sixth place as Carl Mays and Sad Sam Jones, a combined 37–18 the previous year, were only 19–31 this season before Carl Mays was traded to the Yankees. He was 9–3 there and would have several big seasons for them. Perhaps the biggest change in Boston's pitching was that Babe Ruth was limited to 17 games and a 8–5 mark as he became a full-time everyday player.

Ruth became the full-time right fielder and led the league with 29 home runs and 114 RBIs, while batting .322. His home run total exceeded that of four other teams in the league. This was just a harbinger of what was to come. Soon baseball would be changed forever.

Chicago topped the loop with 87 complete games, while Washington was last with 67. Although 11 pitchers had 20 or more complete games, none reached the 30 plateau.

Pitcher/Team	G	GS	CG	W	L	Pct	ERA	SO	W	IP
Ed Cicotte, Chgo	40	35	29*	29*	7	.806*	1.82	110	49	307*
Stan Coveleski, Clev	43	34	24	24	12	.667	2.52	118	60	296
Lefty Williams, Chgo	41	40*	27	23	11	.676	2.64	125	58	297
Hooks Dauss, Detroit	34	32	22	21	9	.700	3.55	73	63	256
Bob Shawkey, NY	41	27	22	20	11	.645	2.72	122	92	261
Allan Sothoron, STL	40	30	21	20	13	.606	2.20	106	87	270
Walt Johnson, Wash	39	29	27	20	14	.588	1.49*	147*	51	290

Again a weak team deprived Johnson of several more wins, as noted by his 1.49 ERA. In the World Series Cicotte was 1–2, but with a respectable 2.90 ERA, while Williams was 0–3 with a 6.62 ERA. Only Dickie Kerr and a 2–0 mark with a 1.42 ERA stood out for Chicago.

Ty Cobb won his twelfth and final batting title with a .384 mark. Although he would play until 1928 and never hit below .323, this was his last batting crown. Hitting was on the rise, starting with the next season. For the ensuing two decades, averages, runs and home runs would skyrocket as ERAs would soar.

NATIONAL LEAGUE: AN UNKNOWN AND UNWILLING PARTICIPANT

Little did the Cincinnati team realize what was happening in their first World Series. They just thought Chicago had a bad Series. During the regular season Cincinnati was a surprise winner, with a ten-game margin over New York and 21 over Chicago. The latter thought it had the pennant wrapped with the return of Pete Alexander from the war, but although he had the league's best ERA (1.72), he was only 16–11. He appeared in only 30 games after averaging 47 for his first seven years.

No one knew it at the time, but the effects of being gassed in the war were starting to show up, and he would suffer from epilepsy for the balance of his life. This led to a severe drinking problem, which only tended to heighten his epileptic condition.

Hippo Vaughn chipped in with 21 wins, but the Cubs could finish only a distant third. Cincinnati benefited from the only 20-win seasons from pitchers Hod Eller and Slim Sallee. Jesse Barnes of the Giants led the league with 25 wins.

Sallee won 174 games in a 14-year career, with only five losing seasons. This was his only 20-win year as he was 21–7 for the Reds. Twice earlier he had won 18 and once 19; thus he was not a stranger to being a frontline pitcher, but the 20-win mark had eluded him until this season.

Teammate Eller didn't last as long; his career was finished by the time he reached 26. While posting a 60–40 mark for his five years, he never had a losing season. This was his premier year at 20–9 with a 2.40 ERA.

Barnes was by far the league's premier pitcher as he led the loop with a 25–9 mark; it was also his career-best season. Barnes lasted 13 years in the big leagues and pitched winning ball in six of them. Twice he would exceed 20 wins, but also twice he lost 20 or more. As a result of the war, he was limited to nine games in 1918 and was 6–1, but in his two previous full seasons Barnes won 19 while losing 35, including 21 in 1917.

Vaughn had another fine year for Chicago with 21 wins, and with his 1.79 ERA could have won at least another half dozen given any decent support. The Chicago fans had come to expect big seasons from the big fellow, and from 1914 through 1920 he didn't disappoint them as he rolled up 143 wins in that span.

For the second straight season Wilbur Cooper failed to win 20 games; he had his second consecutive 19-win season. Certainly the shortened year cheated him: given a full year he undoubtedly would have exceeded 20 in both seasons, which would have given him five consecutive years at 20 or more victories.

Brooklyn topped the loop with 98 complete games, while seventh-place St. Louis had only 55. Again, no pitcher topped the 30 mark in complete games, with nine reaching the 20 level.

Pitcher/Team	G	GS	CG	W	L	Pct	ERA	SO	W	IP
Jesse Barnes, NY	38	34	23	25*	9	.735	2.40	92	35	296
Slim Sallee, Cinn	29	28	22	21	7	.750	2.05	24	20	228
Hippo Vaughn, Chgo	38	37*	25	21	14	.600	1.79	141*	62	307*
Hod Eller, Cinn	38	30	16	20	9	.690	2.40	137	50	248

Sallee became the first pitcher to win 20 games and not appear in at least 30 games. It would be almost a quarter of a century before this feat would be duplicated. In the Series Eller was 2–0, as Cincinnati won in six games.

Alexander won the shutout title with nine, while Dutch Ruether (19–6) won the percent crown with .760 for the champion Cincinnati Reds.

3

1920–1929

1920

AMERICAN LEAGUE: LANDIS LAUNDERS THE BLACK SOX

As the 1920 season began, rumors of a thrown 1919 World Series became more rampant. By year's end the stars of the Chicago team were expelled permanently from baseball. "Shoeless" Joe Jackson, who potentially had many brilliant years in front of him, and a sure Hall of Fame position, was barred from baseball for life, as were seven other White Sox players, including Ed Cicotte, who won 21 games in 1920.

Kenesaw Mountain Landis had been made Commissioner of Baseball and would rule like a czar for the next 25 years and return stability, integrity and honesty to the game.

Starting with this season, hitting would dominate the game for almost a quarter of a century. Babe Ruth hit an unbelievable 54 home runs, a total greater than any of the other seven teams in the league. Despite this hitting feat, Carl Mays' 26 wins and Bob Shawkey's 20 wins, the Yanks finished third with a 95–59 record, three games off the pace.

Cleveland won out over a dispirited Chicago team by two games for their first pennant. Jim Bagby's 31 wins, Stan Coveleski with 24 and Ray Caldwell with 20 paved the way. Meanwhile, Chicago had four 20-plus-game winners in Red Faber, Lefty Williams, Dickie Kerr and Eddie Cicotte. This was the first time it ever happened, and a foursome wouldn't be duplicated until 50 years later by the Baltimore Orioles.

Urban Shocker won 20 games for St. Louis, giving the league a total of ten 20-game winners. There were also three pitchers to lose more than 20. Hooks Dauss of Detroit was 13–21 as they finished seventh, while last-place Philadelphia had Scott Perry at 11–25 and Rollie Naylor at 10–23.

Bagby's career spanned nine seasons and in only six of them was he an everyday pitcher. From 1916 through 1921 he averaged 44 games per year, which includes two shortened seasons. Prior to this year his high-water mark had been 23 wins in 1917, but this season Bagby put it all together as he won 31 games (tops in the league). He also led in appearances (48), games started (39) and complete games (31). It was truly a career-best season.

Coveleski by now could just as easily have been called steady Stan, as he chalked up another big season with 24 wins to help Bagby pitch Cleveland to its first-ever pennant. Teammate Caldwell also had his best year as he won 20 for the only time in his career. The three were an awesome 75–36, leaving the balance of the staff with a 23–20 mark.

Faber led the White Sox with 23 wins. This was his first of three straight seasons in the charmed circle and also the first of three straight at 300 or more innings pitched. He also tied Bagby for starts at 39. Teammate Williams won 22 games, but at age 26 would be barred from baseball for life after this season. A potentially great career was lost.

Kerr, who pitched his heart out in the 1919 Series and won two games, was a 21-game winner in this tragic season. Kerr would pitch one more full season and then was out of baseball until 1925, when he appeared in 12 games with the White Sox before calling it a career. Cicotte was the fourth mound member of the team to win 20 or more, and he too would be banished from the game after this season. As stated earlier, his chances for the Hall also went south with his banishment.

Mays had a difficult season. On the bright side, he won 26 games—his tops to date—but on the down side, he was faced with tragedy. On August 16 at the Polo Grounds, he beaned Cleveland shortstop Ray Chapman. Chapman passed out, never regained consciousness and died the following day—the only fatality in major league baseball. It is believed by many that this, coupled with Mays' temperament and lack of personality, kept him out of the Hall despite a brilliant career.

Shawkey turned in another great season for the Yankees as he posted 20 wins for the second consecutive season. Starting with the 1916 campaign when he became a full-time starter for the club, he never won fewer than 13 games in any full year through 1924. The lone exception was the war year of 1918, which we have already discussed. Perhaps his last three seasons (1925–27) have hurt him as he was only 16–24, but a career should be viewed in its entirety.

Shocker had 12 years in the big time. He won 187 games and never had a losing season, but doesn't get consideration for the Hall. In 1920 he won 20 for the first of four straight years. From 1919 through 1927 he never won fewer than 12 games, averaging almost 19 wins a season for the St. Louis Browns and, in the latter years, for the New York Yankees.

Dauss' ERA was almost identical to 1919, but he went from 21 wins to 21 losses. It would take a couple more seasons before he rebounded into the winning column as a top-drawer pitcher. Meanwhile, Scott Perry had a horrendous 11–25 for last-place Philadelphia, giving him a two-year mark of 15–42 and 61 losses in three seasons. After the 1921 season he would be out of major league baseball.

The final 20-game loser was Rollie Naylor, who was 10–23 for Philadelphia.

His career lasted seven seasons, of which only one was a winning year. His career mark of 42–83 is not very envious.

Chicago, bolstered by its big four, led with 112 complete games, while Washington was last with 80. For the first time since 1909, Walter Johnson did not win 20 or more games as an arm injury limited him to 21 games and an 8–10 record. Ironically, in a subpar season he pitched his only no-hitter. Fifteen pitchers topped 20 complete games, with only Bagby at the 30 level.

Pitcher/Team	G	GS	CG	W	L	Pct	ERA	SO	W	IP
Jim Bagby, Cleve	48*	38*	30*	31*	12	.721*	2.89	73	79	340*
Carl Mays, NY	45	37	26	26	11	.703	3.06	92	84	312
Stan Coveleski, Cleve	41	37	26	24	14	.632	2.48	133*	65	315
Red Faber, Chgo	40	39*	28	23	13	.639	2.99	108	88	319
Lefty Williams, Chgo	39	38	26	22	14	.611	3.91	128	90	299
Dickie Kerr, Chgo	45	28	20	21	9	.700	3.37	72	72	254
Eddie Cicotte, Chgo	37	35	28	21	10	.677	3.27	87	74	303
Urban Shocker, STL	38	28	22	20	10	.667	2.71	107	70	246
Ray Caldwell, Cleve	34	33	20	20	10	.667	3.86	80	63	238
Bob Shawkey, NY	38	31	20	20	13	.606	2.45*	126	85	268

In an experiment that lasted only a couple of seasons, Cleveland won a planned eight-game Series in seven games, 5–2. Highlights were Coveleski's 3–0 and .67 ERA mark, and shortstop Bill Wambsganss' unassisted triple play—the only one in Series history.

NATIONAL LEAGUE: NOT AN OUTSTANDING SEASON

Neither overall events nor the race were as exciting in the National League, as Brooklyn won by seven games over New York. Burleigh Grimes led the way with 23 wins, while New York had a trio of 20-game winners but lacked the overall depth of Brooklyn's pitching staff.

Pete Alexander had his last really big season, although he would twice more exceed 20 wins, and pitch losing ball only in his final season in 1930. Alexander was 27–14 with a league-leading 1.91 ERA. Without Alexander, Chicago was 48–65. Bill Doak of St. Louis and Wilbur Cooper of Pittsburgh were the other 20-game winners.

This was Grimes' fifth season in the big time, but prior to this year he had only one winning season: 1918 when he was 19–9. His other three years he was a combined 15–30, including a terrible 3–16 in 1917. However, starting with this year he would win another 236 games to finish with 270 wins and enter the Hall of Fame. This was his first of five 20-plus-win seasons.

Fred Toney was the first of the trio of pitchers to win 20 for the Giants as he posted his second 20-plus-win season with a 21–11 mark. Toney had one more big season, winning 18 the next year before finishing with two losing campaigns.

Art Nehf pitched in the big leagues for 15 years, 13 of them winning seasons. He won 184 games, but this was the first time he broke the 20-win barrier.

He was 21–12 for the highest victory total of his career. However, from 1917 through 1924 he never won fewer than 14, while averaging 17 wins per year.

The third member of New York's winning trio was Jesse Barnes, who followed his 25-win campaign with a 20-victory season, giving him two years in a row. Barnes would not win 20 again, but did have winning marks his next two years before falling on hard times. From 1923 through the end of his career in 1927, he didn't have another winning year, going 51–72 for the five seasons.

The season lasted 154 games. Cooper finally got his 20 wins and did it in a big way by winning 24, after being deprived the two prior years with shortened seasons. He was not to be denied this year as he appeared in 44 games, started 37, and completed 28 while posting a 2.39 ERA. This was the first of Cooper's three straight 20-plus-win seasons.

Alexander was once again the darling of National League pitchers as he led with 27 wins, 40 starts, 33 complete games, 363 innings pitched, 173 strikeouts and a 1.91 ERA. He certainly came back in a big way. Although he pitched winning ball for the next nine seasons and twice topped 20 wins, he was never again as devastating as from the years 1911 to 1920. The war had taken its toll.

Hippo Vaughn was again a workhorse for the Chicago team, but fell one win short of the 20-win club; he had to settle for a 19–16 record, despite a fine 2.54 ERA. Vaughn pitched only one more season, finishing 3–11 with Chicago in 1921, and then called it a career.

Doak had a checkered career; he did finish with a winning record, 169–157, but had nine losing seasons in 15. However, this year he wouldn't be denied as he won 20 games on the button for his only time in the charmed circle. He also posted a fine 2.53 ERA in an era when scoring was on the rise.

Eppa Rixey lost 20 or more for the second time in three years when he posted a 11–22 mark, giving him a composite 33–55 mark for the years 1918–20. However, he would soon recover and pitch winning ball through 1928, including three 20-plus-win and two 19-victory seasons.

While the National League had no home run threat to match Babe Ruth, as Cy Williams led with 15, they did have Rogers Hornsby, who batted .370 in his first of six consecutive seasons in which he led the league. Over those six years he averaged better than .400, exceeding that hallowed mark three times.

Chicago, largely on the strength of Alexander's arm, led the way with 95 complete games, while St. Louis, although tied with Chicago for fifth, finished last with 72 complete games. Thirteen pitchers had 20 or more complete games, with only Alexander over 30.

Pitcher/Team	G	GS	CG	W	L	Pct	ERA	SO	W	IP
P Alexander, Chgo	46	40*	33*	27*	14	.659	1.91*	173*	69	363*
Wilbur Cooper, Pgh	44	37	28	24	15	.615	2.39	114	52	327
Burl Grimes, Bklyn	40	33	25	23	11	.676	2.22	131	67	304
Fred Toney, NY	42	37	17	21	11	.656	2.65	81	57	278
Art Nehf, NY	40	33	22	21	12	.636	3.08	79	45	281

Pitcher/Team	G	GS	CG	W	L	Pct	ERA	SO	W	IP
Bill Doak, STL	39	37	20	20	12	.625	2.63	90	80	270
Jess Barnes, NY	43	35	23	20	15	.571	2.65	63	56	293

The shutout title was captured by Pittsburgh's Babe Adams (17–13) with eight, one more than Alexander. Brooklyn was pathetic in the Series, scoring only eight runs in seven games as they lost to Cleveland.

1921

AMERICAN LEAGUE: THE FIRST OF MANY TO COME

Chicago had both pennant winners in 1906, and now for the first time New York would have the pennant winner from both leagues, a feat that was to be repeated many times over. When the Yankees won the pennant in 1921, no one dreamed or realized a dynasty was being created. Over the next 44 seasons, they would win 29 pennants and 20 World Series, far and away the best record of any team in the game.

Carl Mays led the way with a 27–9 mark, to tie St. Louis' Urban Shocker for the league high in victories. Cleveland was second, 4½ games back, as Coveleski had another 20-plus-win season with 23 wins. Sad Sam Jones won 23 for fifth-place Boston, but perhaps the most outstanding achievement was by Chicago's Red Faber. The team finished seventh, but he led the league in ERA with 2.48 and won 25 games. Certainly a better team would have seen his total over 30. Without Faber, Chicago was 37–77.

Dickie Kerr was 19–17 and also deserved a better fate. The rest of the staff was 18–60, highlighted by Roy Wilkinson's 4–20 mark. However, Philadelphia again captured team futility by losing 100 games and finishing last. Eddie Rommel won 16 but lost 23.

Again the real news of the league was Babe Ruth, who broke his own home run record by hitting 59. Only St. Louis with 67 and Philadelphia with 82 hit more home runs. Ruth had perhaps the greatest single season of any player in the history of baseball. He played in 152 games, had 177 runs, 204 hits, 44 doubles, 16 triples, 59 home runs, 170 RBIs and hit .378. The latter was good only for third place behind Harry Heilmann's .394 and Ty Cobb's .389.

Mays had his best season at 27–9, while completing 30 games and leading the league in appearances with 49. For the two seasons, he was an outstanding 53–20. While he wouldn't approach these numbers again, he still had a few good seasons left, which would be with Cincinnati later in the 1920s.

Coveleski completed his four-year run with 23 wins, while Cleveland was a bridesmaid for the third time in four seasons, interrupted only by their 1920 championship. He would not win 20 again for Cleveland, although he did win

45 games over the next three years. He would later surface with Washington to pick up his final 20-win season. But that's a story for another day.

Shocker had his biggest season as he tied for the lead in wins with 27, while completing 31 of 37 starts and making eight relief appearances and garnering four saves. Only Mays and Detroit's Jim Middleton with seven had more. Shocker was in the second year of a four-year run of 20 wins or more, during which he posted 91 victories.

Jones is another pitcher with a mixed career. He won 229 games but lost 217. He is credited with pitching in 22 seasons, 19 of them full campaigns. In only nine of his years did he pitch .500 ball or better. He twice won 20 or more and twice lost the same amount. This season was his first juncture at that stage; he was 23–16 for a fifth-place Boston team that would have finished lower without him.

Faber turned in perhaps the best pitching job in the league as he won 25 games for the hapless White Sox, who might have finished last without him. His 32 complete games and 2.48 ERA were the league's best and with a better team could have won 30 or more games. This was to be Faber's fate, saddled with a weak team, even though he would spend his entire 20-year career with them and eventually win 254 games and acceptance to the Hall of Fame. Undoubtedly he could have won over 300 given a decent team behind him.

Rommel pitched for 13 seasons and finished with 171 wins and a .590 winning percentage. Much of the reason for his 16–23 record could certainly be traced to the hopeless A's ineptitude. Rommel made 46 appearances, 32 starts and logged 285 innings. He would soon reverse his record.

New York led with 92 complete games while Detroit was last with 73. A total of 12 pitchers had 20 or more complete games, with three reaching the 30 plateau.

Pitcher/Team	G	GS	CG	W	L	Pct	ERA	SO	W	IP
Carl Mays, NY	49*	38	30	27*	9	.750*	3.04	70	76	337*
Urban Shocker, STL	47	39	31	27*	12	.692	3.55	132	86	327
Red Faber, Chgo	43	39	32*	25	15	.625	2.48*	124	87	331
Stan Coveleski, Cleve	43	40*	29	23	13	.639	3.36	99	84	316
Sad Sam Jones, Bos	40	38	25	23	16	.590	3.22	98	78	299

Waite Hoyt won two games in the Series and Mays one, but the Yankees lost in eight, five games to three. Ruth hit his first series home run. Walter Johnson, although not a 20-game winner, did return to winning form, as he won 17 games.

NATIONAL LEAGUE: FINALLY A CHAMPIONSHIP IN THE FIRST SUBWAY SERIES

There would be nine subway Series between the Yankees and either Brooklyn or the Giants. In this first season that it happened, the Giants edged out

Pittsburgh by four games and St. Louis by seven. Art Nehf won 20 for the Giants, but it was their hitting that paced the way as George Kelly, Frankie Frisch and Ross Youngs all hit over .300, and each drove in over 100 runs. Six of the regulars batted over .300 and a seventh was at .299.

Hitting was on the rise. St. Louis led the league with a .308 team batting mark, paced by Rogers Hornsby's .397. Except for home runs, his season paralleled Ruth's. He had 131 runs, 235 hits, 44 doubles, 16 triples, 21 home runs, and 126 RBIs to go with his league-leading mark.

Despite 22 wins from Burleigh Grimes, Brooklyn slipped to fifth place. Wilbur Cooper with 22 wins kept Pittsburgh in the chase. Boston's Joe Oeschger won 20 to help the Braves to fourth place. Oeschger's greatest fame would be pitching a 26-inning game with Leon Calderon in a 1–1 tie.

This marked Nehf's second straight 20-plus-win season and his final one, although he would win 19 the next year. For the 1917–22 period, Nehf won 109 games, averaging 18 wins per season. While never posting victory totals in the high 20s, he was a model of consistency, as during that period his victories ranged between 15 and 21. More pitchers should be blessed with his consistency. Even after his big win days were over, he won 38 and lost 23 for New York over a three-year period. Managers would love to have a pitcher of that caliber.

Cooper continued his excellent pitching for the Pirates as he garnered 22 wins, while starting a league-high 38 games and completing 29 of them. When we talk of consistency, Cooper's name must be added to the list. From 1917 through 1924, he ranged between 17 and 24 wins, averaging 20 wins for the eight seasons. This is what pennant-winning staffs are made of.

Oeschger pitched all or part of 12 seasons in the majors and posted only a 82–114 record, with just three full-season winning records. This was his high-water mark as he made 20 wins. The next two years he won only 11 games while losing 36. His greatest claim to fame is being one of two pitchers to pitch an entire 26-inning game.

Grimes was in his heyday as he spitballed his way to 22 wins, while pitching 302 innings and a league-high 30 complete games. Grimes would take his consistency in five-year stretches. He won 105 games from 1920 to 1924, ranging from 17 to 23 victories. He then slumped for a couple of seasons but bounced back to win 94 from 1927 through 1931 with a little wider range of 16 to 25 wins. Still a heck of a pitcher was "Ol' Stubblebeard."

Epilepsy and drinking began to take their toll on Pete Alexander. He appeared in only 31 games and was 15–13 for the Cubs, who had many problems and finished in seventh place. Pittsburgh grabbed team complete game honors with 88, while St. Louis was last with 70, one less than New York. Only six pitchers achieved 20 or more complete games, topped by Grimes' 30.

Pitcher/Team	G	GS	CG	W	L	Pct	ERA	SO	W	IP
Burl Grimes, Bklyn	37	35	30*	22*	13	.629	2.84	136*	76	302
Wilbur Cooper, Pgh	38	38*	29	22*	14	.611	3.25	134	80	327*

Pitcher/Team	G	GS	CG	W	L	Pct	ERA	SO	W	IP
Art Nehf, NY	41	34	18	20	10	.667	3.62	67	55	261
Joe Oeschger, Boston	46	36	19	20	14	.588	3.52	68	97*	299

It was obvious that hitting was on the increase as shutouts were limited to 3, posted by several pitchers. Boston had the most as a team with 11. St. Louis' Bill Doak took winning percent honors with a .714 mark off his 15–6 record. The league boasted 38 players who batted .300 or better and had at least 300 official at bats.

The Giants dominated the Series as Phil Douglas and Jess Barnes (both 15 game winners during the regular season) each won two. Strangely, Nehf, who had the best ERA at 1.38, was only 1–2.

—————— 1922 ——————

AMERICAN LEAGUE: TWO IN A ROW, BUT NO BRASS RING

The Yankees won their second consecutive pennant in a one-game squeaker over the St. Louis Browns, who had a franchise record 93 wins. Even in their lone pennant winning season (1944), they would not equal this total. Most sports historians consider this the best Brownie team of all time.

The Yankees repeated even though Ruth played in only 110 games and Bob Meusel in 121. Both had been suspended by Judge Landis for barnstorming after the 1921 season and didn't play until May 20. Despite this, Ruth hit 35 home runs to finish second, one of only two times he didn't win the home run crown between 1918 and 1931.

Bullet Joe Bush, despite a finger injury, won 26 games, while Bob Shawkey again won 20 to pace the Yankees' mound staff. Waite Hoyt won 19, but Carl Mays slipped to 12–14. They basically relied on a six-man pitching staff, a throwback to earlier days.

St. Louis was led by 24-game winner Urban Shocker and Elam Vangilder won 19. George Uhle of Cleveland, Red Faber of Chicago and Eddie Rommel of Philadelphia were the other 20-game winners. Rommel won 27 games for seventh-place Philadelphia, the first time in eight seasons they didn't finish last. Without Rommel the team was 38–76, good enough for the cellar.

Bush spent all or part of 17 seasons in the big time, but only four with the Yankees—and they were the most productive. During that time, he won 76 while losing 52. For the rest of his career he was 119–131, giving him a composite 195–183 record. This was certainly his high-water mark, as he logged 26 wins and lost only seven for a league-leading .788 percentage. His next-highest victory total was 19 the next season.

Shocker continued turning in big numbers for St. Louis. He won 24 games while appearing in 48 games, starting 38 and completing 29. He was a real workhorse as he logged 348 innings, posted a 2.97 ERA and led the league with 147 strikeouts. Another Shocker and the Browns would have won the pennant.

A new pitcher came to the forefront, and for the next couple of seasons he would be a dominating force in the league. Uhle won 22 games for Cleveland, while appearing in 50 games and starting a league-high 40. This was his first of two straight 20-plus-win seasons and three overall. While Uhle won 200 games in his career, he was not a consistent pitcher, as from 1921 through 1929 his victory totals varied from eight wins to 27. One could never be certain which Uhle would show up for the season.

Faber had another 20-win season as he won 21 for Chicago, and despite a league-best 2.80 ERA he lost 17 games, no doubt thanks to a weak Chicago team behind him. Faber also led with 352 innings and 31 complete games. To show the unfairness of the situation, teammate Charlie Robinson had a 3.64 ERA but posted a 14–15 mark. Faber deserved a better fate.

Rommel virtually reversed his 1921 record as he won a league-high 27 games for a Philadelphia team that finished seventh. Rommel was in a league-high 51 games. Remember, this was the era when a starting pitcher normally led the league in appearances. We are still several decades from the time when each team has its own relief specialist. Without Rommel, Philadelphia was a last-place finisher.

Walter Johnson, though posting a 2.99 ERA, was only 15–16. It looked like the end was near for the 34-year-old great. The Yankees led with 98 complete games, while Boston was last in the league and complete games with 71. Ten pitchers had 20 or more complete games, but only Faber could reach 30 or more.

Pitcher/Team	G	GS	CG	W	L	Pct	ERA	SO	W	IP
Ed Rommel, Phila	51*	33	22	27	13	.675	3.28	54	63	294
Joe Bush, NY	39	30	20	26	7	.788	3.32	92	85	255
Urban Shocker, STL	48	38	29	24	17	.585	2.97	149*	57	348
George Uhle, Cleve	50	40*	23	22	16	.579	4.08	82	89	287
Red Faber, Chgo	43	38	31*	21	17	.553	2.80*	148	83	353*
Bob Shawkey, NY	39	33	19	20	12	.625	2.91	130	98	300

George Sisler tied the modern American league hitting mark by batting .420, while teammate Ken Williams batted .332 and had a league-high 39 home runs and 155 RBIs. The Browns produced four 100-plus RBI hitters, and six of the regulars batted .312 or better.

The Yankees lost in the Series for the second straight time, this time four games to none as Ruth batted only .118, but brighter days were just ahead.

NATIONAL LEAGUE: TWO IN A ROW AND THREE IN A ROW

The New York Giants won their second straight pennant, this time by seven games over Cincinnati. The margin probably would have been greater if not for pitching ace Phil Douglas (11–4) being banned from baseball for life in midseason after it was discovered that he wrote a letter wherein he said he would accept a bribe to throw a game. Although New York lacked a 20-game winner, they had enough depth and hitting attack to take the title.

Cincinnati, while finishing second, had the unique honor of having a 20-game winner (Eppa Rixey, 25–13) and a 20-game loser (Dolf Luque, 13–23). Wilbur Cooper had another 20-plus-win season in helping Pittsburgh to third place, while Dutch Reuther rounded out the 20-game winners by winning 21 for sixth-place Brooklyn. They also unveiled Dazzy Vance, who won 18 games in his first full season at age 31. He would eventually win 197 games and become a Hall of Famer. Too bad he didn't break in six or seven years earlier.

Hitting continued to be on the rise as three teams batted over .300, led by Pittsburgh's .308. However, individually it was Rogers Hornsby who led the way with his third batting title in a row. His final mark showed 141 runs, 250 hits, 48 doubles, 14 triples, 42 home runs, 152 RBIs and a .401 average. The only number not to lead the league was the triples, in which he tied for third.

Rixey had the biggest season of his career with a league-high 25 wins and 312 innings pitched. He also led in starts with 38 while completing 26 of them. Had teammate Luque reversed his record, Cincinnati would have won the pennant. This was the low point of his career, while next year would mark the high spot.

Cooper's 23 victories made it three years in a row in the charmed circle. Had 1918–19 been full seasons, he probably would have had five in a row. Cooper just missed pitching 300 innings as he twirled 295, but he did lead with 27 complete games.

Ruether had the biggest winning season of his career with 21 victories for a sixth-place Brooklyn team. He previously had posted a 19–6 mark for Cincinnati in 1919 and followed with 16 in 1920. He would later help Washington win the American League pennant in 1925 with 18 wins and then help the Yankees in 1926–27 with a combined 27–15 mark. While never again achieving 20 wins, he did have several good and important winning seasons.

Pete Alexander continued to have problems with his epilepsy and drinking and finished with a 16–13 mark. Pittsburgh led with 88 complete games, and St. Louis (finishing fourth mainly on its hitting) was last with only 60 complete games—a low total for this era.

Pitcher/Team	G	GS	CG	W	L	Pct	ERA	SO	W	IP
Eppa Rixey, Cinn	40	38*	26	25*	13	.658	3.54	80	45	313*
Wilbur Cooper, Pgh	41	37	27*	23	14	.622	3.18	129	81	295
Dutch Ruether, Bklyn	35	35	26	21	12	.636	3.54	89	92	267

Cincinnati's Pete Donahue, with his 18–9 record, had the best winning percentage at .667, while Vance and Pittsburgh's Johnny Morrison each had five shutouts. The ERA title went to Rosy Ryan of New York at 3.00, another indication of the increased hitting.

In the World Series it was all New York Giants, as they steamrolled the Yankees in four straight. They batted .309 to the Yankees .203.

1923

AMERICAN LEAGUE: REVENGE FOR EVICTION

At the end of the 1922 season the Giants informed the Yankees that they were no longer welcome to play in the Polo Grounds. Thus the Yankees went out and built Yankee Stadium, and with an exciting team became the premier draw in baseball. They also went on to win their third straight pennant in easy fashion, by 11 games over Detroit. In October they would get their revenge on the Giants.

Once again the Yankees relied primarily on six pitchers, with Sad Sam Jones leading the way with 21 wins, but Herb Pennock and Joe Bush were 19-game winners, Waite Hoyt won 17, while Bob Shawkey had 16. There were four other 20-game winners, including George Uhle, who led the league with 26 wins as he helped pitched Cleveland into third place. The most interesting was probably Howard Ehmke, who won 20 games for last-place Boston.

Babe Ruth regained the home run title by hitting 41 and scoring a league-high 151 runs and driving home 130, tops in the league. Hitting continued to dominate the game as Cleveland hit .301 and Detroit batted .300, paced by Harry Heilman's .403.

This was the high-water mark of Jones' career with the Yankees; in fact, his only decent season. In the other four he was a combined 46–48, including a 9–15 mark in 1925. However, this season all the pieces came together and Jones garnered a 21–8 mark.

Hooks Dauss found his way back to the charmed circle as he won 21 for Detroit while helping pitch them to a second-place finish. This year marked Dauss' return from the downside; he had been 36–49 the prior three years. It seems as if this was the season of recuperation for several pitchers. He proved to be a real workhorse, appearing in 50 games, of which 39 were starts.

However, Uhle was the man of the hour and garnered most of the league honors. His 26 victories paced all pitchers, as did his 44 starts, 29 complete games and 358 innings. He also appeared in 54 games and had five saves. He certainly was a savior for the Cleveland ball team. Only Boston's Jack Quinn with seven and Washington's Alan Russell with nine had more saves.

Urban Shocker made it four years in a row for St. Louis as he won an even 20 games. Shocker would have one more season with the Browns where he won 16 before he was traded to the Yankees, where he won 49 games from 1925 to 1927. Shocker has to be the best pitcher in the history of the St. Louis Browns. No other pitcher ever won 20 or more four times in a row for the club, and given its total lack of success, Shocker would have to rate as the best.

For his career, Ehmke was 166–166, but this was his shining hour. Boston was 41–74 without him and even with Ehmke they were dead last. He appeared in 43 games, started 39, completed 28 and won 20. With a better team he might have achieved 25 or more wins. Ehmke would win 19 the next season for Philadelphia.

In a reversal of fortunes, Ed Rommel, who led the league with 27 wins in 1922, was tied with Detroit's Herman Pillette as the biggest loser with 19, although Rommel did win 18. Walter Johnson captured the strikeout crown as he showed flashes of old with his 17–12 mark. New York topped the circuit with 102 complete games while second-place Detroit was last with 61. Only seven pitchers made 20 complete games and none achieved the 30 level.

Pitcher/Team	G	GS	GC	W	L	Pct	ERA	SO	W	IP
George Uhle, Cleve	54	44*	29*	26*	16	.619	3.77	109	102	358*
Sam Jones, NY	39	27	18	21	8	.724	3.63	68	69	243
Hooks Dauss, Detroit	50	39	22	21	13	.615	3.62	105	78	316
Urban Shocker, STL	43	35	25	20	12	.625	3.41	109	49	277
Howard Ehmke, Bos	43	39	28	20	17	.541	3.78	121	119	317

St. Louis fell to fifth, primarily because George Sisler missed the entire season due to a severe sinus infection that almost ended his career. Although he returned the next year and enjoyed several good years, he was never quite the same hitter as previously.

Stan Coveleski of Cleveland, who was ill part of the season and could fashion only a 13–14 record, ironically led in ERA with 2.76 and shutouts with five. Even though Cleveland led in runs scored, it seemed as if they couldn't do it when Coveleski took the mound. Pennock garnered winning percentage honors with a .760 fashioned from his 19–6 mark.

The Yankees got their revenge on the Giants in the fall classic when they won four games to two. Ruth had a big Series, batting .368, scoring eight runs and hitting three home runs. Pennock won two games and saved a third.

NATIONAL LEAGUE: THREE STRAIGHT AND FOUR IN A ROW

For the third straight season the Giants won the pennant, but this one was not as easy as previous seasons. They had to battle Cincinnati and Pittsburgh, finally finishing 4½ and six games, respectively, ahead of them. The Giants did it without the aid of a 20-game winner; the highest was 16, posted by two pitchers. The Giants again relied on hitting as they had four men hitting over .300 and three driving in over 100, paced by Irish Meusel's league-high 125.

Cincinnati flashed three 20-game winners in Eppa Rixey, Dolf Luque and Pete Donohue, but didn't possess enough hitting to keep pace with the Giants. Pittsburgh had the hitting and 25-game winner Johnny Morrison; their old reliable Wilbur Cooper won 17 but lost 19.

Pete Alexander rebounded to win 22 and put Chicago into fourth place, slightly ahead of fifth-place St. Louis, which had 20-game winner Jesse Haines.

Brooklyn's Burleigh Grimes won 21 while Dazzy Vance chalked up his second straight 18-win season, but they were sixth at 76–78. While no team batted .300, hitting still continued to dominate, as every team except Boston scored at least 708 runs.

In almost a complete reversal of form, Luque led the league with 27 wins following his 23-loss season, and lost only eight times to lead with a .771 winning percentage. He also had the best ERA at 1.91, while leading with six shutouts. It certainly was a premier year for the "pride of Havana." Never again did he approach these heights, as his next-highest total was in 1921 when he posted a 17–19 record. For the rest of his career he was just 167–171. Take away this season and he is a sub-.500 pitcher.

Teammate Rixey garnered his second straight 20-win season and third straight year pitching over 300 innings with 309. His 20 wins gave him a three-year total of 64. Teammate Donohue played in the big leagues for all or part of 12 seasons, but it is the years 1922–26 for which we remember him. During that time he won 96 while losing 61. This year he won 21 for his first time at that level. He would achieve it two more times. The other seven seasons he was just 38–57—not quite enough over the long haul to put him in the upper echelon of career pitchers.

This was Morrison's one big season. The next closest was the prior year when he won 17, but this year was all his as he won 25 games. Morrison appeared in 42 games, of which 37 were starts, completed 27, while pitching 302 innings. This season evidently took a real toll on him: next year he slipped to 11–16 and fell to 238 innings pitched.

Cooper continued to be a workhorse for the Pirates as he made the league-high 38 starts and completed 26 of them. However, he had the misfortune to be on the wrong end of too many games, became the league's big loser with 19, and lost his chance for four years in a row of 20 or more wins.

Alexander had his biggest year since 1920. He rebounded to win 22 games while completing 26 of 36 starts. He showed there was still some life left in that arm, although he continued to have problems with his epilepsy, which would be worsened by his drinking.

Haines won 20 games for the first time, a feat he would accomplish two more times. He would win 210 games and be the all-time Cardinal win leader until Bob Gibson broke the record in the 1970s. Haines would eventually be elected to the Hall of Fame. Unfortunately, the next season would see a complete reversal as he fell to his low ebb with a 8–19 and 4.40 ERA mark.

Grimes had missed the charmed circle in 1922 with only 17 wins, but bounced back this year to win 21 for Brooklyn. This was his third in four years and the first of two in a row again. He tied for the lead in starts with 38, while leading in complete games with 33. Teammate Vance was serving notice on the league of what to expect as he won 18 for the second straight season, giving him 36 for his first two full years.

Brooklyn grabbed complete game honors with 94, while Boston finished seventh and had only 54 for last. Ten pitchers made 20 or more complete games, but only Grimes could exceed 30.

Pitcher/Team	G	GS	CG	W	L	Pct	ERA	SO	W	IP
Dolf Luque, Cinn	41	37	28	27*	8	.771*	1.93*	151	88	322
John Morrison, Pgh	42	37	27	25	13	.658	3.49	114	110*	302
Pete Alexander, Chgo	39	36	26	22	12	.647	3.19	72	30	305
Pete Donohue, Cinn	42	36	19	21	15	.583	3.38	84	68	274
Burl Grimes, Bklyn	39	38*	33*	21	18	.538	3.58	119	100	327*
Jess Haines, STL	37	36	23	20	13	.606	3.11	73	75	266
Eppa Rixey, Cinn	42	37	23	20	15	.571	2.80	97	65	322

In hitting, once again it was Rogers Hornsby as he batted .384. Although missing a third of the season, which reduced his overall numbers, he had sufficient plate appearances to qualify for the title. Cy Williams of last-place Philadelphia set a new National League record with 41 home runs.

In the World Series, the Giants' pitching didn't hold up well, allowing 30 runs in six games and a composite .293 Yankee average. Casey Stengel led the Giants with a .417 mark and two home runs.

1924

AMERICAN LEAGUE: A NEW CHAMPION IS CROWNED

For the first time ever, Washington won the pennant in a hotly contested, three-team race. They edged out New York by two games and were six over Detroit. It was the old master, Walter Johnson, who led the charge with a league-high 23 wins and a league-leading 2.72 ERA. For a change, they had hitting to back the pitching as Goose Goslin hit .344 and drove home a league-high 129.

The Yanks tried hard, as Herb Pennock won 21. Babe Ruth had another monstrous year, leading with 143 runs, 46 home runs and a league-high .378 mark. His home run total exceeded five other clubs.

This was Johnson's first 20-win season in five years and his eleventh over-all, and it marked the first time he played for a pennant winner as Washington won their first pennant. He led in strikeouts for a record eleventh time while leading in shutouts for the seventh and last time. It was truly a magnificent year for the big right-hander.

Pennock followed his 19–6 season with a 21–9 mark, his first time to break the 20-win circle. From 1923 through 1928, Pennock won 115 games for the Yankees, an average of better than 19 per season. For his career Pennock won 240 games, a number that eventually earned him a Hall of Fame spot.

Joe Shaute had an up-and-down career. He finished after 13 full and part seasons with a 99–109 record, but did manage to win 20 games for sixth-place Cleveland. The team had strong hitting but weak pitching; without Shaute they were only 47–69.

For his career Sloppy Thurston was only three games over .500 at 89–86. Like many pitchers, however, he had one prime season, and 1924 was it. He won 20 games for the last-place White Sox and led the league with 28 complete games. Hall of Famers Ted Lyons and Red Faber were 12–11 and 9–11, respectively, for the same team.

Missing from the roster of 20 game winners were Urban Shocker (16–13), Stan Coveleski (14–15), Hooks Dauss (12–11), Eddie Rommel (18–15), Bob Shawkey (16–11) and George Uhle (9–15). All but Uhle had produced winning seasons, but he slipped from a league-high 26 wins to six games under .500 and a 4.78 ERA.

Cleveland paced the league with 87 complete games while Detroit was last with 60. Only seven pitchers had at least 20 complete games, with a high of 28 by the aforementioned Thurston.

Pitcher/Team	G	GS	CG	W	L	Pct	ERA	SO	W	IP
Walt Johnson, Wash	38	38*	20	23*	7	.767*	2.72*	158*	77	278
Herb Pennock, NY	40	34	25	21	9	.700	2.83	101	64	286
Sloppy Thurston, Bos	38	36	28*	20	14	.588	3.80	37	60	291
Joe Shaute, Cleve	46	34	21	20	17	.543	3.75	68	83	283

Johnson grabbed the shutout crown with six, while Howard Ehmke led in innings pitched with 315. The first real relief pitcher surfaced as Washington unveiled Firpo Marberry in that role. He led in game appearances with 50, of which 15 were starts. His record was only 11–12, but he had 15 saves. Over the next several years we would slowly see the emergence of this pitching position.

Washington won its first World Series as Tom Zachary (15–9) won two games. Johnson won the Series finale, but it was his only win as he was 1–2.

NATIONAL LEAGUE: A FOUR-TIME WINNER AND A NEW BATTING RECORD

The New York Giants were favored to repeat, and won their fourth consecutive pennant in an extremely tight three-team race. New York finished with 93 wins, Brooklyn with 92 and Pittsburgh with 90. Once again New York failed to have a 20-game winner, as their top winner was again 16, but a .300 team batting average paved the way to the title. They had six .300 hitters and two 100-plus RBI men, including league-leader George Kelly with 136.

Dazzy Vance won the MVP as he led Brooklyn to second place with a 28–6 mark, while Burleigh Grimes chipped in with 22 more. Pittsburgh got another 20-win season from Wilbur Cooper. Cincinnati picked up Carl Mays after the Yankees released him and finished fourth, mainly on the strength of his 20–9 season.

Rogers Hornsby established a new high for the modern era when he batted .424, a mark that stands until this day. This was his fifth straight batting crown. However, the best St. Louis could do was finish sixth.

Pete Alexander had another 20-win season in the making, but he broke his wrist and had to settle for a 12–5 record. Brooklyn, mainly on the arms of Vance and Grimes, led with 97 complete games while Philadelphia was last with 59.

If Vance could have made the majors by the time he was 24 or 25, his victory total probably would have reached or even exceeded 300. As it was he still managed 197, even though he was 31 when he won his first major league game. This was his premier season as he won a league-high 28, had the best ERA (2.16), led with 262 strikeouts and had 30 complete games in 34 starts. For his first three full seasons he had won 64 games. From 1922 through 1930, Vance had only one losing season and won 164 games—an average of better than 18 per season. As late as 1930, at age 39, he still had enough steam left to win 17 games.

This marked Grimes' second straight 20-plus-win season and the fourth in the last five years. Teamed with Vance, the duo won 50 games and almost put Brooklyn into the World Series. Grimes led in starts (36) and tied Vance with 30 complete games. The next two seasons would be downers for Grimes, and it wouldn't be until he was traded to the Giants in 1927 that he would bounce back to his winning ways.

Cooper returned to his winning ways by recording his fifth and last 20-win season with an even 20 victories. Cooper had given Pittsburgh many great years of pitching. He was traded in the off-season to the Chicago Cubs and spent 1925 with them, then split 1926 with the Cubs and Detroit Tigers before calling it a career. He was just 14–19 for his last two seasons. After an off-season in 1922 with the Yankees and limited action in 1923, Carl Mays was sent to Cincinnati where he had his final 20-win season. Mays appeared in 37 games, of which 27 were starts, as he fashioned a 20–9 record. He would be injured and see limited action in 1925 before coming back for one last big season in 1926.

The Dodgers led in complete games with 97, while Philadelphia was last with 59. Only five pitchers had 20 or more complete games, with Vance and Grimes hitting 30. Slowly the days of relievers were coming into play.

Pitcher/Team	G	GS	CG	W	L	Pct	ERA	SO	W	IP
Dazzy Vance, Bklyn	35	34	30*	28*	6	.824*	2.19*	262*	77	309
Burl Grimes, Bklyn	38	36*	30*	22	13	.629	3.62	135	91	311*
Carl Mays, Cinn	37	27	15	20	9	.690	3.15	63	36	226
Wilbur Cooper, Pgh	38	35	25	20	14	.588	3.28	62	40	269

The Giants were again losers in the Series as Jack Bentley (16–5) lost twice and Virgil Barnes (16–10) had a 5.09 ERA.

1925

AMERICAN LEAGUE: A MAJOR
STOMACHACHE AND THE START OF A STREAK

Babe Ruth had built a reputation as a prodigious hitter on the field and a lover of night life off the field. It finally caught up with him in the spring of 1925 when he was forced to miss the game until June with an intestinal abscess that required surgery. When he returned he hit .290 with 25 home runs and 66 RBIs in 98 games—his lowest marks for the period 1919–1933.

In May, Lou Gehrig took over first base and would remain there until ill health forced him out of the lineup in 1939. In the interim, he would become known as the "iron man" of baseball by playing in 2,130 consecutive games.

In a reversal of form, the Yankees finished seventh—their lowest standing until 1966, when they finished last. Washington won its second straight pennant with a franchise high 96 wins, as Stan Coveleski and Walter Johnson each won 20 games. Philadelphia returned to the fray as Ed Rommel won 21 to help place them second. They also had a young slugger named Al Simmons who batted .384 with 24 home runs and 129 RBIs.

Ted Lyons won 21 games for a fifth-place Chicago team. Cleveland was one of two teams to pitch over 50 percent complete games; they led with 93. The other team was New York with 80. Philadelphia trailed the field with 61. Firpo Marberry led in appearances with 55; he was 8–6 and tops in saves with 15.

After a three-year absence Coveleski returned as a 20-game winner with a 20–5 mark that gave him the league's best winning percentage at .800 while also posting the top ERA with 2.84. This was the fifth and last time he would win 20 or more games in a season. This was also his second trip to the World Series. He was with Cleveland in 1920, and after being with that team since 1916, he was traded to Washington before the 1925 year.

Johnson was also a 20-game winner with a 20–7 mark; this was the twelfth and last time he would achieve that status. Only Christy Mathewson and Warren Spahn have more 20-game seasons in the 20th century. Johnson finished the year three wins short of 400.

Although he would pitch winning ball for the next six seasons, this would be Rommel's last big winning year. He posted a 21–10 mark to lead the league with 21 victories. This was the lowest leading total in the 20th century. Rommel continued to show his versatility as he appeared in 52 games, of which only 28 were starts. The A's truly got their money's worth.

Lyons won 21 games to tie Rommel for the league lead. It was the first of three times he would achieve the charmed circle. His fate was the same as teammate Red Faber: pitching for a ball club that would be mired in the second division during most of his career. Lyons would finish his 20-year career with 260 victories and earn a Hall of Fame slot, but a better team certainly could have made him a member of the elite 300-victory club.

In a reversal of form, Howard Ehmke, winner of 39 games the two prior seasons, was only 9–20 for last-place Boston. They also had young Red Ruffing, who was 9–18, en route to his 39–96 mark with the team for five seasons. No one would believe he would eventually win 270 games and enter the Hall of Fame, but that's a long way off.

Cleveland had the tops in complete games with 93, while Philadelphia had the fewest at 61. The league produced only three pitchers with 20 or more complete games, all on second-division teams. The game was changing.

Pitcher/Team	G	GS	CG	W	L	Pct	ERA	SO	W	IP
Ed Rommel, Phil	52	28	14	21*	10	.677	3.69	67	95	261
Ted Lyons, Chgo	43	32	19	21*	11	.656	3.25	45	83	263
Stan Coveleski, Wash	32	32	15	20	5	.800*	2.84*	58	73	241
Walt Johnson, Wash	30	29	16	20	7	.741	3.07	108	78	229

The only team in double figures for shutouts was Chicago with 12, of which Lyons had five to lead the league. The A's rookie Lefty Grove led in strikeouts with 116 and walks with 131 while posting a 10–12 record, his only losing season in a 17-year career that produced 300 wins. In a few years he would be the premier pitcher in the league, if not in baseball.

Johnson had won only one game in the 1924 Series, but it was the deciding game. This time he won twice but lost the deciding game as Pittsburgh downed the Senators, four games to three.

NATIONAL LEAGUE: SIX IN A ROW, BUT NOT FIVE

The Giants were looking for a fifth straight pennant, but came up short as they had to settle for second place, 8½ games behind Pittsburgh. Neither team boasted a 20-game winner. Lee Meadows topped the Pirates with 19 wins; they had five starters to win 15 or more. It was Pittsburgh's hitting that led the way as the team batted .307, with seven regulars batting over .300 and an eighth at .298. They also had four players to score 100 or more runs and four to drive in 100 or more.

The league had only three 20-game winners, two of whom played for third-place Cincinnati: Eppa Rixey and Pete Donohue. Dazzy Vance continued his brilliant pitching with a 22–9 mark, but Brooklyn fell to sixth place. A reversal of form by Burleigh Grimes from 22 wins to a 12–19 mark certainly didn't help their cause.

St. Louis, with only mediocre pitching, made it to fourth place mainly on the bats of Jim Bottomley (44 doubles, 12 triples, 21 homers, 126 RBIs and a .367 mark) and Rogers Hornsby, who took his sixth straight batting title (.403). He also had a league-high 133 runs, 39 home runs and 143 RBIs to capture the triple crown.

Rixey was in the middle of an eight-year run during which his record was over .500. When one considers the caliber of some of the teams he played for, his career mark of 266–251 isn't bad. Some eyebrows were raised when he was elected to the Hall because of his low winning percentage, but taking into account his lack of support is important. This year he had a fine 21–11, 2.89 ERA mark. Although it was his last 20-win season, he still had several decent years ahead for him.

Donohue won 20 for the second time in three years. This was the fourth year of a five-year run in which he won 96 games. At age 26, it looked like big things were ahead, possibly a spot in the Hall. However, from this point on, except for 1926, it was all downhill. He won only 31 games while losing 51 for the remainder of his career, which ended in 1932. In this last big year, he won 21 while leading in games (42), starts (38), complete games (27), and innings pitched (301).

Vance put together another brilliant season, even though his Brooklyn club finished sixth. He led the league with 22 wins and 221 strikeouts. He also managed 26 complete games in just 31 starts.

Cincinnati led with 92 complete games while Philadelphia was last with 69. The National League fared a little better in the complete game department as eight pitchers had 20 or more.

Pitcher/Team	G	GS	CG	W	L	Pct	ERA	SO	W	IP
Dazzy Vance, Brklyn	31	31	26	22*	9	.710	3.53	221*	66	265
Eppa Rixey, Cinn	39	36	22	21	11	.656	2.89	69	47	287
Pete Donohue, Cinn	42	38*	27*	21	14	.600	3.08	78	49	301*

Cincinnati was the only team in double-digit shutouts with 11, four by Dolf Luque (16–18), who tied with Vance for the league lead. The four shutouts by Vance were all Brooklyn had. St. Louis' Bill Sherdel (15–6) took winning percent honors with .714.

Ray Kremer (17–8) and Vic Aldredge (15–7) each won two games for the Pirates in the World Series. Meadows didn't appear again after an opening game loss, although the Series went seven games.

1926

AMERICAN LEAGUE: A RETURN TO THE TOP

The Yankees looked like runaway winners in mid-August, but late-season challenges reduced their final margin to four games over Cleveland. Herb Pennock showed the way with 23 wins, ably supported by Urban Shocker's 19. Waite Hoyt was the only other pitcher in double-digit wins with 16.

Once again, it was Yankee hitting led by Babe Ruth that dominated the league, as he turned in 138 runs, 47 home runs, 155 RBIs and a .372 average, all league tops except the last. Lou Gehrig got his first of 13 consecutive 100-plus RBI years, and Tony Lazzeri also broke the 100 barrier.

Cleveland had another strong pitching performance from George Uhle, who won 27 to lead the league, but couldn't match the Yankee firepower. Philadelphia, continuing its return to respectability, finished third although no pitcher won more than 13 games; they had six in double digits, plus Joe Pate at 9–0 with six saves. There were no other 20-game winners in the league. The champions of the past two years, the Washington Senators, fell to fourth place as their trio of Walter Johnson, Stan Coveleski and Dutch Ruether slipped from 58–19 to 41–33.

Cleveland led the way with 96 complete games while Boston, finishing last for the fourth time in five years, was last with 53 as they compiled a 46–107 mark. They had unveiled Red Ruffing in 1924 and after two full years he was 15–33. He would remain with Boston through early 1930 and have a 39–96 mark, when he was traded to the Yankees. From that point on he would be 234–129 and eventually enter the Hall of Fame.

Pennock had his second 20-plus-win season in three and his biggest year as he won 23 games. He saw double duty as he appeared in 40 games, starting 33. This was Pennock's last 20-plus-win season, although he had several more productive years ahead of him.

Uhle continued his Jekyll and Hyde performance. Three seasons ago he won 26 games, then followed with a 9–15 mark. Last year he gained some respectability again with a 13–11, and now he had his career-best year with a 27–11 mark. He was also tops in winning percentage (.711), games started (36), complete games (32) and innings pitched (318)—a truly super season, and it almost put Cleveland into the World Series. But they were bridesmaid once again. Uhle would revert to Mr. Hyde next year as he would slip to 8–9. Despite winning 200 games, it was probably erratic performances such as this that kept him out of the Hall of Fame.

Cleveland topped the league with 96 complete games while Boston was last with 53. Only four pitchers achieved 20 complete games or more, with only Uhle over the 30 mark. Walter Johnson was only 15–16, but did have 22 complete games and finished the season with 412 wins.

Pitcher/Team	G	GS	CG	W	L	Pct	ERA	SO	W	IP
George Uhle, Cleve	39	36*	32*	27*	11	.711*	2.83	159	118*	318*
Herb Pennock, NY	40	33	19	23	11	.676	3.62	78	43	266

Lefty Grove replaced Johnson as the strikeout king. He won his second title in a row with 194 during a string of what would be seven consecutive seasons. Ed Wells of Detroit, despite a 12–10 mark, would lead with four shutouts. Firpo Marberry continued as the relief ace of baseball with a league-high 64 games, 22 saves (the record then) and a 12–7 season.

Although Pennock was great in the Series (2–0, 1.22), the Yankees would lose in seven games as they were held to 21 runs. Ruth hit four home runs and Gehrig batted .348, but to no avail.

NATIONAL LEAGUE: AT LONG LAST, THEY POP THE CHAMPAGNE CORK

The last time St. Louis had tasted championship was in the 1880s. All other National League teams had won pennants. In fact, only St. Louis was without a title, as neither the Cardinals nor Browns had ever captured the crown. This was their breakthrough year. Flint Rheem won 20 games to pace a balanced pitching staff, and for a change Rogers Hornsby didn't win the batting title, but he did guide his team to the pennant.

The Cardinals picked up 39-year-old Pete Alexander, who finished at 9–7 despite a sore arm and team suspension for his drinking problem—but it would be in the World Series that he would shine.

At the finish, St. Louis was only two games ahead of Cincinnati, four and one-half ahead of Pittsburgh and seven ahead of Chicago.

Pete Donohue posted 20 wins for Cincinnati and Carl Mays had his last big year with 19. Rixey fell from 20 to only 14, thus costing them a chance for first place. The other two 20-game winners were Ray Kremer and Lee Meadows of Pittsburgh, but the rest of the staff were only 44–54.

Rheem spent all or part of 12 seasons in the big leagues, mostly with the Cardinals. For most of that career he was just a so-so pitcher, showing a 85–90 record, but in 1926 he was something else. Rheem fashioned a 20–7 mark to tie for the lead in wins. He also garnered 20 complete games. His next-best year was a split season between St. Louis and Philadelphia in 1932, when he was 15–9.

Donohue enjoyed his second consecutive 20-win season to gain a share of the victory lead. This marked the third time in four years he had won 20 or more and concluded a five-year run in which he won 96 games. It was also his last big winning year in the majors. He appeared in 47 games, including a league-high 38 starts.

Meadows won 20 games for the only time in his career, but it was the middle season sandwiched between two 19-win campaigns. This was his fourth year of a five-year run in which he won 88 games. For his career he was 188–180 over 13 full and two part seasons. For the other ten seasons he was just 100–126, after his 88–54 performance for the period 1923–27.

Teammate Kremer not only had 20 wins but the best winning percentage (.769) and ERA (2.61). Kremer would win 20 again in 1930. From 1924 through 1930 he had winning seasons with a range of 15 to 20 each year, totaling 127 for the seven seasons. Kremer was another of the late starters, as he was 31 when he won his first game in 1924. An earlier start might have given him a chance for a much higher career total.

St. Louis led the loop with 90 complete games while Boston was last with

60. Only five pitchers could muster 20 or more complete games, topped by Mays with 24.

Pitcher/Team	G	GS	CG	W	L	Pct	ERA	SO	W	IP
Ray Kremer, Pgh	37	26	18	20*	6	.769*	2.61*	74	51	231
Flint Rheem, STL	34	34	20	20*	7	.741	3.21	72	75	258
Lee Meadows, Pgh	36	31	15	20*	9	.690	3.96	54	52	227
Pete Donohue, Cinn	47	38*	17	20*	14	.588	3.37	73	39	286*

Donohue led with five shutouts. Dazzy Vance, limited to 24 games and a subpar 9–10 season, led in strikeouts for the fifth straight year with 140.

St. Louis won the Series in classic Hollywood fashion. Alexander fanned Tony Lazzeri with the bases loaded, two out and a one-run lead in the bottom of the seventh. Alexander already had two complete game victories, including one the day before. Many have contended that he was hung over from a night of celebrating, as he didn't expect to pitch. But when Jesse Haines got into trouble in the seventh, Hornsby summoned the ol' warhorse, who responded in storybook fashion in what has now become one of the most celebrated and legendary moments in World Series history.

The Cardinals would capture nine flags and six World Titles over the next 21 seasons. While not quite equal to the Yankees pace, it still was quite exceptional. From 1926 through 1994 they would win 15 pennants, nine World Series, finish second 16 times and third 13 times. Thus, out of 69 seasons, they were in the top three almost 70 percent of the time. St. Louis became one of the perennial challengers.

1927

AMERICAN LEAGUE: THE GREATEST TEAM EVER

Many sports people and fans have called the 1927 Yankees the greatest team ever assembled. If not the greatest, it certainly would rank in the top handful. They won a new American League record 110 games and finished 19 games ahead of a strong Philadelphia team that boasted seven .300 hitters, whose averages ranged from .304 to .392 (Al Simmons), including Ty Cobb's .357 at age 40. Simmons' mark was good only for second place to Heine Manush, who hit .398.

However, none of this could compare to the Yankee team, as Waite Hoyt paced the mound crew with 22 wins, while Herb Pennock and rookie Wilcy Moore each won 19 games. Moore was in 50 games, of which he started 12, and took over the league honors as relief ace with his 19–7 mark and league-high 13 saves, tied by Washington's Garland Braxton who replaced Firpo Marberry as the team's ace reliever, since Marberry was now starting and relieving.

This was the year of Babe Ruth's fabled 60 home runs, league-high 158 runs, .356 average, and second-best 164 RBIs, as teammate Lou Gehrig had 47 home runs, 149 runs, .373 average and a league-high 175 RBIs. Never before or since had such a dynamic duo existed. They would terrorize the league for the next eight seasons. Tony Lazzeri and Bob Meusel also cleared the 100 RBI mark. Ruth's 60 home runs were more than any other team in the league, as well as five of the National League clubs.

Lefty Grove won 20 games for the first time, beginning a string that would eventually reach seven consecutive years. Chicago's Ted Lyons won 22 despite a weak team behind him.

This was the first of two successive 20-win seasons for Hoyt. He led the loop with 22 and a .759 winning percentage while posting a 2.64 ERA. After only a 10–12 record with Boston for parts of three seasons, Hoyt was traded to the Yankees before the 1921 campaign and from then through 1931 had only one losing year. For the Yankees from 1921 to 1928, he won 145 games, an average of better than 18 wins per season.

This was Grove's maiden 20-win season as he hit the mark with exactly that number. Grove led the league with 174 strikeouts for the third of seven successive seasons. He showed his versatility by starting 28 games, relieving 23 times and posting nine saves. This is a pattern that would be followed for the rest of his career with Philadelphia, which lasted through 1933.

Lyons had another big season, despite a weak team. He tied for the lead league in wins with 22, while leading with 30 complete games in just 34 starts. He also relieved five times, saving two. His 308 innings were a league high. Without Lyons, the White Sox were a candidate to challenge Boston for last place.

Chicago, mainly on the strength of Lyons' arm, led with 85 complete games, while Washington was last with 62. This was Walter Johnson's last season, as he was limited to 18 games and a 5–6 mark because of a broken leg. He retired with 417 wins, 3,506 strikeouts and a career 2.17 ERA, all remarkable achievements when you consider that Washington played less than .500 ball during his career. Only four pitchers had 20 or more complete games, with only Lyons at the 30 level.

Slim Harriss, while pitching for Boston, led the loop with 21 losses, the second time he had 20 or more defeats in a season. In a nine season career he had one winning year, going 19–12 for Philadelphia in 1925. Harriss finished with a 95–135 record.

Pitcher/Team	G	GS	CG	W	L	Pct	ERA	SO	W	IP
Waite Hoyt, NY	36	32	23	22*	7	.759*	2.64	86	54	256
Ted Lyons, Chgo	39	34	30*	22*	14	.611	2.84	71	67	308*
Lefty Grove, Phila	51	28	14	20	13	.606	3.20	174*	79	262

Washington's Hod Lisenbee (18–9) was shutout king with four, while Moore had the best ERA at 2.28.

The Yankees won the Series in four games as Hoyt, Moore, Pennock and George Pipgras each won one game. Moore also saved Hoyt's first game win, in addition to his final complete game victory. Ruth hit the only two Series home runs and had seven RBIs in four games.

NATIONAL LEAGUE: A DOGFIGHT DOWN TO THE WIRE

The pennant wasn't decided until the final day of the season. Pittsburgh nosed out St. Louis by 1½ games, with New York two behind, and Chicago nine out as they faded in September.

Pittsburgh boasted a strong pitching staff, paced by Carmen Hill's 22 wins, with 19 each from Ray Kremer and Lee Meadows. St. Louis got 20-plus wins from Jesse Haines and Pete Alexander, who at age 40 won 21 games.

Charlie Root had a league-high 26 wins, but the rest of the Chicago staff pitched only 59–54. Paul Waner led the league with .380 and 131 RBIs, while brother Lloyd hit .355 with a league-high 133 runs to pace the Pirate offense.

At the age of 32, Hill had spent parts of six seasons in the majors, dating back to 1915, compiling a 9–8 record. Everyone was surprised when he posted a 22–10 mark to lead the Pirates to the National League pennant. Hill appeared in 43 games, 31 as a starter, and completed 22. He would follow this with a 16–10 record before fading into oblivion and out of the majors by 1930.

Haines had his biggest season, winning 24 games, leading the league with 25 complete games and six shutouts. This was his first of two successive 20-win seasons in a career that would see him join the charmed circle three times. Starting in the 1930s, Haines would become a combination spot starter and reliever. He spent 19 seasons in the big leagues, the last 18 with St. Louis.

Alexander had one last year of glory as he racked up 21 wins to make it the ninth time he had won 20 or more. Only Christy Mathewson and Warren Spahn in the National League had more 20-plus-win seasons during the 20th century. Alexander would pitch two more winning years with St. Louis before closing out his career with his old club, the Philadelphia Phillies, in 1930.

Root, in only his second year, topped the league with 26 wins, a career best. He showed his durability and versatility as he appeared in 48 games, starting 36 and pitching 309 innings. Although he had several more productive years, the closest he ever came again was 19 wins in 1929. Root retired with 201 victories, but has no Hall of Fame membership. It's a tough club to get into.

After two poor seasons in which he was 24–32, including a 12–19 and 5.03 ERA in 1925, Burleigh Grimes bounced back with a fine 19–8 mark in his only season with the New York Giants. Meanwhile, Dazzy Vance recovered from his injury to win 16 games for a weak Brooklyn team. Pittsburgh led with 90 complete games and seventh-place Boston was last with 52. Six pitchers had 20 or more complete games.

Pitcher/Team	G	GS	CG	W	L	Pct	ERA	SO	W	IP
Charlie Root, Chgo	48*	36	21	26*	15	.634	3.76	145	117*	309*
Jesse Haines, STL	38	36	25*	24	10	.706	2.72	89	77	301
Carmen Hill, Pgh	43	31	22	22	11	.667	3.24	95	80	278
Pete Alexander, STL	37	30	22	21	10	.677	2.52	48	38	268

Dazzy Vance led in strikeouts for the sixth straight season with 184 as he posted 16 wins for a sixth-place Brooklyn team. New York's Larry Benton (17–7) led with a .707 winning percentage. The National League was still without a standout relief hurler; St. Louis' Bill Sherdel (a starter) led with six saves during a 17–12 season. Teammate Haines led in shutouts with six.

In this World Series, the Pirates were pathetic in losing four straight. They scored only ten runs in four games, while the Yankees had 23.

1928

AMERICAN LEAGUE: A HARBINGER OF THINGS TO COME

It was a dogfight all the way, with the final margin only two and one-half games, as the Yankees edged Philadelphia with a 101–53 to 98–55 mark. No doubt Philadelphia was back, and they served notice regarding what the league could expect over the next several seasons.

New York had its usual firepower from Babe Ruth, Lou Gehrig and company, but a strong pitching staff paced by 24-game winner George Pipgras and 23-game winner Waite Hoyt led the way. Wilcy Moore slipped to a 4–4 mark, but Hoyt picked up the slack by leading the league with eight saves in addition to his 23 wins.

Lefty Grove tied Pipgras with 24 wins and the league lead in strikeouts for the third straight year. St. Louis made it to third place mainly on the arms of 20-game winners General Crowder and Sam Gray, who were a composite 41–17, while the rest of the staff were 41–55.

Boston had now replaced Philadelphia as tailenders and finished last for the fourth straight season. Red Ruffing led the league with 25 losses despite 25 complete games and a 3.90 ERA, while teammate Ed Morris won 19 games for the cellar dwellers. Ruffing was one of baseball's best hitting pitchers, often used as a pinch hitter.

This was Pipgras' big season. In addition to sharing the lead in wins at 24, he appeared in 46 games, had the most starts (38) and pitched the most innings (301). Pipgras continued to pitch winning ball for the Yankees through the early 1930s, but the highest number of games he ever won again was 18.

This was Hoyt's biggest season with a 23–7 mark and his league-high eight shutouts. It also marked the end of an eight-year run during which he won 145 games. Although he had several winning seasons over the next decade, he was never again a big winner, with his tops being 15 for Pittsburgh in 1934.

Grove was blossoming into his own as the premier pitcher in the league, if not in baseball. This was the first of four times he would lead the league in victories. He also led in strikeouts for the fourth consecutive season. Grove appeared in 39 games, with 24 complete games among his 31 starts, and he added four saves for good measure. His fastball was as explosive as his temper, which became legendary. Sometimes hitters didn't know which they feared most.

Crowder started his career with Washington in 1926, was traded to St. Louis in mid–1927 and would be traded back to Washington in early 1930. However, this season he was all St. Louis as he went 21–5 with a league-best .808 winning percentage. From 1928 through 1933, he would win 124 games for St. Louis and Washington combined.

Teammate Gray had spent his first four seasons with Philadelphia and had a 44–33 mark, with a best of 16–8 in 1925. In his first year in St. Louis he won 20 games for the only time in his career. After following that with an 18-win season in 1929, things went downhill fast. Over 1930–32 Gray was 22–51, including marks of 4–15 and 11–24 in 1930 and 1931.

Chicago paced the loop with 88 complete games while Detroit was last with 65. Eight pitchers completed 20 or more games, with the most being 25 by Red Ruffing, who also lost 25.

Pitcher/Team	G	GS	CG	W	L	Pct	ERA	SO	W	IP
Lefty Grove, Phila	39	31	24	24*	8	.750	2.57	183*	64	262
George Pipgras, NY	46	38*	22	24*	13	.649	3.38	139	103	301*
Waite Hoyt, NY	42	31	19	23	7	.767	3.36	67	60	273
General Crowder, STL	41	31	19	21	5	.808*	3.69	99	91	244
Sam Gray, STL	35	31	21	20	12	.625	3.19	102	86	263

Washington's Garland Braxton, who had moved into the starting rotation, was the league leader in ERA with 2.52. Herb Pennock, limited to 24 games because of illness, led with five shutouts en route to a 17–6 season.

The Yankees got their revenge against St. Louis by winning four straight as Hoyt was 2–0 and Pipgras and Tom Zachary each won one game. Ruth hit three home runs and batted .625, but he was overshadowed by Gehrig who hit four homers and drove in nine runs while batting .545. New York outscored St. Louis 27–10.

NATIONAL LEAGUE: ANOTHER RACE DOWN TO THE WIRE

When all the dust had settled, only four games separated first-place St. Louis from third-place Chicago, and sandwiched between was New York, down by two despite winning 25 games in September.

St. Louis again had two 20-game winners, and this time it brought them home first. Forty-one-year-old Pete Alexander chipped in with 16 wins. The

Cardinals had a potent hitting attack and boasted four .300 hitters, with Chick Hafey having 111 RBIs, while Jim Bottomley had a league-high 136 RBIs and 31 home runs (also tops).

New York also had two 20-plus game winners in Larry Benton and Freddie Fitzsimmons. The Cubs, boasting no 20-game winners, had six pitchers who won 10 to 18. Burleigh Grimes tried to keep Pittsburgh in it with 25 wins, but there wasn't quite enough other mound help and they finished nine games back, despite leading the league in hitting with a .309 batting mark and in runs scored.

Sherdel spent 15 seasons in the majors, with over 13 of them in a Cardinal uniform. This was his best season as he won 21 games, most ever for a Cardinal left-hander, although later tied by Howard Pollet and John Tudor. This was Sherdel's only 20-win season, but he had five others between 15 and 17 for the Redbirds. When he retired in 1932 Sherdel had won 165 games, with 153 in a St. Louis uniform.

The old master, Haines, turned in another fine season, posting 20 wins for the second straight year and third and final time in his career. Haines would pitch for nine more seasons and have only one losing year (1932) when he was 3–5, but in most of those years he was limited to a spot starter and reliever role. His top wins after this year were 13 in 1929 and 1930.

Larry Benton pitched for the Boston Braves, Cincinnati Reds and New York Giants over a 13-year career and was a lackluster 127–128. But in 1928 he was king of the hill, as he tied for the league lead with 25 wins while losing only 9, which also gave him the league's best percentage at .735. His 28 complete games were tops, while his 310 innings ranked second. Benton also relieved seven times and was credited with four saves.

In a 19-year career that included 16 full seasons, Fitzsimmons had losing records in only four of them. This was his only 20-win season, but was in the midst of a ten-year run of winning marks for the New York Giants during which he won 154 games. For his career he had 170 wins and 114 losses while pitching for New York. The balance of his career he was 47–32 for Brooklyn, mostly built on a 16–2 mark in 1940.

At age 35, Grimes had his biggest winning season. He won 25 games for the Pirates and posted a 2.99 ERA. He led with 48 appearances, 28 complete games and 331 innings pitched. This was his fifth and last 20-plus-win season, but he would win 50 games over the next three seasons for Pittsburgh, Boston and St. Louis combined. The old master wasn't finished yet.

Dazzy Vance was 22–10 for sixth-place Brooklyn and led in strikeouts with 200 for his seventh straight title. This was his third and final season as a member of the charmed circle, but even after reaching age 39 he still had enough left to pitch effective winning ball in three of the next four seasons.

St. Louis captured complete game honors with 83, and lowly Philadelphia (43–109) had only 42, a new major league low. Only five pitchers would hurl 20 or more complete games for the season. Russ Miller had an unenviable 0–12, 5.42 ERA record for the Philadelphia Phillies.

Pitcher/Team	G	GS	CG	W	L	Pct	ERA	SO	W	IP
Larry Benton, NY	42	35	28*	25*	9	.735*	2.73	90	71	310
Burleigh Grimes, Pgh	48*	37*	28*	25*	14	.641	2.99	97	77	331*
Dazzy Vance, Bklyn	38	32	24	22	10	.688	2.09*	200*	72	280
Bill Sherdel, STL	38	37	20	21	10	.677	2.86	72	56	249
Jesse Haines, STL	33	28	20	20	8	.714	3.19	77	72	240
F Fitzsimmons, NY	40	32	16	20	9	.690	3.69	67	65	261

Grimes and Vance tied with two others for the shutout lead with four. In the Series, St. Louis batted only .206, while their pitchers had a composite 6.08 ERA.

—————— 1929 ——————

AMERICAN LEAGUE: THE RETURN OF THE WHITE ELEPHANT

If Connie Mack had known in 1914, when he dismantled his pennant winners of that year, that it would take 15 years—including seven straight in the cellar—to return to the top, it is quite unlikely he would have done so. When Philadelphia did return, they came back with a vengeance: their final margin of victory was 18 games, based on a 104–46 record. George Earnshaw and Lefty Grove were 20-game winners to pave the way. They also had a potent attack that included five .300 hitters, five to score 100 runs and two with over 100 RBIs, paced by Al Simmons (.365) and his league-leading 157 RBIs.

The Yankees, champions the three prior seasons, finished a distant second, as Herb Pennock and Waite Hoyt, 40–17 in 1928, slipped to 19–20. Despite a great year from Babe Ruth and Lou Gehrig, the Yankees could do no better than second.

Rookie Wes Ferrell helped pitch Cleveland into third place as he won 21 games. No other pitcher won 20, but Washington's Firpo Marberry continued double duty. He logged a 19–12 mark while leading the league in appearances with 49, of which 28 were starts, and saves with 11.

Earnshaw was 29 and in his second big league season when he blossomed into a big winner. He paced the league with 24 wins while appearing in 44 games, 33 as a starter. Over the 1929–1932 period, Earnshaw won 86 games, failing to win 20 only in 1932 when he copped 19. In the late 1920s and early 1930s, Earnshaw, Grove and Rube Walberg provided a tough pitching trio for the Mack men.

Grove copped an even 20 and lost only six en route to his third straight 20-win season during a string of seven. He led the league in winning percentage with .769. This is a feat he would accomplish five times and would finish over .700 on eight different occasions. His 170 strikeouts gave him his fifth consecutive strikeout title.

Ferrell pitched and batted his way to 21 victories. Ferrell is one of the games' greatest hitting pitchers, retiring with a lifetime .280 mark and a career-record 37 home runs. Ferrell logged a lot of double duty; he had 18 complete games in 25 starts, but also relieved 18 times and was credited with five saves. Ferrell would exceed 20 wins in each of his first four seasons.

Boston (last for the fifth straight season) led in complete games with 84, while Washington was last with 62. Seven pitchers had 20 or more complete games.

Pitcher/Team	G	GS	CG	W	L	Pct	ERA	SO	W	IP
Geo Earnshaw, Phila	44	33	13	24*	8	.750	3.28	149	125*	255
Wes Ferrell, Cleve	43	25	18	21	10	.677	3.59	100	109	243
Lefty Grove, Phila	42	37	21	20	6	.768*	2.82*	170*	81	275

Four pitchers, three from St. Louis, tied for the lead in shutouts with four. Philadelphia had a league-high 24 saves shared by nine pitchers, showing that relief specialists were still several years away. Red Ruffing lost 22 games to give him a five-year record of 39–93. He was only a season away from not only a change in uniforms, but in fortune.

The A's completed their return to stardom with a convincing four-games-to-one win over Chicago, as Grove was used in relief and saved two of the games.

NATIONAL LEAGUE: ANOTHER
FORMER WINNER RETURNS TO THE TOP

For the past four seasons, St. Louis and Pittsburgh had alternated winning the title, with the former winning in even years and the latter in odd years. In 1929, Chicago stormed out front and won by almost ten games over Pittsburgh to take the title. Pat Malone paced the loop with 22 wins, with Charlie Root (19–6) and Guy Bush (18–7) close behind.

However, it was the Chicago hitting that paved the way, with five .300 hitters including Rogers Hornsby (.380, 131 runs, 39 home runs, 149 RBIs) and Hack Wilson (.360, 135 runs, 39 home runs and a league-high 159 RBIs). Home run honors went to Philadelphia's Chuck Klein with 43.

Pittsburgh finished second, but failed to have a 20-game winner. St. Louis, which had been first or second the past four seasons, slipped to fourth. There were no other 20-game winners in the league.

Malone spent ten seasons in the big leagues, the first seven in a Chicago Cub uniform, when he did his most illustrious pitching. In his second full season, he won 22 games to be the league's only 20-game winner after posting 18 wins in his rookie season. Malone was a workhorse, appearing in 40 games, of which 30 were as a starter. From 1928 through 1932, Malone won 91 games for the Cubs.

St. Louis paced the loop with 83 complete games while Brooklyn was last with 59. Only one pitcher had 20 or more complete games—the first time this happened in either league. Red Lucas had 28 in 32 starts as he was 19–12 for seventh-place Cincinnati. Lucas also batted .293 and was another one of baseball's best hitting pitchers. He was often used as a pinch hitter, including 44 times this season.

Pitcher/Team	G	GS	CG	W	L	Pct	ERA	SO	W	IP
Pat Malone, Chgo	40	30	19	22*	10	.688	3.57	166*	102	267

Malone broke Dazzy Vance's seven-year reign as strikeout king and was also the leader in shutouts with five. The ERA title went to New York's Bill Walker at 3.08, while Root had the league's highest percentage at .760. Walker's ERA was an indication of the hitting that now was dominant. Philadelphia had a team ERA of 6.13, and New York was the only team below 4.00, at 3.87.

In the Series Chicago, which batted .303 for the season, hit only .249 and had a team 4.33 ERA, as Malone was 0–2 with a 4.16. Only Bush won as he was 1–0 with a .81 ERA.

4

1930–1939

— 1930 —

AMERICAN LEAGUE: THE WHITE ELEPHANT LEADS THE CHARGE

The 1930 season has been heralded as the greatest hitting year of all time: the American League batted a phenomenal .288. The A's continued their dominance by an eight-game margin over surprising second-place Washington. Lefty Grove had a brilliant 28–5, while George Earnshaw chipped in with 22 wins. Grove also paced the loop with nine saves.

Al Simmons led the league with .381, but his 36 home runs and 165 RBIs were not the best. Babe Ruth took home run honors with 49, and Lou Gehrig wore the RBI crown with 174. However, Yankee pitching wasn't up to the task.

Washington made it to second place without any pitcher over 16 wins, but they had four at the 15-win level, including Firpo Marberry, who was now primarily a starter.

The Yankees slipped to third, as their pitching didn't hold up to support 1,062 runs scored and a .309 team batting average. They did acquire Red Ruffing from the Red Sox. He was 15–5 for them and soon would team with Lefty Gomez to form a dynamite lefty-righty duo throughout the 1930s.

Wes Ferrell pitched Cleveland to fourth place with 25 wins, while Lefty Stewart won 20 games for the sixth-place Brownies. Ted Lyons chalked up 22 wins for the Pale Sox, who finished seventh, and without him may have been last. That distinction went to the Red Sox, who finished there for the sixth straight season and had two 20-game losers, giving them six over the same period.

Grove was a virtual superman as he led the league with 28 wins, nine saves, 50 appearances, 209 strikeouts and a 2.54 ERA. What is even more amazing is his low ERA, when Washington as a team had the league's low at 3.96. He also posted the best winning percentage at .848 as he lost only five times.

Earnshaw was another hard-working moundsman as he won 22 games while appearing in 49, of which 39 were a league-high for starts. This was the second of three straight seasons he exceeded 20 victories.

Ferrell, in only his second season, won 25 games to give him 46 wins for his first two big league years. Ferrell again did double duty as he started 35 and relieved another eight while logging 297 innings. He also swung a mean bat, hitting .297, appearing as a pinch hitter on several occasions.

Stewart had only three winning seasons during his nine-year career, but he chose this year to be his big one and won 20 games. Without him St. Louis would have been 44–78 and would have challenged Boston for last place.

Lyons would pitch through 1942, enter the service for three years and then return to finish in 1946, but this was his last big season as he won 22 games for the inept Chicago White Sox. He also led the loop with 29 complete games. After suffering a career-threatening injury in 1931, he became a weekly pitcher starting in 1935, and posted some excellent winning seasons for the lowly Chicago team.

Washington and the Red Sox paced the league with 78 complete games, the only teams with a 50 percent or better ratio, while New York was last with 65. There were seven pitchers to have 20 or more complete games.

Pitcher/Team	G	GS	CG	W	L	Pct	ERA	SO	W	IP
Lefty Grove, Phila	50*	32	22	28*	5	.848*	2.54*	209*	60	291
Wes Ferrell, Cleve	43	35	25	25	13	.658	3.30	143	106	297
Geo Earnshaw, Phila	49	39*	20	22	13	.629	4.44	193	139*	296
Ted Lyons, Chgo	42	36	29*	22	15	.595	3.77	69	57	298*
Lefty Stewart, STL	35	33	23	20	12	.625	3.45	79	70	271

Washington was the only team to finish the season with an ERA under 4.00, and just barely did so at 3.96. Earnshaw and George Pipgras tied for the lead in shutouts with three, as Philadelphia had the most with eight.

In the World Series, the A's made it two in a row. Earnshaw and Grove each won two with respective ERAs of .72 and 1.42.

NATIONAL LEAGUE: IT'S EVEN YEARS — OUR TURN AGAIN

The St. Louis Cardinals continued their pattern of winning in the even years, edging out Chicago by two games. In fact, only six games separated St. Louis from fourth-place Brooklyn, with New York five out in third.

The highest number of wins by any St. Louis pitcher was 15 by Wild Bill Hallahan. The Redbirds relied on firepower, with ten hitters batting .300 or better, each of whom batted at least 227 times. They led the league in runs scored with 1,004, and were third in hitting with .314.

Six of the teams batted .300 or better, topped by New York's .319 as Bill Terry hit .401 and became the last National Leaguer to do it. Last-place Philadelphia hit .315, but had a team ERA of 6.71.

Pat Malone of Chicago and Ray Kremer of Pittsburgh were the league's only 20-game winners, each reaching that plateau exactly.

This was Malone's second straight 20-win season. He tied Kremer for the league lead but led with 22 complete games. Malone also appeared in 45 games, 35 as a starter, and had four saves while pitching 272 innings.

Kremer won 20 games for the second and last time in his career as he led the league with 276 innings pitched and 38 starts. This was his seventh successive big winning season for the Pirates, and his last. He pitched three more years, winning 16 while losing 18. During these seven seasons he had won 127 games, an average of better than 18 per year.

Freddie Fitzsimmons was close with a 19–7 mark, while appearing in 41 games, of which only 29 were starts. Red Lucas had only a 14–16 mark, but batted .336 while pinch-hitting 47 times.

Brooklyn had the league-low ERA at 4.03, as Dazzy Vance was the only hurler to have an ERA under 3.00; he was 17–15 with a 2.61. One wonders how, with all Brooklyn's hitting and his low ERA, he didn't win 25 games. Pittsburgh was the only team to complete at least 50 percent of its games. It led with 80 while the Phillies were last with 54.

Pitcher/Team	G	GS	CG	W	L	Pct	ERA	SO	W	IP
Pat Malone, Chgo	45	35	22*	20*	9	.690	3.94	142	96	272
Ray Kremer, Pgh	39	38*	18	20*	12	.625	5.02	598	63	276*

For a further indication of the type of year this was, compare Vance's record to Kremer's. The latter's ERA was almost double, and he allowed 366 hits versus 241 for Vance, yet he had a considerably better win-loss mark.

Charlie Root and Vance tied for the shutout lead with four each, as Brooklyn had 13—an amazing total considering the year of the batter. The next two teams had only six each.

The World Series was a different story as Philadelphia batted .197 and St. Louis .200, but St. Louis scored only 12 runs as opposed to Philadelphia's 21. Pete Alexander called it a career with Philadelphia and had an 0–3 mark. When he retired he had 373 wins and 90 shutouts, second to Walter Johnson. Certainly the epilepsy, which led to his drinking problem, cost him a career of 400 or more wins.

Hack Wilson set the National League home run mark at 56 and the major league RBI mark at 190. Both records still stand 66 years later.

1931

AMERICAN LEAGUE: THE ELEPHANT RUNS WILD

The Philadelphia A's won an unprecedented third straight title, and seemed a shoo-in for a third straight World Series title. They had three 20-game winners led by MVP Lefty Grove, who was 31–4 with a 2.05 ERA. While hitting had returned to a more normal level, the big guns for Philadelphia were Jimmy Foxx, Al Simmons and Mickey Cochrane.

The Yankees managed 94 wins, but were still 13½ games behind the A's, who were 107–45. Lefty Gomez paced the mound staff with a 21–9 mark. Babe Ruth and Lou Gehrig tied for the home run lead with 46, while Gehrig set the American League RBI mark with 184.

Washington came in third, two games behind the Yankees, with a balanced pitching staff and adequate hitting. Wes Ferrell continued winning 20 or more for Cleveland, and helped them to fourth place. Boston finally escaped the cellar, finishing sixth.

Grove continued to be almost invincible as he won 31 games, and would be the last American League pitcher to do this until Denny McLain in 1968. Grove had the best winning percentage (.886) as he lost only four times. He led with 27 complete games in 30 starts, relieved 11 times, saved five more and had the best ERA (2.05) and most shutouts (four). He also led for the seventh straight season in strikeouts with 175. He had the distinction of leading the league for his first seven seasons in the majors. No other pitcher before or since has equaled this mark.

During 1929–1931 Grove was an amazing 79–15. He also logged 18 saves and appeared in 133 games, 34 as a reliever. Grove was truly a remarkable athlete.

George Earnshaw had his best career percentage mark as he won 21 and lost only seven, giving him three straight 20-plus-win seasons, and each time Philadelphia won the pennant. He was once again a workhorse, appearing in 43 games, 30 as a starter, of which he completed 23. He also had six saves.

The third member of the trio, Rube Walberg, had his career-best season as he was 20–12 while appearing in 44 games, 35 as a starter. This season marked a culmination of a long climb for Walberg, who had posted winning seasons for the five prior years but had never made it to 20 wins. He followed this with a 17–10 mark in 1932, but then it was downhill for the last five years of his career, with four of them losing, as he was relegated to the role of a spot starter and reliever.

From 1931 through 1942, Gomez had only one losing season. He was given the nickname "Goofy" for some of the crazy or ridiculous things he would do or say, but on the mound he was far from that as he posted a career 189–102, .649 winning percentage, which eventually put him in the Hall of Fame. This was his first of four 20-plus-win seasons. In this hitting era he had a fine 2.61 ERA, while appearing in 40 games, only 26 as a starter.

Some baseball critics don't believe Red Ruffing belongs in the Hall of Fame, as his record was enhanced because of the strong New York Yankee teams for which he pitched. With Boston he was 39–96, with Chicago (his last season in 1947) he was 3–5, and with New York he was 231–124. His ERA declined once he started pitching for New York and from 1930 through 1946—sans 1943–45 for World War II service—he had only one losing year and was a 20-game winner four times. In his second New York season he was 16–14.

Pat Caraway lasted only three years in the big leagues and was 22–40, including a 10–24 and 6.22 ERA this year. No wonder he was gone in three seasons.

The A's led the pack with 97 complete games, while last place Chicago had only 54. Only five pitchers managed at least 20 complete games. It had been a long time since someone had 30.

Pitcher/Team	G	GS	CG	W	L	Pct	ERA	SO	W	IP
Lefty Grove, Phila	41	30	27*	31*	4	.886*	2.05*	175*	62	289
Wes Ferrell, Cleve	40	35	27	22	12	.647	3.75	123	130*	276
Geo Earnshaw, Phila	43	30	23	21	7	.750	3.67	152	75	282
Lefty Gomez, NY	40	26	17	21	9	.700	2.63	150	85	243
Rube Walberg, Phila	44	35	19	20	12	.625	3.74	106	109	291*

Shutouts were still scarce, as Philadelphia was the only team to have more than ten; they led with 12. Grove and Earnshaw tied for the lead with three each. Washington led the league with 24 saves, as Bump Hadley appeared in a high of 55 games and had eight saves, while Firpo Marberry (16–4) did double duty and had seven. However, the leader was Wilcy Moore, who had ten while posting an 11–13 mark for Boston.

Philadelphia was heavily favored to win the Series but lost in seven games as Grove took two; Earnshaw, despite a 1.88 mark, was only 1–2. This was Connie Mack's last taste of glory.

NATIONAL LEAGUE: A DASH OF PEPPER MAKES IT SPICY

The Cardinals broke their pattern of winning in the even years by having a runaway title with a 13-game bulge over second-place New York. St. Louis again had no 20-game winners, but got 19 victories from Bill Hallahan, 18 from youthful Paul Derringer and 17 from old Burleigh Grimes.

The hitting attack again was potent, although somewhat subdued from the prior year. Chick Hafey won the batting crown in the closest race ever, with .3489 to Bill Terry's .3486.

New York finished second and failed to have a 20-game winner, but Carl Hubbell (14–12) was just a couple of seasons away from becoming the Giants' meal ticket.

No pitcher won 20 as Pittsburgh's Heine Meine and Philadelphia's Jumbo Jim Elliott each had 19. The Meine story is quite interesting. He had a cup of coffee with the St. Louis Browns in 1922, and then returned to his tavern in South St. Louis. He kept telling his patrons he could pitch as well as some of those "hamburgers" in the league. Finally, he got a chance in 1929 at age 33 with the Pirates. He pitched through 1934 and won 66 games, having only one losing season. One must wonder what he could have accomplished if he could have broken in a few years earlier.

Walks were Hallahan's bugaboo during his career and kept him from a more successful foray during his pitching days. He finished with a 102–94 mark, but from 1930 through 1933 he won 62 and lost only 38. Unfortunately, he couldn't sustain that pace over the other eight seasons he pitched.

Derringer was a real double-duty pitcher for St. Louis as he started 23 games and relieved another 12 times. He lasted only one more season with St. Louis before moving on to Cincinnati, where he gained his greatest fame. The first two years there he was only 22–46, despite a respectable 3.45 ERA. Once they got their act together he began to win. He eventually would be in the charmed circle four times and twice help pitch Cincinnati into the World Series. Derringer finished with a 223–212 mark and to date has been overlooked for Hall of Fame consideration.

Elliott spent six full seasons and four part seasons in the big leagues, but this was his only really decent year. With a weak Philadelphia team, he won 19 games. Elliott was in a league-high 52 games, starting 30, and he also had five saves. He proved to be very durable and versatile during the 1931 campaign. The balance of his career he was only 44–60, not much to write home about. Hallahan led in strikeouts and walks, while Derringer led in winning percentage. New York's Bill Walker (16–9) wore the ERA crown (2.26), while Red Lucas with last-place Cincinnati had the most complete games: 24. Teamwise, New York was first with 90 and Philadelphia last with 60.

In the World Series, Hallahan and Grimes each won two games, with the former also saving the final game and posting a .49 ERA. The real hero was Pepper Martin, who had 12 hits, five runs, 5 RBIs and five stolen bases.

—————————— **1932** ——————————

AMERICAN LEAGUE: THE BABE'S LAST SERIES

The Philadelphia A's were picked to make it four in a row, but New York put together a pitching staff to go with their vaunted power that short-circuited that dream. A quartet of pitchers, led by Lefty Gomez's 24 wins, posted a 75–27 mark to pace the Yankees to a 13-game margin over the A's, as New York's final mark was 107–47.

The Yankees scored over 1,000 runs again, and also had the league's best ERA at 3.98, which paved their way to victory. This would be Babe Ruth's final super season, although he had a couple more decent years. He finished with 120 runs, 41 home runs, 137 RBIs and a .341 mark.

The A's had a record that would have won in many seasons, but not this year, despite Lefty Grove's 25 wins. George Earnshaw added 19 for his last big season. Washington, showing a harbinger of things to come, finished third, one game behind Philadelphia, on the strength of 20-plus-win seasons from General Crowder and Monty Weaver.

Gomez had his second straight 20-plus-win season as he registered 24 wins against only seven losses. Gomez appeared in 37 games, 31 as a starter, of which he completed 21. In Gomez's first four years as a Yankee starter he won 87 and lost only 31. Red Ruffing didn't win 20, but began to win some of the skeptics to his side. His final 18–7 and impressive 3.09 ERA won many a convert. His ERA was very impressive considering the league's was around 4.50. He also broke Grove's reign as strikeout king as he edged him by two whiffs (190–188).

Grove "slipped" a little from his prior two seasons, but was still good enough to win 25 while losing just ten, and to place second in total victories. His 2.54 ERA was the league's best and his second straight ERA crown, a feat he would accomplish nine times. Grove continued double duty as he completed 27 of 30 starts, relieved 14 times and had seven saves—almost a one-man army.

Crowder had come to Washington in an early season trade in 1930 from St. Louis. His first two seasons he had a 33–20 mark; not bad, but the best was yet to come. This year he led the league with 26 wins while appearing in 50 games, starting a league-high 39. He also was the league workhorse as he logged 327 innings.

In his first full season, Weaver had his best year as he was 22–10 for the Washington club. Weaver started 30 times and relieved another 13 as he piled up 234 innings. Weaver would never again approach these heights, as his next best two seasons (12 and 11) were only one win greater than his total this year. He finished his career with the Red Sox in 1939 by going 1–0 in nine games.

Wes Ferrell continued his 20-victory seasons, as he won 23 to help put Cleveland in fourth place. This gave Ferrell 91 wins in his first four full seasons in the majors. He pitched one more year for Cleveland and was only 11–12 before he was traded to the Boston Red Sox. With Boston he would eventually regroup and have two more 20-win seasons before finishing out his career with Washington, the Yankees and the Dodgers.

Ted Lyons had recovered from arm problems and posted a fine 3.28 ERA for the hapless White Sox; but he could go only 10–15 due to their ineptitude. They were 49–102.

The Yankees led with 95 complete games, while Boston, again last, had a new league low of 42. No pitcher had 30 complete games, but seven did make it to the 20 level.

Pitcher/Team	G	GS	CG	W	L	Pct	ERA	SO	W	IP
G Crowder, Wash	50	39*	21	26*	13	.667	3.33	103	77	327*
Lefty Grove, Phila	44	30	27*	25	10	.714	2.84*	188	94	292
Lefty Gomez, NY	37	31	21	24	7	.774	4.21	176	105	265
Wes Ferrell, Cleve	36	34	26	23	13	.639	3.65	105	104	288
Monty Weaver, Wash	43	30	13	22	10	.688	4.08	83	112	234

Grove and Detroit's Tommy Bridges tied for the shutout lead with four, while New York rookie Johnny Allen took the winning percentage honors with .810, based on his 17–4 mark. Firpo Marberry continued his dual role for

Washington and led in appearances with 54, while logging an 8–4 mark and a league high 13 saves.

The Series was all New York as they won in four games, outscoring Chicago 37 to 19. Lou Gehrig hit three home runs and Ruth hit his last two, including the controversial "called shot" to center field off Charley Root.

Jimmy Foxx staged the first serious threat in the American League on Ruth's magic 60 when he belted 58 home runs during the season.

NATIONAL LEAGUE: FIRED WHILE IN FIRST PLACE

Since the Cardinals had won in 1926, 1928, 1930 and 1931, many thought they would repeat, but such was not the case. The prior season Bill Hallahan, Paul Derringer and Burleigh Grimes were 54–27. In 1932 Hallahan was 12–7, Derringer 11–14 and Grimes went to the Cubs, where he was 6–11. Only rookie Dizzy Dean's 18 wins kept them from falling into the basement, as the Redbirds finished seventh.

In August, Chicago fired its manager, Rogers Hornsby, even though they were in first place at the time. There was a dispute over club policy. Charley Grimm took over and finished guiding them to a pennant. Lon Warneke took league pitching honors with 22 wins, and Charley Root added 19.

Pittsburgh finished second without a 20-game winner, doing it more on hitting. Watty Clark won 20 for Brooklyn to help them to third place. These were the league's only two 20-game winners.

Warneke was nicknamed "The Arkansas Hummingbird" because he hailed from that state and loved to hum. He had appeared in one game in 1930 and 20 in 1931 for the Chicago team, but this was his first full season as a starter and he made the most of his opportunity. Warneke led with 22 victories, .786 winning percentage, four shutouts and a classy 2.37 ERA. He also registered 25 complete games, but came in second to Cincinnati's Red Lucas with 28. Lucas also hit .287 and made 45 pinch-hitting appearances.

Clark, the league's other 20-game winner, had been a pitcher who was a few games over .500 prior to this season, and would return to the same level afterwards. Again, as with several pitchers, this was his one hour of glory. Clark started a league-high 36 games and went 20–12. His next closest had been 16 in 1929, but he lost 19 that year. He spent most of his career with Brooklyn and finished in 1937 with a 111–97 record.

While Carl Hubbell didn't win 20 games, the New York Giants had in him a pitcher who—starting next season and for the ensuing five years—would be rated with Dizzy Dean as one of the two best pitchers in the league, if not in baseball. He was completing his first five seasons in the big leagues and finished with an 18–11 record, the second time he achieved that. Hubbell would be 30 when the next season started and had won 77 games through the 1932 season, but nothing indicated the stardom he would achieve. He developed a screwball, and the rest is history.

Last place Cincinnati led with 83 complete games while New York was last with 57. The pickings for complete games were thin, as only Warneke, Hubbell and Lucas had 20 or more.

Pitcher/Team	G	GS	CG	W	L	Pct	ERA	SO	W	IP
Lon Warneke, Chgo	35	32	25	22*	6	.786*	2.37*	106	64	277
Watty Clark, Bklyn	40	36*	19	20	12	.625	3.49	99	49	273

Warneke and Dean tied for the lead in shutouts with four. Dean also led in strikeouts with 191 and innings pitched at 286.

The Cubs should have stayed home for the World Series. They batted .253, but their pitching staff had a horrendous 9.26 ERA for the four games.

1933

AMERICAN LEAGUE: A FINAL CHAMPIONSHIP

The Yankees still had their powerful hitting attack, although at 38 Babe Ruth was showing signs of slowing down. He had his lowest totals since 1925. He finished with 34 home runs, 103 RBIs and a .301 batting mark—great for anyone else, but not the Babe. However, the real downfall was in pitching. Lefty Gomez fell from 24 wins to 16 and Red Ruffing from 18-7 to 9-14, his only losing season in 15 with the Yankees.

Washington won its third and final pennant. Never again during the remainder of their years in Washington would they reach this pinnacle of success. Led by General Crowder's 24 wins and Earl Whitehill's 22, they finished with 99 wins (a franchise record) to edge out the Yankees by seven games.

Lefty Grove tied Crowder for the league lead with 24 wins, but Philadelphia didn't have much else in pitching and finished third, 19½ games back. Cleveland's Wes Ferrell came down with a sore arm and won only 11 while losing 12.

This was Crowder's last big year as he tied Grove for the lead with 24 wins, while leading with 299 innings pitched. He once again showed his durability and versatility as he started 35 times, relieved 17 and was credited with four saves. After this year he was only 4–10 with Washington when he was traded in 1934 to Detroit, where he finished the season with a 5–1 mark. He spent his final two years in Detroit compiling a 20–13 record for the two years before retiring at the end of the 1936 campaign.

While this was Whitehill's only trip to the charmed circle, he had a long and effective career. Whitehill pitched for 17 seasons, the first ten with Detroit. This was his maiden season with Washington and he responded with his biggest year (22-8). Whitehill pitched three more years in Washington, winning 14 games each time before he was traded to Cleveland where he spent two seasons.

His final year (1939) was with the Chicago Cubs. In 1933, Whitehill led with 37 starts and had a 3.33 ERA, good for this high-scoring era. For his career Whitehill was 218–185.

Grove made it seven years in a row at over 20 wins with his 24, which gave him a seven-season total of 172. He also led with 21 complete games, the lowest to date of any pitcher in the majors. Grove was still a workhorse, appearing in 45 games, 28 as a starter, throwing 275 innings and having six saves. In the last eight seasons, the fewest innings he pitched totaled 258 in 1926, and the lowest number of games in which he appeared was 39 in 1928. After this season Grove would be used almost exclusively as a starter, making only 24 relief appearances in his final eight seasons, of which 20 were in the next three.

In his first nine seasons, Grove made 135 relief appearances while starting 267 games. He was a real double-duty hurler. He was credited with 51 saves during that time. He would have only four saves for the rest of his career. Grove also lost out on the ERA crown after being number one for four straight years. However, he would win that title four more times before he retired.

Bump Hadley had his second straight 20-loss season with the St. Louis Browns as they finished last. Hadley pitched for the Senators, Browns and White Sox before surfacing with the Yankees in 1936. He stayed with them through 1940 as a spot starter and reliever, compiling a 50–31 record. For the rest of his career he was 111–134.

For the first time no team had 50 percent complete games, as Cleveland led with 74 while Chicago was last with 53. Grove was the only pitcher to reach the 20-game completion plateau.

Pitcher/Team	G	GS	CG	W	L	Pct	ERA	SO	W	IP
Lefty Grove, Phila	45	28	21*	24*	8	.750*	3.21	114	83	275
G Crowder, Wash	52*	35	17	24*	15	.615	3.97	110	81	299
Earl Whitehill, Wash	39	37*	19	22	8	.733	3.33	96	100	270

ERA honors went to Cleveland's Mel Harder at 2.95, while Gomez led with 163 strikeouts. Washington had traded Firpo Marberry in the off-season to Detroit, where he went 16–11 as a starter, but they came up with Jack Russell who led the league with 13 saves.

Whitehill won Washington's only game in the Series with a 4–0 third-game shutout. They had little else to cheer about as the New York Giants stopped them cold.

This was the first year of the All-Star Game, which would become an annual event.

NATIONAL LEAGUE: A NEW PITCHING KING ARRIVES

Carl Hubbell had been a good pitcher for his first five seasons, winning 77 games, but over the next five he would be a standout, winning 115. It was pitching that put New York back into the World Series with a four-game margin over Pittsburgh. Hubbell led the way with 23 wins, ably assisted by Hal Schumacher, who had 19.

Although Pittsburgh led the league in hitting and had good pitching, they had no hurler to match Hubbell. Other 20-game winners included Guy Bush who helped pitch Chicago into third, while Ben Cantwell pitched Boston to fourth place, and Dizzy Dean for St. Louis who, although finishing fifth, were 11 games over .500.

Hubbell was the MVP winner hands down in the league. He did it all. His 23 wins were tops as was his sparkling 1.66 ERA. Hubbell was a real worker, pitching in 45 games, 33 as a starter, and posting five saves while pitching a league-high 309 innings. He was also the shutout king with ten. His screwball had turned him from a good pitcher into a superstar. Hubbell was noted for his great control and issued just 47 passes during the season.

This was Bush's best season among several good ones with the Cubs. This was the middle of three years during which he won 57 games over the 1932–34 period. He had 19 in 1932 and followed with 18 in 1934. Bush had 13 full seasons and parts of four others in the majors, the bulk of which were spent with Chicago. He joined them in 1923 and lasted through 1934, winning 152 while losing 101. After he left the Cubs, Bush pitched for Pittsburgh, St. Louis, Boston and Cincinnati, with little success, as he was only 24–35.

Cantwell had a career 76–108, 3.91 ERA, but 1933 was his year. Cantwell was 20–10 with a league-best .667 winning percentage and an excellent 2.61 ERA. He appeared in 40 games, of which only 29 were starts. Before and after this season Cantwell was only 56–98, which covered ten other years.

Dean served notice that he was about to become the best pitcher in baseball. Known for his braggadocio, he could back up whatever claims he made. This was his first of four straight 20-win seasons and except for a career-ending injury at age 27, he probably would have exceeded 300 wins. As it was he had to settle for a 150–83 record. Dean appeared in 48 games, started 34, completed a league-high 25, led with 199 strikeouts and also had four saves.

Larry French was 18–13 for the Chicago team and appeared in 47 games, starting 35. French never won 20 games, but it is worth noting that he was a good pitcher who won 197 games over 14 seasons, then left for World War II and never returned to baseball. He spent 27 years in the navy, retiring as a captain. Had French returned he would have been in his late 30s, but possibly could have won enough to reach 250.

Another pitcher worth noting is Lon Warneke. Although he didn't win 20, he finished with 18, tied for the league lead with 26 complete games and was in the middle of a four-year run in which he won 82 games, this being the only time he didn't win 20 or more.

On the downside was Paul Derringer with Cincinnati, who was 7–27, but in a few years would help pitch Cincinnati into two World Series. Derringer deserved a better fate as he had a respectable 3.30 ERA, but pitched for the weakest-hitting and lowest-scoring team in the majors.

Chicago paced the loop with 95 complete games while Philadelphia was last with 52.

Pitcher/Team	G	GS	CG	W	L	Pct	ERA	SO	W	IP
Carl Hubbell, NY	45	33	22	23*	12	.657	1.66*	156	47	309*
Ben Cantwell, Bos	40	29	18	20	10	.667*	2.61	57	54	255
Guy Bush, Chgo	41	32	20	20	12	.625	2.59	87	70	264
Dizzy Dean, STL	48*	34	26*	20	18	.526	3.04	199*	64	293

Hubbell dominated the World Series, winning two games and allowing no earned runs in 20 innings. Mel Ott was the hitting star with a .389 mark and two home runs.

1934

AMERICAN LEAGUE: A WESTERN CHAMPION

After 14 seasons of Eastern champions, finally one from the West emerged, as Detroit beat out the Yanks by seven games, winning 101 to New York's 94. Schoolboy Rowe with 24 wins and Tommy Bridges with 22 paved the way. The Tigers also had a potent attack with six .300 hitters and three driving in 100 or more. They led the league at .300 and in runs scored.

Lefty Gomez bounced back to take league honors with 26 wins, Red Ruffing had his biggest year yet with 19, and Lou Gehrig won the triple crown, but all to no avail. This was also Ruth's last season with New York. He had 22 home runs, 88 RBIs and a .288 mark, the lowest overall totals in his Yankee career.

Mel Harder garnered 20 wins to help put Cleveland third, while Wes Ferrell, traded to Boston, started a comeback with a 14–5 mark for them. Boston had counted heavily upon the players they received in a trade with Philadelphia, especially Lefty Grove, but he had a sore arm and was only 8–8.

Rowe is credited with 15 active seasons, but three years he pitched in 11 games or less and the fourth was his rookie season in which he appeared in 19 games. This was his first full season and after a 7–4 rookie mark, he really blossomed. He won his career-high 24 games, the only time to reach 20, and appeared in 45 games, of which 30 were starts.

Rowe was also an excellent hitting pitcher, batting .303, and he was used on several occasions as a pinch hitter. Over the three-year period of 1934–36, Rowe won 62 games, but then arm injury made him almost useless from 1937–39, when he was 11–18. He did respond with several winning seasons in the 1940s, but never again approached his halcyon days of the mid-30s, as his highest win total was 16.

Bridges' career spanned 16 seasons, 13 full and three part-time, all with Detroit where he carved out a 194–138 record. This was Bridges' fifth season in the majors; the first four had been undistinguished as he was a composite 39–42. However, in 1934 Bridges blossomed into the pitcher many thought he could be as he won 22 games for the first of three consecutive 20-win seasons with the Tigers. Bridges and Rowe formed the backbone of a Tiger pitching staff that gave them two pennants, a World Series title and a second-place finish in three years.

Gomez returned to the charmed circle with a vengeance. He led the league in most major categories. He was first in victories (26), winning percentage (.839), complete games (25), innings pitched (282), strikeouts (158), shutouts (six) and ERA (2.33). It was truly an outstanding season! This gave Gomez 87 wins for his first four full seasons as a Yankee starter—quite an enviable record.

Harder spent his entire 20-year career with the Cleveland Indians and won 223 games. This was Harder's seventh season and his first of two successive 20-plus-win seasons. Harder also was a double-duty pitcher as he started 29 times and relieved 15 times, receiving credit for four saves. He also tied for the lead in shutouts. As good a pitcher as Harder was, perhaps his greatest claim to fame was as a pitching coach for the Cleveland Indians in the 1940s and 1950s. Among his pitchers were Bob Feller, Early Wynn, Bob Lemon, Herb Score and Mike Garcia. The first three are Hall of Famers, and except for a career-ending injury, Score probably would have made it.

Red Ruffing won 19 and started a string of 11 consecutive winning seasons. Over the next six seasons, Ruffing won 117 games. Another pitcher we should mention is Bobo Newsom, as some think he should be in the Hall of Fame. Newsom is the much-traveled right-hander who spent 20 years in the majors and pitched for nine teams, some of them on two and three different occasions. It seems he was always being traded to someone by someone for someone. This was his first full year; he was 16–20 and appeared in 47 games, 32 of them as a starter. Three times during his career he lost 20 and three times he won 20. His final mark was 211–222.

New York led in complete games with 83 while St. Louis was last with 50. Four pitchers made the list of those who completed 20 or more games.

Pitcher/Team	G	GS	CG	W	L	Pct	ERA	SO	W	IP
Lefty Gomez, NY	38	33	25*	26*	5	.839*	2.33*	158*	96	282*
S Rowe, Detroit	45	30	20	24	8	.750	3.45	149	81	266
Tommy Bridges, Det	36	35*	23	22	11	.667	3.67	151	104	275
Mel Harder, Cleve	44	29	17	20	12	.625	2.61	91	81	255

Gomez and Harder led with six shutouts, while Firpo Marberry was now doing double duty for Detroit, with a 15–5 mark in 38 games, of which 19 were starts.

The Tigers lost the Series in seven games after leading three games to two, losing the last two at home. No Tiger pitcher won more than one game.

Lou Gehrig won the triple crown with a .363 batting mark, 49 home runs and 165 RBIs, but was deprived of the MVP. It went to Detroit's Mickey Cochrane for guiding them to the pennant.

NATIONAL LEAGUE: DIZZY, DAFFY AND THE GASHOUSE GANG

In spring training Dizzy Dean said, "Me and Paul will win 45 games and if the rest of you guys equal that we'll go to the World Series." Well it really took 94 games to win, as the Giants finished with 93 and St. Louis was two in front with 95 victories. However, Dizzy and Daffy, as Paul was called, actually won 49, with brother Dizzy taking 30 to become the last National League pitcher to reach that mark.

The Giants got 20-plus-win seasons from Hal Schumacher and Carl Hubbell, and another 18 from Freddie Fitzsimmons. Lon Warneke won 22 for the Cubs, who finished third, eight games out.

Dean was the National League MVP and deservedly so. He had the league's best winning percentage (.811), appeared in 50 games, completing 24 of 33 starts, and had seven saves. His 312 innings were third behind Van Lingo Mungo's 315 and Hubbell's 313. Dean was tops with seven shutouts and 195 strikeouts to go with his 2.65 ERA. This was the second of four straight 20-plus-win seasons during which he won 102 games.

His brother Paul had a very fine rookie season, winning 19 games and two more in the World Series. Had a rookie of the year award been available, I feel certain Paul Dean would have been the recipient.

Schumacher was a pretty fair pitcher who toiled for the Giants for 13 seasons, winning 158 games. Most of the time he was in the shadow of Hubbell, but this year he outshone the "Meal Ticket," as Hubbell had been nicknamed. Schumacher won 23 games and was in the midst of his three finest seasons for the Giants. He won 19, 23 and 19 for the 1933–35 years. After 1935 he never approached those levels again, but he was a winner every season but one and pitched consistent ball. He won 13 each year from 1937 through 1940 and 12 each in 1941 and 1942.

Hubbell racked up his second consecutive 20-win season with 21 victories. He also led the league with eight saves, again demonstrating his versatility. Hubbell had the low ERA (2.30) while appearing in 49 games and completing a league-high 25 in 34 starts. He also walked only 37 men in 313 innings. No wonder they called him the Meal Ticket. Is it any wonder that Dean and Hubbell were coming to be known as the two best pitchers in the league, if not in all of baseball?

Warneke returned to the 20-win club with his 22 wins for the second time in three years. He would follow with one more season at the 20-win level. Once again he was a dual-role pitcher, starting 35 times and used in relief eight times, as he completed 23 games and hurled 291 innings.

No other pitcher won 20, but Curt Davis had 19 for the seventh-place

Phillies. Davis appeared in league-high 51 games, starting 31 and receiving credit for five saves. His 2.96 ERA shows how well he pitched, and his 19–17 record could have been much superior given a better team behind him. This was Davis' rookie season; he would last for 13 years, winning 158 games pitching for Chicago, Brooklyn and St. Louis as well as Philadelphia.

Cincinnati finished last again while Paul Derringer went 15–21 and Si Johnson was 7–22. This gave Derringer the unenviable record of 48 losses in two seasons, although he had pitched well in both years, but had a very weak team behind him. Once again he was a workhorse, starting and relieving for a total of 47 games, with 31 of them starts. Johnson was completing a four-year record that was pretty dismal. From 1931 through 1934, he won 38 while losing 74. For his career he was 101–165. Brighter days were a few years ahead for the Reds.

St. Louis led the loop with 78 complete games and last-place Cincinnati trailed with 51. Five pitchers did have 20 or more complete games.

Pitcher/Team	G	GS	CG	W	L	Pct	ERA	SO	W	IP
Dizzy Dean, STL	50	33	24	30*	7	.811*	2.65	195*	75	312
Hal Schumacher, NY	41	36	18	23	10	.697	3.18	112	89	297
Lon Warneke, Chgo	43	35	23	22	10	.688	3.22	143	66	291
Carl Hubbell, NY	49	34	25*	21	12	.636	2.30	118	37	313

We were still in the era when starting pitchers were used consistently in relief, and often led the league in appearances. A quick check of the leading pitchers will show how often they were called on for relief duty.

The Cardinals outscored Detroit 34–23, outhit them .279 to .224, and outpitched them (2.34 ERA to 3.74). Dizzy and Daffy each won two games with Dizzy taking the finale, 11–0. Unfortunately, this would be their only Series appearance. Both would see their careers cut short abruptly.

In the All-Star Game, Carl Hubbell gained immortality when he fanned Babe Ruth, Lou Gehrig, Jimmie Foxx, Al Simmons and Joe Cronin in order. What a feat!

1935

AMERICAN LEAGUE: AT LAST A CHAMPIONSHIP

Detroit had been the bridesmaid often, but never the bride. They had been to the Series four times, and came away a loser each trip. The 1935 year would be different. Detroit beat out the Yankees by five games as Tommy Bridges won 21 and Schoolboy Rowe had 19. They also got 18 from Eldon Auker and 16 from General Crowder.

New York, although boasting the best ERA (3.60) in the league, slipped mainly because Lefty Gomez went from 26–5 to 12–15. A mark somewhere in the middle would have brought New York another title.

Mel Harder passed the 20 mark again to put Cleveland in third place. Wes Ferrell regained his old form and led the loop with 25 wins for Boston. Lefty Grove returned to form to win 20 and with Ferrell helped pitch Boston into the final First Division spot.

Philadelphia finished last but had one of the strongest teams ever to be cellar dwellers. Jimmy Foxx led the league with 36 home runs, had 115 RBIs and hit .346, while teammates Pinky Higgins hit .296 with 23 home runs, Wally Moses batted .325, Doc Cramer hit .332 and Bob Johnson had 28 home runs, 109 RBIs and batted .299. Johnny Marcum also won 17 games, but they still finished last.

Bridges logged his second straight 20-plus-win season as he garnered 21 wins to lead the Detroit staff. He also led the league with 163 strikeouts. Bridges completed 23 of 34 games he started as he logged 274 innings. Bridges would have one more season at the 20-win level. Even though he would not make it after 1936, he would still have several good winning seasons, chalking up a losing mark only in 1941 at 9–12.

Harder had his second straight 20-win season and career high with 22 wins. Harder, too, would not again win 20 games, but continued to pitch effective winning ball for Cleveland through 1947, with seven seasons in double-digit victories and four at 15 or better. His only losing seasons were 1942 at 13–14 and 1945 at 3–7.

After a two-year absence, Ferrell was back in the 20-win circle as he matched his career high with 25 victories. Not only did Ferrell lead in wins, he became the first American Leaguer since Ted Lyons in 1927 to pitch 30 or more complete games. He had 31 in 38 starts, which gave him 322 innings pitched. Ferrell also batted .347 with seven home runs and made 34 pinch-hitting appearances—almost a one man show.

Grove bounced back from a sore arm to win 20 games for the eighth and last time in his career and capture his sixth ERA title with a 2.70 mark. While Grove never again won 20, he pitched for six more seasons, twice winning 17. He never had a losing year, led in ERA three times and in winning percentage once. Finally, in 1941 he won his 300th game and retired with a 300–141 record for a .680 winning percentage, fourth highest on the all-time list for pitchers over 100 wins and highest of pitchers with over 300 wins.

Detroit led with 87 complete games while St. Louis was last with 42. Four pitchers had 20 or more complete games, topped by Ferrell's 31. Bobo Newsom again led in losses, but this time the number was only 18.

Pitcher/Team	G	GS	CG	W	L	Pct	ERA	SO	W	IP
Wes Ferrell, Boston	41	38*	31*	25*	14	.641	3.52	110	108	322*
Mel Harder, Cleve	42	35	17	22	11	.667	3.29	95	53	287
Tommy Bridges, Det	36	34	23	21	10	.677	3.51	163*	113	274
Lefty Grove, Boston	35	30	23	20	12	.625	2.70*	121	65	273

Rowe led with six shutouts. Auker had the best percentage at .720, based on his 18–7 mark.

In the World Series, Bridges was 2–0 and Rowe and Crowder each won a game as Detroit took the title in six games.

NATIONAL LEAGUE: THREE IS THE LUCKY NUMBER

The Chicago Cubs were on a pattern to win the pennant every three years: they won in 1929, 1932 and now again in 1935. The Cardinals were the pre-season favorites, but a 21-game winning streak by the Cubs in September put them four ahead of St. Louis and eight and one-half ahead of New York.

Bill Lee and Lon Warneke each won 20 to pace the Cubs' mound force, while Larry French added 17 and Charley Root another 15.

St. Louis got 47 wins from the Dean brothers, with Dizzy winning 28 and Paul 19 again. No one realized it, but this would be Paul's last big year at age 21: he injured his arm the next season. In two years Diz would be finished at 27. It was hard to believe about two pitchers who could have rewritten the record books.

Carl Hubbell fashioned another 20-plus-win season, and with 19 more from Hal Schumacher the Giants finished third. Cincinnati began showing signs of life as they finished sixth, primarily on the arm of Paul Derringer, loser of 48 the last two seasons, as he fashioned 22 wins.

Lee spent 14 seasons in the big leagues and won 169 games. Most of that time and all of his successful seasons were spent with the Chicago Cubs. This was Lee's second year and he broke the 20-game barrier with a 20–6 mark, which gave him the league's best winning percentage (.769). Lee fashioned a 2.96 ERA over 252 innings in 32 starts and seven relief appearances.

Warneke completed his four-year run with his second successive 20-win season and third in the past four years as he had an even 20 victories. Warneke continued double duty as he started 30 times and relieved another 12, which allowed him to have four saves. As has been stated before, this was still the era when managers went to their starters in key situations when needing a relief pitcher. In another decade or so this would start to change.

Dizzy, or "The Great One" as he was sometimes called, had another banner season, winning 28 games to lead the league. It looked for a while like he would hit the 30 mark again. Dean also had the most starts (36), complete games (29), innings pitched (324) and strikeouts (182). In addition, he relieved 14 times and had five saves. His mastery was unbelievable.

Hubbell won 20 or more for the third straight season but posted his highest ERA (3.27) for the 1931–39 period. It should be noted that a 3.27 ERA in this era of high scoring was quite acceptable. Hubbell again logged over 300 innings with his 303 and was in 42 games, with 35 of them being starts.

Derringer won 20 games for the first time in his career. This season he won 22 games as he appeared in 45 games, completing 20 of his 33 starts. From 1935 through 1940, Derringer had only one losing season, 1937, when he was 10–14. Four times he won 20 or more and a fifth time he checked in with 19, with only 1937 being a downer. However, it is probably the 48 losses in 1933–34 and the losing years in the early 40s that have kept him out of the Hall, despite his 223 wins.

Boston was dead last with a 38–115 mark and Ben Cantwell was 4–25. Chicago topped the loop with 81 complete games while Philadelphia was last with 53, one less than Boston. Five pitchers had 20 or more complete games.

Pitcher/Team	G	GS	CG	W	L	Pct	ERA	SO	W	IP
Dizzy Dean, STL	50	36*	29*	28*	12	.700	3.11	182*	82	324*
Carl Hubbell, NY	42	35	24	23	12	.657	3.27	150	49	303
Paul Derringer, Cinn	45	33	20	22	13	.629	3.51	120	49	277
Bill Lee, Chgo	39	32	18	20	6	.769*	2.96	100	54	252
Lon Warneke, Chgo	42	30	20	20	12	.625	3.06	120	50	262

Five pitchers tied with four for the shutout lead, including Freddie Fitzsimmons, who had an arm injury and was only 4–8, a major reason New York could only finish third. Pittsburgh's Cy Benton (18–13) wore the ERA crown at 2.59.

Warneke was brilliant in the Series, posting a .54 ERA and a 2–0 record, but no other Cub could win a game, even though they basically pitched well enough.

Babe Ruth ended his career with the Boston Braves. They had figured he would bring fans to the park and he did, but the Babe thought he would be given the opportunity to manage, which he wasn't. Babe batted only .181, but hit six home runs in just 72 at bats, including three in a game at Pittsburgh — sort of a last hurrah. When he retired he had 714 home runs, 2,209 RBIs and a .342 career average. While Hank Aaron would surpass the first two, he would have 3,965 more official trips to the plate. Let's not even conjecture what Ruth's final numbers would be given those additional at bats.

1936

AMERICAN LEAGUE: START OF A
NEW DYNASTY AND BEGINNING OF A NEW HERO

Given the power and pitching Detroit possessed, many thought they would make it three in a row. However, two tragedies struck Detroit. Hank Greenberg, their powerhouse first baseman, broke his wrist and was lost for the season after just 12 games. Mickey Cochrane's health gave out and he had to spend most of the year in Wyoming recuperating. Thus they finished a distant second, 19½ games out, despite 23 wins from Tommy Bridges and 19 more from Schoolboy Rowe.

The Yankees put it all together as Red Ruffing won 20. Monte Pearson chipped in with a 19–7 mark to help the cause, as the Yankees won 102. They also unveiled a rookie, Joe DiMaggio, who would soon become their new super-star. This season Lou Gehrig did win the MVP.

Ruffing continued to confound the skeptics as he had his first of four straight 20-win seasons for the Yankees. Over the next four seasons Ruffing was 82–33, and while there would remain some diehards by the time the 1940s arrived, most believed that Ruffing was a great pitcher and deserved to be in the Hall of Fame. For the season he completed 25 of his 33 starts and batted .291, hit five home runs and made 20 pinch-hitting appearances.

Bridges had his biggest winning season with 23 as he won 20 or more for the third straight year and en route captured his second successive strikeout title. After this season, Bridges continued as a winning pitcher, although he never topped 20 again.

Teammate Schoolboy Rowe had another fine season, garnering 19 wins to give him 62 over the three seasons. Next year tragedy would strike, and for the 1937–38 seasons Rowe was limited to 14 games and a 1–6 record. He was able to get into 28 games in 1939 but had only a 10–12 mark with a 4.99 ERA. Winning ways weren't seen again until 1940, and he never did regain the form of the mid-1930s.

Chicago's Vern Kennedy was 29 years old but only in his second season when he posted a 21–9 record, giving promise perhaps of greater things to come. They never materialized. Kennedy pitched in the big leagues through 1945 and the most he ever won again was 14. He fashioned a 72–110 mark for the balance of his career—another example of one season in the spotlight.

Johnny Allen had broken in with the Yankees in 1932 with a 17–4 mark and league-leading .810 winning percentage. In four seasons with the New York club he was 50–19. Then the temperamental Allen was traded to Cleveland, where in 1936 he enjoyed his biggest season with a 20–10 record. Allen pitched for Cleveland through 1940 and never had a losing record. Following a brief stint with the St. Louis Browns, he was traded to the National League where he finished out his career with the New York Giants and Brooklyn Dodgers. His only losing season was his last, when he was 4–7 in 1944 with the Giants. For his career he was 142–75, had a winning percentage of .654, and was eleventh on the all-time list of pitchers with over 100 career victories.

For Boston, Wes Ferrell turned in his second straight 20-win season and sixth overall. It also proved to be his last. He led with 39 starts, 28 complete games and 301 innings pitched. Ferrell was still dangerous with the bat, hitting five home runs while batting .267 and getting into 22 games as a pinch hitter. After this season Ferrell slipped and was 14–19 for Boston and Washington the next season and 15–10 for Washington and the Yankees in 1938, which proved to be his last full season. He played through 1940 but appeared in only eight games over the three years, posting a 3–3 mark. Ferrell retired with a 193–128 mark.

Chicago led with 80 complete games and seventh-place St. Louis was last with 54. Seven pitchers had 20 or more complete games.

Pitcher/Team	G	GS	CG	W	L	Pct	ERA	SO	W	IP
Tom Bridges, Detroit	39	38*	26	23*	11	.676	3.60	175*	115	295
Vern Kennedy, Chgo	35	34	20	21	9	.700	4.63	99	147*	274
Johnny Allen, Cleve	36	31	19	20	10	.667	3.44	165	97	243
Red Ruffing, NY	33	33	25	20	12	.625	3.85	102	90	271
Wes Ferrell, Boston	39	38*	28*	20	15	.571	4.19	106	119	301*

ERAs were high as the league ERA was 4.92, with New York the lowest at 4.17. Pearson took winning percent honors with .731, while Lefty Grove (17–12) had the most shutouts (six) and led in ERA with 2.81.

The Yankees took the Series in six games, including scores of 18–4 in game two and 13–5 in the finale. Gomez was 2–0, while Ruffing failed to win a game. A 17-year-old kid from Van Meter, Iowa stunned the baseball world when he tied the American League record for strikeouts by fanning 17 Philadelphia Athletic players. The young hurler's name was Bob Feller, and in a few years would become the premier pitcher in baseball. Had it not been for four lost years during World War II, he would probably have won over 350 games. He amassed six 20-plus-win seasons.

NATIONAL LEAGUE: THE MEAL TICKET COMES THROUGH

In a hard-fought season, New York finally won out over St. Louis and Chicago by five games, mainly on the strength of Carl Hubbell's MVP season, 26–6, 2.31 ERA, both best in the league. No other pitcher on the staff won over 14.

St. Louis again relied on Dizzy Dean as he chalked up 24 wins. Little did he know this would be his last big season. Brother Paul developed a sore arm, was only 5–5 and basically at 22 was through, although he hung around for several years.

Hubbell had his finest season as he led the league with 26 wins, .813 winning percentage and 2.31 ERA. This was his fourth consecutive 20-plus-win season and the second time he led in victories. It also marked the second time he was chosen league MVP. Only one other pitcher has that distinction in the 20th century: Hal Newhouser for the Detroit Tigers in 1944–45. Hubbell amassed 304 innings on 25 complete games in 34 starts and eight relief appearances. What a season he had. What a pitcher!

The other pitcher considered to be one of the two best in the game turned in another fine year. Dean won 24 games for a faltering second-place St. Louis. Dean led in appearances with 51, saves with 11, complete games at 28 and innings pitched (315). This gave Dean 102 wins over the past four years, by far more than any other pitcher. The closest to him was Hubbell with 93. Tragedy would strike next season and end a brilliant career. It already struck down his younger brother Paul, winner of 38 games in his first two seasons.

No other pitcher could claim 20 wins. Paul Derringer won 19 for Cincinnati, but also lost 19, while future teammate and pitching ace Bucky Walters was 11–21 for the last-place Philadelphia team.

Chicago led with 77 complete games and Philadelphia was last with 51.

Pitcher/Team	G	GS	CG	W	L	Pct	ERA	SO	W	IP
Carl Hubbell, NY	42	34	25	26*	6	.813*	2.31*	123	57	304
Dizzy Dean, STL	51*	34	28*	24	13	.649	3.17	195	53	315*

Brooklyn's Van Lingle Mungo led with 238 strikeouts and 110 walks. Seven pitchers tied for the shutout lead with four.

Hubbell was 1–1 in the Series with a 2.25 ERA. The rest of the staff were over 7.00 ERA.

1937

AMERICAN LEAGUE: THE
BARRAGE CONTINUES UNABATED

Detroit had a healthy Hank Greenberg, who batted .337 with 40 home runs and 183 RBIs, plus rookie Rudy York who hit 35 home runs and 103 RBIs in only 375 at bats. When added to the rest of their firepower and their great pitching, you would have thought they would dethrone the Yankees. Such was not the case.

Schoolboy Rowe injured his arm, and would never again be the same pitcher. He fell to 1–4 and it would be three years before he could pitch effective winning baseball again. Tommy Bridges dipped to 15–12 and the Tigers had the second-worst ERA (4.87) in the league. An example was Roxie Lawson who had a 5.22 ERA, but was 18–7 thanks to Detroit's six runs per game. Only last-place St. Louis with its 6.00 ranked lower.

Meanwhile, the Yankees produced the only two 20-game winners in the league in Red Ruffing and Lefty Gomez. When added to their tremendous hitting, they won by 13 games as young Joe DiMaggio led the league with 46 home runs and had 167 RBIs while batting .346. Lou Gehrig and Bill Dickey also had big years in batting average, home runs and RBIs.

Gomez had another big season as he turned in 21 victories for his fourth and final time in the charmed circle. Gomez logged 278 innings on 25 complete games in 34 starts, was the strikeout leader with 194 and ERA king at 2.33, almost two and one-half runs below the league average. While Gomez never won 20 again, he pitched winning ball for the rest of his career with the Yankees. He pitched one game for the Washington Senators in 1943, lost it and then retired.

With each passing season, Ruffing was silencing most of his doubters. This year he notched his second straight 20-win season despite missing a month because he was a holdout. Ruffing posted a 2.99 ERA (exceptional in this high-scoring era), with 22 complete games in 31 starts and a 20–7 record. He continued as a pinch hitter deluxe for the Yankees, being in that role 23 times during the season.

Young Bobby Feller came down with an arm injury and made only 19 starts as he was 9–7. The Yankees led the league with 82 complete games, while the hapless Browns (46–106) were last with 55.

Pitcher/Team	G	GS	CG	W	L	Pct	ERA	SO	W	IP
Lefty Gomez, NY	34	34	25	21*	11	.656	2.33*	194*	93	278
Red Ruffing, NY	31	31	22	20	7	.741	2.99	131	68	256

Gomez was the leader with six shutouts, while Wes Ferrell led in complete games (26) and innings pitched (281). Cleveland's Johnny Allen had the top percentage mark at .938, based on his 15–1 mark, the loss coming on the final day of the season.

It was all Yankees again in the subway Series as they outscored the Giants 28–12 and won four games to one. Gomez was 2–0, and Ruffing and Monte Pearson picked up the other wins.

NATIONAL LEAGUE: ANOTHER TRAGEDY, THE SAME CHAMPION

The St. Louis Cardinals had figured to bounce back, as they added Lon Warneke to their staff and were hopeful of a comeback from Paul Dean. After all, they already had his brother, Dizzy. Warneke won 18, but Paul had a sore arm and appeared in only one game. Dizzy was on his way to another 25-win season when tragedy struck.

In the All-Star game he was hit by a line drive from Earl Averill and it broke his toe. He went back to pitching too soon, put a strain on his shoulder and was never the same pitcher again. At 27, the winner of 134 games was through, as was brother Paul at only 23.

The Cubs made a gallant run for the pennant, but fell short by three games as the Giants got 22 wins from Carl Hubbell and rookie Cliff Melton added 20. Boston had two rookies to win 20 games, which put them over .500. Thirty-year-old Lou Fette was 20–10, while 33-year-old Jim Turner was 20–11.

Hubbell was again the master as he led with 22 wins, 159 strikeouts and a .733 winning percentage. This was his fifth and final 20-plus-win season and for the five years he was 115–50. Hubbell would pitch another six years and have only one losing season, 11–12 in 1940. In his latter years he was a spot starter, but won between 11–13 games in five of the six years. He retired with a 253–154, .622 winning percentage and a spot in the Hall of Fame. He is 37th on the all-time winning percentage list of pitchers with over 100 wins and tenth for pitchers with over 200 wins.

Melton showed great promise when he broke in with a 20–9 mark. The Giants thought they had another Hubbell on their hands, but after this season the only resemblance was that they both threw left-handed. Melton turned in a great performance, leading in saves with seven and posting a 2.61 ERA. He was in 46 games, starting 27 of them. Thus he was a durable and versatile pitcher. However, after this season the best he could do was 14–14 in 1938. Melton lasted until 1944 and never again pitched .500 ball until his last year, when he was 2–2. He finished with a career 80–86 record.

Much has been written about the tragedy that struck the Dean brothers, whose careers were cut down in the prime of their lives. At least in Dizzy's case he did get his chance at some glory as he had six full seasons, but brother Paul had only two. One can only conjecture what they might have achieved. If you assumed another ten seasons for Diz and 13 or 14 for Paul, it is quite conceivable that Diz could have exceeded 300 wins and Paul at least 250. But injuries are part of the game, and we must accept the records they achieved.

Fette was a 30-year-old rookie when he posted a fine 20–10, 2.88 ERA mark with 23 complete games in 33 starts. The Braves thought they had a real winner, even though he was already 30. However, Fette would never again approach these heights. In fact he lasted only four more seasons and won a total of 21 games while losing 30 during that time. He hung around until 1940 with little success, then was out of the majors until 1945. After the war Boston gave him one last chance, and at age 38 he was 0–2 in five games.

His partner Turner fared a little better. He was a 33-year-old rookie and went 20–11 with a league-high 24 complete games and best ERA at 2.38. However, the best he could do was 14 wins the next season, but he lost 18; he then won 14 in 1940 for Cincinnati, when he lost only seven. He pitched through 1945 but was strictly a relief pitcher after 1940. He finished with a 69–60 record. Both Turner and Fette are examples of pitchers who had that one year of glory amidst an otherwise undistinguished career. I believe it also points out the difficulty of pitching consistent winning ball season after season.

Boston led the loop with 85 complete games while seventh-place Philadelphia was last with 59. Only three pitchers could achieve 20 or more complete games as managers were using the bullpen more and more, even though starters were still called on to perform double duty.

Pitcher/Team	G	GS	CG	W	L	Pct	ERA	SO	W	IP
Carl Hubbell, NY	39	32	18	22*	8	.733*	3.19	159*	55	262
Cliff Melton, NY	46	27	14	20	9	.690	2.61	142	55	248
Lou Fette, Boston	35	35	23	20	10	.667	2.68	70	81	259
Jim Turner, Boston	33	30	24*	20	11	.645	2.38*	69	52	257

St. Louis' Joe Medwick won the triple crown with a .374, 31 home runs and 154 RBIs. No National League player has turned the trick since then. Hubbell won the only game for the Giants in the Series, while the rest of the staff had an ERA above 5.00.

─────────────── **1938** ───────────────

AMERICAN LEAGUE: ANOTHER
CHALLENGE, MORE TRAGEDIES

Boston, Cleveland and Detroit were all set to challenge for the title, but when it was over the Yankees had won by 11 over Boston, 13 over Cleveland and 17 over Detroit. Red Ruffing paced the loop with 21 wins and Lefty Gomez added 18 for the Yankees.

The Yankees had banner years from Joe DiMaggio, Bill Dickey and Joe Gordon. No one knew it, but this was the last full season for Lou Gehrig, who hit .295 with 29 home runs and 114 RBIs. That would be great for 99 out of 100 hitters, but not for the Iron Horse.

Bobo Newsom won 20 for seventh-place St. Louis, which was 36–81 without him. Injuries played a prominent part in the season. Any hope Boston had faded when ace Lefty Grove was sidelined in mid-July. He finished 14–4, but his loss for almost two months doomed an already weak pitching staff.

Cleveland also was dealt a setback, when Johnny Allen (14–8) was lost for almost two months. However, Bobby Feller served notice about what to expect, as at the age of 19 he won 17 games for Cleveland. He also led the loop with 240 strikeouts and 208 walks. Postseason tragedy struck when Chicago star right-hander Monte Stratton blew off his leg in a hunting accident and ended a promising career.

Ruffing had his third straight 20-plus-win season as he led the league with 21 wins and the top winning percentage at .750. There seemed little he had to prove to the skeptics, although there were still a few doubting Thomases who felt the Yankees firepower benefited him. Of course it did, just like it did all other staff pitchers. Lefty Gomez chipped in with 18 wins.

Newsom surfaced again with the St. Louis Browns and was 20–16, but had a 5.07 ERA. He got into 44 games, including a league-high 40 starts, and had 31 complete games, the most since Wes Ferrell turned the trick in 1935. Newsom also amassed a league-high 330 innings, showing what a real workhorse he was.

The Yankees topped the loop in complete games with 91 while Philadelphia was last, both in standings and complete games (56). Five pitchers had at least 20 complete games, led by Newsom's 31. A new relief ace was emerging as the Yanks' Johnny Murphy was 8–2, with a league-high 11 saves.

Pitcher/Team	G	GS	CG	W	L	Pct	ERA	SO	W	IP
Red Ruffing, NY	31	31	22	21*	7	.750*	3.32	127	82	247
Bobo Newsom, STL	44	40*	31*	20	16	.556	5.07	226	192	330*

Lefty Gomez led the league with four shutouts, as hitting continued to dominate, with only the Yankees having a team ERA (3.91) below 4.00. In the

World Series, New York swept the Cubs in four straight as Ruffing won two and Pearson and Gomez one each.

Hank Greenberg made an assault on Babe Ruth's home run record, but fell two short. He finished with 58.

NATIONAL LEAGUE: A SIZZLING RACE AND COSTLY INJURY

In contrast to the runaway in the American League, the National was a hard-fought, four-team donnybrook, eventually won by Chicago on the basis of a 21–4 September. Only six games separated the first-place Cubs from fourth-place Cincinnati. Between them were Pittsburgh, 2½ games out, and New York, five back.

Bill Lee paced the Cubs and the loop with 22 wins, and Clay Bryant added 19. No other Cub pitcher won more than 10. Pittsburgh was second, more on its hitting than pitching. New York lost its chance at three in a row when ace Carl Hubbell (13–10) was shelved with a sore arm in August and lost his chance for six straight 20-win seasons. Teammate Cliff Melton fell from his rookie 20–9 mark to a 14–14 season.

Cincinnati produced the loop's other 20-game winner as Paul Derringer won 21 in pacing Cincinnati to fourth place. Bucky Walters came over shortly before midseason and won 11 games. In 1939, a lot more would be heard from these two.

Lee had his career-best season for the Cubs. He had a league-high 22 wins that included the league's best winning percentage (.710), most shutouts (nine) and lowest ERA (2.66). This was the second and last time Lee would win 20 games. He had one more big season before falling on hard times, as he won 19 the next year. From 1934 through 1939 Lee posted a 106–70 mark. In the balance of his career split between Chicago, Boston and Philadelphia, he was only 63–87.

Derringer won 21 games for his second time as a 20-game winner. This was the first of three successive 20-plus-win seasons for the right-hander. Starting in 1939, he and Walters would team up to pace Cincinnati to two pennants and one World Series title. Derringer was masterful as he appeared in 41 games, completed 26 of his 37 starts, posted a 2.93 ERA and pitched 307 innings. The games started, completed and innings pitched were all league highs.

However, the real drama this season was provided by Johnny Vander Meer in Cincinnati. An otherwise journeyman pitcher, he did something this season no one ever did before or any pitcher has done since. Vander Meer pitched two consecutive no-hit, no-run games, thus earning him the nickname "Double No-Hit." He no-hit Boston 3–0 on June 11th and no-hit Brooklyn 6–0 on June 15th. For the season he was 15–10. Vander Meer pitched for Cincinnati through 1950 and was 119–120. He pitched one game for Cleveland in 1951 and was 0–1. The highest number of games he ever won was 18 in 1942. During their pennant years of 1939 and 1940, Vander Meer was only 8–10 for the two years. In 1940 he was in only ten games with a 3–1 record.

Only Boston had more than 50 percent complete games as they led with 83, while Brooklyn was last with 56.

Pitcher/Team	G	GS	CG	W	L	Pct	ERA	SO	W	IP
Bill Lee, Chicago	44	37*	19	22*	9	.710*	2.66*	121	74	291
Paul Derringer, Cinn	41	37*	26*	21	14	.600	2.93	132	49	307*

Lee had nine shutouts to pace the league, while Bryant led with 135 strike-outs. Dick Coffman of New York led in appearances with 51 and in saves with 12, to become the first bonafide relief specialist in the league. Larry French, an otherwise good pitcher and winner of 197 career games, had a terrible season as he was 10–19 for the first-place Cubs, thus becoming the only pitcher ever to lose 19 games for a first-place team.

Chicago scored only nine runs in four Series games. Lee was 0–2 despite a 2.45 ERA. The rest of the staff performed horribly.

——————— **1939** ———————

AMERICAN LEAGUE: A NEW
STAR, BUT THE END OF AN ERA

The Yankees won by their biggest margin in four years when they finished 17 games ahead of Boston, as they posted a 106–45 mark. Red Ruffing again showed the way with 21 wins, and while no other pitcher won more than 13, there were six with ten wins or more.

The Yanks had great seasons from many. Joe DiMaggio won his first batting crown with a .381 mark. However, there was a note of tragedy. Lou Gehrig, after playing 2,130 consecutive games, took himself out of the lineup, never to return. He had a rare neuromuscular disease—amyotrophic lateral sclerosis—that would claim his life in two years. It has become known as Lou Gehrig's Disease.

Although he was limited to 23 games, Lefty Grove turned in a fine 15–4, 2.54 ERA mark for Boston, with the latter leading the loop. However, the big news out of Boston was a 21-year-old rookie named Ted Williams, who batted .327 and led the loop in homers (31) and RBIs (145). He would be a force for the next 20 years, but Boston would win only one pennant during that time.

Bob Feller pitched Cleveland into third place as he led the league with 24 wins. Bobo Newsom and Dutch Leonard were the league's other 20-game winners. New York led with 87 complete games, even though Johnny Murphy had 19 saves, while Philadelphia was last with 50. Four pitchers recorded 20 or more complete games. The hapless St. Louis Browns were last with a 43–111 mark.

Ruffing won 20 or more for the fourth straight season as he matched his previous year's mark with another 21–7 record. Ruffing appeared in only 28 games and completed 22. Thus he achieved a rarity in baseball—winning 20 while appearing in less than 30 games. It is a feat that has been accomplished only a few times. Ruffing also posted a 2.94 ERA. I think his record should put to rest the speculation as to whether he belongs in the Hall or not.

Feller embarked on a career that only World War II could—and did—interrupt. This was his first of three straight and six 20-win seasons. Feller led the league with 24 victories, appeared in 39 games, started 35 and completed 24, best in the league. His 297 innings pitched and 246 strikeouts were the league's best marks. Over the three years (1939–41) Feller was 76–33, and if we add 1946 for his four full seasons he was 102–47. Thus it is easy to see why so many say he could have retired with 350 or more wins and 3,500 to 4,000 strikeouts.

The irrepressible Newsom did it again, this time in a split season with St. Louis and Detroit, although most of the time was spent with the latter. For the second time in his career, Newsom won 20 games and tied Feller for the league high with 24 complete games. If ever there was a pitcher who was an anomaly, it was Newsom.

Leonard had been in the big leagues with Brooklyn and Washington since 1933, but this was his first and only time to record 20 wins. He had the misfortune to pitch for Brooklyn, Washington, the Philadelphia Phillies and Chicago Cubs when they were on the downside. Thus his final career record was only 191–181 for 20 years. With better teams and support he could have won at least 250 games and perhaps earned a spot in the Hall of Fame. Leonard was 20–8 this season.

Pitcher/Team	G	GS	CG	W	L	Pct	ERA	SO	W	IP
Bob Feller, Cleve	39	35	24*	24*	9	.727	2.65	246*	142*	297*
Red Ruffing, NY	28	28	22	21	7	.750	2.94	95	75	233
Dutch Leonard, Wash	34	34	21	20	8	.714	3.55	88	59	269
Bobo Newsom, Det	41	37*	24*	20	11	..645	3.58	192	126	292

Ruffing was shutout king with five, while Grove grabbed winning percent honors at .769. The Yankees had a new opponent in the World Series—Cincinnati—but swept them four straight by outscoring the Reds, 20–8. No pitcher won over one game in the Series.

NATIONAL LEAGUE: A NEW CHAMPION EMERGES

Chicago and New York had each won two of the last four pennants, but were never really in the chase. Chicago got 47 wins from Bill Lee, Larry French and Claude Passeau, but the rest of the staff were 37–38. New York had 18 wins from Harry Gumbert, with no one else over 13.

Converted infielder Bucky Walters paced Cincinnati to first place with 27 wins, which made him the MVP. He was also ably assisted by Paul Derringer's

25 wins. St. Louis made a gallant run, but fell short despite Curt Davis' 22 victories.

Walters spent 1935 through 1938 pitching for Philadelphia until he was traded to Cincinnati in mid-1938. Prior to this season he amassed a 49–59 record, of which he was 38–53 with Philadelphia. With Cincinnati he hit his stride and was the winningest pitcher in the National League from 1939 through 1944. He posted a 121–73 record, which included three times as a 20-game winner. However, in 1939 he was just superb. He won a league-high 27 games, and had there been a Cy Young Award he would have won hands down. He did win the MVP, and based on his record there can be no argument. He led with 36 starts, had 31 complete games, the most innings pitched (319) and the lowest ERA (2.29). His 31 complete games marked the first time a National League pitcher had 30 complete games since 1924 when Dazzy Vance and Burleigh Grimes turned the trick.

Teammate Derringer probably would have won the MVP in any other season, but he was overshadowed by Walters. This was Derringer's second straight 20-plus-win season, and his best ever, as he posted a 25–7 mark that included the league's best winning percentage (.781), 28 complete games, 301 innings pitched and a 2.95 ERA. What a magnificent duo they proved to be.

Davis had his best season as he won 22 games, appeared in 49 games, 31 as a starter, and posted seven saves. Strangely, after going 0–4 in 14 games the next year, he was traded to Brooklyn. He helped them to a pennant in 1941 with a 13–7 record and was 15–6 in their spirited second-place finish in 1942. Davis also batted .381 for the Redbirds this season.

Luke Hamlin helped pitch Brooklyn into third place as he won 20 games. Hamlin is another of those pitchers who had one bright spot in an otherwise undistinguished career. Prior to this season Hamlin had been 26–31, and he would be 27–32 for his four remaining years after 1939. However, in 1939 he stood tall. He won 20 games, tied Walters for the most starts at 36 and pitched 270 innings.

Cincinnati topped the loop with 86 complete games. St. Louis was last with 45, but they topped the league with a new record in saves: 32. Only three pitchers had 20 or more complete games; the use of relief pitching was on the rise.

Pitcher/Team	G	GS	CG	W	L	Pct	ERA	SO	W	IP
Bucky Walters, Cinn	39	36*	31*	27*	11	.711	2.29	137*	109	319*
Paul Derringer, Cinn	38	35	28	25	7	.781*	2.93	128	35	301
Curt Davis, STL	49	31	13	22	16	.579	3.63	70	48	248
Luke Hamlin, Bklyn	40	35*	19	20	13	.606	3.63	88	54	270

Lou Fette of Boston, although only 10–10 for the season, led with six shutouts. Davis, in addition to his 22 wins, had seven saves and batted .381, often being used as a pinch hitter. St. Louis' Don Padgett batted .399 in 233 official at bats.

In the Series, it was a different story. Walters was 0–2 with a 4.91 ERA, and Cincinnati lost to the Yankees in four games.

5

1940–1949

— 1940 —

AMERICAN LEAGUE: THE CRY BABY TEAM

Most sports enthusiasts thought the Yankees would make it five in a row. After a disastrous start, they got hot but came in only third, two games off the pace. The loss of Lou Gehrig, Bill Dickey hitting .247, Lefty Gomez (3–3) with a sore arm and Red Ruffing falling to 15 wins all contributed to their fall from grace.

However, the real story was in Cleveland. At a time when the status quo was the order of the day, Cleveland's ballplayers revolted and presented a petition to management for the removal of manager Ossie Vitt. It was rejected and they made a fainthearted drive down the stretch, losing by one game to Detroit.

Bobo Newsom won 21 to pace Detroit. After two years of virtual inactivity and a third of ineptitude, Schoolboy Rowe returned with a 16–3 record to help Detroit capture the flag. The balance of the staff were 53–56. They continued getting big years from Hank Greenberg, Rudy York and Charley Gehringer.

The pitching star again was Bob Feller, who paced the league with 27. Al Benton of Detroit emerged as a new bullpen ace when he saved 17 games.

For Newsom this was his second straight 20-win season and third and final of his career. This season proved to be his best, as he had a 2.83 ERA while hurling 264 innings with 20 complete games in 34 starts. After this year, Newsom didn't fare well as he had losing records in five of the next eight years. He was then out of the majors from 1949 to 1951, returning in 1952 and 1953 with Washington and the Philadelphia A's and posting a combined 6–5 for the two years.

Feller left no doubt as to who was the best pitcher in baseball as he led the league in most major categories. His 27 wins, 43 appearances, 37 starts, 31 complete games, 320 innings, 261 strikeouts, four shutouts and 2.61 ERA were the best for each area in the league. This was the second straight season he led in wins and innings pitched. All told, he would lead in victories six times and innings worked five times. It was also his third straight strikeout crown enroute to a total of seven in his career. It is conceivable that he would have had 11 straight strikeout titles had World War II not intervened. He led from 1938 through 1941, missed all of 1942–44, most of 1945 and then led in 1946–48. No need to belabor the issue of what the war cost Feller, as he believed serving his country to be more important. He joined the navy right after Pearl Harbor and was awarded six battle stars.

Dutch Leonard, pitching for the Washington Senators, tied for the lead in losses with 19, but had 14 wins and a respectable 3.49 ERA, which was about one run below the league average. A better team could have provided him with a reversed record at the minimum. George Caster of the tailender Philadelphia team tied him with a 4–19 mark and 6.57 ERA. In 1938 Caster was 16–20; he was ill part of 1939 and was 9–9. He was traded to St. Louis in the off-season and became a relief pitcher, recording a 24–25 mark and 29 saves over 4½ seasons. He finished with Detroit in 1946 and was 8–4 with six saves for his 1½ years.

Chicago, with six pitchers winning between 10–14 games, paced with 83 complete games while Boston was last with 51. The league boasted seven pitchers with 20 or more complete games.

Pitcher/Team	G	GS	CG	W	L	Pct	ERA	SO	W	IP
Bob Feller, Cleve	43*	37*	31*	27*	11	.711	2.62*	261*	116	320*
Bobo Newsom, Det	36	34	20	21	5	.806	2.83	164	100	264

Feller tied teammate Al Milnar (18–10) for the shutout lead at four, while Rowe grabbed winning percent honors at .842.

The World Series was again a different story. Newsom was great, with a 2–1 and a 1.38 ERA record, but Rowe was 0–2 with a 17.18 ERA. The Tigers lost in seven games.

NATIONAL LEAGUE: TWO IN A ROW AND FINALLY A CHAMPIONSHIP

Brooklyn had won their first nine games, highlighted by a no hitter by former Cardinal Tex Carleton against Cincinnati on April 30. From that point on, Cincinnati made its move and eventually won by 13 games over Brooklyn. Pacing the way again were 20-game winners Bucky Walters and Paul Derringer.

St. Louis, which provided the major challenge in 1939, got off to a slow start, and when finally righted could do no better than third. Chicago boasted the league's only other 20-game winner in Claude Passeau.

While not quite as dominating as in 1939, Walters still was a highly effective pitcher. He posted a league-high 22 wins while leading with 29 complete games and 305 innings pitched. His 2.48 ERA was also the best in the league. This gave Walters a 60–27 mark for a little over two and half seasons with Cincinnati. Although he would pitch very effectively over the next three years, with ERAs well below 3.00 twice, he was only 49–44 because he didn't have the same level of support as in 1939–40.

Derringer checked in with his third straight 20-win season at exactly that number, while starting a league-high 37 games and completing 26. This was his last winning season with Cincinnati as he was only 12–14 and 10–11 the next two years despite good ERAs. Traded to Chicago for the 1943 season, he was 10–14 and 7–13 before going 16–11 in 1945 to help the Cubs to their last pennant. Thus Derringer pitched on three teams in four World Series during his career.

Passeau had broken in with Pittsburgh in 1935, was in one game and lost it. Traded to Philadelphia, he was 38–55 for the club from 1936 through early 1939. It should be remembered that Philadelphia had some woefully weak ball-clubs at that time and Passeau's record could have been easily reversed or even better. Joining the Cubs in early 1939, he finished with a 13–9 mark for them and pitched winning ball through 1946.

During the 1939–45 time period Passeau compiled a 113–80 record, highlighted by his 20 wins this year. From 1940 through 1942, he had at least 20 complete games each season. Passeau was a real workhorse in 1940, appearing in 46 games, 31 as a starter. He was credited with five saves, pitched 281 innings and had an excellent 2.50 ERA. His final season was 1947 and Passeau finished at 2–6 for Chicago.

Brooklyn had two pitchers who had a strong season for them. Freddie Fitzsimmons at 38 got into only 20 games and started 18, but he posted a brilliant 16–2 record with a 2.82 ERA and the league's best winning percentage at .889. Meanwhile, Whit Wyatt, who had pitched in the American League with Detroit, Cleveland and Chicago since 1929, proved to be an effective pitcher for the Dodgers. Wyatt would drift between the majors and the minors during the period from 1929 to 1937 and was only 26–44 for his efforts. There was certainly nothing to indicate his usefulness to a team trying to rebuild.

When Wyatt joined the Dodgers in 1939, he was already 32. One could question what value he would be, as his past record didn't indicate the possibility of what was to happen. In his first year Wyatt was 8–3. Then, between 1940 and 1943, he won 70 games and lost only 36—a truly unexpected development. This season he was only 15–14, but had a creditable 3.46 ERA and was the league's best shutout pitcher with five. The best was yet to come.

Hugh Mulcahy posted a 13–22 for the hapless last-place Phillies, who lost 103 games. This ran his four-year record with Philadelphia to 40–76, including two seasons of 20 or more losses. He was in the service from 1941 through 1944, and then pitched with Philadelphia until 1947, ending with a 45–89 career mark.

Cincinnati again led with 91 complete games while fourth-place Pittsburgh was last with 49. Five pitchers had 20 or more complete games, including Philadelphia's Kirby Higbe, who led the league with 137 strikeouts, a low total by today's standards. Higbe was 14–19, but soon would be with the Dodgers and a key part of their pennant-winning team.

Pitcher/Team	G	GS	CG	W	L	Pct	ERA	SO	W	IP
Bucky Walters, Cinn	36	36	29*	22*	10	.688	2.48	115	92	305*
Paul Derringer, Cinn	37	37*	26	20	12	.625	3.06	115	48	297
Claude Passeau, Chgo	46	31	20	20	13	.606	2.50	124	59	281

Cincinnati became the first National League World Series winner since St. Louis in 1934. Derringer and Walters each won two games, with Walters having a 1.50 ERA for his two complete game victories. Ironically, Detroit outscored Cincinnati 28–22.

This was Dizzy Dean's last season in the majors. He pitched four innings in 1947 for the St. Louis Browns in the last game, more as a joke, although he held the opposition scoreless. Dean was only 3–3, had a sore arm and was through. His career mark stood at 150–83 with a .644 winning percentage, sixteenth on the all-time list of pitchers with 100 or more wins.

1941

AMERICAN LEAGUE: TWO GREAT EVENTS AND ONE SAD MOMENT

The 1941 season will be remembered as the year Ted Williams batted .406 to become the last major leaguer to hit .400, and as the year of Joe DiMaggio's 56-game hitting streak. These were two of the greatest sports achievements of all time. However, it is also the year of the untimely death of baseball great Lou Gehrig, who undoubtedly would have set records for runs and RBIs that might never have been surpassed.

On the more mundane task of winning a pennant, the Yankees returned to the top, after a one-year hiatus, by a 17-game margin over second-place Boston, although neither team flashed a 20-game winner. The Yankees had eight pitchers to win eight to 15 games, with Johnny Murphy (8–3) also leading the league with 15 saves.

The only 20-game winners were on also-ran teams. Third-place Chicago (77–77) had 22-game winner Thornton Lee and fourth-place Cleveland (75–79) had the league's biggest winner again in Bobby Feller.

Feller again walked off with many of the individual honors. He was the top winner with 25, but had to settle for second place in complete games even though he had 28. Feller led in appearances (44) for the second straight year and in innings pitched (343) for the third consecutive season. His six shutouts were the league's best as were his 260 strikeouts, giving him the title four years in a row. We would not see him for almost four years; shortly after the bombing of Pearl Harbor, Feller enlisted in the navy.

Lee pitched all or part of 16 seasons from 1933 through 1948, with all but the last year spent in the American League. He was with Cleveland from 1933 to 1936, then with Chicago until 1947, finishing with the Giants in 1948. For his career Lee was only 117–124; thus his 1941 season was an anomaly. Lee was 22–11, with a league-best 2.37 ERA, and completed a league-high 30 games out of 34 starts while pitching 300 innings. Never before or after did Lee approach those heights. His two closest were 15–11 in 1939 and 15–12 in 1945.

Bobo Newsom did a complete reversal of his 1940 season as his ERA shot up to 4.61. He managed only 12 complete games in 36 starts and posted a dismal 12–20 record. Detroit had two pitchers from whom would be heard in a few years: Dizzy Trout was 9–9 and Hal Newhouser was 9–11.

Chicago became the first team to exceed 100 complete games since the New York Yankees completed 101 in 1923; they had 106, while Detroit was last with 52. Boston was the last National League team to reach that mark with 105 in 1917. Lee and Feller were the only two pitchers to have at least 20 complete games.

Pitcher/Team	G	GS	CG	W	L	Pct	ERA	SO	W	IP
Bob Feller, Cleve	44*	40*	28	25*	13	.658	3.15	260*	164*	343*
Thornton Lee, Chgo	35	34	30*	22	11	.667	2.37*	130	92	300

Feller led in shutouts with six, while Lefty Gomez (15–5) captured the winning percent title with .750. Lefty Grove retired at the end of the season after posting a 7–7 mark, but left with a career 300–141 record. Detroit fell to fifth place as Bobo Newsom lost 20 games, and after only 19 games their power-house first baseman Hank Greenberg was drafted and all-star Charlie Gehringer batted just .220.

The Yankees won their eighth straight World Series title, dating back to 1928. The big break came in game two when catcher Mickey Owen missed strike three with two out and no one on in the ninth and the Yanks down by one run. When it was all over, they had won 7–4. The Yankees then defeated the demoralized Brooklyn Dodgers the next day to capture the title.

NATIONAL LEAGUE: A TWO-TEAM RACE RESTORES A LONGTIME LOSER

After 21 years, the Brooklyn Dodgers finally made it to the top when they edged out St. Louis by 2½ games with a 100–54 record to St. Louis' 97–56. The Bums were paced by 22-game winners Kirby Higbe and Whit Wyatt. Pete Reiser, playing his first full year, led in runs (117), doubles (39) and batting average (.343).

The Cardinals had six pitchers to win between 10 and 17 games, but injuries to Terry Moore and Enos Slaughter derailed their pennant chances. Late in the season they introduced a young outfielder—Stan Musial—who would become the superstar of the league for the next two decades.

Higbe came over from Philadelphia in a trade and immediately paid dividends. He had his career-best year with a 22–9 mark, tying for the lead in victories. His appearances (48) and games started (39) were the league's highest, while he was second in innings pitched at 298. While Higbe never again equaled this season, he did give the Brooklyn team some solid pitching for several seasons. He was 16–11 and 13–10 the next two years before going into the service for 1944–45. On returning in 1946 he went 17–8, his last big season. Higbe finished his career with Pittsburgh and the Giants and a career mark of 118–101.

The other half of this pitching duo was Wyatt, who also logged 22 wins, fashioned a 2.34 ERA and completed 23 of 35 starts as he worked 288 innings. This dynamic duo accounted for almost half of the Dodgers' victories as they paced them to a pennant, but couldn't bring home a World Series title.

Cincinnati was third, mainly on the arms of 19-game winners Elmer Riddle and Bucky Walters. Riddle was a Jekyll and Hyde character in the early 40s for Cincinnati. He was a brilliant 19–4 with the league's best ERA (2.24) and winning percentage (.826) this year. Then he slipped to 7–11 in 1942 only to bounce back and tie for the lead in wins with 21 in 1943.

Meanwhile, Walters led the league in complete games for the third straight season with 27 and in innings pitched with 302. This made the third straight time his innings pitched exceeded 300 as well as leading the league. Walters also showed a respectable 2.83 ERA, but the Cincinnati bats couldn't provide the needed support and he suffered 15 losses. Quite easily, several could have been logged in the win column.

However, Walters' partner Paul Derringer couldn't keep pace; he was 12–14. Cincinnati again led with 89 complete games while last-place Philadelphia (43–111) posted a new league low with only 35. The only other pitchers who had 20 or more complete games were on also-rans. Claude Passeau (14–14) and Boston's Jim Tobin (12–12) each had 20.

Pitcher/Team	G	GS	CG	W	L	Pct	ERA	SO	W	IP
Kirby Higbe, Bklyn	48*	39*	19	22*	9	.710	3.14	121	132*	298
Whit Wyatt, Bklyn	38	35	23	22*	10	.688	2.34	176	62	288

Brooklyn batted just .182 and scored only 11 runs in a losing effort in the Series. Wyatt garnered their only win. Hugh Casey did double duty for the Dodgers as he was 14–11 with seven saves. Soon he would become the first bonafide relief ace in the National League.

1942

AMERICAN LEAGUE: THE WAR BEGINS ITS TOLL, BUT THE YANKS REIGN SUPREME

World War II began decimating team rosters, but enough talent was left to continue. The Yankees again dominated, this time winning by nine games over Boston. Cleveland and Detroit suffered the most. The former would be without their pitching ace, Bob Feller, for the next four seasons, while Detroit would lose Hank Greenberg through the middle of 1945.

Ernie Bonham led a mound staff that had depth and quality with a 21–5 mark, while the team relied on the bats of Joe DiMaggio, Charlie Keller and Joe Gordon. Johnny Murphy again led in saves, this time with 11.

Bonham broke in with the Yankees in 1940 and from then through 1944 he was 66–31, with his ERA never exceeding 2.99. However, from 1945 his ERA ranged from 3.28 to 4.25 and he had losing seasons in three of the five years. He finished with Pittsburgh and died late in the 1949 season. But in 1942 he was superb. He posted a 2.27 ERA (not best in the league) and won 21 while losing only five to give him the percentage title with .808, while also leading with 22 complete games. He became one of the few pitchers to win 20 games while pitching in fewer than 30; he was in only 28. This was a feat last performed by teammate Red Ruffing in 1939.

The league's other 20-game winner, Hughson, led with 22 victories, tied for the most complete games and had the top innings pitched with 281, while posting a 2.59 ERA. Hughson appeared in 38 games and was credited with four saves. This was the first of two 20-win seasons for Hughson as he would win that number in 1946 after returning from the service. An early call to the army in 1944 deprived him of a chance for 20 and he finished at 18–5.

The ERA crown went to Chicago's Ted Lyons, who appeared in only 20 games, starting and completing them all. He was 14–6 with a 2.10 ERA. It was a real shame he didn't have better teams behind him for his career.

Bobo Newsom didn't win or lose 20 this season, but he came close. With Washington he was 11–17 with a 4.92 ERA. Then late in the season he was waived out of the American League and picked up by the Dodgers for their stretch pennant drive. He was 2–2 with a 3.38 ERA in six games. This gave him a composite 13–19 mark for the season.

The Yankees led with 88 complete games and Cleveland, minus Bobby Feller, had the fewest with 61. Only Bonham, Hughson and Lyons had 20 or more complete games.

Ted Williams won his first triple crown with 36 home runs, 137 RBIs and a .356 batting mark. Tex Hughson won a league-high 22 games, but despite a 93–59 mark they still trailed by nine games at the finale.

Pitcher/Team	G	GS	CG	W	L	Pct	ERA	SO	W	IP
Tex Hughson, Bos	38	30	22*	22*	6	.786	2.59	113*	75	281*
Ernie Bonham, NY	28	27	22*	21	5	.808*	2.27	71	24	226

The Yankees were heavy favorites to repeat their Series win, but after an opening-game victory by Red Ruffing, they lost four straight to the young St. Louis ball club.

NATIONAL LEAGUE: CULMINATION OF YEARS OF WORK

St. Louis had been rebuilding since the loss of the Dean brothers in the mid-30s and had two second- and one third-place finish in the past three years. Finally, in a hotly contested race with Brooklyn, they won out by two games with a 106–48 mark to 104–50 by winning 43 of their last 51 games.

Mort Cooper with 22 and Johnny Beazley with 21 wins led a strong pitching staff. Meanwhile, Enos Slaughter (.318) and Stan Musial (.315) batted either one-two or two-three in the league, depending on which baseball bible you use. Some credit Ernie Lombardi (.330) with the batting crown although he batted only 309 times. Others give it to Slaughter.

Brooklyn had six pitchers to win between 10 and 19 games, plus Hugh Casey in relief at 6–3 with a league-high 13 saves, but still finished second with the second best record ever for a runnerup. No other team could produce a 20-game winner. Cincinnati fell to 76–76 as Bucky Walters and Elmer Riddle fell from a 38–19 mark to 22–25.

Cooper, along with his brother Walker, formed a potent battery combination for the Redbirds in the early 1940s. Cooper had broken in with St. Louis late in 1938 and from 1939 was 36–27. In 1942 he came into his own. Cooper won the MVP on the strength of his 22–7, 1.77 ERA record, both best in the loop. Cooper fashioned ten shutouts, had 22 complete games in 35 starts and hurled 279 innings. This was the first of three straight 20-win seasons. He would pitch the Cardinals to three straight pennants as he was 65–22 for the 1942–44 seasons.

Beazley is another player who was a victim of World War II. This would be his only season in double-digit wins as he developed a sore arm. On returning from the service he could pitch in only 32 games between 1946 and 1949, compiling a 9–6 mark. In 1942, though, Beazley was brilliant. He appeared in 43 games, 23 as a starter and won 21 while losing just six and posting a 2.14 ERA. What a career he might have had—but that could be said of many a player.

Two pitchers almost made the charmed circle, but each fell one win short. Whit Wyatt was 19–7 with a 2.74 ERA for the Dodgers in 31 games. Claude Passeau didn't have as good a team behind him as he posted an even better ERA at 2.69 with 24 complete games, but lack of batting support cost him several wins. He finished at 19–14.

Walters had a fine 2.66 ERA but was only 15–14 as Cincinnati batted just .231 and scored just over three runs per game. Boston's Jim Tobin, although only 12–21, led with 28 complete games. He was kept in the game because of his bat as much as his arm.

Philadelphia was last with 42–109 as Rube Melton, a 20-game winner a few years earlier, was 9–20. Cincinnati was tops in complete games with 80, while Philadelphia was last with 51. Five pitchers registered 20 or more complete games.

Pitcher/Team	G	GS	CG	W	L	Pct	ERA	SO	W	IP
Mort Cooper, STL	37	35	22*	22*	7	.759	1.77*	152	68	279
Johnny Beazley, STL	43	23	13	21	6	.778	2.14	91	73	215

Cooper led with ten shutouts, while Brooklyn's Larry French (15–4) had the best winning percentage (.789). Ace Adams of the Giants was developing into an ace relief pitcher as he led with 61 appearances and was second in saves with 11.

The Cardinals, after an opening game defeat to New York, 7–4, swept the next four to take the title with Beazley winning two games. Cooper lost one start, and was kayoed in another.

—————— 1943 ——————

AMERICAN LEAGUE: ONE MORE
TIME—ONE MORE CHAMPIONSHIP

As more and more stars departed for the service, the rosters of many clubs were greatly altered, but the talent-rich Yankees had enough left to wrap up one more pennant, this time by 14½ games over surprise second-place finisher Washington. This was their highest finish since their pennant in 1933. Pacing the Senators' mound staff was 23-year-old Early Wynn, future Hall of Famer and 300-game winner, with a 18–12 record.

The Yankees had lost Joe DiMaggio to the military, but Charlie Keller and Nick Etten provided the main firepower, while the dominating factor was the Yankee pitching staff. They were led by MVP winner Spud Chandler with a 20–4 and 1.64 ERA record. Johnny Murphy continued to shine in relief as he was 12–4 with eight saves.

Chandler is another one of those pitchers who didn't win his first major league game until he was 30 in 1937, but by the time he retired after the 1947 season at age 40 he had a 109–43, .717 mark. This is the highest lifetime percentage of any pitcher with over 100 victories, but as most statisticians require at least 1,500 innings, Chandler doesn't qualify because he pitched only 1,485. Thus, on a technicality, he is left off the list.

From 1937 through 1943 Chandler was 78–29, capped by his 1943 MVP season of 20–4 and an incredible 1.64 ERA, and he was the league's only pitcher with 20 complete games. His .833 winning percentage was also the league's best. He was nearly unhittable and unbeatable in 1943. Although 37, Chandler spent almost all of 1944 and 1945 in the service; he was in only five games and had a 2–1 record. Chandler returned to win 20 again in 1946 and then retired after a 9–5 season in 1947. It's nice to conjecture what he could have achieved had he made the majors at 23 or 24. He might have had 250 wins or more and a spot in the Hall of Fame.

Trout finally blossomed into the winning pitcher the Tigers thought he would be by winning 20 games in 1943. He tied Chandler for the lead in shutouts with five as he posted a 2.48 ERA. This was still the day of starters being used in relief, and Trout was no exception as he appeared in 44 games, completing 18 of 30 and being credited with six saves. Next season would be his super year.

A year later Trout would team with Hal Newhouser for one of the greatest one-two pitching duos ever in a single season. But this year 22-year-old Newhouser was only 8–17, although he had a fine 3.03 ERA. This followed on the heels of an 8–14 record when he had a 2.45 ERA. In two seasons Newhouser had a 2.75 ERA, but could only record a 16–31 mark. He certainly pitched in a pair of tough-luck seasons, but that was soon to change.

A new relief star appeared in Chicago: Gordon Metzberger had 14 saves to top the circuit. The Yankees led in complete games with 83 while Washington was last with 61.

Tex Hughson was only 12–15 for the season although he had virtually the same ERA (2.64) as the prior year when he was 22–6. He had the misfortune to play for a weak Boston team that had lost much of its power to the military.

Pitcher/Team	G	GS	CG	W	L	Pct	ERA	SO	W	IP
Spud Chandler, NY	30	30	20*	20*	4	.833*	1.64*	134	54	253
Dizzy Trout, Det	44*	30	18	20*	12	.625	2.48	111	101	247

This time the Yankees were the underdogs in the World Series but turned the tables on St. Louis by winning in five games. Chandler had two complete game victories and a .50 ERA.

NATIONAL LEAGUE: A RUNAWAY AND THEN A FALL FROM THE TOP

St. Louis had lost Terry Moore, Enos Slaughter, Jimmy Brown and Johnny Beazley to the service, but had enough talent in their farm system to win by 18 games over Cincinnati. Morton Cooper again led the way with 21 victories, and the staff had the top three ERA pitchers in Howie Pollet (1.75), Max Lanier (1.90) and Cooper (2.30). Pollet, after a brilliant first half, was called into the service.

Stan Musial won his first of seven batting titles with a .357 mark and his first of three MVP awards. Elmer Riddle rebounded to gain 21 wins and help put Cincinnati in second place. Meanwhile, Rip Sewell garnered 21 victories to shove Pittsburgh past Chicago into the first division.

Cooper turned in another brilliant performance as he tied for the league lead with 21 victories in his second of three successive 20-plus-win seasons. Cooper was in 37 games, 32 as a starter, of which he completed 24, and he threw six shutouts while posting a fine 2.30 ERA. He also was credited with three saves.

Riddle put on his Dr. Jekyll uniform for 1943 and grabbed a share of the league lead for victories as he went 21–11 with a 2.63 ERA. His looked like a promising career, as he had two good seasons out of three and was 40–15 for those two years. Then disaster struck. A shoulder injury forced him to miss much of 1944. Then he was suspended by the team for part of 1945 and was out of the league in 1946. When he returned in 1947, he appeared in only 16 games and was traded to Pittsburgh, where he finished his career with a 12–10 record in 1948 and a 1–8, 5.35 ERA record in 1949. Thus, another promising career was lost.

Sewell was another late bloomer. He broke in with Detroit for five games and no decisions in 1932. His next appearance in the majors was in 1938 when he got into 17 games and had no record with Pittsburgh, with whom he would stay until his career ended in 1949. When Sewell recorded his first win in 1939, he was already 32; he finished the year at 10–9. Over the next three years, for a team whose combined record for those seasons was less than .500, Sewell won 47 while losing 37.

At the age of 36, he won 21 games to grab a share of the title for most wins, while also completing the most games (25). In the process he registered a 2.55 ERA. Sewell is probably best known for his famous "blooper ball" pitch, which just floated to the plate but played havoc with the hitter's timing. One hitter it didn't fool was Ted Williams in the 1946 All-Star Game. He hit it for a home run. Sewell followed this year with another 21-win season in 1944.

Pitching in tough-luck conditions were Jim Tobin and Nate Andrews for Boston. The Braves averaged less than three runs a game as the lowest-scoring team in the league. Tobin was 14–14 with a 2.66 ERA and 24 complete games in 30 starts. From 1941 through 1944, Tobin completed 100 of his 125 starts, but could only post a 56–66 record even though his ERA was a quite respectable 3.20.

Andrews fared even worse. He had a 2.57 ERA but was only 14–20 with 23 complete games in 34 starts. Andrews had spent part of four seasons with three teams since 1937, appearing in 23 games and posting a 1–3 record before he was picked up by the Boston Braves. Andrews ERA jumped the next season to 3.22, but he posted a winning mark at 16–15. After two more years he finished his career with the Giants in 1946.

While the Giants finished last, they had the league's top reliever in Ace Adams, who led the team with an 11–7 mark while appearing in 70 games and garnering a league-high nine saves. Brooklyn finished third as a sore arm slowed down Whit Wyatt and a broken finger sidelined Curt Davis. In 1942 they had been 34–13; in 1943 they were 24–18, with Wyatt having a 14–5 mark.

St. Louis was tops with 94 complete games while Brooklyn was last with 50. Six pitchers completed 20 or more games.

Pitcher/Team	G	GS	CG	W	L	Pct	ERA	SO	W	IP
Mort Cooper, STL	37	33	24	21*	8	.724*	2.30	141	79	274
Rip Sewell, Pgh	35	31	25*	21*	9	.700	2.55	65	75	265
Elmer Riddle, Cinn	36	33	19	21*	11	.656	2.63	69	107	260

Hi Bithorn (18–12) of Chicago led with seven shutouts. The Series was a reverse of 1942. The Redbirds could garner only one win despite good pitching, and their hitting let them down as the team scored only nine runs and batted .224.

—————————————— **1944** ——————————————

AMERICAN LEAGUE: THE FIRST TIME EVER

For 53 years of existence through 1953, the St. Louis Browns finished in the first division only 12 times, while finishing last 11 times and posting the lowest winning percentage by far in the league at .432. However, 1944 would be a different year. Finally, after years of frustration, they would edge out Detroit by one game and New York by four.

The Browns did not have a 20-game winner, but got 19 from veteran Nels Potter and 17 from Jack Kramer. Shortstop Vern Stephens led the attack and the league in RBIs with 109. This was a far cry from earlier-day numbers.

Detroit had the league's best pitching duo in Hal Newhouser, who won 29 games and the MVP, and Dizzy Trout, who won 27 games and finished second in the MVP voting. Unfortunately for Detroit fans, the balance of the staff posted a dismal 32–43 record.

After two years of frustration and pitching excellent ball, but losing two of three decisions, all the pieces came together for Newhouser. He enjoyed the kind of season not seen since Bobby Feller, and prior to him Lefty Grove. Newhouser started a three-year run in which he won at least 25 each year and compiled a 80–27 mark over the 1944–46 period.

In 1944 he was awarded his first of two successive MVP awards as he barely edged out teammate Trout, who also had a terrific season. Newhouser won a career- and league-high 29 games while losing just nine as he posted a 2.22 ERA. Newhouser led the league with 187 strikeouts and was second in innings pitched at 312. He appeared in 47 games, completing 25 of his 34 starts and receiving credit for two saves. He was second to Trout with six shutouts. It was a truly great season.

Trout followed up his 20-win season with the greatest year of his career as he was 27–14 with the league's best ERA at 2.12. Trout was in the most games (49), started the most (40) and had the highest complete games (33) since Babe Ruth had 35 in 1917. Burleigh Grimes had 33 for Brooklyn in 1933 and Pete Alexander had 33 for Chicago in 1920. Looking back, it almost seems that the Most Valuable Award should have been split between Trout and Newhouser. The final vote was 236–232 in favor of Newhouser.

Trout never approached these numbers again, although he did win 18 the next year and 17 in 1946. After that his figures declined; his record from 1947 through 1952 was only 55–63. For two years he was one of the best, and in 1944 he and Newhouser were a magnificent twosome, winning 64 percent of their team's games.

Potter had joined the Browns in 1943 after an undistinguished career with several teams since 1936. He had been in and out of the league, compiling a lackluster 22–39 mark. Suddenly with St. Louis he learned how to win and posted marks of 10–5, 19–7 and 15–11 for the 1943–45 seasons. After that he was only 23–32 for several more teams, finally finishing with the Boston Braves in 1949.

Kramer was one of those pitchers who seemed to have a lot of potential, but it never materialized. He did win 17 games in 1944, but fell back to 10–15 the next season. Out of 11 full seasons, Kramer had winning marks in only four of them. His best was with the hard-hitting Red Sox in 1948 when he was 18-5 and had a gaudy 4.35 ERA.

The Yankees had lost Charlie Keller and Spud Chandler to the service. Thus their power was Nick Etten and Johnny Lindell. Hank Borowy was the top pitcher with 17 wins. Any chance Boston had faded when Tex Hughson (18–5) left for the service in mid-August. This also cost Hughson the opportunity to win 20 games, as he lost eight to ten starts.

Gordon Maltzberger of Chicago and Lum Harris of Philadelphia tied for the lead in saves with 12. Detroit led in complete games with 87, while last-place Washington had 83 and Cleveland was last in the league with 45.

Pitcher/Team	G	GS	CG	W	L	Pct	ERA	SO	W	IP
Hal Newhouser, Det	47	34	25	29*	9	.763	2.22	187*	102	312
Dizzy Trout, Det	49	40*	33*	27	14	.659	2.12*	144	83	352*

Trout also led the league with seven shutouts, and Newhouser was second with six. The Browns were the underdogs in the Series, but the sentimental favorites. They won the first game 2–1, although they had only two hits. For the Series, the Browns scored just nine runs in six games and lost to their St. Louis rival, the Cardinals.

National League: Three Hundred and Sixteen Wins in Three Years

The question never was which team would win the pennant, but rather by how much and how many games St. Louis would win. They had a chance to tie Chicago's 116-win record, but a late season slump (they lost 15 of the last 20) cost them a chance to tie or break the record. The Cardinals finished with 105 wins and became the first team to win 100 games three years in a row.

Mort Cooper again paced the mound staff with 22 wins, but had plenty of help from the likes of Max Lanier (17), Ted Wilks (17) and Harry Brecheen

(16). George Munger was 11–3 with a 1.34 ERA when he left for the army in mid-season. Stan Musial had another banner year, but shortstop Marty Marion was voted the league's MVP, giving the Cards that honor three years running.

Cooper completed his three-year run by matching his 1942 win-loss mark with another 22–7 record. However, his victory total was only good for second place. Cooper had elbow problems and often had to take aspirin to help kill the pain. He was also known to favor John Barleycorn, and these factors weighed heavily on the balance of his career. Cooper appeared with St. Louis in only four games the next year and was 2–0 when traded to Boston. From there he went to the Giants and then finished with the Cubs, never regaining his old form. Cooper was only 25–25 for the 1945–48 period, which basically ended his career. His career mark of 128–75 with a .631 winning percentage is good for a tie for 23rd place on the all-time list of pitchers with over 100 career wins.

Rip Sewell won 21 again for Pittsburgh to put them in second, 14 out, while Cincinnati was a game back in third as Bucky Walters won 23. This was Sewell's second straight 21-win season and his last. He worked 286 innings while hurling 24 complete games in 33 starts. He also made five relief appearances and had two saves. Sewell pitched through 1949 and was 44–29 for those years. He was 42 when he finally called it quits and retired with a 143–97, .596 winning percentage record. His is another example of what might have been had he reached the majors to stay at, say, age 25 or so. He might have had 250–275 wins and a spot in the Hall.

Walters had his last big season as he won 23 games to lead the league for the third and last time in his career. It was also his third 20-plus-win season. Walters had another fine season as he completed 27 games in just 32 starts, posted a 2.40 ERA and logged 285 innings. Although he pitched effectively for the two years, as his ERAs were 2.40 and 2.68, he got very little support, was only 20–17 for the two seasons and was in only 22 games each year.

Walters began managing the Reds in the mid-1948 season, and then used himself sparingly over the next two years and was only 8–11. He called it quits, although he came back to pitch in one game in 1950 for the Boston Braves. When he retired he was 198–160—not bad for a converted third baseman whose early career was with a weak Philadelphia team.

Bill Voiselle chalked up 21 for New York, as Ace Adams again led in saves with 13. Jim Tobin of Boston had 18 wins, but lost 19. This was Voiselle's one big season as he started a league-high 41 games and completed 25 en route to his 21 wins and a league-leading 313 innings. Voiselle was in the majors for part or all of the years 1942–50 with the Giants, Braves and Cubs, but most of his time was spent with the New York team. His career mark was 74–84.

Cincinnati led with 93 complete games to St. Louis' 89, while New York was last with 47. Five pitchers topped the 20 complete game list, with Boston's Jim Tobin leading the pack with 28.

Pitcher/Team	G	GS	CG	W	L	Pct	ERA	SO	W	IP
Bucky Walters, Cinn	34	32	27*	23*	8	.742	2.40	77	87	285
Mort Cooper, STL	34	33	22	22	7	.759	2.46	97	60	252
Rip Sewell, Pgh	38	33	24	21	12	.630	3.18	87	99	286
Bill Voiselle, NY	43	41*	25	21	16	.568	3.02	161*	118	313*

Cooper regained the shutout title with seven, giving him 23 for three years, during which he was 65–22. The ERA title went to Cincinnati's Ed Heusser (13–11) with a 2.38, while Wilks (17–4) took the winning percentage crown with .810.

Pitching dominated the World Series as Cooper, Lanier, Brecheen and journeyman pitcher Blix Donnelly each won a game to give the Cardinals the title.

1945

AMERICAN LEAGUE: THE GRAND RETURN AND TWO MVPs IN A ROW

St. Louis was hoping for a second successive pennant but fell short as they finished third, seven games out. Nels Potter and Jack Kramer had won 36 games in 1944 but could only go 25–26 this year, with Potter having a 15–11 mark.

Detroit took the title by 1½ games over Washington, who was paced by Roger Wolff with a 20–10 log (his only winning season in the majors). However, it was Detroit who had the real heroes. Hal Newhouser again was outstanding, winning 25 games, and while Dizzy Trout wasn't as dominating as in 1944, he still won 18. However, it took returning serviceman Hank Greenberg's grand-slam homer to turn the trick on the final day of the season against the St. Louis Browns. Greenberg rejoined the team in mid-season and batted .311 with 13 home runs and 60 RBIs in 76 games.

New York finished fourth but had the league leader in RBIs, Nick Etten with 111, while teammate Snuffy Stirnweiss had the lowest batting champion average at .309. Boo Ferris, in his rookie year, racked up 21 wins for Boston, which finished seventh and probably would have been eighth without him.

Newhouser was even more brilliant in 1945 than the previous year, if that was possible. He led the league with 25 wins, .735 winning percentage, 29 complete games, eight shutouts, 313 innings, 212 strikeouts and a remarkable 1.81 ERA. No wonder he was voted MVP the second year in a row, although this time it was a runaway. It seemed Newhouser had little else to prove, but more good years were still in the making.

Whether it was the war year or just one of those unexplainable events, Wolff was terrific in 1945. He won 20 games, chalked up 21 complete games and had a fine 2.12 ERA. He had broken in with the A's in 1941 and in three years was 22–32. Traded to Washington for the 1944 season, he went 4–15. Thus there was nothing in his past to suggest the season he had in 1945. After this year he reverted to form, lasting two more years and going 6–12, finishing with Pittsburgh in 1947. What a strange career.

Ferris broke out of the gate fast and in his rookie year won 21 games for a weak Boston team. Without him they were 50–73 and would have challenged Philadelphia for last place. Ferris had a 2.95 ERA and pitched 265 innings as he completed 26 of 31 starts. He also relieved four times and picked up two saves. He was an excellent hitting pitcher, batting .267, and was used 25 times as a pinch hitter during the season. This was his first of two successive 20-win seasons. After the season Commissioner K. M. Landis died. Albert B. (Happy) Chandler was named to replace the man who saved the game and had been baseball's only commissioner. Cleveland, finishing fifth, boasted two pitchers who won 37 games between them. Steve Gromek had his best season at 19–9 and would stay in the majors until 1957, although it would be nine years before he approached that victory total again. The other was Allie Reynolds who was 18–12, but his real glory years were a few years in the future, after he was traded to the Yankees.

St. Louis led the loop with 91 complete games, while last-place Philadelphia was last also in this category with 65. Five pitchers posted 20 or more complete games.

Pitcher/Team	G	GS	CG	W	L	Pct	ERA	SO	W	IP
Hal Newhouser, Det	40	36*	29	25*	9	.735*	1.81*	212*	110	313*
Boo Ferris, Boston	35	31	26	21	10	.677	2.95	94	85	265
Roger Wolff, Wash	33	29	21	20	10	.667	2.12	108	53	250

Bobo Newsom lost 20 games or more for the third time as he was 8–20 for Philadelphia. It also made the third team with which he had turned the trick. Newsom had eight seasons in which he lost 15 or more games.

Newhouser also led in shutouts with eight. It was a hard-fought Series, but with Newhouser winning two games despite a 6.10 ERA, the Tigers held on to win in seven games.

NATIONAL LEAGUE: A LAST HURRAH

St. Louis was aiming for four straight titles, and it looked like they could do it, although they lost Stan Musial to the navy. Then, in a salary dispute, they traded Mort Cooper to Boston for journeyman Red Barrett. Cooper was 9–4 for the year, had an elbow injury and would never again be the same pitcher, while Barrett had his career-best year, winning 23 for St. Louis. But it was not enough.

Chicago got 22 wins from Hank Wyse, then in mid-season got Hank Borowy in a trade from the Yankees. Between the two leagues Borowy had a 21–7 mark. Phil Cavaretta paced the batting for the Cubs with a league-leading

.355 mark, while Boston's Tommy Holmes fanned only nine times as he led the league with 28 home runs.

Wyse spent six full and two part seasons in the majors. He broke in with Chicago in 1942 and posted a winning record every season but 1947, when he was 6–9. After that he was out of the majors in 1948–49, but returned to the Philadelphia A's in 1950, was 9–14 and finished with a 1–2 mark with them in 1951. Meanwhile, with the Cubs he had winning seasons, but only one or two games over .500 until 1945. This was his one season to shine, and he did. Wyse won 22 games, completed 23 of 34 starts as he posted a 2.69 ERA. He never again approached these numbers, even though he was only 27 and should have been heading into the prime years of his career.

Borowy had been a consistent winner for the Yankees since 1942 when the Cubs acquired him in mid-season 1945. He had records of 15–4, 14–9 and 17–12 for 1942–44 and was 10–5 when traded to Chicago. For Chicago he was 11–2 with a 2.14 ERA. His final record was 21–7, 2.65 ERA, with 18 complete games in 32 starts. After this season Borowy pitched for the Cubs, Phillies, Pirates and Detroit Tigers, but was never again the same pitcher. His composite record was 41–48 for those teams. One often wonders what happens to a pitcher—why, all of a sudden, it's gone. Baseball history is replete with stories of this kind.

Barrett is another one of those pitchers who put it all together in one season, but never before or after showed anything resembling the same level of performance. Barrett had been in 12 games with Cincinnati from 1937 to 1940 and was 3–0. He finally came to stay with Boston in 1943 and quickly posted marks of 12–18 and 9–16 in his first two years. Barrett was 2–3 when traded to St. Louis. Then everything changed. He was 21–9, with a 2.73 ERA and 21 complete games, giving him a final of 23–12, 3.00 ERA and 24 complete games. The wins and complete games were league highs. Barrett was 3–2 for St. Louis in 1946, the year the ball players returned from the service. He was traded back to Boston and played there from 1947 to 1949, finishing out with a 19–21 mark.

Chicago led with 86 complete games while last-place Philadelphia (46–108) set a new major league low with 31. Ace Adams continued to dominate as a relief pitcher, chalking up 15 saves. Only Wyse and Barrett broke the 20 complete game level.

Pitcher/Team	G	GS	CG	W	L	Pct	ERA	SO	W	IP
Red Barrett, STL	45	34	24*	23*	12	.657	3.00	76	54	285*
Hank Wyse, Chgo	38	34	23	22	10	.688	2.69	77	55	278
Hank Borowy, Chgo	33	32	18	21	7	.750	2.66	82	105	254

Chicago's Claude Passeau (17–9) led with five shutouts, while St. Louis' Harry Brecheen (15–4) took the winning percent honors at .789. This gave him a two-year log of 31–9.

Borowy was a workhorse for Chicago in the Series, appearing in four games and posting a 2–2 record with a 4.00 ERA, mostly built on five runs he gave up in the first inning of the last game. This would be Chicago's last entry into the World Series to this date. Over 50 years later they are still waiting to hoist another pennant flag over Wrigley Field. They also last won the World Series in 1908.

1946

AMERICAN LEAGUE: THE DROUGHT ENDS

With returning veterans and players jumping to the Mexican League, no one could be certain how the season would end. Commissioner A. B. Chandler ruled that any player jumping to the Mexican League would be banned from the majors for five years. A few years later this was relaxed.

The last time Boston had won the pennant, Babe Ruth was pitching and playing the outfield. In 1945 they finished seventh, but with the return of the veterans the Red Sox shot to the top and won by 12 games over Detroit. Offensively, Ted Williams led a parade of three .300 hitters and three 100-plus RBI men. However, it was on the mound where the Red Sox, often short, came up with the winners. In only his second season, Boo Ferriss won 25 games, while returning serviceman Tex Hughson added 20. Mickey Harris chipped in with 17.

Detroit was paced by Hal Newhouser with 26 and Dizzy Trout with 17. New York was third, 17 games out, as Spud Chandler won 20 games and Bill Bevans 16, but the rest fell off dramatically.

Ferris wouldn't be 25 until December and the future looked bright for him. He had just completed a 25–6 season, giving him 46 wins in his first two full seasons and exceeding 20 wins each year. The only other pitcher to do that had been Wes Ferrell, so he was in good company. It looked like many great years ahead—perhaps 10 to 15—and based on what he had accomplished so far, he could probably win 300 games. But fate would take an ironic twist.

In 1946 Ferris led with a .806 winning percentage, had 26 complete games in 35 starts, posted six shutouts and was credited with three saves during his five relief appearances. It was indeed a fine season. Then came disaster as he suffered arm problems; the most he would ever win again was 12, and then seven in 1948. He could pitch in only four games in 1949 and one in 1950, then was out of baseball and back to Mississippi to coach college ball. At an age when he should have been racking up 15, 20 or 25 victories, he was through. It was another great tragedy.

Hughson was six years older than Ferris, but still in the prime of his career. His first year back from the service he registered 20 wins for the second time and had a fine 2.75 ERA to go with his 21 complete games, six shutouts and three saves. The future seemed to hold several more good seasons for him, but misfortune reared its ugly head again. Two pitchers from the same team were struck down.

Hughson suffered a finger injury the next season and duplicated Ferris' record at 12–11. Hughson pitched two more seasons, was 7–3 and out of baseball prematurely. He retired with a fine 96–54, .640 winning percentage. Two potentially great careers lost.

Newhouser completed his fantastic three-year run by tying Bob Feller for the league high with 26 wins. Newhouser posted the league's best ERA at 1.94, had six shutouts, logged 293 innings and had 29 complete games in 34 starts. This season in some ways was more satisfying than his two MVP years. There had been the rap on him that his record was built because of the war years. Well, all the players were back, and he had just as good a season—if not better. Thus, any doubting Thomases should have been put to rest.

Finally in 1992 the veterans committee voted Newhouser into the Hall of Fame after a very long wait. It was a deserved honor. Although he never attained these heights again, he did win 17, 21, 18 and 15 over the next four seasons before developing arm trouble. This limited him to 47 games for the 1951–53 seasons and he was 15–16, but he bounced back to help Cleveland to a pennant in 1954 with a 7–2 mark and seven saves out of the bullpen. He finished with a 207–150 record, and given a few breaks early in his career could have added another 15 to 20 wins.

Chandler returned to New York and, at the advanced age of 39, posted an excellent 20–8 record with 20 complete games in 32 starts and a 2.10 ERA. He finished next season with a 9–5 record. One can only wonder what he might have done given an early start and no military service, as he was 37 when he entered the military.

Feller picked up where he left off by winning 26 games for a sixth-place team. Without Feller, the Indians were 40–71. With a better hitting team he probably could have won 30 to 35 games. This may have been Feller's finest season as he posted his best ERA at 2.18. Feller appeared in a league-high 48 games, started the most (42) and completed the most (36), while leading with ten shutouts. He also logged 371 innings as he fanned 348 batters, and was credited with four saves.

In later years Feller has said he was proudest of his 36 complete games, which is far more than 90 percent of what entire teams complete today. Although admittedly the manner in which pitchers are handled has changed, this is much to the chagrin of the Fellers, Bob Gibsons, Newhousers and others of that ilk who believed their job was to go nine innings. You have to go back to 1916 to find a pitcher that completed at least 36 games. You guessed it. Walter Johnson did it, and Pete Alexander had 38.

The bottom fell out for Philadelphia, as they were last at 49–105. The height of futility for the year was by the A's Lou Knerr who was 3–16, 5.41 ERA, giving him a two-year and career mark of 8–27, 5.05 ERA. Detroit led with 94 complete games while Philadelphia was last with 61. Seven pitchers had 20 or more complete games.

Pitcher/Team	G	GS	CG	W	L	Pct	ERA	SO	W	IP
Hal Newhouser, Det	37	34	29	26*	9	.743	1.94*	275	98	293
Bob Feller, Cleve	48*	42*	36*	26*	15	.634	2.16	348*	153*	371*
Boo Ferriss, Bos	40	35	26	25	6	.806*	3.25	106	71	274
Spud Chandler, NY	34	32	20	20	8	.714	2.10	138	90	257
Tex Hughson, Bos	39	35	21	20	11	.645	2.75	172	51	278

In the World Series, the Red Sox were heavily favored but lost in seven games to St. Louis.

NATIONAL LEAGUE: THE FIRST PLAYOFF IN BASEBALL HISTORY

The National League was harder hit by jumpers to the Mexican League. Hardest hit was New York, which, although leading the league in home runs, fell into the basement. The talent-rich Cardinals lost several, including Max Lanier, after a 6–0 start in only six games and a 1.90 ERA.

As a result the league was hosted to a tight race between St. Louis and Brooklyn. Both teams ended in a tie at season's end to force a playoff, which St. Louis won two games to none. Howie Pollet paced the league with 21 wins. The offense was led by Stan Musial, who led the league in everything except home runs and RBIs. This earned him his second MVP, while teammate Enos Slaughter wore the RBI crown. Pollet was a stylish left-hander who in 1946 was at the top of his game, having just returned from two years in the service. Prior to that Pollet had spent parts of three seasons with St. Louis and compiled a 20–11 record with a fine 2.21 ERA and completing 23 of 31 starts. Therefore, his 1946 record of 21–10 with a league-best 2.10 ERA was not surprising. Pollet logged the most innings at 266, had 22 complete games in 32 starts and made eight relief appearances, which gave him five saves. Unfortunately, after this season things went downhill for a couple of years. At an age (25) when he should just be coming into his own, he ran into problems and was 9–11, 4.35 ERA and 13–8, 4.55 ERA the next two seasons before righting himself and winning 20 again in 1949, but we are getting ahead of our story. Had there been a Cy Young Award in 1946, Pollet would have won easily.

Johnny Sain was the only other 20-game winner as he helped pitch Boston into fourth place. Sain won 20 for the first of three consecutive seasons and should have had a higher total based on his 2.21 ERA. He led with 24 complete games and was second with 265 innings. Sain was one of baseball's best hitting pitchers and in 94 at bats he hit .296. He didn't strike out a single time.

St. Louis led with 75 complete games and New York was last with 48. Sain and Pollet were the only pitchers with 20 or more complete games.

Pitcher/Team	G	GS	CG	W	L	Pct	ERA	SO	W	IP
Howie Pollet, STL	40	32	22	21*	10	.677	2.10	107	86	266*
Johnny Sain, Bos	37	34	24*	20	14	.588	2.21	129	87	265

Pollet led with four shutouts, while teammate Murray Dickson (15–6) was the percentage leader at .714. Johnny Beazley, hero of the 1942 Series, was only 7–5, developed a sore arm and would be out of baseball by 1949. A brilliant career went down the drain.

The Cardinals had a history of upsetting the favorites, which included New York twice and Philadelphia. This time they did it to Boston, on Slaughter's famous dash from first on a two-out single by Harry Walker in the last of the eighth. Pollet failed to win in the Series, but Harry Brecheen picked up the slack by going 3 0 with a .45 ERA.

Little did St. Louis know it would be 18 years before they would appear in another Series, although they were second the next three years, plus finishing in the first division many times during the 1950s and early 60s.

1947

AMERICAN LEAGUE: A RETURN TO
THE TOP—THE FIRST BLACK PLAYER

Most sports people figured Boston would repeat, as they had basically the same team returning. Ted Williams won the triple crown, but lost the MVP to Joe DiMaggio. The downfall of the Red Sox (who finished third) was the collapse of their pitching. In 1946 Boo Ferris, Tex Hughson and Mickey Harris were 62–26, while in 1947 they were 29–26; end of story.

The Yankees boasted the deepest pitching staff in the league, led by fireballer Allie Reynolds who won 19 games. But the most important cog was reliever Joe Page, who won 14 games and saved 17, tying him with Cleveland's Eddie Heliman for the league high.

Detroit climbed into second place on the strength of strong pitching and hitting. Bob Feller was the only 20-game winner in the league and this helped boost Cleveland to fourth place.

Feller had his lowest full season total wins since 1938 as he led the league with 20 wins. Feller appeared in 42 games, starting a league-high 37 and completing 20 while pitching 299 innings and leading in strikeouts (196) for the second straight year and his sixth overall. This also marked the fifth time he led in victories and the fourth time with shutouts, as he posted five.

Although he fell one win short of the coveted 20-game club, Reynolds had a fine 19–8 mark, which gave him the league's best percentage at .704. Reynolds had been acquired from Cleveland in the off-season after they had given up on him following a performance of 11–14, 3.89 ERA and only nine complete games in 28 starts in 1946. While Reynolds would win only 20 games once for the Yankees, he won 131 and lost only 60 from 1947 through 1954, helping the Yankees to six pennants and six World Series titles. Reynolds proved effective as both a starter and reliever during that time as he also recorded 41 saves. When he retired after the 1954 season he left behind a 182–107, .630 record. His winning percentage places him 25th on the all-time list of pitchers with over 100 wins. There are many who believe he belongs in the Hall of Fame.

Hal Newhouser didn't win 20 games, but finished at 17–17. He did lead with 24 complete games and had an excellent 2.87 ERA. While the Tigers were a high-scoring team (third in the league), they seemed to have difficulty always getting the runs for Newhouser. With a few breaks he could have won over 20, which with his 1948 season would have given him five campaigns in a row in the charmed circle.

Detroit led the pack with 77 complete games while sixth-place Chicago was last with 47. Phil Marchildon turned in his career-best season for the Philadelphia A's as he was 19–9 with a 3.22 ERA and 21 complete games. One of the other 20 complete game pitchers was Ed Lopat of the light-hitting White Sox. He was 16–13 with a 2.81 ERA and 22 complete games. He would soon be a Yankee and things would improve.

The other pitcher was Early Wynn. He was 17–15 and had 22 complete games, but a 3.64 ERA, which is close to his career ERA. Wynn was also an excellent hitting pitcher and was used on over 20 occasions by the Senators this year. Many of his defeats could also be attributed to the light-hitting Senators, as they averaged only three runs per game.

Pitcher/Team	G	GS	CG	W	L	Pct	ERA	SO	W	IP
Bob Feller, Cleve	42	37*	20	20*	11	.645	2.68	196*	127	299*

Red Ruffing retired at the end of this season with a 273–225 record, 27 wins short of the 300-win club. His years with the Red Sox certainly didn't help his chances, but that aside he still could have made it. Ruffing went into the service in 1943 at age 39 and lost all of 1943–44 and most of 1945. He was 7–3 in 11 games at the end of the 1945 season. In 1946 he was 5–1 when a line drive broke his knee cap, and he was out for the season. Then he tried one last year with the Chicago White Sox. His knee gave him trouble again and he finished 3–5. While many younger players didn't serve, or perhaps only a year or so, Ruffing at the advanced age of 39 lost almost three seasons. Given those years he easily could have made the 300 club.

New York's opponent in the Series was Brooklyn, but this time it took seven games to defeat them. New York outscored Brooklyn 38–29. Spec Shea had two wins and Johnny Lindell led all hitters with a .500 average and seven RBIs.

NATIONAL LEAGUE: THE COLOR LINE IS BROKEN

The big news of 1947 was the breaking of the color line. Brooklyn brought Jackie Robinson to the majors as the first black in the 20th century. He responded by helping to lead the Dodgers to a pennant ahead of favorite St. Louis.

Ralph Branca, with 21 wins, led an adequate pitching staff that backed a potent hitting attack. The Cardinals' fall from grace can be traced to Howie Pollet's reversal of form, going from 21–10 to 9–11. Warren Spahn and Johnny Sain each won 21 games to put Boston in third place. Rookie Larry Jansen won 21 for the Giants to help them finish fourth.

Branca had been with the Dodgers for parts of the 1944–46 seasons, compiling a 8–9 record. In 1947, at the age of 21, no one expected him to become the ace of the staff, but he did. Branca appeared in 43 games, started 36 of them, won 21 and posted a 2.67 ERA while pitching 280 innings. The future looked bright. Already they were counting how many wins this kid might rack up by age 35. He was finished by the time he was 28. What happened? No one can say for certain.

Branca stayed with the Dodgers through 1952 and twice won 13 games and once 14, but that was his best. At his young age they kept expecting him to regain his 1947 form, but he never did. He developed a sore arm in 1952. Finally the Dodgers gave up on him and sent him to Detroit in 1953. He was 7–10 for them during 1953–54 before finishing 1–0 with the Yankees in 1954. Branca pitched in one game for the Dodgers in 1956. He finished with an 88–68 career record.

Sain had his second straight 20-plus-win season as he registered 21 while completing 22 of his 35 starts. Sain also logged 266 innings. He would have two more years in the charmed circle before going to the American League as a spot starter and reliever. Sain's numbers were undoubtedly affected by World War II as he lost three critical years. But so did many others.

Spahn was 26 when he had his first 20-win season, having lost three years to the military during World War II. Little did anyone expect he would eventually reach that level 13 times. From 1947 through 1963, Spahn never won fewer than 14 games and had only one losing season that entire time. He was 14–19 with a 2.98 ERA for a weak Boston team in 1952. In 1947, Spahn was 21–10 as he posted 22 complete games in 35 starts, made five relief appearances and received credit for three saves. He led the league in innings pitched with 290, something he would do four times. His 2.33 was also the best ERA, and he did this twice more. His seven shutouts marked the first of four times he led. All in all, it was a highly productive season.

Jansen was a 27-year-old rookie who burst onto the scene with a 21–5 mark for the New York Giants. His .808 winning percentage was the league's best. He proved to be a real workhorse, appearing in 42 games and completing 20 of his 30 starts. From 1947 through 1951, Jansen won 96 games for the Giants. He seemed destined for a possible career total of 200 wins when he suffered a knee injury in 1952 and was never the same pitcher again. He lasted through 1956, but was only 26–32 the rest of the way.

The league's biggest winner was Cincinnati's Ewell Blackwell with 22 victories. The previous season he had been only 9–13 despite an excellent 2.47 ERA. This was his premier season as he also led with 23 complete games, 193 strikeouts and posted a 2.47 ERA while hurling six shutouts. With his sidearm pitching, he was brutal on right-handed batters. Blackwell was only 24 and it looked like a bright future for the hard-throwing right-hander.

Then fate stepped in and dealt him a cruel blow. He suffered an arm injury and then was ill the next two seasons. He was in 52 games, starting only 24, while posting a 12–14 record with a 4.41 ERA. He did recover and have a couple of fair seasons in 1950–51 when he was 17–15, 2.97 ERA and 16–15, 3.44 ERA, but he was not the same devastating pitcher. A 3–12, 5.38 ERA in 1952 sent him to the Yankees and Kansas City (which had replaced Philadelphia), and his career was over. Here was yet another example of a potentially brilliant career cut short.

The Giants set the major league record for home runs with 221. Johnny Mize and Pittsburgh's Ralph Kiner tied for the lead with 51 each.

Hugh Casey led the league with 18 saves, and he was another factor in putting Brooklyn in first place. Boston was tops with 74 complete games, while last-place Pittsburgh was also last in this category at 44. Only four pitchers could muster 20 or more complete games.

Pitcher/Team	G	GS	CG	W	L	Pct	ERA	SO	W	IP
Ewell Blackwell, Cin	33	33	23*	22*	8	.733	2.47	193*	95	273
Larry Jansen, NY	42	30	20	21	5	.806*	3.16	104	57	248
Warren Spahn, Bos	40	35	22	21	10	.677	2.33*	123	84	290*
Johnny Sain, Bos	38	35	22	21	12	.636	3.52	132	79	266
Ralph Branca, Bklyn	43	36*	15	21	12	.636	2.67	148	96	280

Sain continued his amazing hitting, batting .346, with one strikeout in 107 times at bat, giving him a two-season total of one whiff in 205 at bats.

Brooklyn lost again in the World Series, despite great pitching from Casey, who appeared in a record six games, won two and saved the third, but got no help from anyone else. The cry became, "Wait till next year!"

1948

AMERICAN LEAGUE: A FIRST
PLAYOFF AND FINALLY NUMBER TWO

For the first half of the 20th century, only the New York Yankees had a better winning record than Cleveland. They had been the bridesmaid but rarely the bride. In 1948 that would change: when the season ended Boston and Cleveland were tied for first, with New York only two games back.

In a one-game playoff, Cleveland defeated Boston for the title. They had parlayed good hitting, defense and pitching for the pennant. They were led by 20-game winners Gene Bearden and Bob Lemon and 19-game winner Bob

Feller, who failed for the first time in six years to capture 20 wins or more. They also had the top reliever in Russ Christopher, who had 17 saves.

Boston had the most explosive offense, but lacked the pitching to sustain it. Meanwhile, New York was led by Joe DiMaggio, who had a league-high 39 home runs and 155 RBIs, or one per game. He was the last American Leaguer to accomplish that goal. While New York had no 20-game winners, they had three pitchers who won 52 games and would form the nucleus of the staff that would lead them to five straight pennants, beginning in 1949. They were Vic Raschi (19), Ed Lopat (17) and Allie Reynolds (16).

This was Bearden's rookie season, and what a way to break in. He had the league's best ERA at 2.43, appeared in 37 games, completing 15 of the 29 starts he made and posting a 20–7 record. It looked like Cleveland would also have a strong staff for the future in Bearden, Lemon and Feller. Bearden unexplainably flopped and was out of baseball after 1953. Following this season he pitched for five teams and compiled a 25–31 mark. Who can explain why fate works this way on some pitchers and not others?

Lemon, on the other hand, was a converted infielder à la Bucky Walters and went on to become one of the biggest winners in Cleveland history. He broke in as a pitcher in 1946 and after going 15–10 for his first two seasons, Lemon really blossomed. In 1948 he won 20 games while posting a 2.82 ERA and leading the league with 20 complete games, 294 innings hurled and ten shutouts. He appeared in 43 games, starting 37, and was credited with two saves.

This was the first of three successive 20-plus-win seasons for the big right-hander and seven in total. From 1947 through 1956, Lemon won 186 games and never had a losing season, with his lowest victory total at 17. He had replaced Feller as the ace of the staff. Lemon also became known as one of the best hitting pitchers in the game, often used as a pinch hitter. He batted .286 with five home runs in 1948.

Newhouser checked in with his fourth and final 20-win season as he was 21–12 with 19 complete games and a 3.01 ERA. Newhouser still had a couple of decent seasons left before his arm injury as he won 33 games in 1949–50. Without Newhouser Detroit would have finished deep in the second division.

Feller started slowly and was having great difficulty before he finally righted himself and finished with 19 wins. He was in 44 games, starting a league-high 38 and was credited with three saves. Feller led in strikeouts with 164 for the seventh and last time. Another 19-game winner was Vic Raschi, who starting next season would win 20 or more for three straight years. During the 1948–52 time period, Raschi won 98 while losing only 42.

Reynolds had come to the Yankees in a trade before the start of the 1947 season that sent Joe Gordon to the Indians. The Yankees thought Gordon had washed up, but he was one of the key players in the Indians' pennant victory. Meanwhile, the Indians didn't think that Reynolds would ever develop into a consistent winner, and with the staff potential they had, figured they didn't need him. Reynolds would play a key role in the Yankee pennants over the next eight years.

Ed Lopat, the third member of the Yankees' triumvirate, won 109 while losing 51 for the period 1948–54, despite the fact that he had suffered injuries that slowed him down at times and caused him to miss several starts in different years.

The league had several big losers. St. Louis' Fred Sanford was 12–21 while Chicago's Bill Wight was 9–20. Early Wynn was 8–19 with a 5.82 ERA for Washington—certainly nothing to indicate a future Hall of Famer who would win 300 games. But next season he would be with Cleveland and, under the tutelage of Mel Harder, all that would change.

Philadelphia, which had risen to fourth, was first with 74 complete games, while last-place Chicago had only 35.

Pitcher/Team	G	GS	CG	W	L	Pct	ERA	SO	W	IP
Hal Newhouser, Det	39	35	19	21*	12	.636	3.01	143	99	272
Gene Bearden, Cleve	37	29	15	20	7	.741	2.43*	80	106	230
Bob Lemon, Cleve	43	37	20*	20	14	.588	2.82	147	129	294*

Lemon won two games with a 1.65 ERA in the Series, and Feller lost both his starts. One was a disputed 1–0 loss where Phil Masi was called safe after supposedly being picked off second, and later scored. Feller allowed only two hits in the loss. The Indians would prevail in six games to make them World Champions in their only two trips to that time.

NATIONAL LEAGUE: ANOTHER LONGTIME DROUGHT IS ENDED

Boston last won a pennant when Woodrow Wilson was in the White House, and airplanes and automobiles were in their infancy. However, the year 1948 produced the famous chant "Spahn, Sain and then two days of Rain." This was because the only two dependable, consistent pitchers were Johnny Sain, with 24 wins, and Warren Spahn, who won 15.

St. Louis was again second as Harry Brecheen won 20, and Stan Musial led the league in everything but ticket selling to take his third MVP award. Actually, he was one home run short of the triple crown, but did lead in all other offensive categories.

Sain had his finest year, and had there been a Cy Young Award he would have been a certain winner. He was the league's biggest winner with 24, while completing 28 of 39 starts and appearing in 42 games. He posted a 2.60 ERA, had four shutouts and one save. Boston had a very good team and the difficult question is how Sain lost 15 games. Spahn with a 3.71 was 15–12 while Bill Voiselle with a 3.60 was 13–13. Sain deserved a better fate and probably could have won 30 with a few breaks.

Brecheen had been with the Cardinals since 1943 and always posted winning records, but never a 20-game season. Prior to this season his biggest claim to fame was his three victories in the 1946 World Series. Going into this season Brecheen was 71–41, with his ERA below 3.00 every year except 1947. This year Brecheen had his top season as he had 22 complete games in 31 starts while posting a 20–7 record, which gave him the best percentage in the league at .741 as well as the lowest ERA at 2.10.

Brecheen pitched four more seasons for the Cardinals and had only one losing season. At age 39 he joined the St. Louis Browns in their last season in St. Louis. Although he had a very respectable 3.08 ERA, he was only 5–13. Brecheen didn't win his first major league game until age 29; thus he too got a late start that undoubtedly cost him his share of victories. Still, he finished with a 133–92 mark for a .591 winning percentage, which is 81st on the all-time list. His winning percentage with the Cardinals was .618.

Ewell Blackwell, last year's biggest winner, developed a sore arm and finished at 7–9.

Boston led with 70 complete games and Cincinnati was last with 40. Sain and Brecheen were the only two pitchers with 20 or more complete games.

Pitcher/Team	G	GS	CG	W	L	Pct	ERA	SO	W	IP
Johnny Sain, Bos	42	39*	28*	24*	15	.615	2.60	137	83	315*
Harry Brecheen, STL	33	30	21	20	7	.741*	2.34*	149*	49	233

Cincinnati's Harry Gumbert led with 17 saves.

Boston couldn't prevail in the Series despite excellent pitching. Sain and Spahn each won one game, with the former posting a 1.06 ERA but losing his second start, 2–1.

1949

AMERICAN LEAGUE: CASEY AND HIS BAG OF MAGIC TRICKS ARRIVE

Casey Stengel had been thought of somewhat as a buffoon or clown in his previous managerial attempts. The Yankees were also crumbling as age was creeping up and Joe DiMaggio would miss the first half of the season. Cleveland and Boston were loaded with talent and even Detroit and Philadelphia showed some real potential.

However, DiMaggio on his return had a great second half. Vic Raschi paced the mound corps with 21 wins, while Joe Page won 13 games, but more importantly set an incredible new major league record with 27 saves.

Boston finished a game out because they lost the last two games to New York, blowing a one-game lead. This was despite Ted William's MVP triple crown season, 25 wins from Mel Parnell, and 23 from Ellis Kinder.

Raschi won 21 games for the first of three straight seasons that he would win that exact number. He started a league-high 37 games and had 21 complete games to go with his 3.34 ERA. Raschi never had a low ERA; only in 1952 when he was 16–6 did his ERA go below 3.00. His career ERA was 3.72. However, the story on Raschi was that he was only as good as he had to be. If you gave him three runs he held you to two, but if his team got six you might get five. While this wasn't always true, it did seem to follow a certain pattern. Still he retired with a 132–66 mark and .667 winning percentage, which is fifth for pitchers with over 100 wins. It comes back to the old bromide: does the pitcher make the team, or vice versa? We can argue about that one all night.

This was Parnell's third season in the big leagues and his biggest. He led the league with 25 wins and posted a high of 27 complete games with the most innings pitched (295) and the best ERA at 2.78. Parnell was a consistent winner for Boston from 1948 through 1953 until he injured his arm in 1954. He won 109 games over that six-year period and at age 31 looked like he might easily exceed 200, and maybe get a trip to the Hall of Fame. But a sore arm cut short that dream and he finished with a 123–75, .621 winning percentage, 40th best on the all-time list of pitchers with over 100 victories.

Teammate Kinder was already 34 and didn't win his first game until age 32 in 1946 for the St. Louis Browns. Thus the baseball world was astounded when he posted a 23–6 record, appearing in 43 games, starting 30, throwing six shutouts and registering four saves. The most Kinder ever won again was 14 the next season. Then he became a relief pitcher, and from 1951 through 1956 he was 44–28 with 87 saves. He was 43 when he retired, and left with a 102–71 mark.

Lemon posted his second straight 20-win season as he was 22–10 with a fine 2.90 ERA while making 22 complete games in 33 starts. Lemon would have another 20-win season before his streak would be interrupted, then he would start another three-year run only to be interrupted once again before winning 20 or more for the final time in 1956. He was a very consistent and dependable pitcher for the Indians at this time, starting and relieving.

Bobby Feller produced only 15 wins, his lowest total since 1937, and doomsayers were writing him off. But Rapid Robert still had some smoke left in that arm. The Indians added two pitchers who would soon have big years for them and make them perennial contenders. Mike Garcia was a rookie and was 14–5 in 41 games, of which 20 were starts, and had the league's best ERA at 2.35. They also added Early Wynn, who was 11–7 in his first year at Cleveland. From now until 1957 the fewest games he would win would be 17.

Virgil Trucks had been pitching for Detroit since 1941 and had never won 20 games. He came close with a 19–11 record and 2.81 ERA, and he was in 41 games of which 32 were starts. Since 1942, with two years out for service in 1944 and 45, he had won 14, 16, 10, 14 and now 19. Next season he would be sidelined with an arm injury and be only 3–1. He would later win 20, but some strange things would happen before he made it. More on that later.

Detroit finished fourth on their strong hitting and solid pitching, with four pitchers winning between 15 and 19, while Alex Kellner with 20 wins kept Philadelphia above .500. St. Louis and Washington fought it out for last, with the latter winning as they lost 104 games to the Brownies 101.

Kellner was a 25-year-old rookie who won 20 games for Philadelphia with the promise of greater things to come, but they never developed. He stayed in the major leagues through 1959 and the most he ever won again was 12. Along the way he posted an 81–100 mark for those seasons. What happened to that 20-game winner of 1949? Who can say? Was he a one-year wonder? He seems to be like many pitchers who had that one big year and never approached it again.

Philadelphia led with 85 complete games, while St. Louis was last with 43, one less than Washington. Four pitchers achieved 20 or more complete games.

Pitcher/Team	G	GS	CG	W	L	Pct	ERA	SO	W	IP
Mel Parnell, Bos	39	33	27*	25*	7	.781	2.78*	122	134	295*
Ellis Kinder, Bos	43	30	19	23	6	.793*	3.36	138	99	252
Bob Lemon, Cleve	37	33	22	22	10	.688	2.90	138	137	280
Vic Raschi, NY	38	37*	21	21	10	.677	3.34	124	138	275
Alex Kellner, Phila	38	27	19	20	12	.625	3.75	94	129	245

Kinder and Detroit's Virgil Trucks (19–11) tied for the shutout lead at six, while Hal Newhouser (18–11) led with 144 strikeouts.

The Yanks again met the Dodgers and once more took their measure, this time four games to one. Raschi, Allie Reynolds (17–6), Ed Lopat (15–10) and Page each won a game and Reynolds and Page each were credited with a save. Bobby Brown was the hitting star with a .500 average that included four runs, five RBIs and two triples.

NATIONAL LEAGUE: CHOKING DOWN THE STRETCH

The Dodgers and Cardinals battled all season long, and Brooklyn finally won by one game on the last day of the season. St. Louis had enjoyed a two-game lead with five to go, but lost four of five to last-place Chicago and sixth-place Pittsburgh in blowing the pennant.

Stan Musial had his usual great season, and the Cardinals gave him ample support and the best pitching in the league, led by Howie Pollet, who returned to 20-win game form.

Brooklyn couldn't match the St. Louis pitching, but had a powerful attack led by Jackie Robinson's MVP year. This was the team that would dominate the league through the mid-1950s.

Boston fell to fourth despite 21 wins from Warren Spahn, and Johnny Sain posted the worst record of his career at 10–17. Philadelphia had moved into third with the team that would win next season. Included was a 22-year-old hurler named Robin Roberts (15–15), who would dominate the league starting in 1950.

After two off years, Pollet bounced back with his second 20-win season as he was 20–9 with a fine 2.77 ERA. At age 28 it looked like he was just rounding into form and St. Louis could expect several good seasons from the talented left-hander, but such was not to be. Pollet won 14 the next season and after an 0–3 start in 1951 was traded. He bounced around several teams and stayed in the majors until 1956, but never won over eight in a season. What happened? Who can explain why a pitcher is a star one day and a virtual bum the next? This is what makes managers and pitching coaches gray.

Spahn had his second 20-win season and his first of three straight. With 21 wins, he led the league for what would be the first of eight times. He also led with 151 strikeouts, the first of four straight years. His 302 innings were the most in the league as were his 25 complete games. From 1947 through 1963, Spahn never hurled fewer than 246 innings. He was a real workhorse.

Brooklyn had added two pitchers who would prove very helpful over the next several seasons. Preacher Roe had pitched for Pittsburgh from 1943 to 1947 and was 34–47, with ERAs over 5.00 the last two years. He joined the Dodgers in 1948 and was 12–8. From 1948 through 1953, Roe was 90–33, helping the Dodgers to three flags and two second-place finishes.

The other pitcher was Don Newcombe, who would prove to be even more successful. In this his rookie year, he was 17–8 and for 1949–56, sans 1952–53 while he was in the service, Newcombe was 112–48, including three 20-game seasons, an MVP and the first-ever Cy Young Award. We will revisit him shortly.

No other pitchers won 20 games, although Ken Raffensberger won 18 for seventh-place Cincinnati. Raffensberger had a career that spanned 15 seasons, although several were partial ones. He finished with a 119–154 record. This was his biggest winning season, though he did lose 17.

Boston and New York tied for the most complete games at 68, while Chicago had the fewest at 44. Spahn and Raffensberger were the only pitchers with 20 or more complete games.

Pitcher/Team	G	GS	CG	W	L	Pct	ERA	SO	W	IP
Warren Spahn, Bos	38	38*	25*	21*	14	.600	3.07	151*	86	302*
Howie Pollet, STL	39	28	17	20	9	.690	2.77	108	59	231

Four pitchers tied for the lead in shutouts with five, while New York's Dave Koslo, with only a 11–14 mark, had the best ERA at 2.50. Brooklyn's Preacher Roe had the top winning percentage (15–6, .714).

Brooklyn continued its ineptitude against New York by losing in five games, as Don Newcombe lost twice, a pattern that would continue throughout his career. Despite several successful seasons, he was considered a pitcher who couldn't win the big game.

6

1950–1959

AMERICAN LEAGUE: THE
CONTINUANCE OF A DYNASTY

New York was in the process of building a dynasty that would last through 1964. Over this period (1949–1964) they won 14 pennants and nine World Series. They finished second and third the two years they didn't win it all. An MVP season from Phil Rizzuto, another fine year from Joe DiMaggio and 21 wins from Vic Raschi, plus fine backup support, carried the Yankees to 98 wins.

The Yankees needed all of their 98 victories as fourth-place Cleveland won 92, helped by Bob Lemon's league-high 23 wins. Detroit, second with 95, and Boston, third with 94, failed to post a 20-game winner, but both had potent hitting attacks. Boston was the last team to bat over .300, as they hit .302 and scored 1,027 runs.

Boston's pennant chances probably went up in smoke when Ted Williams fractured his elbow in the All-Star Game. Through 89 games, he had 28 home runs, 97 RBIs and a .317 mark. Boston had nine players who batted over 400 times to hit .300. Billy Goodman, who didn't have a regular position, won the batting title, as various players took time off to give him enough times at the plate to qualify for the crown.

Raschi won 21 for the second straight year, but wasn't the league's big winner. However, he did have the best winning percentage at .724. His ERA was 3.99, once again showing that he pitched only as effectively as he had to. The other viewpoint is that the strong Yankee team behind him built his fine record. If that be true, then why didn't other hurlers win 21 games and two out of three decisions?

Lemon had his third straight 20-plus-win season and his first time to lead in victories as he won 23 games. Lemon was in 44 games, starting a league-high 37 and completing the most (22), while also leading the league with 288 innings pitched. He also was credited with three saves.

Early Wynn was coming into his own. He went 18–8 and had the league's best ERA at 3.20, as this was a high-scoring season. Bob Feller rebounded with a 3.34 ERA and 16–11 mark. Next year he would post his final 20-win season.

Art Houtteman was a real workhorse for the Tigers, appearing in 41 games, starting 34, and completing 21 as he won 19 and saved another four. A break here or there would have given him his only year in the charmed circle. Houtteman was another of those Jekyll and Hyde pitchers. In 1948 he was 2–16, then 15–10 in 1949. In 1951 he was in the army, in 1952 he was 8–20, 9–13 in 1953 and then 15–7 in 1954. Will the real Art Houtteman please stand up?

Mickey Harris surfaced as the league's top reliever with 15 saves for Washington, while Joe Page got 13 for the Yankees.

Detroit led with 72 complete games and Philadelphia was last with 50. Four pitchers had 20 or more complete games.

Pitcher/Team	G	GS	CG	W	L	Pct	ERA	SO	W	IP
Bob Lemon, Cleve	44	37*	22*	22*	10	.676	3.84	170*	146	288*
Vic Raschi, NY	33	32	17	21	8	.724*	3.99	155	116	257

Detroit's Art Houtteman (19–12) led with four shutouts, while Cleveland's Early Wynn (18–8) had the top ERA at 3.20.

The Series was a low-scoring affair, as New York swept all four games, outscoring Philadelphia 11–5. Connie Mack retired after 50 years as manager of the Philadelphia Athletics. He won eight pennants and five World Series and gave integrity, honesty and credibility to the game. It will be a long time before the likes of Mack are seen again.

NATIONAL LEAGUE: THE WHIZ KIDS MAKE IT

Philadelphia had not been in a World Series since 1915, which was their only trip. They had been in a rebuilding program for seven years, and it culminated with a final day victory over Brooklyn that gave them the pennant by one game. Robin Roberts paced the staff with 20 wins, but it was reliever Jim Konstanty who carried the team, as he was voted MVP over Stan Musial. He won 16 and saved 22.

Brooklyn had a potent hitting attack to go with 19-game winners Preacher Roe and Don Newcombe. New York finished third, mainly because Larry Jansen won 19, and returning Mexican expatriate Sal Maglie was 18–4. Commissioner A. B. Chandler had eased the five-year suspension and allowed the players who had jumped to the Mexican League to return.

Boston completed the first division on the arms of Warren Spahn (21), Johnny Sain (20) and Vern Bickford (19), plus a strong hitting game.

Roberts had his first of six consecutive 20-plus-win seasons. The last National Leaguer to accomplish this was Christy Mathewson and the last American Leaguer was Lefty Grove. In the 20th century only Mathewson, Grove, Roberts, Walter Johnson, Ferguson Jenkins and Warren Spahn have had six consecutive 20-win seasons. Roberts was a hard-working and -throwing right-hander who led the league with 39 starts while hurling 304 innings. Roberts made three starts in the last five days of the season. He also made two relief appearances and garnered one save in addition to his five shutouts. This was Roberts' third season, and second full one. Prior to this year he was 22–24. More would be heard from him over the next few years as he established himself as one of the top three or four pitchers in the game.

Spahn registered his second straight 21-win season as well as leading the league in wins for the second consecutive year. Spahn tied Roberts for most starts and hurled 293 innings while pitching 25 complete games. He was used in relief three times and made one save. His 191 strikeouts were the best in the league.

Sain came back from his worst season to win 20 games for the fourth and last time. After this year he would only be 5–13 when Boston traded him to the Yankees, where he would sparkle as a spot starter and reliever through 1954. Over that period of time, Sain won 33 and lost 20 while completing 19 of 39 starts. More important, he developed into a top-flight relief pitcher and made 92 relief appearances, highlighted by his last full season as a Yankee when he was strictly in a relief role and appeared in 45 games, with a league high of 22 saves. Sain ended his career with a 2–5 mark with Kansas City in 1955 and then became a pitching coach for several teams. His final career mark was 139–116.

Newcombe was another hard worker as he appeared in 40 games, starting 35 and pitching four shutouts while saving three games. In the final week of the season he beat the Phils in a doubleheader, going nine innings in the first game and seven in the nightcap. Newk won 123 games in seven seasons with the Dodgers, then finished with Cincinnati and Cleveland and left the majors at age 34 with a final record of 149–90. Many sports critics believe that if he had pitched longer and taken better care of himself, he could have posted 200 wins or more. However, during the first half of the 1950s, he was awesome.

Roe matched Newcombe's record as he appeared in 36 games, of which 32 were starts. Roe was in the midst of a six-year string for the Dodgers during which he won 11 or more each season and had no year below .600 winning percentage. For the six seasons, Roe won over 70 percent of his decisions.

For Jansen this marked his fourth consecutive season with at least 15 wins. It was his biggest since his rookie year, when he posted 21 victories. Jansen completed 21 of 35 starts while appearing in 40 games. He tied for the league lead with five shutouts and also recorded three saves.

Maglie had broken in with the Giants in August 1945 as a 28-year-old right-hander and was 5–4 that first season. Then in 1946 he jumped to the Mexican League and was banned from baseball for five years. When the commissioner relented in 1949, he returned to the Giants for the 1950 season and posted a dazzling 18–4 mark, with the league's best ERA at 2.71. He started out the season as a relief pitcher and appeared in 45 games, but in the second half was made into a starter and completed 12 of 16 starts. He tied for the league lead in shutouts, even though other pitchers started 15 to 20 more games.

During the 1950–52 period, Maglie won 59 while losing only 18. He was one of the best pitchers in either league. It's a shame he missed four years when he jumped to the Mexican League, as based on his early 1950s performance he probably would have won another 80 games or more. Those lost years cost him a chance at 200 career wins and possible consideration for the Hall.

Bickford had his career-best season in 1950 as he tied for the lead in games started, had the most complete games (27) and innings pitched (312). Bickford broke in with Boston in 1948 and posted a 11–5 log. The next season he was 16–11 and the Braves were expecting big things from him, especially after his 1950 season. However, fate took a bad turn for him when Bickford suffered a broken finger, made only 20 starts and had to settle for an 11–9 season. Bickford never was the same pitcher again, posting a 19–17 mark through one game in the 1954 season, when he left the majors. He died at age 39 in 1960.

This was still the era when there were only one or two top relief pitchers in the league, although this would change within the next decade. Boston led with 88 complete games while last-place Pittsburgh had only 42. Six pitchers had 20 or more complete games.

Pitcher/Team	G	GS	CG	W	L	Pct	ERA	SO	W	IP
Warren Spahn, Bos	41	38*	25	21*	17	.553	3.16	191*	111	293
Robin Roberts, Phila	40	38*	21	20	11	.645	3.02	146	77	304
Johnny Sain, Bos	37	37	25	20	13	.606	3.95	96	70	278

By the time the Series rolled around, Philadelphia was a worn-out ball club. Although they pitched well, they were no match for New York. They would have to wait another 30 years before they could claim a World Championship.

1951

AMERICAN LEAGUE: GOOD-BYE JOE, HELLO MICK!

The Yankee Clipper, Joe DiMaggio, called it a career with the 1951 season, while a young lad from Oklahoma, Mickey Mantle, made his debut and would become Joe's replacement. This would give the Yankees three Hall of Fame center fielders, beginning with Earle Combs in 1925 through Mantle's retirement in 1968.

The final victory margin was five games for the Yankees, as Eddie Lopat and Vic Raschi each won 21, assisted by Allie Reynolds' 17. Cleveland almost duplicated Chicago's 1920 feat of four 20-game winners, but fell one short as Bob Lemon racked up only 17. Probably the most outstanding pitching job was by Ned Garver of the last-place St. Louis Browns.

Raschi racked up his third straight 21-win season and best-to-date ERA at 3.28. Raschi tied Wynn and Lemon for most starts at 34, an usually low number for league high. This season gave Raschi 82 wins in his first four full seasons.

Though Raschi would be past 33 when the next season started, it looked like he would have a few more years at this level, but this was his last 20-win season. He posted two more winning seasons before finishing his career with the St. Louis Cardinals and Kansas City A's with a 12–16 mark for the 1954–55 years.

Lopat enjoyed the finest season of his career as he was 21–9 with a 2.91 ERA that included 20 complete games in 31 starts. This was a culmination of four fine seasons for the Yankees and gave him 71 wins during that time. Injuries would plague Lopat over the next few years, although he posted a fine 38–13 winning record in limited duty. He finished out his career with the Yankees and Baltimore in 1955 at 7–12, which gave him a final career mark of 166–112 and a .597 winning percentage, 73rd best on the all-time list.

Throughout his career Reynolds had performed double duty, starting and relieving. In 1951 he accelerated that pace as he was 17–8 while appearing in 40 games, 26 as a starter, of which he completed 16. Reynolds led the league with seven shutouts while also posting seven saves. He would follow this same pattern for the rest of his career, which ended in 1954. Over these four years, Reynolds was 63–27 with 50 complete games, 18 shutouts and 33 saves.

After a three-year absence from the 20-win circle, Feller responded with his biggest win total since 1946 as he posted a 22–8 mark. This was Feller's sixth and final 20-win season as well as the sixth time he led in total wins. Feller pitched through the 1956 season with mixed results. He was only 36–31, highlighted by a 13–3 mark in the Indians' pennant-winning year, and the low mark was 1952 when he was 9–13.

This was the first of two successive 20-win seasons for Garcia, who proved to be a real workhorse. Garcia appeared in 47 games, completing 15 of 30 started, and posted six saves. Throughout his career with the Indians, Garcia was a double-duty pitcher. From 1949 to 1957 Garcia won at least 11 games each year and had only one losing season. His top years were 1951–54 when he was 79–41.

Wynn became a 20-game winner for the first of five times (four with Cleveland) in 1951. Since joining Cleveland in 1949, he had slowly improved each year, going from 11 to 18 and then 20 wins this season. During his Washington career, his years had been erratic, starting in 1939 with 0–2, then 3–1 in 1941, 10–16 in 1942, 18–12 in 1943, 8–17 in 1944, 8–5 in 1946, 17–15 in 1947 and 8–19 in 1948 for a composite 72–86. There was nothing to indicate a future 300-game winner and Hall of Famer, but the years 1949–56 would cement his career.

The Browns had the worst pitching and defense and the weakest hitting, but Garver won 20 games. Without Garver, the Browns were a dismal 32–90. Many teams coveted Garver and thought he could be a perennial big winner with a good ball club. Garver later played for Detroit and Kansas City, but in a 14-season career had only four years at .500 or above. His final career mark was 129–157, 3.73 ERA. Perhaps he was one of those overrated pitchers who wasn't as good as everyone thought he was—or should have been.

Cleveland topped the loop with 78 complete games, while third-place

Boston was last with only 46. Only three pitchers had 20 or more complete games.

Pitcher/Team	G	GS	CG	W	L	Pct	ERA	SO	W	IP
Bob Feller, Cleve	33	32	16	22*	8	.733*	3.40	111	95	250
Ed Lopat, NY	31	31	20	21	9	.700	2.91	93	71	235
Vic Raschi, NY	34	34*	15	21	10	.677	3.28	164*	103	258
Ned Garver, STL	33	30	24*	20	12	.625	3.73	84	96	246
Mike Garcia, Cleve	47	30	15	20	13	.606	3.15	116	82	254
Early Wynn, Cleve	37	34*	21	20	13	.606	3.02	133	107	274*

Slowly relief pitching was becoming a specialty, but there were still many teams using starters in critical relief situations, a la Cleveland's Garcia. Boston's Ellis Kinder topped the league with 14 saves, as he was now primarily a relief pitcher. Chicago's Saul Rogovin had the best ERA, 2.78.

The Yankees had a new opponent for the third straight year, but the result was the same, as they brought down the Giants four games to two. DiMaggio batted .261 in his final Series, but had five RBIs.

NATIONAL LEAGUE: THE MIRACLE OF COOGAN'S BLUFF

When writing the history of baseball, the 1951 National League race can be viewed in two ways: a total collapse of the Brooklyn Dodgers, who had a 13½ game bulge on August 12, or a tremendous comeback by the New York Giants. Although several players had better statistics, Willie Mays is credited with providing the spark that ignited the Giants' stretch drive. That drive enabled them to overtake Brooklyn and win in a dramatic play-off, when Bobby Thompson hit the home run that will live forever. His home run turned sure defeat into a 5–4 victory and a trip to the World Series.

Sal Maglie and Larry Jansen paved the way with 23 victories each, while Brooklyn also flashed two 20-game winners in Preacher Roe and Don Newcombe.

Warren Spahn continued his 20-plus seasons with a 22–14 campaign, while Robin Roberts got his second in a row. Murray Dickson picked up 20 wins for a seventh-place Pittsburgh ball club.

Jansen tied with teammate Maglie for the league lead with 23 victories. Besides making 18 complete games in 34 starts, he also made five relief appearances. This was Jansen's last big season as he suffered a back injury and would never be the same dominating pitcher again. For the balance of his career, which ended with Cincinnati in 1955, Jansen was only 26–32. It was a disappointing end to a career that had a great start, with 96 wins in its first five seasons.

Maglie had his greatest season ever and showed what was missed with those four years in the Mexican League. Maglie finished at 23–6, 2.93 ERA and 22 complete games in 37 starts. He also made five relief appearances and was credited with four saves. Maglie had another big year at 18–8 in 1952 before slipping to 8–9 in 1953. He would rebound with 14–6 to help New York to another pennant in 1954, then was 13–5, which helped Brooklyn to a pennant in 1956. His final mark of 119–62 could have been so much better.

Roe was nearly unbeatable as he was 22–3 to post the finest season of his career. At age 36 he still took his turn every fifth day and sometimes every fourth day, completing 19 of his 33 starts. Starting in 1952 he would become a once-a-week pitcher and post a 22–5 mark for Brooklyn during their pennant winning seasons of 1952–53. He then retired after the 1954 campaign with a 127–84 mark, which had been weakened by those poor seasons in Pittsburgh with their hapless ball clubs.

Newcombe posted his first of three 20-win seasons with a 20–9 mark. He spent 1952–53 in the army, returning to only a 9–8 mark for 1954 before righting himself and posting two successive 20-plus win seasons in 1955–56. But more on that later. We should point out here that Newcombe was also one of baseball's best hitting pitchers, often used as a pinch hitter.

Spahn just did what became second nature for him during the late 1940s, 1950s and early 1960s, and that was to win 20 games. During this time he would exceed 20 wins on 13 occasions. This year his 22 wins were good only for third place, but his 26 complete games were tops as were his 164 strikeouts. He was second with 311 innings pitched and first with seven shutouts.

Roberts posted the second of his six consecutive 20-plus-win seasons, and as would be the situation in several years, there were four to six more victories he should have had each year. This, plus a failure to develop another pitch to go with his fastball, cost him a 300-win career, but more on that later. Roberts was becoming a real workhorse, appearing in 44 games, starting a league high 39 times and leading with 315 innings. He also had 22 complete games and was second with six shutouts.

Dickson kept the Pirates from finishing last as he won 20 games. With another team, he may have made 25. Even though he had a high ERA (4.02), much of that could be attributed to a weak infield defense and, except for Gus Bell, a slow-moving defensive outfield. Dickson pitched 289 innings as he appeared in 45 games, starting 35 and completing 19. He was also credited with two saves. Dickson finished his career at 172–181, but had a record of 72–54 with St. Louis. Thus many of his defeats came while playing for the doormats of the league, especially the Pirates during the 1950s.

Boston led with 73 complete games while Pittsburgh was last with 40, of which 19 were by Dickson. Only three pitchers had 20 or more complete games, as relief pitching was taking on added importance.

Pitcher/Team	G	GS	CG	W	L	Pct	ERA	SO	W	IP
Sal Maglie, NY	42	37	22	23*	6	.793	2.93	146	86	298
Larry Jansen, NY	39	34	18	23*	11	.676	3.03	145	56	279
Preacher Roe, Bkln	34	33	19	22	3	.880*	3.03	113	64	258
Warren Spahn, Bos	39	36	26*	22	14	.611	2.96	164*	109*	311

Pitcher/Team	G	GS	CG	W	L	Pct	ERA	SO	W	IP
Robin Roberts, Phila	44	39*	22	21	15	.583	3.03	127	64	315*
Don Newcombe, Bkn	40	36	18	20	9	.690	3.28	164	91*	272
Murray Dickson, Pgh	45	35	19	20	16	.556	4.02	112	101	269

Spahn led the league with seven shutouts, while Pittsburgh's Ted Wilks had 12 saves to be number one in that department. The Giants had spent all their energies in beating the Dodgers, and they fell apart in the Series. Only journeyman Dave Koslo had a decent ERA at 3.00. The rest were astronomical.

Stan Musial won his second consecutive batting title and five in nine years. He finished second in the MVP voting for the third straight season, giving him a record of six first- or second-place finishes in his first nine seasons.

—— 1952 ——

AMERICAN LEAGUE: MORE
MAGIC FROM THE OLD MASTER

New York entered the season minus Joe DiMaggio and several key players in the military. To compound problems, they got off to a slow start and lost ace Ed Lopat for almost half a season. Meanwhile, Cleveland boasted the best pitching staff in the league, especially starters, with four proven 20-game winners.

At the end, New York won by two games. Allie Reynolds picked up the slack and won 20 with the league-low ERA. He also saved six games. Vic Raschi chipped in with 16 wins and former Brave star Johnny Sain won 11 and saved seven more.

Cleveland once again had three 20-plus game winners, led by Early Wynn. However, longtime ace Bob Feller dropped to 9–13, his worst season ever, to keep the Tribe from the pennant.

This was Reynolds' finest hour as he posted a 20–8 mark with the league's best ERA (2.07) and the most shutouts (six). Reynolds completed 24 of 29 starts and also made seven relief appearances, picking up six saves. He truly was the man of the hour for the Yankees. Many have wondered why he isn't in the Hall of Fame as he has a career 182–107 mark, .630 winning percentage (25th among pitchers who won at least 100 games). His record with the Yankees is even more remarkable: 131–60, .686 winning percentage for eight seasons.

Wynn posted his second consecutive 20-win season as he won 23 to pace the Indians and finish in second place in the league for total victories. Wynn had a 2.90 ERA as he posted four shutouts and three saves. His record included 19 complete games in 33 starts and nine relief appearances. From 1949 through

1956, Wynn won 149 games for Cleveland in the most successful period of his career.

Garcia also had his biggest year as he won 22 games and posted a 2.37 ERA, best on the Cleveland staff. He tied Lemon for the most starts (36), of which he completed 19. Garcia tied Reynolds for the lead in shutouts and also had four saves as he made ten relief appearances. He was truly a double-duty workhorse. Garcia would be 37–17 with eight shutouts, five saves and a composite 2.95 ERA for the next two seasons before he tapered off.

From 1955 through 1959, Garcia was only 38–39 for the Indians. He retired after 1961 when he had been 0–1 as relief pitcher in 31 games for the Chicago White Sox and Washington Senators during 1960–61. His final career mark was 142–97.

Lemon rejoined the 20-game circle with his 22–11 season and had the league's most complete games with 28. He turned in a 2.50 ERA as he led with 310 innings while hurling five shutouts and picking up four saves in six relief appearances. Lemon followed this season with two more successive 20-win seasons, giving him three in a row twice. From 1948 through 1956, he posted seven 20-win seasons, one 18-win and one 17-win year.

Feller had the worst season of his career with a 9–13 mark, 4.73 ERA and only 11 complete games in 30 starts. To show how far he had fallen, Feller fanned only 81 batters in 192 innings.

The Indians relied mainly on their big three as they pitched 15 of the team's 17 shutouts, had 66 of the 80 complete games and 11 of its 18 saves. The balance of the staff were only 26–27 with a composite 4.48 ERA. A little help from one or two pitchers would have put Cleveland in the World Series.

Shantz was only 5'6" and weighed 139 lbs. One might think a good wind would blow him off the mound, but he played 16 years in the majors and posted a 119–99 mark. This was his peak season as he led with 24 wins, had 27 complete games in 33 starts and the league's best winning percentage at .774. Shantz had won 18 games the previous season; thus it looked like the A's had a sound starter for many years to come, as Shantz was only 26.

However, he developed a sore arm the next season and was only 5–9, and after that the most games he won was 11 for the Yankees in 1957. After his sore arm, Shantz pitched mostly in relief and accumulated 48 saves for his career—not many by today's standards, but given the time he pitched, it is a respectable amount.

Detroit was the team of frustration as journeyman Ted Gray was 12–17, but there were two bigger losers on the staff. Jekyll and Hyde pitcher Art Houtteman was 8–20 and Virgil Trucks was 5–19. Trucks was a good pitcher posting, a 177–135 mark for his career of 16 full seasons. Ten times he was in double digits during his career. While Trucks won only five games, two of them were no-hitters.

Cleveland was tops with 80 complete games, while St. Louis was last with 46. Only three pitchers had 20 complete games or more.

Pitcher/Team	G	GS	CG	W	L	Pct	ERA	SO	W	IP
Bobby Shantz, Phila	33	33	27	24*	7	.774*	2.49	152	63	280
Early Wynn, Cleve	42	33	19	23	12	.657	2.90	153	132*	286
Bob Lemon, Cleve	42	36*	28*	22	11	.667	2.50	131	105	310*
Mike Garcia, Cleve	46	36*	19	22	11	.667	2.37	143	87	292
Allie Reynolds, NY	36	29	24	20	8	.714	2.09*	160*	97	244

Reynolds and Garcia led in shutouts with six. Note that the starters were still in relief a large number of games. Cleveland's big three had 11 saves, while the rest of the staff had seven.

Ted Williams was called to the service after only six games, at the age of 33, and would miss all of 1952 and most of 1953. There have always been rumors that he had some enemies in Washington and was therefore recalled to active duty, especially since he was a fighter pilot who was well past the prime age for that category.

The Yanks faced a new opponent in the Series for the fourth straight season, although they were an old familiar foe. However, with Reynolds and Raschi each winning two games, they took the Dodgers' measure in seven games.

NATIONAL LEAGUE: MAKING UP FOR THEIR FAILURE

Most thought New York would be a repeat winner, but many obstacles were placed in their way. Monte Irvin (121 RBIs in 1951) broke his ankle in spring training and had only 21 for the year. Willie Mays was drafted after 34 games and ace Larry Jansen had arm trouble and was 11–11. Only Sal Maglie held up, and he was 18–8.

Meanwhile, the Dodgers put together a potent hitting attack to bolster their pitching, and with rookie Joe Black winning 15 and saving the same number, they would edge out New York by four and a half games.

Perennial 20-game winner Warren Spahn was only 14–19 (despite a 2.98 ERA) for seventh-place Boston, who would move to Milwaukee in the off-season. The league's only 20-game winner was Robin Roberts with a 28–7 mark.

Roberts had his premier season as he did it all. His 28 wins were by far the best, ten more than second-place Maglie. He also had 30 complete games in 37 starts and pitched 330 innings. His ERA was 2.59 and he made two relief appearances and was credited with two saves. This was Roberts' third consecutive 20-win season and he would follow with three more. During the 1950–55 period he won 138 games, an average of 23 per season. This was also his first of five consecutive seasons leading in complete games and his second of five leading in innings pitched.

Pitcher/Team	G	GS	CG	W	L	Pct	ERA	SO	W	IP
Robin Roberts, Phila	39	37*	30*	28*	7	.800	2.59	148	45	330*

Philadelphia's Curt Simmons led with six shutouts, while Spahn was strikeout king with 183. St. Louis' Vinegar Bend Mizell was predicted to be a left handed Dizzy Dean, but the most games he ever won was 14. New York's Hoyt Wilhelm took the percentage title at .833, based on his 15–3 record. The save leader was St. Louis' Al Brazle at 16.

The Dodgers thought they would finally break through against New York, but when it was all over, they had lost again. Black had a fine ERA (2.53), but lost two of three decisions.

Stan Musial captured his third consecutive batting crown, and sixth over-all in ten seasons. Ralph Kiner led with 37 home runs for a National League record of seven straight seasons.

1953

AMERICAN LEAGUE: A NEW RECORD

No team had ever won five straight pennants, a record New York was soon to establish. New York boasted the league's top offense, and while having no 20-game winners, had five pitchers with a composite 74–30, with four of the five being 34 years of age or older.

Cleveland produced only one 20-game winner, Bob Lemon, as Mike Garcia and Early Wynn slipped slightly, with 18 and 17 respectively.

Meanwhile, Virgil Trucks picked up his only 20-win season with Chicago while Mel Parnell notched 21 with Boston. The league leader in victories was Washington's Bob Porterfield at 22. St. Louis completed its last season in St. Louis by losing 100 games and finishing last.

Lemon posted his second consecutive 20-win season with his 21 victories. He had a league-high 36 starts and 23 complete games and also made five relief appearances. In 1952 the big three appeared in 130 games, making 25 relief appearances, posting 11 saves, had 67 wins and 66 complete games with a 2.59 ERA. In 1953 they made 115 appearances, ten in relief and Lemon had the only save. They won 56 games and had 60 complete games with a 3.56 ERA.

Virgil Trucks rebounded from his worst season ever to have his only 20-win campaign in a split season between St. Louis and Chicago. He was 5–4, 3.07 at St. Louis and 15–6, 2.86 at Chicago. The highest number of wins Trucks had previously was 19 in 1949, and he would win 19 again in 1954 before dropping to 13 in 1955. Trucks pitched through 1958 and posted a 17–14 mark, mostly in relief for those three seasons.

Porterfield pitched part or all of 12 seasons in the big leagues and came away with a 87–97 record. The highest number of wins he had other than this year was 13 (twice) in 1952 when he lost 14 and 1954 when he lost 15. This season was his one great moment as he led the league with 22 wins, 24 complete games and nine shutouts. Never before or again did he approach such brilliance. It is hard to explain, but it happens on many occasions.

Parnell had his last big season as he won 20 or more for the second time, this year having a 21–8 record. Parnell was only 31 and already had 113 victories to his credit. Thus the chances looked good for a 200-career-win total, but he developed a sore arm the following year and was never the same pitcher again. Parnell tried to pitch until 1956, but was only 12–16 for his efforts. He finished with a 123–75 record, .621 winning percentage.

Cleveland again led the way with 81 complete games, while St. Louis set a new modern low record (for the time) at 28. Again only three pitchers posted 20 or more complete games.

Pitcher/Team	G	GS	CG	W	L	Pct	ERA	SO	W	IP
Bob Porterfield, Was	34	32	24*	22*	10	.688	3.35	77	73	255
Mel Parnell, Bos	38	34	12	21	8	.724	3.06	136	116*	241
Bob Lemon, Cleve	41	36*	23	21	15	.583	3.36	98	110	287*
Virgil Trucks, Chgo	40	33	17	20	10	.667	2.93	149	99	264

New York entered the Series against their perennial challengers, Brooklyn, the underdogs, and won in six games. Billy Martin was the hitting star with 12 hits, .500 average, eight RBIs, two triples and two home runs.

Ted Williams returned late in the season and in just 91 at bats smashed 13 home runs and hit .407. Two years away hadn't dulled his hitting one iota.

NATIONAL LEAGUE: FINALLY A REPEAT WINNER

Brooklyn dominated the league with five .300 hitters, including Carl Furillo, the batting champ at .344, as he broke Stan Musial's hold on the title. They had six players to score over 100 runs and a seventh 85, and five to bat in 92 runs or more. They also flashed a 20-game winner in Carl Erskine and won by 13 games over Milwaukee (Boston's replacement).

Warren Spahn tied for the lead in victories with 23, as Milwaukee set a new National League attendance mark at 1,826,397. Eddie Mathews hit 47 home runs to break Ralph Kiner's hold on the home run derby.

Robin Roberts also won 23 as he helped pitch Philadelphia to third place. However, with a little more support he could have won another five or six games. This would be the story over the next three years, and those victories alone kept him from 300 for his career.

Erskine posted his only 20-win season by winning that exact number. He pitched for the Dodgers (both Brooklyn and Los Angeles) and had one losing season, his last in 1959 at 0–3. Erskine was never noted for his low ERA as he had a career 3.99, but was a smart pitcher who was as good as he had to be. He also benefited from those powerful Dodger bats, especially the days in Brooklyn, where Erskine spent most of his career. He won 68 games from 1951–54. He finished with a 122–78, .610 winning percentage record.

The Braves moved to Milwaukee and Spahn rejoined the charmed circle as he and Roberts tied for the lead in wins with 23 each. In addition, Spahn had the lowest ERA (2.10), completed 24 starts in 32 games, made three relief appearances, got three saves and pitched five shutouts. Spahn would win 20 or more eight of the next ten seasons, interrupted only by a 17-win campaign in 1955 and an 18-win season in 1962.

Roberts won 20 for the fourth straight time and posted 23 for the first of three consecutive years. This was his second year in a row leading in victories, as well as his second straight with the most complete games (33), which also was his career high. He led with 347 innings, another career high. Some have speculated that the excessive pitching wore out Roberts' arm. After 1955 he never won 20 games again and posted five losing seasons in his last ten. From 1950 through 1955 the fewest number of innings he hurled was 304 in 1950. For his career he had five more seasons with at least 250 innings and another three over 200. There may be some truth to the theory or speculation that he wore out his arm.

Rookie Harvey Haddix won 20 for St. Louis, his lone season at that level. Haddix looked like a world-beater as he led the league with six shutouts, had 19 complete games and a fine 3.02 ERA in a heavy hitting season. However, the closest he ever came again was 18 the next season.

Murray Dickson led in losses for the second straight season en route to three consecutive seasons as the league's top loser. He certainly deserved a better fate, but pitching for Pittsburgh in those days offered a pitcher little hope. For the two seasons he was 24–40, a record that could have been reversed or better with a decent team behind him.

Al Brazle again led in saves, this time with 18. Philadelphia was tops in complete games with 76 while seventh-place Chicago was last with 38. Spahn and Roberts were the only two to achieve 20 complete games or more. The advent of the relief pitcher was here. Maybe the closer wasn't in full bloom, but managers were going to their bullpen a lot more.

Pitcher/Team	G	GS	CG	W	L	Pct	ERA	SO	W	IP
Warren Spahn, Milw	35	32	24	23*	7	.767	2.10*	148	70	266
Robin Roberts, Phila	44	41*	33*	23*	16	.590	2.75	198*	61	347*
Carl Erskine, Bkln	39	33	16	20	6	.769*	3.53	187	95	247
Harvey Haddix, STL	36	33	19	20	9	.690	3.06	163	69	253

Brooklyn entered the Series favored to win their first battle with New York. While their hitters batted .300, their pitching let them down and in the end they would lose four games to two.

1954

AMERICAN LEAGUE: A NEW RECORD

During their five consecutive pennant winning seasons, the Yankees' highest victory total was 99, but in 1954 they won 103 games and finished eight games out of first place. The reason? Cleveland set a new American League record (which still stands) with 111 victories.

Bob Lemon and Early Wynn each won 23, while Mike Garcia added 19 and the team had a 2.78 ERA. New York got 20 wins from Bob Grim, but no other pitcher won 20, although Virgil Trucks came close at 19.

Baltimore's first season was reminiscent of the old St. Louis Browns as they lost 100 games. Even so, they only finished seventh, as Philadelphia was still in the league, although next year they would be in Kansas City. To show Baltimore's futility, we look at Don Larsen and his 3–21 mark with a 4.37 ERA. Larsen was a journeyman pitcher who was more renowned for his carousing with Mickey Mantle, Whitey Ford and Billy Martin than for his pitching.

In a 14-year career that covered seven teams, the highest number of games Larsen ever won was 11 for the Yankees in 1956. However, he is the only pitcher in World Series history to pitch a perfect game, as he won the deciding seventh game of the 1956 Series with a 9–0 whitewashing of the Dodgers. Seemingly, he had everything going for him: he was 6'4" and weighed 215 lbs., but he enjoyed the nightlife more than pitching. His five-year record with the Yankees was 45–24, while the balance of his career he was 36–67; enough said.

Lemon won 20 or more in a row for the third time and this was the second time he had turned this trick in the past seven seasons. His 23 wins tied him with Wynn for the league's best and marked the second time he led in that category. His 21 complete games tied with Bob Porterfield for first in that department, making the fourth time Lemon had led the league. This was also the sixth year in seven that he posted at least 20 complete games.

This for Wynn was his second successive 20-win season and the third time he had reached this level. It marked the first time he had led in victories, but his 271 innings pitched marked the second time he was the leader in that department. Wynn led with 36 starts, had 20 complete games and made four relief appearances, garnering two saves. He and Lemon both finished with a 2.72 ERA.

Garcia fell one short in a bid for his third 20-win season, but led the league with a 2.64 ERA and five shutouts. He also continued his double duty pitching as he started 34 games, relieved 11 times and posted five saves. This was his last big season, although he remained in the majors through 1961 when he finished with Washington. As a starter for the next three years, he was only 34–33; then he pitched primarily relief for the balance of his career.

The Yankees thought they had another right-handed pitcher in the mold of Waite Hoyt, Red Ruffing, Vic Raschi or Allie Reynolds when Grim won rookie of the year with his 20–6 mark. Grim appeared in 37 games, starting 20. However, he developed a sore arm the next season and finished at 7–5. The highest number of games he won after 1954 was when he posted a 12–8, 2.63 ERA record with 19 saves for the Yankees in 1957. However, that hope quickly faded when he was 0–1, 5.63 ERA in 11 games the next season and was promptly traded to Kansas City. He journeyed to several teams after that, finally finishing again with Kansas City in 1961. His career mark was 61–41.

However, the Yankees did have another pitcher who would eventually land in the Hall of Fame. Whitey Ford broke into the majors in mid–1950 with a 9–1 mark and then spent 1951–52 in the service. He returned in 1953 and posted an 18–6 record and followed with 16–8 this season. Ford never had a losing season until his last two (1966–67), when he was a combined 4–9. Meanwhile, he won 232 while losing 97. Three times he led in wins, twice in innings pitched, twice in ERA and three times in winning percentage. Ford would continue pitching winning ball, but wouldn't break the 20-win barrier until 1961.

Trucks had another big year with Chicago, giving him 39 wins in two seasons. This was his last big season, although he did manage 13 wins in 1955. After that he pitched three more years, mostly in relief, and finally retired at the end of the 1958 season. He fell 23 wins short of the coveted 200, which can be traced to two lost years in the service during World War II. The two seasons before entering the service he had 30 wins and his first year back he posted 14.

The last pitcher we need to review is Steve Gromek, who posted a brilliant 18–16 and 2.74 ERA with a weak Detroit team that scored less than four runs a game. With any decent support, he could have won 22 to 25. His biggest season had been in 1945, when he was 19–9 and the Indians thought they had another pitcher to compliment Feller; but that was not to happen.

In 1946 when Feller returned, Gromek was only 5–15 with a 4.32 ERA. Although he stayed with the Indians through early 1953, his best total was a 10–7 record in 1950. Over the years he was bypassed with the likes of Lemon, Wynn and Garcia and became relegated to a spot starter and relief role. Perhaps if his 1946 year had been better, he might have enjoyed more starting opportunities. Gromek finished his career at 123–108 for 14 full and three part seasons.

Cleveland was complete game leader with 77 while Boston had the fewest with 41. Only Lemon, Wynn and Porterfield made the 20 complete game club. Boston also welcomed the return of Ted Williams, who had 29 home runs, 89 RBIs, and a .345 average in 117 games, as a shoulder injury sidelined him for over a month.

Pitcher/Team	G	GS	CG	W	L	Pct	ERA	SO	W	IP
Bob Lemon, Cleve	36	33	21*	23*	7	.767	2.72	110	92	258
Early Wynn, Cleve	40	36*	20	23	11	.676	2.72	155	83	271*
Bob Grim, NY	37	20	8	20	6	.769	3.26	108	35	199

Chicago's Sandy Consuegra (16–3) had the top winning percentage at .842.

The World Series was a disaster for Cleveland. They batted only .190 and lost four straight, with Lemon being 0–2, 6.76 ERA. Over 40 years later Cleveland finally went back to the fall classic.

NATIONAL LEAGUE: THE RETURN OF THE "SAY HEY" KID

Willie Mays returned from the service and came of age as a ballplayer, as he led the league with a .345 mark, had 41 home runs and 110 RBIs, and won the MVP. This was a great year for hitters: Ted Kluszewski led with 49 home runs and 141 RBIs, while Stan Musial became the first player to hit five home runs in a doubleheader.

Despite this heavy hitting, it was the pitching that carried New York to the title by five games over Brooklyn, as Johnny Antonelli won 21, Ruben Gomez 17 and a bullpen tandem of Hoyt Wilhelm and Marv Grissom was 22–11 with 26 saves.

Brooklyn was second with Don Erskine its top winner with 18, while Don Newcombe, returning from the service, was only 9–8. Warren Spahn had another 20-plus season, as Milwaukee finished third and unveiled a rookie named Hank Aaron, from whom more would be heard.

Robin Roberts kept completing and winning games and chalked up 23. Again, with a little more support he could have been several victories higher. St. Louis led in every offensive category except home runs but finished sixth, although their pitching ERA was only .19 higher than Brooklyn.

Antonelli had been one of the first bonus babies when he was signed by the Boston Braves in 1948, and through 1950 he was only 5–10. Antonelli spent two years in the service; when he returned the team was in Milwaukee and he posted a 12–12 mark. Traded to the Giants for the 1954 season, Antonelli began a somewhat Jekyll and Hyde career. He was brilliant in 1954, winning 21 and losing only seven as he had the top winning percentage (.750) and best ERA (2.29) while leading with six shutouts. He also relieved twice and recorded two saves. Then in 1955 he was 14–16, although he had a respectable 3.33 ERA. He then would win 20 in 1956 and go 12–18 with a 3.78 ERA in 1957 before going 16–13 and 19–10 the next two seasons. It's probably true, at least in Antonelli's situation, that the rules of the days requiring bonus babies to stay with the team hurt him. From 1948 through 1950 he pitched only 158 innings, thus losing valuable time he could have been learning in the minors. His final career mark was 126–110.

Spahn won 21 for the second successive season at that level or better. Also the staff that would help Milwaukee to pennants in the mid–50s was being formed. Lew Burdette was 15–14 with a 2.76 ERA. In another season Bob Buhl would become the third member of a trio that would become quite dominating during the middle and late 1950s.

Roberts continued his Herculean work, winning 23 and leading in wins and complete games (29) for the third straight season. He also led in innings pitched (337) for the fourth straight year. He fashioned a fine 2.96 ERA and garnered his second strikeout title as he fanned 185. When we review his record it can be seen that with a little help, Roberts could have won four to six more games in each of the 1951 and 1953–55 seasons. Had he done this he would have exceeded 300 victories, instead of falling short by 16.

Harvey Haddix was headed for his second successive 20-win season as he was 13–5 when hit in the knee by a line drive. Thereafter he wasn't the same pitcher, finishing at 18–13. He never again won over 13 in a season. Haddix, like Roberts, was also used in relief; each appeared in 45 games and was credited with four saves.

Complete games were really falling off, but Philadelphia amassed 78, while Cincinnati was last with only 34 (a new National League low). Roberts, Spahn and Curt Simmons were the only pitchers with 20 or more complete games.

Pitcher/Team	G	GS	CG	W	L	Pct	ERA	SO	W	IP
Robin Roberts, Phila	45	38*	29*	23*	15	.605	2.96	185*	56	337*
Johnny Antonelli, NY	39	37	18	21	7	.750*	2.29*	152	94	259
Warren Spahn, Milw	39	34	23	21	12	.636	3.15	136	86	283

New York was the underdog in the World Series, but shocked the baseball world by sweeping Cleveland in four games. Their team ERA was 1.46, but the real hero was a reserve outfielder, Dusty Rhodes, who was four for six with two home runs and seven RBIs, as he had the game-winning hit in each of the first three games.

1955

AMERICAN LEAGUE: STARTING ANOTHER STRING

New York returned to its old ways of winning less than 100 games but won the pennant on the strength of a 98–56 season, five games better than Cleveland. Mickey Mantle, Yogi Berra and Bill Skowron provided the firepower, and Berra won the MVP. The pitching was led by Whitey Ford (18–7), who tied for the league lead in victories.

Cleveland's big three went from 64–27 to 51–31, enough for them to finish second, although Bob Lemon shared the lead in victories with Ford and Boston's Frank Sullivan. There was a change in Cleveland's big three as Mike Garcia was replaced by Herb Score, who looked like a left-handed Bob Feller. In his rookie year he was 16–10, with a 2.85 ERA, and fanned 245 batters in 227 innings.

Billy Pierce of Chicago carted off the ERA crown at 1.97, while Tommy

Byrne was the winning percentage champ at .762, based on his 16–5 record. Billy Hoeft had seven shutouts to lead, while Ford was complete game leader with 18. Ray Narleski was 9–1 with 19 saves for Cleveland.

Ted Williams continued to suffer injuries. He was limited to 98 games, during which he hit 28 home runs, 83 RBIs and batted .356. Only once in the past six seasons was he able to play a full year. Two were lost to the service and three were cut short by serious injuries.

This was the first time in the history of the American League that a pitcher did not win 20 games as Ford, Lemon and Sullivan each won 18 to share the lead. Ford also led with 18 complete games, marking the first time no pitcher had at least 20 complete games. In another 20 years this would be commonplace. Ford posted a 2.62 ERA, his second of five in a row below 3.00. From 1953 through 1956 Ford was 71–27 with a 2.73 composite ERA. He would have shoulder problems in 1957 and his record from then through 1960 slipped a little; it was 53–31, fine for anyone else but a little off for Ford.

Lemon in some ways had an off year. He tied for the lead in wins, but completed only five of his 31 starts. This was his lowest complete game total to date. In 1947 he had only six, but only made 15 starts. His ERA at 3.88 was also the highest of his career to this point. Lemon would bounce back to have one more 20-win season.

This was Sullivan's third season and second as a starter. He never developed into the pitcher the Red Sox had hoped for, but did pitch competently during the mid–1950s. From 1954 through 1958 he was 74–52 for mediocre Red Sox ball clubs. After 1958 he slipped badly and for the Red Sox, Philadelphia and Minnesota he was only 22–47, giving him a final career mark of 97–100. However, in 1954 he was tough as he won 18, led with 260 innings and posted a fine 2.91 ERA.

Detroit led with 66 complete games while Kansas City was last with 29. The Yankees were facing their old rivals, the Brooklyn Dodgers, and everyone figured them to take the crown. This time the Yankee fans were disappointed. They went down to defeat in seven games, despite Ford winning twice.

NATIONAL LEAGUE: WE WON'T HAVE TO WAIT UNTIL NEXT YEAR

For several seasons after the World Series, the perennial cry in Brooklyn had been, "Wait until next year!" It wouldn't have to be that way this season. Brooklyn featured its usual heavy-hitting attack, but this year they led in team ERA. Don Newcombe returned to form and won 20 games, while Clem Labine and Ed Roebuck won 18 and saved 23 between them.

Milwaukee was second on the strength of hitting by Ed Mathews and young Hank Aaron. Spahn slipped to 17 wins, and no one else won more than 13.

Newcombe posted a 20–5 mark for the top winning percentage (.800).

This was his second 20-win season and he would have his greatest year in 1956. Newcombe also batted .359 with seven home runs and 23 RBIs in just 117 at bats. He was used as a pinch hitter 23 times.

Milwaukee was developing the nucleus of their staff. Spahn had 17 wins, while Lew Burdette and Bob Buhl each posted 13. The three started 92 while relieving 27 times, a pattern that would be followed for several seasons, although not quite as frequently out of the bullpen.

New York was third, 19 games off the pace, mainly because Johnny Antonelli and Ruben Gomez went from 38–16 to 23–26. Robin Roberts kept Philadelphia in the first division with his league-high 23 wins and almost half of their 58 complete games. Without Roberts, Philadelphia was a seventh-place team.

Roberts certainly deserved a better fate than his 23–14 record as he led with 26 complete games in a league-high 38 starts and 305 innings while posting a 3.28 ERA. Again, better support could have won him a few more games. Roberts also was credited with three saves. From 1949 through 1957, Roberts made 46 relief appearances and was credited with 23 saves. This is in addition to his 332 starts, of which he completed 208.

Some claim that Roberts faded because of overwork and cite his six successive seasons of 300 innings or more. Others say that it was more related to starting every fourth day, frequent relieving and all the complete games he threw. However, the best reason is his failure to develop another pitch. Manager Mayo Smith tried to get him to develop a new pitch, perhaps a slider, but to no avail. Thus when his fastball went, so did his game. From 1950 to 1956 he won 157 games. From 1957 through 1966 he won 107 games but lost 126. In his last ten seasons he posted five losing campaigns and five times his ERA was over 4.00. Thus a combination of inadequate support at times, the failure to develop another pitch and perhaps some overwork deprived him of probably 325 to 350 career wins.

Complete games continued to decline as Milwaukee was high with only 61, while Cincinnati was last with only 38. Roberts was the only hurler with 20 or more complete games, and the next closest was Newcombe with 17.

Pitcher/Team	G	GS	CG	W	L	Pct	ERA	SO	W	IP
Robin Roberts, Phila	41	38*	26*	23*	14	.622	3.28	160	53	305*
Don Newcombe, Bkn	34	31	17	20	5	.800*	3.19	143	38	234

Cincinnati's Joe Nuxhall (17–12) topped the league with five shutouts, while Pittsburgh's Bob Friend (14–9) had the best ERA (2.84).

Friend had his first winning season with a 14–9 mark. For his career he was 197–230, but it must be remembered that he pitched for some pretty terrible teams during the early to mid–1950s. From 1950 through 1957, Pittsburgh was last six times and seventh the other two seasons. It is quite difficult to build any type of decent record with a team like that behind you. For his first four years, Friend was 28–50.

Friend became a real workhorse, twice leading the league in innings pitched, and he had over 200 for 11 straight years. However, he did become somewhat of a Jekyll and Hyde character when it came to his record. He would have a good year, then a bad year, then a good season. From 1955 through 1964 he was 14–9, 17–17, 14–18, 22–14, 8–19, 18–12, 14–19, 18–14, 17–16, 13–18 and 8–12—not as consistent as a manager would like. Admittedly, in the early years there were some weak teams behind him.

In the World Series, Johnny Podres, only 9–10 with 3.96 ERA during the regular season, won two complete games with a 1.00 ERA, while Duke Snider hit four home runs, drove in seven and batted .320.

Roy Campanella won his third MVP title, tying Stan Musial for the National League record, although based on stats Snider had the better season.

Brooklyn also introduced a 19-year-old rookie, Sandy Koufax, who was 2–2.

—————— 1956 ——————

AMERICAN LEAGUE: A NEW
CHAMPION AND HERO ARRIVES

Mickey Mantle finally exploded into the type of season everyone expected as he won the triple crown and MVP with 52 home runs, 130 RBIs, a .353 average, and league-leading 132 runs. He was backed up by a fine hitting attack and pitching staff, which, although missing a 20-game winner, did posses depth. Whitey Ford led the team with 19 wins (losing his chance for 20 on the final day of the season).

Cleveland was again second and had three 20-game winners again. This would be the last season that would happen, as two would suffer injuries, one ending the chance for a brilliant career. More on that later. Billy Pierce, with 20 wins, helped Chicago to third, while Frank Lary and Billy Hoeft were each 20-game winners and put Detroit at 82–72, although they finished fifth.

Ford had another fine season even though he failed to win 20 games. His 19–6 record was good enough for the best winning percentage (.760), while his 2.47 ERA led the league. This was the first time he led in each category.

Early Wynn pitched his fourth and final 20-win season for Cleveland as he posted a 20–9 mark with a fine 2.72 ERA. He logged 278 innings while hurling 18 complete games, four shutouts and also recording two saves. This was his last winning season with Cleveland. He was 14–16 next year and then was traded to Chicago, where in 1959 he would help pitch them to their first pennant in 40 years.

Bob Lemon enjoyed his last 20-win season. He was 20–14 while pitching a league-high 21 complete games, the seventh time in the last nine years he had reached that plateau. Lemon would suffer a leg injury in 1957 and an elbow injury the following season, which limited him to 32 games, 18 starts and a 6–12 record for the two years. Lemon finished with 207–128, .618 winning percentage, 44th on the all-time list. Although he was elected to the Hall, injuries short-circuited his chances for 250 or more victories.

The real tragedy would be Herb Score. This year he was superb, winning 20 while losing only nine and posting a 2.53 ERA. He also fanned 263 men in 249 innings. Comparisons were being made to Bob Feller. Score was only 23 and the future certainly looked bright, but tragedy was lurking just around the corner.

This was Pierce's ninth season in the league. His best year had been 1953 when he was 18–12. Three times he had been a 15-game winner but had no 20-win seasons until this year, when he was 20–9 and tied Lemon for the league high with 21 complete games. This was his first of two successive 20-win seasons for the White Sox. From 1950 through 1962, only once did he fail to win at least ten games (9–10 in 1954 with 3.48 ERA), and only three times was he below .500.

Lary reached the charmed circle for the first time with 21 wins, which was good enough for first place in the victory category. Lary had the most starts (38) while pitching the league-high 294 innings. From 1955 through 1961, Lary won 117 games, posting losing marks in 1955 (14–15) and 1957 (11–16). In the other five seasons he won between 15 and 23 games. He acquired the nickname "Yankee Killer" because of his ability to beat the Bronx Bombers.

Take away 1955–56 and Hoeft was a poor 61–80. Hoeft was 16–7 in 1955 and followed this with a 20–14 mark this year. The Tigers thought with Lary and Hoeft (and soon to add Jim Bunning), they were all set to challenge the Yankees. However, Lary had a bad season in 1957 and Hoeft won only as many as ten games one more time, in 1958 when he was 10–9. Hoeft pitched for five more teams before calling it a career in 1966 with San Francisco. The promise that was there never matured.

A pitcher's record can be affected by the team for which he plays. In 1956 Art Ditmar played for Kansas City, which finished last. He was in 44 games, 34 as a starter and was 12–22 with a 4.43 ERA. Then, from 1957 through early 1961, he was with the Yankees and posted a 47–32 mark with respectable ERAs each year. He returned to Kansas City where he finished out his career for the balance of 1961 and all of 1962 with a 0–7 mark.

Tom Brewer also had 19 for fourth-place Boston. This was Brewer's biggest season as the closest he came was 16 wins the next year. For his eight-year career, all with the Red Sox, Brewer was 91–82.

Cleveland again topped the loop with 67 complete games, while last-place Kansas City (formerly Philadelphia) had 30. The American League had seen two of the original franchises switch in the past three seasons, with St. Louis and Philadelphia moving to Baltimore and Kansas City, respectively. Lemon, Pierce and Lary were the only pitchers with 20 or more complete games.

Pitcher/Team	G	GS	CG	W	L	Pct	ERA	SO	W	IP
Frank Lary, Det	41	38*	20	21*	13	.618	3.15	165	116	294*
Early Wynn, Cleve	38	35	18	20	9	.690	2.72	158	91	278
Herb Score, Cleve	35	33	16	20	9	.690	2.53	263*	129	249
Billy Pierce, Chgo	35	33	21	20	9	.690	3.33	192	100	276
Bob Lemon, Cleve	39	35	21*	20	14	.588	3.04	94	89	255
Billy Hoeft, Det	38	34	18	20	14	.588	4.06	172	104	248

Score led with five shutouts, while Ford (19–6) had the top winning percentage at .760. Baltimore's George Zuvernik topped the league with 16 saves. Bob Feller ended his career this year with an 0–4 record, but had a career total of 266 wins. There is no doubt that World War II service cost him a chance for 350 victories.

In the World Series, after two games New York was down 2–0, having been outscored 19–11. From that point on New York hurlers threw five straight complete games, two of them shutouts, winning four. Included in the group was Don Larsen's perfect game, the only one ever in World Series history. Stengel had his revenge as New York took the Series four games to three.

NATIONAL LEAGUE: AN OLD-FASHIONED THREE-HORSE RACE

Brooklyn, Milwaukee and Cincinnati battled all season. At the end only two games separated the three teams, as they finished in that order. Brooklyn's hitting fell off, but Don Newcombe made up for it by winning 27 games, the MVP and the first Cy Young Award. In those days only one award was given for both leagues.

Warren Spahn returned to 20-victory status and was aided by 19 from Lew Burdette and 18 from Bob Buhl. Cincinnati was in third, based on their home run power. They tied the existing record at 221, as they had eight in double digits and five to hit at least 28.

Robin Roberts won 19, the most he would win for the rest of his career, but also lost 18 and had a 4.46 ERA. Johnny Antonelli won 20 for sixth-place New York, while Bob Friend captured 17 for seventh-place Pittsburgh.

Newcombe was the whole show for the Dodgers as he had his career-best season with a 27–7 mark. His .794 winning percentage also gave him league honors in this category. Although he was only 30, this was Newcombe's last big season. He fell to 11–12 next year, then was traded to Cincinnati after an 0–6 start in 1958 when the Dodgers moved to Los Angeles. Newcombe finished out his career with Cleveland in 1960. One can't help but think his career total of 149 wins could have been much higher if he had taken better care of himself. As it was, he was finished at age 34.

With 20 wins, Spahn started a six-year string of 20-plus-win seasons, during which time he would lead or tie for the high in victories five consecutive seasons (1957–61). Spahn worked 281 innings while hurling 20 complete games and posting three shutouts to go with his three saves. The trio of Spahn, Burdette and Buhl would soon send Milwaukee to a World Series.

Antonelli had his second and last 20-win season for the New York Giants as he also fashioned a 2.86 ERA and posted five shutouts. Antonelli would slump in 1958 to 12–18, but bounce back to win 16 in 1959 and 19 in 1960. He then finished out his career in 1962 with Cleveland and Minnesota.

Roberts again led with 22 complete games and appeared in 43 with six in relief, and he also had three saves. He did relinquish the innings pitched title to Friend (314), but still logged 297. This year he couldn't blame lack of support for his 18 losses, as he had a poor ERA (4.45)

Brooks Lawrence came close with his best season at 19–10, but his ERA was only 3.99. He was undoubtedly helped by the 221 home runs off the Cincinnati bats. Lawrence pitched in the big leagues for seven seasons, the first two with St. Louis and the last five with Cincinnati. He had four winning seasons and three losing ones as he finished with a 69–62 record. He broke in 15–6 with St. Louis in 1954 and then was 3–8. He then came to Cincinnati and won 19, then 16–13, followed by 8–13, 7–12 and 1–0.

Milwaukee led with 64 complete games and New York was last with 31. Only Roberts and Spahn had 20 or more complete games.

Pitcher/Team	G	GS	CG	W	L	Pct	ERA	SO	W	IP
Don Newcombe, Bkln	38	36	18	27*	7	.794*	3.06	139	46	268
Warren Spahn, MIlw	39	35	20	20	11	.645	2.79	128	52	281
Johnny Antonelli, NY	41	36	15	20	13	.606	2.86	145	75	258

Burdette (19–10) led with six shutouts and 2.71 ERA, while Chicago's Sam Jones was tops in strikeouts with 176.

Brooklyn looked like a shoo-in after the first two games, when they outscored New York 19–11, but then they had only eight runs in the next five games, to revert to their old ways—losing. Newcombe failed in both starts, with a 21.21 ERA, but was charged with only one loss. His career World Series record was 0–4, fueling the argument that he choked in the clutch. It's difficult to say about a pitcher who three times won 20 or more and won 149 games with a career .623 winning percentage. It seems that without those victories, Brooklyn might not have been in the World Series a few times.

1957

AMERICAN LEAGUE: TRAGEDY STRIKES AND A GREAT CAREER IS ENDED

Many were touting the Cleveland Indians to replace New York as the champions based on their great pitching staff, but tragedy struck. Cleveland fell to sixth place as age and injuries caught up with Bob Lemon and he was only 6–11, while 37-year-old Early Wynn was 14–16. Then 24-year-old Herb Score was struck in the eye by a line drive off the bat of Gil McDougald. His career ended almost 20 years to the day after Dizzy Dean was injured.

However, at least Dean had five good full seasons, four times a 20-game winner, including a 30-game season and a World Series Championship. Score's career was over after two seasons. He would hang around for a few years, but never again be an effective pitcher. Meanwhile, the injury so shook McDougald that he was not the same hitter again.

New York got another MVP year from Mickey Mantle but had to use a patchwork pitching staff to win the title, as Whitey Ford had a sore arm and could win only 11 games. New York had six pitchers to win ten games or more.

Chicago was a surprising second as Billy Pierce was 20–12. Pierce tied for the lead with 20 wins and led with 16 complete games, the fewest to date to lead the league. He also recorded two saves, as starters were still being used in relief, although less frequently. Pierce never won 20 games again, but did have five consecutive seasons of ten or more victories and only one losing year. His final career mark was 211–169, but he has never had a nibble for the Hall.

The league's other 20-game winner was Detroit's Jim Bunning. Bunning had broken in with Detroit in mid–July 1955, and over the next two years he appeared in 30 games and was 8–6. This was his first season as a full-fledged starter, and he made the most of it by appearing in 47 games, of which 30 were starts. Bunning was 20–8 with a 2.70 ERA. At 25, it looked like he had many more seasons at this level or better. But Bunning would never again win 20 games, even though he pitched through 1971. However, he turned in a quite credible 224–184 mark for his career, and has been selected to the Hall. I think it shows how difficult it is to be elected, based on the number of excellent pitchers we have seen not selected to date. Bunning's record would have been much better but for three of his last four seasons. In 1968 he was 4–14 with Pittsburgh and for 1970–71 he was 15–27 with Philadelphia. The balance of his career he was 205–143 with only two other losing years, 11–14 in 1960 and 12–13 in 1963. For his career he won 19 in four different years and was a 17-game winner three times.

Ted Williams became the oldest batting champ at 38 when he led the league with a .388 mark. Chicago had the lowest total of complete games to lead the league at 58, while Kansas City set a new low with 26. Three pitchers had more than 10 saves as New York's Bob Grim led with 19, while also winning 12 games.

Pitcher/Team	G	GS	CG	W	L	Pct	ERA	SO	W	IP
Jim Bunning, Det	45	30	14	20	8	.714	2.70	182	72	287*
Billy Pierce, Chgo	37	34	16*	20	12	.625	3.26	171	71	257

Wynn was the strikeout leader with 184, while Chicago's Jim Wilson led with five shutouts. The ERA title went to New York's Bobby Shantz (11–5) at

2.45 while teammate Tom Sturdivant (16–6) had the top winning percentage at .727.

The World Series, except for games three and four, was primarily a pitching Series, but this time the title went to newcomer Milwaukee, four games to three.

NATIONAL LEAGUE: CHAMPIONSHIP FOR THE YOUNG, GLORY TO THE OLD

Brooklyn finished third as many of its players were starting to slow down with age—especially the pitching staff. Don Newcombe was only 11–12, while newcomer Don Drysdale led the way with a 17–9 mark.

However, it was Milwaukee getting an MVP year from Hank Aaron, who barely edged out 36-year-old Stan Musial, and 21 wins from Warren Spahn, with help from Lew Burdette and Bob Buhl that won the pennant.

St. Louis gave a great chase but didn't have the pitching depth to stay with Milwaukee, although Musial racked up his seventh batting title. Only Honus Wagner has more batting crowns in the National League.

Spahn led the loop with 21 wins and 18 complete games. He posted a 2.69 ERA, had four shutouts, and still being used in relief on occasion had three saves. Spahn would lead the league in wins for the next five seasons, while he would lead in complete games in six of the next seven years. Although he was already 36, he was getting better with each season and he would win 23 games at age 42. One can project that, had he started sooner, he might have made 400 wins.

Robin Roberts had the worst year of his career as he was only 10–22, although his 4.04 ERA was better than the previous season when he won 19. He still worked 250 innings and appeared in 39 games, of which 32 were starts.

No other pitcher won 20 games for the season. Milwaukee was tops with 60 complete games while seventh-place Chicago was last with 30 (a new low).

Pitcher/Team	G	GS	CG	W	L	Pct	ERA	SO	W	IP
Warren Spahn, Milw	39	35	18*	21*	11	.656	2.69*	111	78	271

Brooklyn's Johnny Podres led in shutouts (6) and ERA (2.68). Five pitchers had ten or more saves, headed by Brooklyn's Clem Labine with 17. Spahn won the Cy Young Award.

In the World Series, Aaron was the batting star with a .393 mark, three home runs and seven RBIs, but the real hero was Burdette (17–9) who had three complete game wins and a .67 ERA.

1958

AMERICAN LEAGUE: THE YANKEE EXPRESS CONTINUES

The Yankees got their usual good power years from Mickey Mantle, Yogi Berra and Bill Skowron, but it was the magic worked with the pitching staff that carried them to the ten-game margin over Chicago. Only Bob Turley (21–7) and Whitey Ford (14–7) were in double digits, but six other pitchers won between six and nine games each. Ryne Duren emerged as the new bullpen ace with a league-high 20 saves.

Turley had his career-best year as he was 21–7 with the league's top winning percentage (.750). He tied Billy Pierce and Frank Lary for the most complete games at 19. After this season Turley never won over nine games in a year, although he pitched until 1963. In fact, three of his last five years were losing campaigns. Prior to this season he had won 14 for Baltimore in 1954, then 17 with New York in 1955 before slumping to eight in 1956. He had rebounded in 1957 with 13–6 before his big season in 1958.

Pierce had a fine 2.69 ERA, but could only muster a 17–11 year. Lary was 2.91 with the most innings pitched (260), but Detroit didn't give him the necessary support and he finished at 16–15.

Pedro Ramos led in losses for the first of four consecutive seasons. The first three were with Washington and then, when they were transferred to Minnesota, he led the first season there. Ramos lost 75 games over the next four seasons. In a career that covered 13 full and two part seasons, only twice did he finish over .500, as most of the time his teams were deep in the second division. His final career mark was 117–160.

No other pitcher in the league made the charmed 20-win circle. Detroit was tops with 59 complete games, while Washington was last in the standings and complete games with 28.

Pitcher/Team	G	GS	CG	W	L	Pct	ERA	SO	W	IP
Bob Turley, NY	33	31	19*	21*	7	.750*	2.98	168	128*	245

Ford topped the circuit in ERA (2.01) and shutouts (7), while Early Wynn, now with Chicago, led in strikeouts at 179. Bob Turley was the Cy Young Award winner. Ted Williams won his sixth and final batting title at .328.

The Yanks fell behind in the World Series three games to one. They became the first team since 1925 to rally from such a deficit, as they swept the last three games. The pitching hero was Bob Turley with two wins and a save, while Hank Bauer was the hitting star with six runs, ten hits, four home runs, eight RBIs and a .323 average.

NATIONAL LEAGUE: THEY
DID WHAT GREELEY SAID

The big news in the National League was the moving of the Brooklyn and New York Giant franchises to Los Angeles and San Francisco, respectively. Both had been anchors of the league and their fans, especially in Brooklyn, were heartbroken. LA set a new attendance record with 1,845,556, while San Francisco, playing in the old Seals ballpark, drew 1,272,625, almost double their last year at the Polo Grounds.

On the field it was a different story. Los Angeles slipped to seventh place as Roy Campanella was paralyzed from an accident and other veterans were showing their age. The pitching also suffered as the team ERA soared to 4.47. Sandy Koufax was 11–11, his stardom still a few years away.

San Francisco moved into third place on the strength of their attack, especially rookie Orlando Cepeda (25 home runs, 96 RBIs, and a .312 average).

Milwaukee won their second straight title as Warren Spahn and Lew Burdette were 20-game winners. Pittsburgh, after nine years in the second division, made it to second place as Bob Friend won 22 games.

Spahn was again the master as he led with 22 wins, 23 complete games and 290 innings pitched. When the season ended he stood at 246 career wins, with still a long way to go to his final 363, third-most in National League history.

Burdette had pitched two games for the Yankees in 1950 and three for the Braves in 1951 with no record, but his career really began with a 6–11 mark for the old Boston Braves in their final season, 1952. After that he pitched winning ball through 1962, with the last being his fewest wins at ten. Prior to this season Burdette had won 79 games in five seasons as he steadily improved his record. His tops had been 19 in 1956. This was his first of two successive 20-win seasons and would give him 114 for the six-year period 1956–61.

Friend was in his Jekyll season as he had the premier year of his career. He tied Spahn for the lead in victories with 22 and also made the most starts (38). Next season he would have the worst year of his career, 8–19. Throughout his long career he had difficulty putting together successful back-to-back seasons. Only twice did he have as many as two successive winning years. This is another reason he finished with a 197–230 mark.

Philadelphia finished last, but it looked like Robin Roberts was on his way back; after all, he was only 31. Here was Spahn 37 and winning 22 games, so why not Roberts? He posted a 17–14, 3.23 ERA record with 21 complete games for the last-place Phillies. With a break or two he could have won 20 games. However, what looked like the start of a comeback wasn't. He would be 28–43 over the next three seasons, although it should be pointed out that Philadelphia was last each year.

Roberts would then move to the American League and find a new lease on life with Baltimore, where he won 37 games in three winning seasons over

1962–64 before returning to Houston and Chicago in the National League to finish out his career in 1966. His final record was 286–245, but it undoubtedly could have been much better with some breaks and support in his earlier years and when the Phillies were last for four straight seasons. It is conceivable he could have finished with a 325–350 career-win total.

Pittsburgh's Roy Face emerged as the new bullpen hero with a league-high 20 saves. Milwaukee was first with 73 complete games, while Chicago set a new low with only 27. Spahn and Roberts were the only pitchers with 20 or more complete games.

Pitcher/Team	G	GS	CG	W	L	Pct	ERA	SO	W	IP
Warren Spahn, Milw	38	36	23*	22*	11	.667*	3.07	150	76	290*
Bob Friend, Pgh	38	38*	16	22*	14	.611	3.68	135	61	274
Lew Burdette, Milw	40	36	19	20	10	.667*	2.91	113	50	275

Milwaukee's Carl Wiley led with four shutouts, while San Francisco's Stu Miller (6–9) had the best ERA, 2.47. St. Louis' Sam Jones led the league with 225 strikeouts.

Los Angeles and San Francisco both planned new stadiums to be opened the following season, although the Dodgers would have to wait a little longer.

Milwaukee looked like a sure repeat winner in the Series, especially after they took a 3–1 game lead. However, from then on they scored only five runs in three games. Spahn was 2–1 with 2.20 ERA, but last year's hero, Burdette, had a reversal of form and was 1–2 with a 5.64 ERA.

It would be many years before a Braves team would again be in the Series.

1959

AMERICAN LEAGUE: THE SPELL
IS BROKEN, AND A CHANCE FOR ATONEMENT

The Yankees were favored as usual and shocked the world when they fell into last place on May 20. They regrouped to finish third.

Early Wynn showed there was still life in the old arm as he won 22 games, the Cy Young Award and paced Chicago to their first pennant in 40 years, thus giving them a chance to atone for the Black Sox scandal of 1919.

At 39, father time had not yet caught up with Wynn, even though his two prior seasons had been losing ones (14–16 in 1957 and 14–17 in 1958). This year was all Wynn's as he was the league's only 20-game winner. It marked the fifth and last time he would reach that level. He also led with 256 innings pitched. When the season ended Wynn still was 29 victories short of the coveted 300-win club, and time could be running out as he would turn 40 next season.

Cal McLish had been bouncing around the majors, in and out, up and down, since 1944. From 1944 to 1955 he pitched in 65 games scattered over six seasons with a 8–21 mark. It wasn't until 1956 that he landed with Cleveland to stay in the majors. Finally, in 1958—at the age of 31—he became a big winner as he was 16–8. He followed that with his 19–8 record this year, the best of his career. After this season he played for three more teams and finished with Philadelphia in the National League in 1964. His final career mark was 92–92. He probably holds the record for the longest name: he was christened Calvin Coolidge Julius Ceasar Tuskahoma McLish, with the nickname "Buster."

No other pitcher won 20 games. Chicago had two top relief aces in Turk Lown and Gerry Staley, who between them won 17 and saved 29. Cleveland had the most complete games (58), while Boston was last with 38. Ted Williams had his first subpar year at .254, and many were writing his baseball obituary.

Pitcher/Team	G	GS	CG	W	L	Pct	ERA	SO	W	IP
Early Wynn, Chgo	37	37*	14	22*	10	.688	3.16	179	110*	256*

The ERA leader was Baltimore's Hoyt Wilhelm (15–11) at 2.19, while Detroit's Jim Bunning (17–13) led with 201 strikeouts. Wynn's teammate Bob Shaw had the top winning percentage at .750 off his 18–6 record. One of the best records was by last-place Washington's Camilio Pascual who was 17–10 with a 2.64 ERA and had the most complete games (17).

While the White Sox played a good Series, they could not completely atone for their 1919 predecessors, as they lost four games to two. The hitting star of the Series was Ted Kluszewski, who batted .391, had three home runs and ten RBIs.

NATIONAL LEAGUE: FINALLY A WINNER

San Francisco had its new stadium, Los Angeles was still in the offing and we had a donnybrook of a race, eventually won by Los Angeles in a two-game playoff over Milwaukee. It was a sweet victory after losing in the playoffs in 1946 and 1951.

Don Drysdale was the Dodgers' top hurler with 17 wins and Duke Snider the top hitter with 88 RBIs. It was a far cry from the glory days of Brooklyn, but enough to win the pennant.

Warren Spahn and Lew Burdette each won 21 for Milwaukee, while Sam Jones did the same for San Francisco. Roy Face had a remarkable record for Pittsburgh as he saved ten and was 18–1, all in relief.

For the third straight season Spahn grabbed a share of the total win title as he, Burdette and Jones posted identical 21–15 records. Spahn had a 2.96 ERA and was tied with six others for the shutout lead at four. His 292 innings and 21 complete games were the league's best. He was now 38, but like 'Ol Man River, he just kept rolling along.

Burdette posted his career-high victory total while also leading the league in starts with 39. He was second in innings pitched with 290, and his 20 complete games were also second to Spahn. Burdette was noted for his pinpoint control and walked only 38 men for the season.

Meanwhile Jones grabbed the ERA title with a 2.82 mark, but lost the strikeout crown to Drysdale. Jones had led in three of the four prior seasons. After a 2–4 mark with Cleveland in the early 50s, Jones found his way to the Cubs where he was 14–20 and 9–14 in two seasons. Then it was on to St. Louis, where he was 12–9 and 14–13 before coming to San Francisco in a trade for Bill White. This would be Jones' biggest season. He followed with 18 wins in 1960 and then was just 14–14 for four teams from 1961–64, finally retiring in the latter year. His career mark was 102–101.

Milwaukee led with 69 complete games while Chicago was last with 30. Vernon Law joined Spahn and Burdette as 20 complete game pitchers. Law was 18–9 before his big 1960 season that would help Pittsburgh win their first pennant in 33 years.

Pitcher/Team	G	GS	CG	W	L	Pct	ERA	SO	W	IP
Sam Jones, SF	50	35	16	21*	15	.583	2.82*	209	109*	271
Warren Spahn, Milw	40	36	21*	21*	15	.583	2.96	143	70	292*
Lew Burdette, Milw	41	39*	20	21*	15	.583	4.07	105	38	290

Seven pitchers tied with four shutouts. Don Drysdale was the new strikeout king at 242, and Face the percentage champion at .947. Baseball was also writing the death knell for Cardinal great Stan Musial, as he batted only .255.

The Dodgers blended timely hitting and pitching for their Series win, but it was an unknown who was the Series hero. Larry Sherry won two and saved two for the champion Dodgers.

7

1960–1969

—————— **1960** ——————

AMERICAN LEAGUE: STENGEL'S LAST HURRAH

The Yankees tied with Baltimore for the best team ERA and finished 12 games ahead in the standings, mainly on the potent bats of Mickey Mantle, Roger Maris and Bill Skowron. No Yankee pitcher won over 15 games.

No pitcher won 20 games, as Baltimore's Chuck Estrada and Cleveland's Jim Perry were the big winners at 18 each. Chicago's Frank Bauman captured the ERA title (2.68), Perry the winning percentage (.643), Frank Lary led with 15 complete games, Jim Bunning with 201 strikeouts and three pitchers tied with four shutouts.

Baltimore had been in the second division for many seasons but rose to second place this year. One of the main reasons was 22-year-old Chuck Estrada, who tied for the league lead with 18 victories.

Estrada was in 36 games, starting 25 of them. Baltimore thought they had a longtime pitching ace, but Estrada never equaled this season again. He was 15–9 in 1961 and only 8–17 the following year before he had elbow problems. By 1967 he was out of the majors, never to return—another promising career lost.

Perry and his brother Gaylord have 529 career wins, second to the Niekro brothers, Phil and Joe, who have 539 victories. This was Perry's second season and he not only tied for the lead in victories, he also started the most games (36) while leading with four shutouts. Perry was just 24 and the Indians also thought they had found another Bob Lemon or Bob Feller, but such was not to be. After 10–17 and 12–12 seasons, he was traded to Minnesota, but fame didn't come immediately.

In his first six seasons he was only 54–39. While respectable, certainly this is not the pace of a 200-career-win pitcher. It wasn't until 1969 that he became a big winner, and over the next six seasons for Minnesota, Detroit and Cleveland he won 105 games, including a league-high 24 in 1970. This is a story whose threads we will pick up later.

Ted Williams bowed out gracefully, hitting .316 with 29 home runs and 72 RBIs in just 310 at bats to atone for his one bad season.

The Yankees outscored Pittsburgh 55 to 27, out-homered them ten to four, out-batted them .338 to .256, had half the ERA, 3.54 to 7.11, but lost the Series four games to three. They won 16–3, 10–0 and 12–0, but lost 6–4, 3–2, 5–2 and 10–9.

Mickey Mantle batted .400 with three home runs and 11 RBIs, while Bobby Richardson had 11 hits, 12 RBIs and hit .367.

NATIONAL LEAGUE: A GREAT RACE AND AN UNBELIEVABLE FINISH

It had been 33 years since Pittsburgh last won a pennant and then they were steamrolled in four games by the Yankees. This year they fought off Milwaukee and St. Louis to win by seven and nine games respectively.

Vernon Law led the way with a 20–9 mark and the Cy Young Award. Warren Spahn won 21 for Milwaukee as did Ernie Broglio for St. Louis.

Law had been with the Pirates since 1950 and went through those dark, dismal last-place finishes that the Pittsburgh team was noted for in the early and mid–1950s. In his first five seasons, with 1952–53 out for military service, he was only 40–57 with an ERA that was over 4.50 per season. Starting in 1957 he began pitching winning ball with corresponding ERAs. He was 10–8, 14–12 and 18–9 going into the 1960 season.

Law not only won 20 games, but tied Spahn and Lew Burdette for most complete games at 18. The next season Law developed a sore arm, and although he never won 20 games again he did recover and by 1965 was able to win 17. He played his entire career with Pittsburgh, finishing with a 162–147 record.

For Spahn, winning 20 games was becoming old hat. This was his fifth straight and 11th overall. It also marked the fourth consecutive season and seventh in which he led or tied for the most victories. This was also the fifth time he led or tied for complete games, and he would accomplish this three more consecutive years. Although now 39, he pitched like a man ten years younger.

The Cardinals thought they had a real find in Broglio as he tied Spahn for the most victories and had the league's best winning percentage (.700). Broglio appeared in 52 games, of which he started 24. However, this was his only 20 win season. He was 9–12 and 12–9 the next two years before he recovered for a 18–8 year in the spirited drive that the Cardinals made for the pennant in 1963.

Broglio is best remembered as the man traded to the Chicago Cubs for Lou Brock, who went on to become the second-greatest base stealer, to accumulate over 3,000 hits and enter the Hall of Fame. Meanwhile, Broglio developed arm trouble, was only 7–19 in three abbreviated seasons with the Cubs and was out of baseball by 1966. It was another ironic twist to a pitching career.

Roy Face won ten games and set a new National League mark for saves with 24. San Francisco was first with 55 complete games and Cincinnati last with 33.

Pitcher/Team	G	GS	CG	W	L	Pct	ERA	SO	W	IP
Ernie Broglio, STL	52	24	9	21*	9	.700*	2.75	188	100	226
Warren Spahn, Milw	40	33	18*	21*	10	.677	3.49	154	74	268
Vernon Law, Pgh	35	35	18*	20	9	.690	3.08	120	40	272

San Francisco's Mike McCormick (15–12) had the top ERA (2.70), while Don Drysdale led with 246 strikeouts.

Pittsburgh didn't seem to be the team of destiny entering the Series, and when you review the statistics, they lost everything *but* the Series. Law won two games, and Face had three saves.

1961

AMERICAN LEAGUE: EXPANSION AND A NEW RECORD

The first expansion in almost 70 years took place as Los Angeles was granted an American League franchise, as was Washington after the original Senators moved to Minneapolis.

However, equally big news was the pursuit by Roger Maris and Mickey Mantle's of Babe Ruth's fabled 60 home runs in a single season. When it was all over, Maris had 61 in game 162, while Mantle had 54. Because it was not achieved in the old format of 154 games, an asterisk was added to denote that it took an additional eight games to break the Babe's record. Many baseball purists objected to the record being broken, as it was considered a sacred cow.

Meanwhile, on the field Detroit won 101 games but finished in second, eight games behind the Yankees, under new manager Ralph Houk. Casey Stengel had been fired after the Yanks lost the Series. All he did was win ten pennants and seven World Series in 12 years!

The league was replete with power, reminding some of the 1920s or 1930s, although the averages weren't as astronomical. For example, Detroit had Norm Cash (41 HR, 132 RBIs, .361) and Rocky Colavito (40 HR, 140 RBIs and .290).

New York and Detroit had the only two 20-game winners in Whitey Ford and Frank Lary.

Ford had been in the majors since 1950, sans 1951–52 in the army, had a career mark 133–59 and had never had a losing season—nor had he won 20 games. Ford had been on a five-day rotation and only three times had he started 30 or more games. Manager Houk decided to put him on a four-day rotation, and it paid great dividends as Ford started a league-high 39 games and finished with his best record ever—25–4—and the league's top winning percentage

(.862). The question was, Why hadn't Ford been on a four-day rotation all this time?

From 1961 through 1965, at the age of 33 to 37, Ford would average 37 starts per season and win 99 games, with the fewest being 16 in 1965. Twice during that stretch he would exceed 20 wins. During the 1953–60 period he averaged 28 starts and 15.5 victories per year, when he was 25–32. Who was the wiser manager, Casey Stengel or a combination of Houk, Yogi Berra and Johnny Keane? You be the judge.

Lary had last won 20 or more in 1956, then after falling to 11–16 the next year rebounded to win 48 games over 1958–60. He had also led in innings pitched in the even seasons (1956, 58 and 60) as well as complete games in 1958 and 1960. This was his biggest season, with a 23–9 mark and 22 complete games. At 31, Lary looked poised to have several more big seasons, and with 117 wins under his belt seemed certain to break the 200 barrier. However, next year he developed a sore arm and although he tried with several teams through 1965, he could manage only an 11–23 record.

Detroit topped the loop with 62 complete games, and Los Angeles, finishing eighth in a ten-team league, set a new low with 25. The Yankees' Luis Arroyo also set a new save record with 29, while compiling a 15–5 record. Lary was the only pitcher with 20 or more complete games.

Pitcher/Team	G	GS	CG	W	L	Pct	ERA	SO	W	IP
Whitey Ford, NY	39	39*	11	25*	4	.862*	3.21	209	92	283*
Frank Lary, Det	36	36	22*	23	9	.719	3.24	146	66	275

Camilio Pascual led with 221 strikeouts, while Baltimore's Steve Barber (18–12) was tops with eight shutouts. Ford captured the Cy Young Award.

The Yankees were seething for revenge and took it out on Cincinnati, beating them in five games, as Ford won two games and broke Ruth's scoreless consecutive innings string.

NATIONAL LEAGUE: STATUS QUO AND A SURPRISE WINNER

The National League opted not to expand until 1962 and therefore played the standard 154 games, while the junior circuit was playing 162. Next season it would all even up.

Cincinnati, a preseason second division pick, surprised the experts and fought off challenges at various times from Los Angeles and San Francisco to finish four and eight games in front, respectively.

Frank Robinson paced the offense, but it was a surprisingly strong pitching staff that made the difference as Joey Jay won 21, Jim O'Toole 19 and Jim Brosnan and Bill Henry were 12–5 with 32 saves.

Los Angeles got 18 wins each from Johnny Podres and Sandy Koufax, who had finally emerged after several years of mediocrity. Warren Spahn was the loop's other 20-game winner.

Except for 1961–62, Jay's career was less than mediocre as he posted only a 57–67 record for those other seasons. He had several tries with the Milwaukee Braves in the early and mid–50s with little success. Finally, in 1958 he landed a permanent spot on their staff, but over the next three years the best he could do was 9–8 in 1960, and he was a combined 22–24 for the three years. In 1961 he broke through and won 21 games to tie Spahn for the most wins in the league and also for the most shutouts at four. He followed this with another 21-win season in 1962.

At age 40 Spahn was just like good wine: he got better with age. Once again, he won 21 games (the eighth time in his career) as he broke the 20-game circle for the 12th time, one shy of Christy Mathewson's record and tying Walter Johnson for the second-most times winning 20 or more. Spahn again led in complete games, this time with 21, and in a hitters' year had the best ERA at 3.01. He was also used in relief on four occasions, but had no saves.

One pitcher was on his way down while another was on his way up. Lew Burdette had his last big season, winning 18 for the Braves. After this year he would pitch until 1967, but never win over ten again, posting a 40–38 mark for the period. Meanwhile, Koufax was arriving as a top-flight pitcher; he too won 18 games. Prior to this season he had been 36–38, but with his control now in hand he became baseball's best pitcher. Only arthritis forced him into early retirement after the 1966 year. He was 129–47 for the 1961–66 era, and that total was shortened because two of the seasons he was forced to miss at least ten starts each year.

Robin Roberts had a knee injury and was forced to suffer through a 1–10, 5.85 ERA for his last year in Philadelphia. He ended his career with the Phillies with a 234–199, surpassing Pete Alexander's 190 career wins in a Philadelphia uniform. However, it should be remembered that Alexander did his in seven years. Milwaukee led with 67 complete games while last-place Philadelphia had the fewest at 29. Only Spahn had 20 or more complete games.

Pitcher/Team	G	GS	CG	W	L	Pct	ERA	SO	W	IP
Joey Jay, Cinn	34	34	14	21*	10	.677	3.53	157	82	247
Warren Spahn, Milw	36	34	21*	21*	13	.618	3.01*	115	64	263

Spahn and Jay tied for the shutout lead with four, while Koufax took his first strikeout crown with 200. Podres, on his 18–5 mark, led with a .783 winning percentage.

In the World Series, Cincinnati was no match for the Yankee firepower and after knotting the Series at one game apiece, quickly fell apart and lost the last three.

1962

AMERICAN LEAGUE: ONE LAST CHAMPIONSHIP

The Yankees won their third straight pennant, and 12th in 14 seasons, by five games over Minnesota (the old Washington Senators). Ralph Terry paced the Yankee mound corps with 23 wins, while Camilo Pascual picked up 20 for Minnesota.

Los Angeles surprised everybody by finishing third in a season when their top pitcher, Dean Chance, had only 14 wins.

Ray Herbert for Chicago and Dick Donovan for Cleveland were the league's other 20-game winners. Dick Radatz of Boston was the top relief man with 24 saves.

Terry had broken in with the Yankees in 1956, was traded to Kansas City in 1957 and back to the Yankees in 1959. His combined record for that time was an undistinguished 22–38. Finally, in 1960 he posted his first winning season, 10–8. He quickly followed with a 16–3 mark, and then came his big year in 1962 with a 23–12 mark for the most victories in the league. He made 43 appearances, of which 39 were starts, had four shutouts, two saves and pitched 299 innings (most in the circuit).

Terry followed this with a 17–15 mark and at 27 seemed headed for some big years, but they never materialized. He played for four teams over the 1964–67 period before finally retiring with the Mets in 1967. He was only 19–23 during that time. Looking back, we can review his career in three phases, with only the middle one on the plus side.

Pascual had pitched with the old Washington Senators (now the Minnesota Twins) since 1954 and had posted only two winning marks during that time. It should be remembered that the Senators-Twins were often near the bottom of the league. The first phase of his career was from 1954 to 1957 and he was 20–54 with an ERA of approximately 5.00 per game. Then in 1958 he was only 8–12, but did have a very respectable 3.15 ERA. From 1959 through 1968 he pitched winning ball every season except 1961, when he was 15–16 with a league-high eight shutouts and his first of three straight strikeout titles with 221. He also logged a 3.46 ERA. He won 142 games during this 10-year stretch. Finally, in 1962 he broke through and became a 20-game winner for the first of two successive seasons. He led with 18 complete games, five shutouts and 206 strikeouts. Pascual had finally arrived as one of the better pitchers in the league.

Herbert had been pitching in the big leagues since 1950 and regularly since 1953, but had only one winning season (1951 when he was 4–0 in five relief appearances). His record coming into this season was a lackluster 58–68. So most baseball experts were surprised when he posted a 20–9 mark, giving him the league's best winning percentage at .690. Although he pitched four more years, the best he could accomplish was a 13–10 mark the next year. Herbert retired after the 1966 season with a career 104–107 record.

This was Donovan's biggest season as he was 20–10 with 16 complete games. However, unlike some other pitchers, he had enjoyed a certain modicum of success. After abortive attempts in the early 1950s with the old Boston Braves and going 0–4 in 25 games over three years, he finally became a regular with the Chicago White Sox in 1955. From then until this season he had only one losing year (9–10 in 1959). Along the way he led in winning percentage (.727) on a 16–6 record in 1957 as well as complete games (16) that season. However, after this year he would not pitch .500 again. He finished his career with Cleveland and was only 19–25 for his last three seasons. His final career mark was 122–99.

Some items worth mentioning. Milt Pappas never won 20 games in a season during his 16 full year career, but won 209 games, the same as Don Drysdale. Drysdale is in the Hall of Fame, but Pappas isn't. He had only three losing seasons and 14 times won in double digits with seven between 15 and 17. Jim Bunning won 19 for the first of four times as he valiantly tried to make the charmed circle, but would fall just short. Early Wynn posted a 7–15 mark and finished the season with 299 wins, but no team. Would fate step in and lend a hand?

Minnesota led the loop with 53 complete games (a new low record for most complete games), while Los Angeles established a new record for low with 23; they had 47 saves between 11 pitchers.

Pitcher/Team	G	GS	CG	W	L	Pct	ERA	SO	W	IP
Ralph Terry, NY	43	39*	14	23*	12	.657	3.19	176	57	299*
Ray Herbert, Chgo	35	35	12	20	9	.690*	3.27	115	74	237
Dick Donovan, Cleve	34	34	16	20	10	.667	3.59	94	47	251
Camilo Pascual, Mn	34	33	18*	20	11	.645	3.31	206*	59	258

Several pitchers tied with five for the shutout lead. In a hard-fought pitchers' Series (only 41 runs scored by both teams in the seven games), the Yankees outlasted San Francisco as Terry won two games.

NATIONAL LEAGUE: EXPANSION AND ANOTHER NEW RECORD

New York regained a team, getting the New York Mets, who would become baseball's buffoons as they lost a modern-day record 120 games in their maiden season. Their five main starters had a composite 30–92 and the team finished 60½ games out of first. Houston, the other expansion team, finished eighth, pushing Chicago who lost 103 games, into ninth.

Los Angeles won the battle of statistics, but lost for the third time in playoffs, this time to San Francisco. When the dust settled, San Francisco was 103–62 and Los Angeles was 102–63.

Maury Wills had set a new major league record with 104 stolen bases, while teammate Tommy Davis led in RBIs with 153 and his .346 mark edged out Cincinnati's Frank Robinson at .342 and St. Louis' 42-year-old Stan Musial at .330, making one last hurrah. Los Angeles also had the Cy Young winner in Don Drysdale, who won 25 games.

What stopped the LA express was a circulatory problem in Sandy Koufax's finger that sidelined him for the last two months of the year. At the time of his departure he was 14–7, 2.54 ERA and had 216 strikeouts in 184 innings.

San Francisco had its own bombers, with Willie Mays leading the way with 49 home runs, a league high, and 141 RBIs. Orlando Cepeda backed him with 35 and 114. However, it was their pitching that won out in the end. Jack Sanford won 24, ably helped by Billy Odell with 19, Juan Marichal with 18 and Billy Pierce in at 16–6.

Cincinnati won 98 games to finish third as Bob Purkey had 23 and Joey Jay another 21. Art Mahaffey pushed Philadelphia over .500 with his 19 wins.

Since Sanford broke in with Philadelphia in 1957 with a 19–8 mark and a league-high 188 strikeouts, the even years had been his losing seasons and the odd years his winning campaigns. He finally broke that chain by posting 24 wins against only seven losses in 1962, as this was the premier season of his career. Sanford won 16 in 1963, but then was short-circuited by a shoulder injury in 1964 that severely impaired his effectiveness for the next two years. He then went to California in 1966 and, used primarily in relief, posted a 13–7 record. He finished his career with Kansas City the next season. His final career mark was 137–101.

Drysdale spent his entire 14-year career with the Dodgers, won 209 games and was elected to the Hall of Fame. With better support he probably could have won 250. Drysdale was also only 33 when he retired, having suffered a shoulder injury in his final season (1969). The 1962 season proved to be his career-best year as he won the Cy Young Award while leading the majors with 25 victories, a league-high 315 innings and posting a 2.84 ERA. He had been in the league since 1956 and his highest win total had been 17, achieved twice. Again, better support could have made him a winner a couple of times more.

From 1962 through 1967, Drysdale averaged over 40 starts per season, falling below that number only in 1967 with 38. The fewest number of innings he hurled was 278, four times he exceeded 300 and his ERA was over 3.00 only once. Yet despite all this he had two losing seasons, both 13–16 in 1966–67 with a composite 3.07 ERA. For the six years he won 111 and lost 86 with an overall 2.75 ERA. Given better-hitting teams of the era, he probably would have won at least 25 more games and broken the 20-win barrier at least four times, if not five, instead of only twice.

Like many before him and after, Purkey had one premier season and this was it, although he did retire with a career winning record of 129–115. Purkey had pitched for Pittsburgh with little success in the mid–50s (5–15) before joining Cincinnati in 1957. From then until this year he alternated winning and losing seasons, starting with an 11–14 in 1957, until he put together back-to-back winning seasons in 1959–60. This season proved to be his best as he posted a 23–5, 2.81 ERA with the league's best winning percentage at .821. After this year he faded and was 27–29 for his last four years, finishing his career with Pittsburgh in 1966.

Jay's 21 wins gave him back-to-back 20-plus-win seasons for the only really good years of his career. The two years were virtually identical, except he lost four more in 1962. As previously stated, after this season it was all downhill for Jay.

Warren Spahn failed to win 20 games for the first time in seven years as he posted an 18–14, 3.04 ERA record, but did lead with 22 complete games, as he, Odell and Mahaffey were the only pitchers to reach that level.

Marichal showed the greatness that soon would unfold beginning with 1963 as he won 18 games this year. This was his second full season and he had improved from 13 to 18 wins. Next year he would jump to 25 and have four straight seasons at 20 or more victories.

Mahaffey looked like he would become a world-beater for the Phillies as he won 19 games and posted 20 complete ones. However, his star quickly faded and by 1966 he was calling it a career with only a 59–64 mark to show for his efforts.

Not only were the Dodgers deprived of the chance for the World Series, but Koufax lost his opportunity for 20 wins. Twice during the 1962–66 period, injuries would short-circuit his season and keep him from reaching 20 or more victories. In the full seasons he pitched, Koufax started 40–41 games, the other two only 28. More on that later.

This was also the season for big losing pitchers as the league had four 20-game losers. Dick Farrell was 10–20 for Houston even though he sported a 3.01 ERA. Dick Ellsworth was 9–20 for Chicago, but had a 5.08 ERA. Ellsworth would virtually reverse that record next year by winning 22, but then three years later lose 22—a real up-and-down career.

The Mets had two 20-game losers and a third to drop 19. Roger Craig was 10–24 in a career that saw him compile a 74–98 record. He did go on to become a successful manager and coach. Al Jackson was 8–20, a mark he would duplicate for the Mets in 1965. For the era 1962–66, Jackson was 53–88. The third member of that vaunted Met staff was Jay Hook, who checked in with an 8–19 record. Two years earlier he was 11–18 for Cincinnati and in 1963 was 4–14 for the Mets. His final career mark was 29–62.

Journeyman Bob Miller, who pitched all or part of 17 seasons in the big leagues, mainly in relief, with eight different clubs, posted a 1–12 mark in 21 starts and 33 appearances for the Mets this season. He was 0–12 until the final day of the year, when he won his last start and pitched his only complete game. Next year he was with the Dodgers, where he had his biggest season ever with a 10–8 mark.

Seven of the ten teams finished above .500. Roy Face led with 28 saves, as more teams were now getting a relief specialist and complete games kept declining. San Francisco was first with 62, while Chicago was last with 29 (another new record).

Pitcher/Team	G	GS	CG	W	L	Pct	ERA	SO	W	IP
Don Drysdale, LA	43	41*	19	25*	9	.735	2.84	232*	78	314*
Jack Sanford, SF	39	38	13	24	7	.774	3.43	147	92	265
Bob Purkey, Cinn	37	37	18	23	5	.821*	2.81	141	64	288
Joey Jay, Cinn	39	37	18	21	14	.600	3.76	155	100	273

Pittsburgh's Bob Friend (18–14) and St. Louis' Bob Gibson (15–13) tied for the shutout lead at five, while Koufax took the ERA title with 2.54. Warren Spahn (18–14) led with 22 complete games.

The heavy hitting didn't materialize in the Series, and Sanford lost two of three decisions despite a 1.93 ERA. The Giants would have to wait until another time for a World Championship.

1963

AMERICAN LEAGUE: THE DOMINATION CONTINUES

Although Roger Maris and Mickey Mantle missed considerable playing time due to injuries, the Yankees had enough firepower left to win it all by ten games over Chicago. However, it was really their pitching that led the way, as Whitey Ford won 24, Jim Bouton 21 and Ralph Terry 17.

Camilo Pascual had another 20-win season for Minnesota to help put them in third, while Steve Barber cranked out 20 for fourth-place Baltimore. Bill Monbouquette picked up 20 for seventh-place Boston, and teammate Dick Radatz was 15–6 with 25 saves, but lost the save title to Baltimore's Stu Miller, who had 27.

For the second time in three years, Ford led the league in victories as he posted an excellent 24–7 mark. He also led with 269 innings pitched. This was the middle year of his five-season string where he averaged 37 starts and 20 wins per season. Although this was his last 20-plus-win season, he still had enough left to win 17 and 16 the next two years before a shoulder injury slowed him down in 1966–67 and forced his retirement and abandonment of any chance for 300 wins.

Bouton was one of those pitchers who bloomed fast and then faded. After a rookie 7-7 season, he won 21 and would add 18 next year, but then quickly fade. He was 4–15 in 1965 and 12–21 for the years 1966–70, pitching for several teams. He tried a comeback in 1978 with Atlanta and was 1–3, 4.97 ERA in five games. Bouton is probably better remembered for his infamous baseball tell-all book, "Ball Four." He finished at 62–63.

Pascual had his biggest year with a 21–9 mark and led with 18 complete games and his third straight strikeout title with 202. After this season Pascual pitched winning ball for five more seasons, but never again approached 20 wins. An arm injury slowed him down for the 1965–66 seasons, but he recovered enough to have winning years in 1967–68 pitching for the second division Washington Senators.

This was Barber's only 20-win season, but coming back from an elbow injury gave high hopes to the Baltimore club. However, he never again approached that level; 15 the next season was his best. Then a second elbow injury in 1966 limited his activity as Barber turned in a 10–5 season. This time he couldn't fully recover from his injury, and although he pitched until 1974 for several teams he was no longer the same effective pitcher, as witnessed by his 30–40 record. His final mark stands at 121–106.

Monbouquette is another of those pitchers who had one good season among several that were mediocre or less. For his career he was 114–112, but take away this 20–10 mark and he is less than .500. Monbouquette had won 43 games while losing 38 the three previous seasons. Ironically, his ERA of 3.81 in 1963 was the highest of the four seasons, when the most he had won prior had been 15 in 1962. After this season he fell to 13–14, then 10–18, and by 1968 was calling it a career.

The Yankees had the most complete games at 59, while Boston and Washington had the fewest at 29. Early Wynn finally got his 300th win as he was 1–2 with Cleveland. After registering that benchmark figure, he promptly retired.

Pitcher/Team	G	GS	CG	W	L	Pct	ERA	SO	W	IP
Whitey Ford, NY	38	37	13	24*	7	.774*	2.74	189	56	269*
Jim Bouton, NY	40	30	12	21	7	.750	2.53	148	87	249
Camilo Pascual, Mn	31	31	18*	21	9	.700	2.47	202*	81	248
B Monbouquette, Bos	37	36	13	20	10	.667	3.81	174	42	267
Steve Barber, Balt	39	36	11	20	13	.606	2.75	180	92	259

Chicago's Ray Herbert led with seven shutouts, while Chicago's Gary Peters (19–8) led with a 2.33 ERA.

New York headed into the World Series against their old rivals, the Los Angeles Dodgers, whom as Brooklyn and LA they had defeated six of seven times. However, this was not their year as they lost four straight with Ford taking two of the losses.

NATIONAL LEAGUE: REVENGE IS SWEET—A FOND FAREWELL

This was the 21st and final full season for Cardinal great Stan Musial. When he retired he owned almost every National League and many major league records. The only two in the National that eluded him were triples, where he was 18th, and home runs, where he was second when he retired.

St. Louis gave a spirited race to Los Angeles and almost caught them with a 19 out of 20 run, but came up a little short. Los Angeles was not to be denied, as Sandy Koufax was fully recovered and came of age. He won 25 games to capture both the MVP and Cy Young Award. Teammate Don Drysdale had 19 and reliever Ron Perranoski was 16–3, 1.67 ERA, 21 saves, but the save leader was Lindy McDaniel with 22.

Juan Marichal tied Koufax with 25 wins for his first of four straight 20-plus seasons. Jim Maloney was a 23-game winner for Cincinnati, as was Warren Spahn for Milwaukee. This marked the 13th and final time Spahn would win 20 games. At season's end he had 350 career victories, and it looked like he would break the National League mark shared by Pete Alexander and Christy Mathewson of 373.

One of the best pitching jobs was by Dick Ellsworth, who with a 22–10 mark put Chicago over .500, as seven teams again scaled the .500 mark.

Koufax was simply brilliant as he led with 25 wins, 1.88 ERA, 11 shutouts and 306 strikeouts. This was the first of three times he led in shutouts, his second strikeout crown and the first of three times he would exceed 300 innings pitched as he worked 311. Koufax achieved 20 complete games, a goal he would reach two more times. Next season he would be limited to 28 starts and step down with a 19–5, 1.74 record with a league-high seven shutouts, although he missed 12 starts. Injuries deprived him of another fine season in 1964, but he would have 1965–66 to recover. His ERA title was his second in a string of five straight from 1962 through 1966, with the highest being 2.54 in 1962 and three of the years below 2.00. His was a truly brilliant career shortened by arthritis at age 31.

Drysdale didn't win 20 but actually had a better ERA—2.63 compared to 2.84—than in his Cy Young season. He certainly deserved better than a 19–17 record. With any breaks he could have posted another 25-win season. Drysdale worked 315 innings, but was second to Marichal's 321.

Marichal's wins tied Koufax for the league lead with 25 wins, and this also marked the first of four straight seasons in which he was in the charmed circle. From 1963 through 1966, Marichal won 93 games and also had 89 complete games, three times over 20. He and Koufax were throwbacks to another era. His 321 innings marked the first of four times he would exceed 300 innings pitched.

Maloney had been with Cincinnati since 1960 and had a career 17–20 mark when he exploded on the scene in 1963 with his best year ever at 23–7. However, Maloney was not like many others who had one season or two at the most and then faded. From 1962 through 1968, Maloney twice won 20 or more, fanned over 200 batters in four seasons and won 105 while losing 55 with a composite 2.90 ERA. Then in 1969 he suffered a foot injury and his career was basically ended, although he hung around until 1971. His final mark was 134–84. Here was yet another potentially great career shortened by injury.

For Spahn this was his swan song. At age 42, he gave it all he had in posting a 23–7, 2.60 ERA record. He had hopes of 400 career wins, or at least surpassing Pete Alexander and Christy Mathewson. Neither would happen. The next season he was 6–13, 5.28 ERA and then finished at 7–16 with San Francisco and the Mets for his curtain call in the majors. When he retired he was the winningest left-handed pitcher (363) in the history of the game, and he still is. He ranks third amongst all pitchers in total wins in the National League.

Ellsworth went from a 9–20, 5.08 ERA to 22–10, 2.10 ERA for a team that, without him, would have finished eighth or ninth in the league. Ellsworth also recorded 19 complete games as he pitched 291 innings. Any hopes that he would continue pitching like this soon faded as he was 36–55 with a 3.85 ERA over the next three seasons. He would be 16–7, 3.03 ERA for the Red Sox in 1968 and then drift with several teams before finishing with Milwaukee in 1971.

New York was again last, this time losing 111. Roger Craig lost 18 in a row enroute to a 5–22 season, although he had a respectable 3.78 ERA. This gave Craig 46 defeats in two seasons. Al Jackson, who had lost 20 the year before, dropped 17 this season.

Milwaukee was number one with 56 complete games while Pittsburgh was last with 34. Spahn led with 22 complete games and Koufax was the only other member of the 20 complete game club.

Pitcher/Team	G	GS	CG	W	L	Pct	ERA	SO	W	IP
Sandy Koufax, LA	40	40	20	25*	5	.823	1.88*	306*	58	311
Juan Marichal, SF	41	40	18	25*	8	.758	2.41	248	61	321*
Warren Spahn, Milw	33	33	22*	23	7	.767	2.60	102	49	260
Jim Maloney, Cinn	33	33	13	23	7	.767	2.77	265	88	250
Dick Ellsworth, Chgo	37	37	19	22	10	.688	2.10	185	75	291

Koufax was number one with 11 shutouts, while teammate Perranoski had the best winning percentage at .842 with his 16–3 mark. The Dodger pitching staff held New York to four runs in four games, as Koufax won twice, both complete game victories. Ironically, Drsydale pitched the LA shutout in game three.

1964

AMERICAN LEAGUE: THE END OF A DYNASTY

No one knew it when the season began, but this would be the last Yankee team to challenge for a pennant for a dozen years. The dynasty was ending with their swan song in the World Series.

The pennant race went down to the wire as only two games separated New York, Chicago and Baltimore in that final order of finish. New York had no 20-game winners, but had 18 from Jim Bouton and 17 from Whitey Ford, while Chicago got 20 from Gary Peters and 19 from Juan Pizzaro.

The only other 20-game winner was Dean Chance for California. He helped put them over .500 and in fifth place. Boston's Dick Radatz was the top reliever with 16 wins and 29 saves.

From 1959 through 1962, Peters pitched in 12 games with a 0–1 mark for Chicago. Then in 1963 he was 19–8 with the league's best ERA (2.33). This season he won 20 for the first time as he tied for the lead in wins and had a 2.50 ERA. It looked like the Sox had a left-handed Ted Lyons or Red Faber, but such was not to be. The most he ever won again was 16 for Chicago in 1967 and the same number for the Red Sox in 1970. He would lead the league with a 1.98 ERA in 1966, but was only 12–10.

Peters had another fine ERA (2.28) in 1967 when he won 16 games for the White Sox, but after that the best he could record was 3.75 the next year, as he was only 4–13. His last four seasons were spent with the Red Sox with ERAs over 4.00 each season and a composite 43–40 mark. He left the majors with a 124–103 record.

Chance had a tremendous year. Looking back, one must wonder how he lost nine games and why he didn't win 25 or even 30. Chance was 20–9 with a sparkling 1.65 ERA, without a doubt the best in the league. He was also first with 15 complete games (fewest ever to lead to this point), 11 shutouts and 278 innings hurled. He also fanned 207 batters.

Chance had two full seasons under his belt and was 27–28 coming into this year, albeit with a very fine 3.09 ERA. Chance would win 20 one more time, in 1967, and although he had very good ERAs he never had the type of consistent winning seasons one would expect. His record with California for the next two years was 15–10, 3.15 ERA and 12–17, 3.08 ERA. Then traded to Minnesota, he was 20–14, 2.73 ERA and 16–16 with 2.53 ERA.

Why didn't he have better seasons? Partly it was the caliber of the teams behind him, primarily in California. However, another factor may be his penchant for having a good time. He and journeyman pitcher Bo Belinsky loved to bask in the limelight of Hollywood and often could be seen squiring beautiful starlets to the nightclubs at all hours of the night. This latter factor probably had more to do with his failure to live up to his promise, especially in California. Then at age 28 in 1969 he suffered an arm injury, and though he hung around three more seasons was finished by 1971. His final career mark of 128–115 is much less than should have been achieved by someone with his talents.

Records were set for lowest number of complete games. The high was only 47 by Minnesota and the low, 18, by last-place Kansas City.

Pitcher/Team	G	GS	CG	W	L	Pct	ERA	SO	W	IP
Gary Peters, Chgo	37	36	11	20*	8	.714	2.50	205	104	274
Dean Chance, LA	46	35	15*	20*	9	.690	1.65*	207	86	278*

Chance was tops with 11 shutouts, while Baltimore's Wally Bunker (19–5) had the best winning percentage at .782. Chance also was the Cy Young Award winner.

New York met St. Louis for the fifth time in the World Series. The teams had split their first four meetings. Bouton won two games. Ford pitched only in the opening game and was the loser, finishing his World Series career with a 10–8 mark, both records.

Ralph Houk had been promoted to general manager at the start of the season and Yogi Berra named field manager, but after losing the Series he was fired and replaced with the winning manager, former Cardinal Johnny Keane.

NATIONAL LEAGUE: A LONG DROUGHT IS ENDED—NEW STARS ON THE HORIZON

During the 1920s, 30s and 40s, the St. Louis Cardinals had been the most dominant team in the league, but then fell out of contention for most of the 1950s, despite having Hall of Famer Stan Musial. However, the acquisition of Lou Brock and bringing Bob Gibson from their farm system paved the way for a run at the pennant in the 1960s.

In a four-team race not decided until the final day of the season, St. Louis edged out Cincinnati and Philadelphia by one game and San Francisco by two. Philadelphia had led by 10½ games on Labor Day, but had a complete collapse.

St. Louis had strong pitching with Ray Sadecki winning 20, Gibson adding 19 and Curt Simmons 18 more. Juan Marichal won 21 for San Francisco, but no one else won over 12 on the staff. The league leader was former Cardinal Larry Jackson, who won 24. Complete games didn't decline as much in the National League as Chicago led with 58, while Houston was last with 30. Houston's Hal Woodeshick was the top relief man with 23 saves, although he had only a 2–9 win-loss mark.

Sadecki pitched in the majors for 18 seasons, compiling a 135–131 record and including this season won in double digits only five times. Without a doubt, 1964 was his year. Sadecki posted 20 wins, becoming the first Cardinal lefty since Harvey Haddix to scale that hill. This was Sadecki's fifth season and the Redbirds thought they finally had another pitcher to compliment their budding right handed ace Gibson. This dream was to be short lived as Sadecki quickly fell to 6–15 with a 5.20 ERA and four complete games in 28 starts. By 1966 he was with San Francisco and this was the beginning of his drifting, which would eventually take him to five other clubs.

Gibson, though falling one short of the charmed circle, continued to improve as his victories over the past four years had climbed from 13 to 15 to 18 and now 19. Next season he would win 20 for the first of five times. This year a rain out deprived him of his possible 20th win as he was leading at the time the game was called. An injury in 1967 would keep him from a 20-game season. Thus, a rain out and an injury cost him a seven-year streak of 20 wins. Only Christy Mathewson and Walter Johnson had more than seven consecutive 20-plus-win seasons.

Marichal picked up his second straight 20-plus win season. His fate would be similar to that of Eddie Plank, as he too would always be the bridesmaid and never win the Cy Young Award. No matter how well he pitched, it seemed as if someone else always had a better year that season. Twice he won 25 and once 26, but still lost out in the race for the pitcher's dream award. Still, in 15 full seasons he posted only two losing years (1972, 6–16 and 1973, 11–15) while posting an overall 243–142, .631 winning percentage, good for a tie for 23rd on the all-time list.

Jackson had been in the majors since 1955 and had always been considered good enough to be the third starter on a team, although he was number one on the Cardinals for many years, due primarily to their weak pitching staffs at the time. Prior to 1964 his biggest season had been 1960, when he led the league with 282 innings pitched and was 18–13. He pitched for St. Louis through 1962 and was 101–86 against a career mark of 194–183. He was traded to Chicago in 1963 and went 14–18 his first year in the Windy City. Then came 1964 and his career-best season as he led the majors with 24 victories. Statistically this was by far his greatest season as he had a career-high 19 complete games as well as 298 innings and his third best ERA (3.14). Jackson pitched one more year with Chicago and then finished with Philadelphia through 1968 with a 41–45 record.

Jim Bunning won 19 games for the second time in his career and the first of three straight seasons for Philadelphia. It seems no matter how hard he tried he always came up one victory short in his quest to join the charmed circle once again. This was also the first of four straight seasons in which he fanned 200 or more batters.

Don Drysdale continued to pitch in tough luck season. He started a league-high 40 games, completed 21 and posted the best ERA (2.19) of his career, but was only 18–16. The Dodgers scored the third-fewest runs in the league and Drysdale suffered more than his share of low-run losses. Compare his earned run average to Sadecki's (3.68) or Jackson's (3.14) and you see the inequity in final pitching records. He also led with 321 innings, his third season in a row over 300.

Pitcher/Team	G	GS	CG	W	L	Pct	ERA	SO	W	IP
Larry Jackson, Chgo	40	38	19	24*	11	.686	3.14	148	58	298
Juan Marichal, SF	33	33	22*	21	8	.724	2.48	206	52	269
Ray Sadecki, STL	37	32	9	20	11	.645	3.68	119	60	270

Los Angeles suffered misfortune as for the second time in three years Sandy Koufax's season was cut short. He led in ERA with 1.74 and winning percentage at .792 based on his 19–5 record. He missed seven weeks of the season. Pittsburgh's Bob Veale (18–12) took the strikeout crown at 250.

Warren Spahn started the season only 23 games behind the all time National League leader, but showed he didn't have it anymore. He was only 6–13, with a 5.28 ERA.

Gibson lost the second game of the Series, but came back to win games five and seven with complete game victories and start a string of seven consecutive complete game wins over three World Series. In August, Cardinal owner Gussie Busch, upset with his team, fired general manager Bing Devine and rumor was that manager Johnny Keane was on his way out. After the Series, Keane became manager of the Yankees, the team he had just defeated.

1965

AMERICAN LEAGUE: THE END OF AN ERA—FINALLY ANOTHER PENNANT

The Yankees started the season as the favorites to win their sixth straight pennant, but key injuries and collapse of other players led to a sixth-place finish, their lowest since 1925 when they finished seventh in an eight-team league. Jim Bouton (38–20 the two previous seasons) was 4–15.

Minnesota (formerly the Washington Senators) finally won a pennant, paced by home run bats, the pitching of 21-game winner Mudcap Grant and 18-game winner Jim Kaat.

Chicago was second, but had no pitcher to win over 15. Nor did Baltimore in third, one game back. Three new pitchers surfaced who would have impact in coming years. Detroit had Denny McLain at 16–6, 2.62 ERA and Mickey Lolich at 15–9, 3.43 ERA, while Cleveland had fireballer Sam McDowell, 17–11, 2.18 ERA with 325 strikeouts (tops in the league).

Grant is another of those pitchers who had one big season and then was just another hurler the rest of his career, pitching just over .500. Grant pitched for Cleveland from 1958 through early 1964, compiling a 67–63 record. However, 1965 was Grant's year as he compiled a 21–7 mark for the league's best winning percentage (.750) and led with six shutouts. He also started 39 games, which meant he had 11 no-decisions. However, this was his season as he pitched Minnesota to its first-ever title, and counting the old Washington Senators, the first one since 1933.

Kaat started a league-high 42 games and was 18–11, which meant he had 13 no-decisions. This was the third time in four years that Kaat had won at least 17 games. Kaat broke in with Minnesota in late 1959 and through 1961 was just 10–24, when finally in 1962 he won 18 games. After that his only full losing season with Minnesota was 1971 when he was 13–14. We will be hearing more about Mr. Kaat next season.

McDowell won his first of five strikeout titles. From 1965 through 1970, the fewest number of batters he fanned in a season was 225 in 1966. Cleveland had images of another Bob Feller or even Herb Score, but neither materialized. From 1964 through 1971 his ERA was above 3.00 only twice, but with relatively weak teams behind him, McDowell was only 122–107. His other problem was control: he walked at least 100 batters every season from 1964 through 1971.

New York had the only other 20-game winner in Mel Stottlemyre as he led the league with 18 complete games. It would be Stottlemyre's misfortune to pitch for the weakest Yankee teams in almost 50 seasons. Nevertheless, in an 11-season career, all with New York, he was 164–139, 2.97 ERA with three 20-win seasons. A shoulder injury in 1974 at age 33 forced him to retire early. Certainly the Yankee teams of earlier years would have produced more wins for the game right-hander.

Complete games were continuing their decline, as 13 pitchers had ten or more saves, headed by Washington's Ron Kline with 29. Detroit was tops with 45 complete games while Kansas City was last in the standings and complete games with 18.

Pitcher/Team	G	GS	CG	W	L	Pct	ERA	SO	W	IP
Mudcap Grant, MN	41	39	14	21*	7	.750*	3.30	142	61	270
Mel Sottlemyre, NY	37	37	18*	20	9	.690	2.63	155	88	291*

Grant won two games in the Series, and Kaat pitched well but lost two of three decisions.

NATIONAL LEAGUE: A CHAMP FALLS AND A NEW ONE TAKES OVER

St. Louis was expected to repeat but fell to seventh place despite Bob Gibson's first 20-win season. MVP Ken Boyer slowed badly, and pitchers Ray Sadecki and Curt Simmons went from 38–20 to 15–30.

The Dodgers and Giants fought it out again just like they did in the old days in New York, with Los Angeles the victor. Sandy Koufax and Don Drysdale won 49 games between them, while Ron Perranoski saved 17. Koufax won the Cy Young Award and was second in MVP voting to Willie Mays.

Juan Marichal had his third successive season in excess of 20 wins, while Cincinnati boasted two 20-game winners in Sammy Ellis and Jim Maloney. Tony Cloninger had 24 to help put Milwaukee into the final first division slot. Jim Bunning won 19 for the second of three straight seasons, which placed Philadelphia at 85–76.

Koufax had his greatest season to date as he led with 26 wins, 27 complete games, 336 innings, 2.04 ERA and a new major league single-season strikeout record at 382. Koufax had truly arrived. This season marked the fifth time in his career he averaged better than ten strikeouts per game. He truly was the greatest pitcher in the game at this time. At only age 30 and 138 victories to his credit, everyone was talking 300 wins and maybe even surpassing Warren Spahn or setting a new National League record for career victories. However, next season would tell us another story.

Drysdale gave the Dodgers another strong pitching effort with a 2.78 ERA on 20 complete games in 42 starts, and this time he got better support, although the team scored six fewer runs than in 1964. At least when Drysdale was pitching they scored enough to allow him his second 20-plus win season. Even though Drysdale continued pitching effective ball, the most he ever won again was 14, and he would be forced to retire in 1969 due to a shoulder injury that ended his career at age 33.

Marichal continued in the role of bridesmaid as he had 22 wins for his third straight season in the charmed circle. He also posted 24 complete games, second in the league, had a brilliant 2.14 ERA and registered ten shutouts. He would have been a cinch Cy Young winner in almost any other season, but not with Koufax in the league at this time.

Maloney won 20 games for the second time in three years as he posted a 20–9, 2.54 ERA record with 244 strikeouts. This was his last 20-win season, although he pitched good winning ball for the next four years. Injuries would force his early retirement in 1971 at age 31—another potentially great career lost to the injury game.

Following a 10–3 mark in 1964, compiled mostly in relief, Ellis was 22–10 for the Reds in 1965 with a relatively high 3.78 ERA. Still, the Cincinnati brass thought they had a strong one-two pitching duo in Ellis and Maloney. Although Maloney would last for several more years and pitch winning ball, Ellis didn't. He quickly faded as he was 12–19, 5.29 ERA in 1966 and by 1969 he was out of the major leagues, never again posting a winning season. He was 30–43 for the rest of his career.

Cloninger spent the bulk of his career with the Milwaukee and then Atlanta Braves. In 1965 he had his career-best season as he won 24 games while hurling 16 complete in 38 starts. This was the middle year of his three best in the majors. He had been 19–14 in 1964 and would be 14–11 the next season. After that he faded quickly, played out with Cincinnati and then finished with St. Louis in 1972. His mark for those years was 32–45. An interesting side note is that he once hit two grand slam home runs in a game, on July 3, 1966.

Gibson posted his first 20-win season as he also pitched 20 complete games. For his career Gibson would have five seasons of 20 or more victories, with the previously mentioned rain out and a broken leg keeping him from seven. Gibson would soon challenge not only for the best right-hander in the league, but its best pitcher. He also proved he was an all-around athlete as he smashed five home runs.

Larry Jackson had almost a complete reversal of his 1964 season as he was 14–21, but with a respectable 3.84 ERA. Al Jackson lost 20 games for the second time in four seasons, giving him 73 defeats during that span. However, teammate Jack Fisher stole the show with 24 losses and only eight wins with a respectable 3.93 ERA. Fisher lasted 11 seasons in the big leagues with only two at or above .500; his final mark was 86–139.

New York lost 112 games to finish last and give them 452 losses in their first four seasons. They had two 20-game losers, giving them six for the four years. Chicago's Ted Abernathy led all relievers with 31 saves as he appeared in 84 games.

Pitcher/Team	G	GS	CG	W	L	Pct	ERA	SO	W	IP
Sandy Koufax, LA	43	41	27*	26*	8	.765*	2.04*	382*	71	336*
T Cloninger, Milw	40	38	16	24	11	.686	3.29	211	119*	279
Don Drysdale, LA	44	42*	20	23	12	.657	2.78	210	66	308
Sammy Ellis, Cinn	44	39	15	22	10	.688	3.78	183	104	264
Juan Marichal, SF	39	37	24	22	13	.629	2.14	240	46	295
Jim Maloney, Cinn	33	33	14	20	9	.690	2.54	244	110	255
Bob Gibson, STL	38	36	20	20	12	.625	3.07	270	103	299

Marichal not only led with ten shutouts, but also hitting catchers with baseball bats: one. On August 22nd, he hit LA catcher John Roseboro in the head with a bat during a heated dispute. Marichal was fined $1,750 and suspended nine days.

Koufax's 382 strikeouts set a new single-season record. It should be noted that batting averages were falling, home runs increasing, although not necessarily runs scored, and strikeouts were up at an alarming rate. Nine pitchers fanned over 200 batters, and a few years ago any one of 15 or more could have led the league. Fifteen players fanned over 100 times, led by Dick Allen's 150. This trend would continue on through the 1990s, although averages would rise again.

Koufax won two more in the World Series, with a .38 ERA as Los Angeles became World Champions. The Milwaukee Braves had asked permission to move to Atlanta at the start of the season but were told they had to wait until 1966. As a result, Milwaukee fans were apathetic, and only 555,000 showed up.

Warren Spahn finished his career with the hapless Mets and San Francisco, compiling a 7–16 mark with an ERA over 4.00. He called it a career with 363 wins and 13 seasons of 20 or more.

1966

AMERICAN LEAGUE: ANOTHER DROUGHT ENDED

Baltimore won its first pennant, and only second for the franchise when we add the St. Louis Browns' 1944 pennant. Baltimore had been the benefactor of a trade in which they received Cincinnati star Frank Robinson. All he did was win the triple crown and MVP as he paced them to the World Series. Baltimore had no pitcher to win over 15 games, but had enough depth and batting power to take it all.

Minnesota finished second mainly on their power and the 25 wins of Jim Kaat, while Mudcat Grant slipped to 13-13. Denny McLain turned in his first 20-win season and New York fell into last place.

Kaat had the biggest season of his long career, which covered four decades from 1959 through 1983, a span of 25 seasons. All but two were complete years. Kaat's 25 wins, 41 starts, 19 complete games and 305 innings pitched were the best in the league. Although he pitched winning baseball for Minnesota in five of the next six seasons, the most he ever won was 14, three years in a row, 1968–70. He would not have a 20-win season again until he pitched for the Chicago White Sox in the 1970s.

McLain posted his first 20-win season, and would shortly add two more. By 1969 he would be considered the best pitcher in the American League, and with Gibson rated as one of the top two in baseball. Then his world would collapse and a potential 300-game winner and sure Hall of Famer would be out of baseball by 28, and in a few years in prison. But we are getting ahead of our story.

Mel Stottlemyre had almost a complete reversal of his 1965 record as he was 12–20, with the Yankees finishing last. Stottlemyre pitched effectively enough, but the Yankees didn't have a hitter over .288 (this was Mantle, as his career was winding down).

Kansas City's Jack Aker was the top reliever with 32, while Minnesota had the most complete games (52) and Kansas City the fewest (19).

Pitcher/Team	G	GS	CG	W	L	Pct	ERA	SO	W	IP
Jim Kaat, MN	41	41*	19*	25*	13	.658	2.74	205	55	305*
Denny McLain, Det	38	38	14	20	14	.588	3.92	192	104	264

Chicago's Gary Peters had the best ERA (1.98), but could go only 12–10, while Cleveland's Sonny Siebert was 16–8 for the top winning percentage at .667. Teammate Sam McDowell had a sore arm, but still led in strikeouts with 225. Chicago's Tommy John (14–11) led with five shutouts.

Baltimore completed a fantastic season by sweeping Los Angeles in four straight in the World Series.

NATIONAL LEAGUE: A REPEAT CHAMPION AND A PREMATURE END

These were still the days of the reserve clause, so Sandy Koufax and Don Drysdale both held out and missed spring training. Koufax signed for $125,000 and Drysdale for $110,000. Missing spring training didn't hurt Koufax as he had his finest season ever at 27–9, with a 1.74 ERA to win his third Cy Young Award and finish second in MVP voting for the second consecutive season. However, Drysdale was not as fortunate; he was only 13–16, with 3.42 ERA.

San Francisco finished 1½ games back of Los Angeles, despite 20-plus-win seasons from Juan Marichal and Gaylord Perry. Chris Short with 20 wins and Jim Bunning with his customary 19 pitched Philadelphia into fourth place. Meanwhile, Atlanta in their new home took fifth, as Hank Aaron garnered the home run crown with 44.

Koufax had his greatest season as he led with 27 wins, 27 complete games in 41 starts, 323 innings, 317 strikeouts, five shutouts and a skimpy 1.73 ERA.

It was all Koufax. It looked like the world was his oyster as he had won 78 games in his last three full seasons. When we add the 19 he won in a shortened season, it can easily be seen that he would have had another 25–27 wins. He was just 30, and many were now talking about him setting a new National League record for victories by pitchers. Even though he had only 165 wins to this point, based on his performance of the past three years, the statisticians quickly calculated that he could reach 400. This certainly boded well for the Los Angeles franchise and baseball in general, as he was a tremendous drawing card wherever he pitched. Then fate dealt him a cruel blow. He was told by doctors that if he continued pitching he could well become a permanent cripple, as the arthritis in his left arm was that advanced and severe. He could probably lead a normal life only if he retired from baseball. With the potential of so many records that could be his, it was a hard decision to make. But with the end of the World Series, he called it a career.

Marichal had another great season as he led with .806 winning percentage based on his 25–6 mark, 2.23 ERA, 25 complete games in 36 starts and 307 innings pitched. However, as great a year as he had, it wasn't enough to earn him the Cy Young, because Koufax was in the league. Once again Marichal was a bridesmaid.

Perry had been in the league since 1962 and was 24–30 for his first four seasons. Nothing in his record indicated he would eventually win 314 games, enter the Hall of Fame and team with his brother Jim to become the second-winningest brother pitching team of all time with 529 wins. In 1966, Perry joined the charmed circle for the first time with his 21–8 mark while posting a 2.99 ERA. This was also the first of four straight and eight overall years that his ERA would be less than 3.00 for the season. For the next 14 seasons, the fewest number of victories Perry had was 12, the only time he won less than 15, with five times exceeding 20 and posting a 255–187 for the period. We will return to Mr. Perry several more times over the next many seasons.

Bob Gibson was the league's other 20-game winner. Not only did he win 20 for the second straight season, but he had his best year to date with 21 wins, 2.44 ERA and a league-high five shutouts (tying Koufax). This was the fifth straight season Gibson won more games than the prior year. Heading into 1967 it didn't seem like he would do otherwise for that year, but fate would enter the picture, as it has and will continue to do with so many pitchers.

For Short this was the culmination of three seasons of fine work, as he progressed from 17 to 18 and finally to 20 victories, giving him a 55–30 mark for the 1964–66 era. When we review Short, we can look at his career in three phases. The first phase is 1960–63, when he had losing records in three of the four seasons, with an ERA of about 5.00 for the first two and just over 3.00 for the last two. His combined record was 32–42. The second phase we have just reviewed. The third begins with 1967 and a knee injury that forced him to miss over a dozen starts; although posting a fine 2.40 ERA, he was only 9–11. He bounced back to win 19 games in 1968, but then a back injury rendered him virtually useless for the 1969 season. He tried a comeback and although he pitched through 1973, he never had another winning season and was 20–36 for the final four seasons. His was another career that "might have been," "could have been," but wasn't better. He retired with a 135–132 record.

Although posting a respectable 3.98 ERA, Dick Ellsworth led the league with 22 losses, marking the second time he had lost 20 or more games in a season. Over the past seven seasons he had one winning year, 1963, when he won 22 games. The other six years he was a composite 62–99. He was another example of a pitcher that had one shining moment in an otherwise gloomy career.

Los Angeles also had the premier relief pitcher in Phil Regan, who was 14–1 with a league-high 21 saves. Los Angeles, San Francisco and Philadelphia tied for the high in complete games with 52, while last-place Chicago (59–103) was last with 28. The New York Mets made it to ninth place, losing only 95 games, the first time less than 109.

Pitcher/Team	G	GS	CG	W	L	Pct	ERA	SO	W	IP
Sandy Koufax, LA	41	41*	27*	27*	9	.750	1.73*	317*	77	323*
Juan Marichal, SF	37	36	25	25	6	.806*	2.23	222	36	307
Gaylord Perry, SF	36	35	13	21	8	.724	2.99	201	40	256
Bob Gibson, STL	35	35	20	21	12	.636	2.44	275	78	280
Chris Short, Phila	42	39	19	20	10	.667	3.54	177	68	272

Six pitchers tied for the shutout lead at five. Milwaukee made its move to Atlanta successfully, and many baseball purists contend this is what enabled Hank Aaron to break Babe Ruth's career home run record. He hit 378 in 12 seasons in Milwaukee, an average of 31 per season, from age 20 to 31. During his nine years in Atlanta he hit 335, an average of 37 per year, from age 32 to 41. Let the reader be the judge.

This season saw the end of Robin Roberts' career. The "Springfield Rifle," a nickname hung on him early in his career, finished with the Cubs and Houston with a 5–8 mark to give him a final career record of 286–245. It is a mark that could have been much higher given a few breaks, and if Roberts had developed another pitch earlier in his career.

The Dodgers lost four straight in the Series, and it would be many years before they would compete again. As already stated Koufax was forced to retire due to an arthritic elbow, which could have made him a cripple if he continued pitching.

1967

AMERICAN LEAGUE: A GOOD
OLD-FASHIONED HORSE RACE

Boston had finished ninth the previous season, and were a hundred-to-one shot to win the pennant. But when the dust settled, the Red Sox held a one-game margin over Detroit and Minnesota, with Chicago only three back. Fifth-place California (formerly called Los Angeles) was only seven and one-half out.

Boston won on the strength of Carl Yastrzemski's triple crown and MVP season. Jim Lonborg, with 22 wins, was the pitching ace and picked up the Cy Young Award. Starting this season, each league would have a winner. Earl Wilson had 22 also for Detroit, while Dean Chance won 20 for Minnesota.

Chicago had a pop-gun attack, batting only .225 with the highest regular at .241, but had terrific pitching with Joe Horlen (19–7), and Gary Peters (16–11). Baltimore slipped to sixth place as their hitters and pitchers both seemed to disappear.

This was Lonborg's third year in the league. After two undistinguished seasons, he was 19–27 with an ERA in excess of 4.00 when he blossomed into the league's top pitcher in 1967. He tied for the lead in wins and had the most starts (39) and strikeouts (246) en route to the Cy Young Award. It looked like the Red Sox would have a longtime pitching ace, but in the off-season Lonborg broke his leg in a skiing accident and would be nearly useless to the team over the next two years, having a combined 13–21. Then in 1970 he started with a 4–1 record, injured his shoulder and was lost for the season. Lonborg was 10–7 the next year before he was traded to Milwaukee. He was 14–12 in his lone season there. Lonborg then moved to the Phillies. They were in a rebuilding program and he met with some degree of success, posting a 17-win season in 1974 and 18 victories two years later. He retired in 1979 after having a 75–59 record with the Phillies, giving him a final career mark of 157–137.

Wilson had been with the Red Sox since 1959. He had pitched mostly in mediocrity through early 1966, logging a 56–58 record, when he was traded to Detroit and went 13–6 to finish with 18 wins for his biggest season to date. Then in 1967 Wilson had his finest year, with a league-high 22 wins. He never again reached that summit, winning 13 and 12 the next two years before finishing out his career with Detroit and San Diego in 1970 with a 5–12 mark.

Chance had last won 20 games in 1964, and although he had pitched effective ball over the past two seasons, could only post a 27–27 record, with one losing and one winning season. This was his last 20-win season as he led with 18 complete games and 284 innings pitched. He also had a 2.73 ERA with five shutouts and 220 strikeouts. Chance pitched even more effectively in 1968, but was rewarded with only a 16–16 record. Then in 1969 came the sore arm and by 1971 he would be forced to retire.

Horlen was one of those pitchers who had the misfortune to spend his entire career with a weak-hitting team. As a result, he finished with a 116–117 record, although a very fine 3.10 ERA. From 1964 through 1968 the highest ERA he had was 2.88, and one year it was below 2.00. Yet during that time he had one season at .500 and two over. The 1967 campaign was his best as he led in winning percentage (.731) and ERA (2.08) while tying for the shutout lead at six. From 1963 through 1969 he won 91 while losing 79 with an ERA below

3.00. Certainly a better hitting team, such as the Red Sox, would have seen him post many more victories.

One more pitcher bears mentioning only because he pitched spasmodically from 1956 through 1971 and had a 69–83 record. However, in the late 1960s George Brunet pitched effective if not winning baseball. His ERA was around 3.15, but for the 1966–68 seasons he was 13–13, 11–19 and 13–17. After that he pitched less effectively and finally finished his major league career in 1971. However, he would continue pitching in the minors until 1985. His professional career covered 1953–85 and he had a 244–242 record in the minors.

California had the leading reliever in Minnie Rojas with 27 saves. Minnesota had the most complete games at 58 and California the fewest at 19.

Pitcher/Team	G	GS	CG	W	L	Pct	ERA	SO	W	IP
Jim Lonborg, Bos	39	39*	15	22*	9	.710	3.16	246*	83	273
Earl Wilson, Det	39	38	12	22*	11	.667	3.27	184	92	264
Dean Chance, Mn	41	39*	18*	20	14	.588	2.73	220	68	284

Boston was looking for revenge for their 1946 loss to St. Louis, but despite Lonborg winning two games and Yastrzemski batting .400, the Red Sox lost in seven games.

NATIONAL LEAGUE: THE YEAR OF CHA-CHA-CHA

Orlando Cepeda had become expendable in San Francisco and joined St. Louis prior to mid-season in 1966. He batted .300, but his real value was to come in 1967. He led the "El Birdos," as he called them, to the pennant with a MVP season. However, in July gloom was cast over St. Louis when pitching ace Bob Gibson suffered a broken leg when hit by a line drive off the bat of Roberto Clemente. But young pitchers Dick Hughes, Steve Carlton, and Nelson Briles picked up the slack, and between them won 44 games for the season while losing only 20.

San Francisco finished in second, 10½ games off the pace, primarily because of a poor season by Willie Mays and a leg injury to Juan Marichal (14–10). Mike McCormick tried to pick up the pitching slack as he won 22.

Chicago had its highest finish in years—third—as Ferguson Jenkins won 20 games for the first of six consecutive seasons. Ted Abernathy, now with Cincinnati, led the league with 28 saves.

McCormick had been pitching in the majors since 1956, when as an 18-year-old he broke in with the New York Giants. McCormick stayed with the Giants after they moved to San Francisco until 1962, when he was traded to Baltimore in the American League. After four seasons over there, split between Baltimore and Washington, he returned to the National League. His record to this point was 84–91 and inconsistency was his pattern, as illustrated by his ERAs. They ran from a league-leading low of 2.70 in 1960 to a high of 5.36 in 1962.

Thus, in 1967 the baseball world was shocked when McCormick won a league-high 22 games with a 2.85 ERA and copped the Cy Young Award. Had McCormick, after all these years of frustration and futility, finally matured as a pitcher? The answer would be no, as this was his one moment of glory. McCormick was 12–14 and 11–9 the next two years before drifting back to the American League and finishing with Kansas City in 1971. He was barely over .500 for his career at 134–128, helped mainly by this one big year.

Jenkins had been acquired by Chicago in a trade with Philadelphia and in only his second full year he blossomed into a 20-game winner. Jenkins eventually would win 20 or more seven times, one of only nine pitchers to ever have that many seasons with 20 or more wins. From 1967 through the end of his career in 1983, he had only two seasons in which he did not win at least ten games. His misfortune, like others before him, was to spend most of his career with teams that spent most of their time in the second division.

Jenkins led the league with 20 complete games, a feat he would accomplish four times, as well as busting the 20 barrier on eight occasions, six in a row. He also fanned 236 batters, the first of five years in a row and six in his career where he fanned at least 200 batters in a season. When Jenkins retired he had won 284 and lost 226, had a winning percentage of .557 and became a Hall of Famer. That's not bad for a pitcher who spent most of his career with teams in the lower half of the division.

Marichal was deprived of a chance for his fifth straight 20-win season. Because he won 20 or more the next two seasons, this would have given him seven in a row. Marichal posted a 2.76 ERA, had 18 complete games in 26 starts and was 14–10 when a leg injury sidelined him, forcing him to miss about 12 starts. This not only stopped his chance for another 20-win season, it dashed any hopes the Giants had for overtaking St. Louis for the title.

Although finishing last, the Mets unveiled a 22-year-old rookie who was 16–13 with a 2.76 ERA. His name was Tom Seaver. He would go on to be one of the dominating pitchers of the late 60s, all of the 70s and part of the early 80s. Eventually he would enter the Hall of Fame with a career 311–205, 2.86 ERA and .603 winning percentage. We will hear more about him later.

San Francisco had the most complete games with 54, Cincinnati had the fewest at 34. New York fell into last place again for the fifth time in six seasons, losing 101 games.

Pitcher/Team	G	GS	CG	W	L	Pct	ERA	SO	W	IP
Mike McCormick, SF	40	35	14	22*	10	.688	2.85	150	81	262
Ferg Jenkins, Chgo	38	38	20*	20	13	.606	2.80	236`	83	289

Jim Bunning, 17–15, led in shutouts (6), strikeouts (253), innings pitched (320) and games started (40), while Atlanta's Phil Niekro had the best ERA at 1.87. With better support, Bunning could have easily won 20 games and probably the Cy Young Award, which went to McCormick.

In the World Series, two players stood out. Lou Brock was the offensive star as he batted .414 and Bob Gibson the pitching hero, as he pitched three complete game victories while fanning 26 men in 27 innings.

1968

AMERICAN LEAGUE: THE YEAR OF REVENGE

The pitchers waited 38 years but got their revenge in this season, as the only batter to hit .300 was Carl Yastrzemski, who at .301 had the lowest batting title win ever. Detroit also got their revenge, 34 years later, by beating the Cardinals in the World Series four games to three.

Detroit coasted to a 12-game margin over Baltimore. The main factor was Denny McLain, who with 31 wins won the MVP and Cy Young Award and became the first pitcher since 1934 to win 30 games or more. Dave McNally, with 22, his first of four straight 20-plus-win seasons, helped put Baltimore in second.

Luis Tiant reversed years of frustration and won 21 as he paced Cleveland to third. Mel Stottlemyre, with 21, helped pitch the Yankees back into the first division with a fifth-place finish.

McLain became the first pitcher in the majors to win 30 games since Dizzy Dean in 1934 and the first American Leaguer since Lefty Grove in 1931. His 31–6, 1.98 ERA year was one of the finest in league history. McLain led in victories, winning percentage (.838), starts (41), complete games (28), and innings pitched (336). He was second in strikeouts with 280. McLain easily was voted the MVP and Cy Young winner. At age 24 he already had 90 victories to his credit and it looked like nothing could ever stop him. It seemed as if he could pitch forever, would easily win 300 games and enter the Hall of Fame. Time would tell a different story.

This was McNally's sixth season and up to this point he had only been a so-so pitcher with one ERA below 3.00 and two over 4.00. His career record entering this year was 48–38. While respectable, it was not one that would cause you to believe a pitcher would win 20 games four seasons in a row. But that's what happened. McNally was 22–10 with a 1.95 ERA and 273 innings pitched, the first of seven straight seasons over 200 and eight overall.

Tiant had pitched very effective ball but had not produced any big winning seasons, partly because of the support behind him. In his first four seasons, three times his ERA was below 3.00, but he had only a 45–35 record to show for his efforts. This year all the pieces came together and he was 21–9 with a league-high nine shutouts and the lowest ERA (1.60). He had 19 complete games and 258 innings, the second of eight times he would achieve over 200. However, all would not continue well and soon there would be a reversal of fortunes. It would be several years before his ship would be righted and dame fortune would smile on him again. After a two-year absence, Stottlemyre returned to the charmed circle, although his being away had more to do with the team behind him than his own pitching efforts. Stottlemyre had a career-high 21 wins while pitching 279 innings and 19 complete games. He was a real workhorse, as the fewest number of innings he hurled between 1965 and 1973 was 251 in 1966. He would win 20 one more year and although still pitching well, never had the support behind him to reach that charmed circle again.

Minnesota's Al Worthington was the save leader with 18, while Detroit's staff had the most complete games at 58 and Chicago the fewest with 20.

Pitcher/Team	G	GS	CG	W	L	Pct	ERA	SO	W	IP
Denny McLain, Det	41	41*	28*	31*	6	.838*	1.96	280	63	336*
Dave McNally, Balt	35	35	18	22	10	.688	1.95	202	55	273
Luis Tiant, Cleve	34	32	19	21	9	.700	1.60*	264	73	258
Mel Stottlemyre, NY	36	36	19	21	12	.636	2.45	140	65	279

Sam McDowell led with 283 strikeouts. McDowell had a fine 1.81 ERA, but could log only a 15–14 record. It seemed no matter how effectively he pitched, somehow, some way he would lose the game.

The Kansas City franchise, which had been moved from Philadelphia, was now transferred to Oakland, where in a few years they would become a dominant force in the league.

Detroit rallied from a three-games-to-one deficit to win the World Series. They were helped greatly by a base running blunder by Lou Brock in the fifth inning of game five, with St. Louis up, 3–2, that broke a potential game-busting rally and Series-clinching victory. Then in the seventh game, Curt Flood misplayed a fly ball that led to three runs and the final victory. Mickey Lolich was 3–0 in Series play, while McLain was 1–2, but did win the crucial sixth game that enabled a seventh to be played. In head-to-head competition, he lost to Gibson twice.

NATIONAL LEAGUE: WHAT HAPPENED TO THE BATS?

Hitting also fell off in the National League, although not quite as dramatically as in the junior circuit. While several Cardinal hitters had poor seasons, Bob Gibson had his career-best year, posting a 22–9 log with a 1.12 ERA and a league-high 13 shutouts. The real question is how he lost nine games. However, he was awarded the Cy Young and MVP trophies. Many observers believed he could have been anywhere from 28–4 to 30–1.

St. Louis won by nine games over San Francisco, despite 26 wins from Juan Marichal. Ferguson Jenkins got his second straight 20–win season as Chicago again finished third. Several other pitchers won 19 games, but no one else made 20. Phil Regan, now with Chicago, led with 26 saves.

This season was Gibson's finest hour. En route to his 22 wins, he also had a 15-game winning streak. In reviewing his season, one can see where a number of his defeats could easily have been in the win column. He led not only in ERA but also in shutouts with 13, and he fanned the most batters (268), while his 28 complete games were second in the league. He would win 20 or more two additional seasons, giving him five overall, in what could just as easily have been seven.

Marichal returned to the 20-win club with his best season as he led the loop with 26 wins, 30 complete games in 38 starts and 326 innings pitched. He would have been a surefire Cy Young winner in any other season, but he ran into Gibson's unbelievable season and thus once again was a bridesmaid. This was to be the destiny of Marichal throughout his career.

The final 20-game winner was Jenkins with this second straight 20-win season, and second consecutive 20 complete games, which he would also reach six years in a row. His 308 innings marked his first time at that level, but proved to be the first of four straight years in which he worked 300 or more innings. When coupled with a 2.63 ERA, this was a performance that in other years might also have won him a Cy Young Award—but not this season.

We should mention four other pitchers. Chris Short won 19 games for an eighth-place Philadelphia team. This season was especially rewarding for Short as he was coming off a serious knee injury. He rebounded strongly by appearing in 42 games, 36 as a starter, and rewarded the Phils with a 19-win campaign, which would prove to be his last winning year. A back injury kept him out of all but two games of the 1969 season, and when he tried a comeback, he was not the same Short of the mid–1960s.

Jerry Koosman broke in with the Mets. Although they finished ninth, he won 19 games with a 2.08 ERA while hurling seven shutouts, pitching 17 complete games and 264 innings. At this point many considered him a better pitcher than Tom Seaver, who had his second straight 16-win season. Time would prove otherwise. Although Koosman won 222, he lost 209, and while he had two 20-win seasons, he also had some big losing years (8–20, 3–15 and 4–13). Meanwhile, Seaver would win over 300 games, be a five-time 20-game winner and a three-time Cy Young winner.

The last hurler we consider is Don Drysdale, who was only 14–12 despite a fine 2.15 ERA. Unfortunately, only the Mets scored fewer runs, and once again he was the victim of weak batting support. During the season he established a new major league record of 58 consecutive scoreless innings. However, that proved to be the only bright spot in an otherwise disappointing season for the big right-hander.

San Francisco led with 70 complete games and Cincinnati was last with 24.

Pitcher/Team	G	GS	CG	W	L	Pct	ERA	SO	W	IP
Juan Marichal, SF	38	38	30*	26*	9	.743	2.43	218	46	326*
Bob Gibson, STL	34	34	28	22	9	.710	1.12*	268*	62	305
Ferg Jenkins, Chgo	40	40*	20	20	15	.571	2.83	206	65	308

Pittsburgh's Steve Blass (18–6) was the percentage leader with .750. St. Louis was favored to win the Series, and except for two bad breaks, probably would have. They were leading three games to one, and 3–2 in the fifth game when Lou Brock, who was the hitting star of the Series, failed to slide at home plate and was out, killing a Cardinal rally and probably Series-clinching victory.

In game seven, Curt Flood misplayed a fly ball by Jim Northrup, which led to three Detroit runs, broke Gibson's seven-game winning streak in World Series play and gave the title to Detroit. Gibson finished 2–1, 1.67 ERA, with 35 strikeouts in 27 innings. In nine Series starts, Gibson was 7–2 with eight complete games.

——— 1969 ———

AMERICAN LEAGUE: A NEW
FORMAT AND DIMENSION TO THE GAME

With expansion to 12 teams, the league now split into two divisions with six teams each. The winner of each division then played for the pennant and the right to represent the league in the World Series.

Baltimore rolled to a 19-game margin over Detroit on the bats of Frank Robinson and Boog Powell and the 20-win seasons of Mike Cuellar and Dave McNally. Detroit got a 24-win season from Denny McLain as he and Cuellar tied for the Cy Young Award. At age 25, McLain was 114–57 and seemed destined for 300–350 wins and a trip to the Hall of Fame. But soon he would fall from grace.

Mel Stottlemyre had another 20-win season for a sub-.500 Yankee team, while Luis Tiant lost 20 games for Cleveland as they fell into the Eastern Division cellar. Minnesota got 20 wins each from Jim Perry and Dave Boswell and won the Western Division. They also had the save leader at 31 in the person of Ron Perranoski.

Cuellar had pitched in two games with no record for Cincinnati in 1959 and then returned with St. Louis in 1964 to stay in the majors. He followed his lone season there with a four-year stint at Houston. Although overall posting quite good ERAs, his record was only 42–41. At the end of 1968 he was sent packing to Baltimore. From here, dame fortune smiled on the happy Cuban.

Cuellar came alive with his first of three straight 20-win seasons as he bagged a 23–11 record with 18 complete games, 291 innings pitched and a 2.38 ERA. From 1969 through 1974 Cuellar won 125 while losing 63, averaging 38 starts, 19 complete games, four shutouts, 282 innings per season and a 2.98 ERA. Along with McNally and Jim Palmer, he formed the nucleus of a great Baltimore pitching staff.

Meanwhile, McNally was posting his second consecutive 20-win season, during which he won 15 straight games. If there was a negative for McNally it was his 11 complete games and 13 no-decisions in 40 starts. On the other side, how many managers who had four pitchers each turn in a 20–7 record would worry about the 52 no-decisions?

McLain won his second straight Cy Young Award as he led the league with 24 wins and 41 starts, but his 23 complete games were second best. He also led with 325 innings pitched, nine shutouts and posted a fine 2.80 ERA. While the numbers weren't equal his 1968 season, they were still high caliber and earned him the award for two years in a row. At this time, no one realized that in three seasons he would be out of baseball and post only a 17–34 mark for those years. It would be a real tragedy for him and the game.

Stottlemyre posted his third and final 20-win season as he also led with 24 complete games, while logging 305 innings and posting a 2.82 ERA. Stottlemyre continued pitching for five more seasons until a shoulder injury in 1974 forced a premature end to his career. While pitching excellent ball from 1970 on, he could put together only a 67–66 mark for those years. A little more batting support was needed.

If we subtract this season from Boswell's career stats, he is only 48–44. Like many others, this was his one good year as he was 20–12 with a 3.23 ERA covering 256 innings in 38 starts. The next season he suffered a knee injury and never fully recovered. By 1971 his career would be ended at only age 26—a tragic footnote for another chapter in our baseball history of pitchers. A side comment: during the season he and manager Billy Martin got into a barroom brawl during which Martin decked his star pitcher. It's unusual for a manager to treat a 20-game winner in such a manner.

It had been nine years since Perry had burst onto the scene as a league-high 18-game winner for Cleveland in 1960. However, this year Perry finally got back on track and posted his finest season to date with a 20–6, 2.82 ERA mark. Perry proved to be a throwback to pitchers from another era, as despite starting 36 games, he also made ten relief appearances. This was quite unusual in an era when starters primarily started and relieving was done basically by the bullpen. This was also the start of a six-year run over which Perry won 105 games, almost half of the 215 he won during a 17-season career.

Sam McDowell led in strikeouts for the fourth time and won 18 games for a last-place Cleveland team that lost 99 games. With better support, he probably could have won 22 to 25 games. Again, as we have seen before, this was to be the albatross of his career. Teammate Luis Tiant would suffer a virtual reversal of his 1968 season as he was 9–20. A shoulder injury next year almost ended his career and it wouldn't be until 1972 that he would again pitch winning baseball.

Detroit topped everyone with 55 complete games, while newcomer Seattle was last in the Western Division and complete games with 21. The other new team was Kansas City, which was now called the Royals.

Pitcher/Team	G	GS	CG	W	L	Pct	ERA	SO	W	IP
Denny McLain, Det	42	41*	23	24*	9	.727	2.80	181	67	325*
Mike Cuellar, Balt	39	39	18	23	11	.676	2.38	182	79	291
Jim Perry, Mn	46	36	12	20	6	.769	2.62	153	66	262
Dave McNally, Balt	41	40	11	20	7	.741	3.21	166	84	269
Dave Boswell, Mn	38	38	10	20	12	.625	3.23	190	99	256
Mel Stottlemyre, NY	39	39	24*	20	14	.588	2.82	113	97	303

McLain was the shutout leader at nine, while Baltimore's Jim Palmer, despite being out for over six weeks with an injury, logged a 16–4 mark to take winning percentage honors at .800. Washington's Dick Bosman took ERA honors at 2.19.

Baltimore was heavily favored in the World Series but went down to defeat in five games, with only Cuellar able to garner a win. Baltimore batted a horrible .146.

NATIONAL LEAGUE: NO LONGER THE DOORMATS

The National League also expanded, adding teams in Montreal and San Diego. Each finished last in their divisions with identical marks of 52–110.

In their first seven seasons, the Mets had lost 737 games, finished last five times and ninth the other two years. There was no reason to expect they would do differently this season. They had a team of misfits and journeyman ballplayers, except for some of their pitchers. Here is where they shone, as Tom Seaver won 25 games and captured the Cy Young Award. Seaver led the team to a 100–62 record with an eight-game margin over the Cubs, who led into September but choked down the stretch.

Ferguson Jenkins had his third straight 20-win season and was joined by teammate Billy Hands in that charmed circle. Bob Gibson picked up another 20 wins to keep St. Louis well above .500.

In the West, Phil Niekro had 23 wins to help Atlanta take first place, as Hank Aaron slammed 44 home runs to continue his assault on Babe Ruth's career home run record. Juan Marichal had his sixth and last 20-win season, and Gaylord Perry added 19 as San Francisco was second.

Los Angeles got 20-win seasons from Bill Singer and Claude Osteen, while Larry Dierker won 20 for Houston, which had the save leader in Fred Gladding with 29.

This season was a bonanza for 20-game winners as the league featured nine of them, led by Seaver's incredible 25–7 record. He also had a 2.21 ERA with 208 strikeouts in 273 innings, covering 18 complete games in 35 starts. This was the second of nine straight seasons, ten overall, that Seaver fanned at least 200 batters. It was also his third straight of 13 years, 16 total, in which he pitched at least 215 innings. From 1967 (his rookie year) through 1978, only once did Seaver fail to win at least 16 games, and never did he pitch less than .500 ball. In 1974 he was at .500 with an 11–11 record.

During that 13-year stretch, he averaged 18 wins, 35 starts, 267 innings, 222 strikeouts and a 2.57 ERA. This outstanding streak would eventually earn him a spot in the Hall of Fame. He also won 20 or more five times and earned three Cy Young Awards. Seaver pitched for another seven years, and although not as effective, still posted winning marks in four of those seasons and was 76–72 overall.

Jenkins posted his third straight 20-win season as he had a to-date career-high 21 wins, and also his third straight with 20 complete games or more (23). Jenkins was first with 273 strikeouts as he posted 311 innings for his second year in a row over 300. His 42 starts were high for the league.

Teammate Hands had an outstanding 2.49 ERA as he pitched an even 300 innings covering 41 starts and won an even 20 games. His career could also be viewed in three segments. Period one (1965–67) he was 15–23. Phase two (1968–70) he was 54–39, and the final portion of his career (1971–75) was again on the losing side of the ledger at 42–48, giving him a lackluster career mark of 111–110.

Gibson had another fine season with a 2.18 ERA, completing a league-high 28 games and fanning 269 batters in 314 innings. What kept St. Louis from winning the pennant was their lack of hitting, as nine teams scored more runs, although St. Louis had the league's best ERA (2.94). With any break at all Gibson could have matched Seaver's 25 wins, if not more. The only consistent bat in the Cardinal lineup was Joe Torre, who drove in 101 runs.

Niekro had been pitching for the Braves since 1964. While pitching effectively, he had not always had proper support and thus had only a 31–27 win-loss record to date. This was to be the cross he would have to bear through much of his career, as often the team would be mired deep in the second division, several times last. However, this season was all Niekro's as he won 23, pitched 21 complete games covering 294 innings and posted a 2.57 ERA. Niekro also performed some double duty, starting 35, relieving five times and receiving credit for one save. Several times over the next many years he would be called upon to relieve at a crucial point in a game or juncture in the season.

From 1967 through 1986, only once did Niekro win less than 11 games, and that was the strike-shortened season of 1981. Most of his pitching was done for the Braves, as he was with them from 1964 through 1984. He then pitched for the Yankees, Cleveland and Toronto, before pitching one final game for Atlanta in 1984. His final career mark was 318–274, 3.35 ERA. Without a doubt, more support would have seen him close to the 400-win mark.

Marichal had his last 20-win season as he posted 21, with a 2.18 ERA, and a league-high eight shutouts among his 27 complete games, while he pitched an even 300 innings. During his career he won 20 or more six times, pitched 20 or more complete games five times, fanned 200 or more six times and pitched over 300 innings four times. Marichal would pitch winning ball for the next two seasons before slumping in 1972, then fading out by 1975, with a career 243–142, 2.89 ERA, .631 winning percentage record.

Singer was a pitcher who twice won 20 games in a season, but still posted a losing career mark at 118–127. He was either very good or very bad—not much middle ground in his career. He had played in seven games with an 0–1 record for Los Angeles from 1964–66 before landing a permanent starting job in 1967. He was 12–8, 2.65 and 13–17, 2.88 the first two years. Then in 1969 he won 20 while posting a 2.34 ERA and pitching 316 innings.

From that point on things turned sour for Singer. He was ill much of 1970 and was 8–5 with a 3.14 ERA in 16 games. He didn't seem to fully recover, as the next two years Singer was a combined 16–33 with an ERA around 4.00. The 1973 season saw him with California in the American League, and he was brilliant again, winning 20, with a 3.22 ERA. However, he suffered a head injury the next year and was 7–4, 2.97 ERA in 14 games. He pitched for three more years for California, Texas, Minnesota and Toronto, but was only 22–33 with an ERA around 4.50 per game. His was a career that might have been different, save the injuries.

In his eighth full season Osteen finally made the 20-win club. He had pitched spasmodically for Cincinnati in the late 50s and early 60s before settling in with Washington as a regular starter in 1962. In three seasons with an ERA under 3.50, he was only 32–40, as the Senators were deep in the second division of the league. Joining the Dodgers in 1965, he would pitch for them for ten seasons and never win fewer than 12 games, twice winning 20. He was a real workhorse, logging over 200 innings every season, and his ERA was always quite good, several times below 3.00. However, his fate was similar to that of other Dodger hurlers of the time: lack of run production, causing numerous low-run defeats. For the ten seasons, he was 149–126—a mark that could have been much better.

Dierker, the final 20-game winner, also had his career-best season. He not only won 20 games but also completed 20, pitched 305 innings and posted a 2.33 ERA. At 23 it looked like he would have many successful years, but the most he ever won again was 15 in 1972. Several injuries played a key part in slowing down his career. He suffered elbow, finger and shoulder injuries, all of which eventually took their toll. The Dierker of the mid–70s was not the Dierker of the late 60s. He retired with a 2–6 mark with St. Louis in 1977, giving him a final mark of 139–123.

San Francisco topped the league with 71 complete games, 53 by Marichal and Perry, while San Diego set a new major league record for fewest at 16.

Pitcher/Team	G	GS	CG	W	L	Pct	ERA	SO	W	IP
Tom Seaver, NY	36	35	18	25*	7	.781	2.21	208	82	273
Phil Niekro, Atl	40	35	21	23	13	.639	2.57	193	57	284
Juan Marichal, SF	37	36	27	21	11	.656	2.10*	205	54	300
Ferg Jenkins, Chgo	43	42*	23	21	15	.583	3.21	273*	71	311
Bill Singer, LA	41	40	16	20	12	.625	2.34	247	74	316
Bob Gibson, STL	35	35	28*	20	13	.606	2.18	269	95	314
Larry Dierker, Ho	38	37	20	20	13	.606	2.33	232	72	305

Pitcher/Team	G	GS	CG	W	L	Pct	ERA	SO	W	IP
Billy Hands, Chgo	41	41	18	20	14	.588	2.49	181	73	300
Claude Osteen, LA	41	41	16	20	15	.571	2.66	183	74	321

Marichal was shutout leader with eight, while teammate Perry (19–14) pitched the most innings (325), and Pittsburgh's Bob Moose (14–3) led with .824 winning percentage. Perry, with his 19 wins, started a string of ten seasons during which four times he won 20 or more, won 191 games, never pitched less than 238 innings and five times exceeded 300. Along the way he picked up two Cy Young Awards, one in each league, the only pitcher ever to accomplish that feat.

The Mets dominated the Series with great pitching as they had a team 1.80 ERA. Led by Jerry Koosman (17–9) with a 2–0 mark, they easily defeated Baltimore in five games.

The Mets had a pitcher named Nolan Ryan, who at 22 fashioned a 6–3, 3.54 ERA mark, with 92 strikeouts and 53 walks in 89 innings. In a few years he would become one of the most dominating pitchers in the game, although playing mostly for poor or weak teams and often pitching in tough luck seasons.

8

1970–1979

AMERICAN LEAGUE: MORE
EXCITEMENT OFF THE FIELD THAN ON

Denny McLain was suspended by Commissioner Bowie Kuhn until July 1 for conduct detrimental to the game. He had been accused of consorting with gamblers and providing money to back book-making operations. When he returned he had lost the zip from his fastball, and was 3–5 when he doused two reporters with water and was suspended again on September 9. At season's end Detroit unloaded him to Washington. In a few years he would be out of baseball and in prison on gambling charges, for which he served four years. McLain's brilliant career went down the drain.

Baltimore won easily with a 15-game margin over the Yankees, who had regained respectability as Fritz Peterson won 20 games. However, Baltimore had three 20-game winners and big seasons from Boog Powell and the two Robinsons.

Sam McDowell won 20 games for Cleveland to help them climb out of the cellar. In the West, Jim Perry tied the league high with 24 wins as Minnesota won for the second straight season with a powerful hitting attack. Oakland finished second, and Clyde Wright, with 22 wins, pitched California into third place.

Mike Cuellar tied Perry and Dave McNally for the league lead with 24 wins, while also tying for the most starts at 40 and leading with 21 complete games as he pitched 298 innings. This was his second straight 20-plus-win season, and he also led with a .750 winning percentage. The man from Cuba had definitely arrived.

McNally had his biggest victory total with 24 as he pitched 296 innings, but like teammate Cuellar gave up first place to another teammate, Jim Palmer. Over the four seasons that McNally won 20 or more, he was 87–31, another reason Baltimore was at or near the top during those years.

The third member of the staff eventually proved to be the most successful.

224

Palmer won his first 20-game season with a 20–10 mark and the best of the three ERAs at 2.71. Palmer is one of those rarities who came back from not only a sore arm, but back injury as well. He missed most of 1967, all of 1968 and a third of the 1969 season. The first two years were due to a sore arm and the latter to a back injury. To most pitchers, it would be the death knell, or time to find another way to make a living, but not to Palmer.

Palmer had broken in with Baltimore in 1965 and was 5–4, then had a 15–10 season before misfortune befell him. Despite injuries during the 1967–69 period, he was an outstanding 19–5, 2.46 ERA when he could pitch. Thus everything was there for a potentially great career if he could get over the injury jinx. He finally did in 1970 by winning 20 games for the first of four straight years and eight out of nine years.

Palmer would suffer another sore arm in 1974 and an elbow injury in 1979. From both of these he would bounce back with winning seasons, although he was more fortunate after the 1974 year. For the next four seasons Palmer won 83 while losing 38, and he was the main cog in the Baltimore pitching wheel.

Peterson had his lone 20-win season in 1970. Most of his career was spent with the Yankees as he pitched for them from 1966 through 1973. He finished with Cleveland and Texas through the 1976 campaign. With New York he was 109–106, and 24–25 with the other two teams. However, he did have one bright stretch in 1968–71, as Peterson won 69 while losing 55 and had the misfortune to play for some of the weaker Yankee clubs at that time.

Detroit had more pitching problems. Mickey Lolich was 14–19 for his first losing season since his 5–9 rookie year in 1963. In between he won between 14 and 19 every year for Detroit. After his rookie season he would not pitch less than 200 innings until 1976, when he hurled 193.

Although Cleveland was again under .500, McDowell finally got a few breaks and won 20 games, a number that still could have been a few wins higher. His 305 innings pitched and 304 strikeouts were the league's best. The latter was the fifth and last time he led in that department.

Perry won the Cy Young award with his 24 wins as he pitched Minnesota to first place in the West Division. This was his finest season and second straight at the 20-win level. Perry was helped in the balloting as Cuellar and McNally both took votes from each other. This is not meant to diminish his efforts, but it did help that these two were also battling for first place.

This was the big, shining moment of Wright's career. Although he won 18 games two years later, this was the apex of his career. In his first four years he was 20–26 and after this season, sans 1972, he was 40–62, which included 19 and 20 game losses in 1973–74. His final career mark was 100–111.

Ron Perranoski was again the save leader with 34, while Baltimore led with 60 complete games and Washington and Chicago, both last in their divisions, were last with 20 complete games.

Pitcher/Team	G	GS	CG	W	L	Pct	ERA	SO	W	IP
Mike Cuellar, Balt	40	40*	21*	24*	8	.750*	3.47	190	69	298
Dave McNally, Balt	40	40*	16	24*	9	.727	3.22	185	78	296
Jim Perry, Mn	40	40*	13	24*	12	.667	3.03	168	57	279
Clyde Wright, Ca	39	39	7	22	12	.647	2.83	110	88	261
Jim Palmer, Balt	39	39	17	20	10	.667	2.71	199	100	305*
Fritz Peterson, NY	39	37	8	20	11	.645	2.91	127	40	260
Sam McDowell, Clev	39	39	19	20	12	.625	2.82	304*	131*	305*

Oakland's Chuck Dobson (16–15) led with five shutouts. In the World Series, Baltimore made easy work of Cincinnati, defeating them in five games. They outscored Cincinnati 33–20, while hitting ten home runs to their five. No Oriole pitcher won over one game.

NATIONAL LEAGUE: THE BEGINNING OF THE BIG RED MACHINE

Chicago continued to play respectable baseball, finishing second in the East to Pittsburgh. They just couldn't grab the brass ring. Ferguson Jenkins won 22 games for his fourth consecutive 20-win season. The Pirates grabbed first mostly on hitting, as no pitcher won over 15 games.

St. Louis finished with a 76–86 mark. They would have been far worse without Cy Young winner Bob Gibson, based on his 23–7 mark. Future Hall of Famer Steve Carlton was 10–19 for the club, although he did fan 19 batters in a 4–3 losing cause to the Mets.

Cincinnati, noted for its hitting, was paced by Pete Rose, Tony Perez and MVP Johnny Bench. Jim Merritt, although missing a month, still won 20 games for the club. San Francisco could only finish third, 16 games out despite Gaylord Perry's 23 wins. Age was catching up with 39-year-old Willie Mays, and Juan Marichal missed a month and won only 12 games.

Atlanta slipped all the way to fifth as Phil Niekro had a reversal of form and was 12–18, although Hank Aaron had another big season as he moved closer to Babe Ruth's hallowed record.

Jenkins had another banner season. He led the league with 24 complete games while winning 22, his fourth straight 20-plus-win season. This was also his third straight 300-plus-inning performance. Although he fanned one more batter (274) than the prior year when he led, he surrendered the strikeout title to Tom Seaver (283), who at 18–12 posted the league's best ERA, 2.81.

Gibson garnered his second Cy Young Award by posting his winningest season. He also had the league's best winning percentage (.767), based on his 23–7 record. His 274 strikeouts tied him with Jenkins for second, and his 23 complete games also put him in second place. This was Gibson's last 20-plus-win season, although he continued to pitch effective winning ball, posting 47 victories and an ERA less than 3.00 over the next three seasons. An injury in the last year cost him six to eight wins and would lead to his career being shutdown by 1975, when he finished with a ghastly 3–10, 5.04 ERA.

Merritt finished his career with an 81–86 record, and we can review him in three phases. From 1965–69, he pitched for Minnesota and had a 37–41 record. Then he came to Cincinnati and was 17–9 and 20–12 the first two years, when injuries took their toll. Over the next two seasons, he appeared in only 32 games and was 2–11. He tried to make a go of it with Texas, but was only 5–13 in 1973, and pitched 31 games for them during 1974–75 with no record, finally calling it a career.

Perry almost matched his brother's victory total. He fell one short, which was good enough to tie him with Gibson for the league lead. Perry worked a league-high 329 innings and was also tied for second with 23 complete games, while starting a league-high 41. Over the years he was accused of throwing a spitball. Whether or not he did has never been definitely proven, but many believed he loaded the baseball with something.

Cincinnati won on the strength of their hitting and bullpen as it set a new record with 60 saves, paced by a new individual high of 35 by Wayne Granger. Chicago had the most complete games at 59, while Philadelphia and San Diego were last with 24.

Pitcher/Team	G	GS	CG	W	L	Pct	ERA	SO	W	IP
Bob Gibson, STL	34	34	23	23*	7	.767*	3.12	274	88	294
Gaylord Perry, SF	41	41*	23	23*	13	.639	3.20	214	84	329
Ferg Jenkins, Chgo	40	39	24*	22	16	.579	3.39	274	60	313
Jim Merritt, Cinn	35	35	12	20	12	.625	4.08	136	53	234

Cincinnati's bats were nearly silent in the Series, as the team batted just .213, although Lee May had a big Series with a .389 mark and eight RBIs. The pitching was horrible as the team had a 6.70 ERA.

When the Cardinals traded Curt Flood to Philadelphia, he protested and challenged the reserve clause. The courts ruled against him, but in a few years that would all change.

1971

AMERICAN LEAGUE: ONE DYNASTY
CONTINUES AND ANOTHER IS BORN

Baltimore easily won its third consecutive division title as they exceeded 100 wins for the third straight season. They also duplicated a feat that last happened in 1920: they had four 20-game winners. It has only happened twice in the game, both times in the American League. The previous team was the Chicago White Sox. Baltimore did it despite Dave McNally missing a month of the season with a sore arm.

Detroit had two 20-game winners, including league leader Mickey Lolich with 25. Denny McLain was now with Washington and had a 10–22 season, would pitch one more year, be out of baseball after 1972 and in prison a few years later. What a shame!

McNally got his fourth straight and last 20-win season despite a sore arm. His .808 winning percentage was the league's best. After this season McNally would have only a 46–44 mark for Baltimore over the next three years, despite posting a respectable 3.25 ERA. He then would challenge the reserve clause and play with Montreal in 1974 without a contract. However, after appearing in 12 games and being only 3–6 with a 5.26 ERA, McNally retired, never to return to the game, although he was only 33. His final record is 184–119, with a .607 winning percentage, but he's had no nibbles from the Hall of Fame. Did his stance on the reserve clause hurt him and help keep him out?

Dobson, who for much of his career was a journeyman pitcher at best, posted a final career mark of 122–129. He spent 11 seasons with six clubs, and 1971 was his standout season as he went 20–8 with a 2.90 ERA and 18 complete games. His next best year was 19–15, with a 3.07 ERA for the Yankees in 1974. However, there were some downer years as well. Following his 20 wins he won 16 but lost 18 for Baltimore, despite a 2.65 ERA. The 1973 season he split with Atlanta and the Yankees at 12–15, ERA around 4.50. After an 11–14 year in 1975 with the Yankees, he finished out his career with Cleveland and a 19–24 record over the 1976–77 years.

Cuellar had his third straight 20-win season. He would "slip" to 18 each of the next two years before bouncing back to win 22 for his final year in the charmed circle. Cuellar had proven to be a real find for the Orioles, helping to strengthen an already strong pitching staff.

Palmer, with a 20–9 mark, completed the quartet of 20-game winners as he notched his second straight season in the charmed circle. His 2.68 ERA made the fourth of six consecutive seasons he would post an ERA below 3.00. Palmer also posted 20 complete games for the first of four times in his career. While McNally and Dobson's stars were beginning to dim, Palmer's was only starting to shine brighter.

Lolich was the league's top winner with 25 wins, a real comeback from his 19 losses of the previous season. Lolich also posted league highs with 45 starts and 29 complete games, while leading with 376 innings and 308 strikeouts. All these marks were career highs for the portly left-hander. Lolich would follow this up with another 20-plus-win season before slumping badly. After going 16–15 for the Tigers in 1973, his record would drop precipitously. He was 16–21, 12–18 for Detroit then 8–13 for the Yankees before going 2–3 as a reliever over two seasons for San Diego. Prior to 1974 Lolich was 179–136, but only 38–55 the rest of his career, thus tarnishing his final mark and diminishing his chances for a spot in the Hall.

This was Coleman's first season with Detroit and he responded by winning 20 games. Over the next two years he would post an additional 42 wins for the most successful period in his career. Then he started to fade and by 1979 was ready to call it quits. Coleman played for Washington from 1965 to 1970, although the first two years he appeared in only 3 games, ironically winning them all. After that he had four straight losing seasons, 40–50, before he was traded to Detroit.

Not to belabor the issue, but the case of Denny McLain is one of baseball's and life's great tragedies. Here was an individual with great talent and personality who threw it all away. McLain tried to burn both ends of the candle and it caught up with him. His nightlife, carousing, gambling and undesirable associations led to the end of his career and eventually a prison term. We understand he has straightened out his life since his release, but what a waste of talent took place.

In the West, Oakland was building a dynasty as Vida Blue won 24 games and captured both the MVP and Cy Young Award. Teammate Catfish Hunter chipped in with 21 wins. Wilbur Wood won his first of four straight 20-win seasons, and Andy Messersmith won 20 for California.

Blue had pitched in 18 games with a 3–1 record for the A's in 1969–70, but this was his first full season and would be the best of his career. His 1.82 ERA and eight shutouts were the league's best and his 24 complete games were only topped by Lolich. Blue would be a holdout next spring and slump badly to 6–10. After that he rebounded and had some good years, including two 20-win seasons, but was never as dominating as in 1971.

This was Hunter's first of five consecutive 20-plus-win seasons, four with Oakland and the final with the Yankees. He not only helped pitch Oakland into three World Series, he also helped the Yankees to get into two, but not during his 20-win season. Hunter was 5–3 in World Series play, with four of the victories coming while in an Oakland uniform, and two of his defeats as a Yankee. His team won four of five Series, three with Oakland and the only loss as a Yankee.

Hunter had broken in with Kansas City (the forerunner of Oakland) in 1965 and for the first five years he was less than a .500 pitcher, posting a 55–64 record with an ERA around 3.50. With better support he could have had a winning record. Finally, in 1970 he arrived and won 18 games, but ironically had his highest ERA since 1966. Over the 1971–75 period, Hunter compiled a 111–49 record and only once was his ERA over 3.00.

Wood had been around the majors for several years, primarily as a relief pitcher, when Chicago decided to make a starter of him, and for the next five seasons he was one of the league's best. With his fluttering knuckleball, he won 20 or more four straight times and 16 in the fifth, while pitching well over 300 innings in each of the first four years and 291 the last.

This was Wood's first season as a starter and he responded beautifully by posting a 1.91 ERA, seven shutouts, 22 complete games and 334 innings pitched. No one expected this type of performance from someone who owned a 37–46 career mark. From 1961 through 1965 Wood bounced around with the Red Sox and Pirates, mostly in relief, and had a 1–8 log. Then the White Sox picked him up in 1967. He became a relief pitcher and was 36–38 with 56 saves while appearing in 292 games over four seasons. He led the league in appearances in 1968–70. Then it was decided to make him a starting pitcher, and the rest became history.

This was Messersmith's fourth season with California. Prior to this time he had performed double duty for the Angels, although he did start 33 and 26 games the past two seasons. He had a winning record each year and good ERAs, but didn't have the support that some other clubs could have provided. However, 1971 proved to be his best season in an Angel uniform as he won 20 games for the first of two times in his career. Next season he had a finger injury that sidelined him. Again he pitched effectively (2.81 ERA), but because of weak support he was only 8–11. He later played with the Dodgers and Atlanta and became embroiled in the first free agent hassle, but more on that later.

Although Milwaukee finished last in the Western Division, they had the league's top reliever in Ken Sanders with 31 saves.

Pitcher/Team	G	GS	CG	W	L	Pct	ERA	SO	W	IP
Mickey Lolich, Det	45	45*	29*	25*	14	.641	2.92	308*	92	376*
Vida Blue, Oak	39	39	24	24	8	.750	1.82*	301	88	312
Wilbur Wood, Chgo	44	42	22	22	13	.629	1.91	210	62	334
Dave McNally, Balt	30	30	11	21	5	.808*	2.89	91	58	224
Catfish Hunter, Oak	37	37	16	21	11	.656	2.96	181	80	274
Pat Dobson, Balt	38	37	18	20	8	.714	2.90	187	63	282
Jim Palmer, Balt	37	37	20	20	9	.690	2.68	184	106	282
Mike Cuellar, Balt	38	38	21	20	9	.690	3.08	124	78	292
Joe Coleman, Det	39	38	16	20	9	.690	3.15	236	96	286
A Messersmith, Ca	38	38	14	20	13	.606	2.99	179	121	277

Baltimore easily defeated Oakland three games to none to move into the World Series as heavy favorites over Pittsburgh. However, after winning the first two, they lost four of the next five. McNally had two wins, while Cuellar lost both his starts.

At the end of the season, the Washington franchise was moved to Dallas, where it has been ever since. While there has been baseball expansion since then, no new team has been moved to Washington in the almost 25 years since the last one left.

NATIONAL LEAGUE: ANOTHER NEW WINNER

For the fourth consecutive season, the National League would be represented by a different team in the World Series. Pittsburgh won out in a hard-fought race with St. Louis, despite Joe Torre's MVP season and Steve Carlton's 20 wins. Gibson's fall to 16 wins didn't help their cause.

Pittsburgh didn't have a 20-game winner, though they got 19 from Dock Ellis. It was their hitting that brought them into the Series, headed by Willie

Stargell's league-high 48 homers. Ferguson Jenkins kept Chicago in the thick of it with his Cy Young season of 24 wins, while Tom Seaver had another big year, winning 20 to keep New York above .500.

Rick Wise won 17 games for a Philadelphia team that finished last and lost 95. San Francisco won in the East without a 20-game winner; Juan Marichal was tops at 18. Al Downing sparked Los Angeles to second place with 20 wins.

Carlton won 20 games for the first of two successive seasons and six overall. Carlton had been with the Cardinals since 1965 but only in 24 games the first two years. In 1967 he became a regular starter and won 44 games over three seasons with ERAs below 3.00 each year. Then he had real problems in 1970 as his ERA soared to 3.72 and his record dipped to 10–19. He was one of the main reasons the Cardinals didn't win the pennant in 1970. However, following his 1971 year it looked like the Redbirds would have a big winner for many years to come. Well, Carlton became a big winner, but someplace else. We'll have more on that story a little later.

Jenkins enjoyed his biggest season to date as he tried to keep the Cubs in competition. Without him they were 59–66 and would have been relegated to the lower part of the division. Jenkins led with 24 wins, 38 starts, 30 complete games, and 263 strikeouts in 328 innings. He also had a 2.77 ERA, and was deservedly given the Cy Young Award. Jenkins was emerging as one of the top pitchers in the league.

Seaver was back in the 20-win circle for the first of two consecutive seasons as he won his second straight ERA title, this time with a scintillating 1.76. He also copped his second consecutive strikeout crown with 289. The 1971–72 years would be the only time Seaver had back-to-back 20-win seasons, even though he reached that level five times. However, he was a very consistent winner if we look at the years 1969–73. He won 25, 18, 20, 21 and 19. A manager sleeps very pleasantly when he knows he has a pitcher he can depend on year after year. He doesn't have to worry whether he will be 22–10 or 11–21 this year.

Downing is another one of the many pitchers who had one big season and never repeated. In fairness it should be pointed out that Downing spent the first nine seasons of his career with the New York Mets when they were basically the doormats of the league. Most years he pitched respectably, but had little support behind him. Strangely, the year the Mets won the pennant (1969), he was just 7–5. His record with the Mets was 72–57—not bad when we consider the caliber of teams he had to pitch for.

Before he joined the Dodgers, he split a season with Oakland and Milwaukee and was 5–13. At age 30 the Dodgers had hoped for some more big seasons from Downing, but it was not to be. Again, although posting respectable ERAs, the most he ever won was nine each of the next two years. He played out his career with the Dodgers, retiring in 1977 with a final career mark of 123–107.

The league's top fireman was Pittsburgh's Dave Guisti with 30 saves. Chicago had the most complete games with 75 while Cincinnati had the fewest at 27.

Pitcher/Team	G	GS	CG	W	L	Pct	ERA	SO	W	IP
Ferg Jenkins, Chgo	39	39*	30*	24*	13	.649	2.77	263	37	325*
Steve Carlton, STL	37	36	18	20	9	.690	3.56	172	98	273
Al Downing, LA	37	36	12	20	9	.690	2.68	136	84	262
Tom Seaver, NY	36	35	21	20	10	.667	1.76*	289*	61	286

Four pitchers tied for the shutout lead with five. In the Series, Steve Blass was the pitching hero for Pittsburgh with two complete game winning performances. Ellis, their big winner, was bombed in his only start.

1972

AMERICAN LEAGUE: A NEW DYNASTY REIGNS

Baltimore won 22 games less than the previous season, as only one of the four 20-game winners repeated. Jim Palmer notched 21 wins, but Mike Cuellar dipped to 18, and Pat Dobson and Dave McNally had losing records. Detroit rode the arms of 22-game winner Mickey Lolich and 19-game winner Joe Coleman to first place. Cleveland, although finishing fifth, had the Cy young winner in Gaylord Perry, who won one-third of his team's games.

Catfish Hunter won 21 and Ken Holtzman 19 as Oakland won in the West by five and one-half games over Chicago, who had MVP winner Richie Allen in his first season in the American League. Oakland's run for the title was made tougher because Vida Blue was a holdout in spring, fell behind, and finished at 6–10 for the year.

Wilbur Wood tied Perry for the high with 24 wins, and teammate Stan Bahnsen added 21 in Chicago's drive to second place. Nolan Ryan won 19 games for a sub-.500 California team that finished fifth.

Lolich had his second successive 20-win season, as well as his second consecutive year with over 20 complete games as he posted 23. His 327 innings, while third in the league, was the second of four consecutive years that he exceeded 300. Lolich fanned 250 batters, giving him four straight years in what eventually would be six. After this year he began to slip as he won 16 each of the next two years, but lost 15 and then 21. After a 12–18 season, he went to the Mets and was only 8–13 before his career-ending stint with San Diego in 1978–79.

Palmer enjoyed his third straight season in the charmed circle as he posted a 21–10 record, his highest wins to date, and his best career ERA, 2.07, although it wasn't good enough to be the best in the league that year. Palmer pitched 274 innings, the fewest he would pitch from 1970–79 except for the injury-ridden season of 1974.

Perry, with his career and league-high 24 wins, kept Cleveland respectable. Without Perry they were 48–68, a pace that would have placed them last in the division. Perry also had a league-best 29 complete games, but his 343 innings and 1.92 ERA were only second best. Wood had the most innings, while Luis Tiant (15–6) had the best ERA at 1.81.

Although Perry won 20 or more five times in his career, he never had back-to-back 20-win seasons. With any support, this year Perry could have won at least 30 games, as only three teams scored fewer runs than Cleveland. Perry is also the only pitcher to win a Cy Young in each league, as he would later win while pitching for San Diego in 1979.

Hunter won 21 games for the second consecutive year and posted the best ERA of his career with a 2.04. His .750 winning percentage was the league's best. Hunter won the same number next season, giving him three years in a row at 21 wins.

With 24 wins, Wood tied Perry for the league lead, but easily won the most games started with 49. Wood worked the most innings—377—which was a throwback to the early part of this century. With a 2.51 ERA, he deserved to win 30 games, but like Perry lacked sufficient support.

Bahnsen pitched in the majors for 16 years and had a 146–149 career mark. His first five years had been spent with the Yankees where he was 55–52, with a tops of 17 in 1968, his first full season in the majors. This would be Bahnsen's only 20-win year as he worked 252 innings and started 41 games, but had only five complete. Bahnsen won 18 and 12 the next two years, but lost 21 and 15 respectively. In early 1975 he was traded to Oakland, where he lasted a couple of seasons. He then spent four years in Montreal, appearing in 181 games, all but four as a reliever, before finishing up with California and Philadelphia in 1982.

This was Nolan Ryan's first big season as he was 19–16 for a very weak California team that averaged less than three runs per game. Ryan worked 284 innings, pitched nine shutouts and posted a 2.28 ERA as he pitched 20 complete games. Ryan could also have been a big winner, with totals reaching the high 20s. He led in strikeouts for the first of 11 times as he fanned 329 men. During his career he would fan over 200 in a season 14 times, and exceed 300 on six occasions. We will revisit Ryan many times before this book is finished.

The Yankees' Sparky Lyle led with 35 saves. Baltimore had the most complete games with 62, while Texas set a new low with only 11.

Pitcher/Team	G	GS	CG	W	L	Pct	ERA	SO	W	IP
Gaylord Perry, Cleve	41	40	29*	24*	16	.600	1.92	234	82	343
Wilbur Wood, Chgo	49	49*	20	24*	17	.585	2.51	193	74	377*
Mickey Lolich, Det	41	41	23	22	14	.611	2.50	250	74	327
Catfish Hunter, Oak	38	37	16	21	7	.750*	2.04	191	70	295
Jim Palmer, Balt	36	36	18	21	10	.677	2.07	184	70	274
Stan Bahnsen, Chgo	43	41	5	21	16	.568	3.61	157	73	252

Rod Carew became the first man to win a batting title without hitting a home run. Oakland took Detroit's measure in five games as Blue Moon Odom (15–6) won two games. Hunter had a 1.17 ERA in two starts, but no decision.

In the World Series, Oakland won four games to three as Gene Tenace, who hit only five home runs in 225 at bats, and hit .225 during the regular season, had four home runs and nine RBIs while batting .348. Hunter had two wins and Rollie Fingers two saves.

NATIONAL LEAGUE: THE BIG RED MACHINE ROARS

Cincinnati, with the addition of Joe Morgan, won handily over surprise second-place finisher Houston. Johnny Bench rebounded to win his second MVP in three seasons. However, no Red pitcher won over 15 games. Claude Osteen had 20 wins and Don Sutton 19 for third-place finisher Los Angeles.

Pittsburgh lost Roberto Clemente after the season in a plane crash after winning for the third straight year in the East, as Chicago again came in second. Ferguson Jenkins won 20 for the sixth straight year, and Tom Seaver made it three out of four seasons. St. Louis, which had traded Steve Carlton over a salary dispute, finished a dismal fourth despite 19 wins from Bob Gibson.

Jenkins pitched his sixth straight 20-win season with a 20–12 record while recording 23 complete games, which also made six straight years he had accomplished that feat. His 289 innings were the fewest he had pitched since he duplicated that number in 1967, the first year of his streak. Jenkins would slump next season to 14–16 with a 3.89 ERA, and even more disturbing would only complete seven games in 38 starts. Then he would be off to Texas, where he would have his biggest season ever in 1974.

Seaver had 21 wins for the second consecutive year, but when he pitched "only" 262 innings it was the fewest since 251 in his rookie year of 1967. Although he didn't lead in strikeouts, he extended his string of at least 200 men fanned in a season to five, en route to nine years in a row.

However, the real pitching story was in Philadelphia, where Carlton won 27 games for a last-place team. His victory total represented 46 percent of the team's wins. He was easily the Cy Young winner. After winning 20 games for St. Louis in 1971, Carlton wanted $75,000 per year, a paltry sum by today's standards, but big bucks for the time. Remember, the reserve clause, which binds a player to a team for life, was still in effect. There is argument pro and con on this subject, but this book is not the place for that debate.

When St. Louis offered $60,000, Carlton balked and took his story to the press. This irked owner Gussie Busch and he ordered Carlton traded. When Carlton heard this, he relented, especially when he found out he was going to the lowly Phils. It was too late. Busch was adamant and Carlton was gone, even though now he was willing to play for $60,000 a season. Carlton's position was that, if Gibson gets $150,000, which he was worth, Carlton ought to get at least half of that because he was at least half as good. Many baseball people believe losing Carlton cost the Cardinals two or three pennants in the 1970s. Sometimes pride gets in our way.

Carlton was outstanding in his career-best season. He easily could have won 30 games given a little more support, but at this time Philadelphia was the doormat of the league. Without Carlton they were 32–87, which would almost have put them in the Three I League. Carlton started a league-high 41 games, had 30 complete, and pitched the most innings with 346, while fanning a league-high 310 and posting the best ERA, 1.98.

Osteen had the second 20-win season of his career as he posted his best ERA, 2.64. Osteen pitched one more season with Los Angeles and had a 16–11 record. Then he spent 1974 with Houston and St. Louis and was 9–11 before finishing up with the White Sox at 7–16 in 1975. That last season cost him his chance for 200 career victories.

Clay Carroll paced Cincinnati and the league with 37 saves. St. Louis led with 64 complete games, mainly because Gibson and Rick Wise not only won 35 games, but were kept in the games because both were excellent hitting pitchers. Cincinnati had the fewest at 25.

Pitcher/Team	G	GS	CG	W	L	Pct	ERA	SO	W	IP
Steve Carlton, Phila	41	41*	30*	27*	10	.730	1.96*	310*	87	346*
Tom Seaver, NY	35	35	13	21	12	.636	2.92	249	77	262
Claude Osteen, LA	33	33	14	20	11	.645	2.64	109	69	252
Ferg Jenkins, Chgo	36	36	23	20	12	.625	3.21	194	62	289

The only honor Carlton didn't gather was winning percentage, which went to Cincinnati's Gary Nolan (15–5, .750).

Cincinnati beat Pittsburgh three games to two, when Bob Moose threw a wild pitch in the bottom of the ninth to allow Cincinnati to score the winning run. In the World Series, Cincinnati actually outpitched Oakland but lost four games to three.

Baseball had experienced its first labor discord, and each team lost approximately eight games from the schedule. The players had walked off the field shortly before the season started, protesting several issues, the main one being the pension plan. After a total of 86 games were lost in 13 days, a settlement was reached and the season began.

1973

AMERICAN LEAGUE: ENTER THE DESIGNATED HITTER

The biggest change in baseball was the introduction of the designated hitter, and with that, the American League produced a record 12 20-game winners during the season. Oakland led the way, as they had three 20-game winners en route to their third straight title. Every team in the Western Division had at least one, except last-place Texas.

In the East, Baltimore got 22 wins from Jim Palmer and shot back to the top. Only New York and last-place Cleveland failed to have a 20-game winner, although the latter got 19 from Gaylord Perry. Detroit's John Hiller had a league-high 38 saves, a new record. The percentage of complete games increased because of the DH, and California led with 72, while Texas had the fewest at 35.

Palmer won his first of three Cy Young Awards with 22 wins. This was his highest victory total to date and his fourth year in a row in the charmed circle. He also led in ERA for the first of two times with a 2.40. His 296 innings represented the second most of his career to that point. Next year a third career-threatening injury would slow him down.

Luis Tiant posted his second 20-win season and the first of two straight at Boston. He had been traded to Boston after the 1970 season. After a dismal 1–7 mark in 1971, he had rebounded to win 15 games and the league's best ERA in 1972. Tiant pitched for Boston through 1978 and had only that one losing season, as from 1972 through 1978 he won 121 games.

With 23 wins, this was Joe Coleman's biggest season, but strangely the highest ERA of the past three years, during which he had won 62 games. After this season Coleman was 14–12, then he slumped to 10–18. Then from 1976 to the end of his career in 1979 he pitched for Detroit, the Chicago Cubs, Toronto, Oakland, San Francisco and Pittsburgh. Most of his pitching was in relief and he had a 13–17 record overall, which gave him a final mark of 142–135.

Jim Colborn is another of those pitchers that had one big season and never really duplicated his efforts. Colborn appeared in 43 games, 36 of them starts and completed 22 as he pitched 314 innings while posting a 20–12 record. However, after this season his ERA shot up and he was 30–41 in three losing seasons for Milwaukee before spending an 18–14 year with Kansas City in 1977. He then finished with Kansas City and Seattle in 1978 at 4–12 for a final career mark of 83–88.

Perry turned in another workhorse season as he pitched 29 complete games (highest in the league) for the second straight season while he logged 344 innings. His efforts paid off with 19 wins, but he also had 19 defeats, many of which could have been on the other side of the ledger.

Even though Catfish Hunter missed over a month with a broken finger, he still won 21 for the third season in a row and also posted the league's top winning percentage (.808). The 256 innings were the fewest Hunter had pitched since he had 247 in 1969.

Ken Holtzman entered the charmed circle with 21 wins for the only time in his career. However, Holtzman was not a stranger to success as he won 19 the prior year for Oakland and would win 19 and 18 the next two seasons for the team. Earlier he had two 17-game winning seasons for the Chicago Cubs. He did however have a Jekyll and Hyde streak with the Cubs as illustrated by the following records beginning in 1966: 11–16, 9–0, 11–14, 17–13, 17–11, and 9–15 before coming to Oakland for the start of the 1972 campaign. He returned to the Cubs late in 1978 and finished his career there in 1979 with a composite 6–12. His final record is 174–150.

Vida Blue didn't hold out this season and was the third member of the staff to win 20, as he was 20–9. This was Blue's second 20-win season and he would join the charmed circle one more time. Blue pitched for Oakland through 1977, winning 17, 18, 22 and 14 over the next four years. His career record with Oakland was 124–86.

Bert Blyleven had his only 20-win season in a career that lasted until 1992, during which he posted a 287–250 record. Blyleven was outstanding this season as he had a 2.50 ERA, led with nine shutouts and had 25 complete games while pitching 325 innings. Based on his ERA and complete games, he lost a lot of one-run tough-luck decisions. During his career he won at least ten games in 17 different seasons. Ten times his ERA was under 3.00, but he had the misfortune to play for weaker teams most of the time.

Paul Splittorff spent his entire career with Kansas City, which included 13 full and two part seasons. He fashioned a 166–143 record and had nine seasons at or above .500. This was his only 20-win year in what was his third full season. His career followed somewhat of a roller coaster, as the next two years he was 13–19 and 9–10. Then he rebounded with three straight winning seasons of 11, 16 and 19 before slumping to a 15–17 and then a winning 14–11 record. His only season below .500 after 15–17 in 1979 was his last, when he was 1–3. While not always spectacular, Splittorff did give solid, steady pitching for many years at Kansas City.

Nolan Ryan had his first of two successive 20-win seasons, which would be the only ones of his career. Ryan had another super year and given a better team behind him could have led the league in wins. This was to be the albatross of his career. Ryan had a 2.87 ERA and pitched 326 innings while completing 26 games and posting a 21–16 record. His 383 strikeouts not only led, but set a new major league record. In time, he would fan over 5,000 batters to hold the all-time record.

Bill Singer proved another workhorse on the California staff as he won 20 games and had a 3.22 ERA. He started 40 games, completed 19 and hurled 316 innings. He and Ryan together started 50 percent of the team's games and completed almost two-thirds while hurling 44 percent of the innings—two really rugged workhorses.

The final 20-game winner was Wilbur Wood, who led in wins for the second straight season with 24. Wood again was a real workhorse as he started 48 games, completed 21 and had a league-high 359 innings. Unfortunately, he lost 20 games, but as in other seasons a little additional batting support and he could have won 30. Wood had one more 20-win season in his arm before tailing off.

Teammate Stan Bahnsen had a reversal of form as he won 18 but lost 21, despite a respectable 3.57 ERA. Wood and Bahnsen together started 90 times, almost 60 percent of the team's games, and their 35 complete games represented almost three-fourths of the team's total.

Pitcher/Team	G	GS	CG	W	L	Pct	ERA	SO	W	IP
Wilbur Wood, Chgo	49	48*	21	24*	20	.545	3.46	199	91	359*
Joe Coleman, Det	40	40*	13	23	15	.605	3.53	202	93	288
Jim Palmer, Balt	38	37	19	22	9	.710	2.40*	158	113	296
Catfish Hunter, Oak	36	36	11	21	5	.808*	2.34	124	69	256
Ken Holtzman, Oak	40	40	16	21	13	.618	2.97	157	66	297
Nolan Ryan, Ca	41	39	26	21	16	.568	2.87	383*	162*	326
Vida Blue, Oak	37	37	13	20	9	.690	3.27	158	105	264
Paul Splittorff, KC	38	38	12	20	11	.645	3.98	110	78	262
Jim Colborn, Milw	43	36	22	20	12	.625	3.18	135	87	314
Luis Tiant, Bos	39	35	23	20	13	.606	3.34	206	78	272
Bill Singer, Ca	40	40	19	20	14	.588	3.22	241	130	316
Bert Blyleven, Mn	40	40	25	20	17	.541	2.52	258	67	325

Oakland defeated Baltimore three games to two to win the right to go to the World Series.

Although Oakland was a much stronger team, they had to win the final two games to defeat New York four games to three. Holtzman won two games while Fingers had two saves. Gene Tenace had no heroics this time, as he batted .063.

NATIONAL LEAGUE: ANOTHER MIRACLE HAPPENS

The National League didn't adopt the designated hitter rule and as a result had only one 20-game winner, Ron Bryant of the San Francisco Giants, who won 24. They finished third to Los Angeles, who trailed three and a half games behind Cincinnati. The Big Red Machine had adequate pitching, but did it again on their hitting.

In the East, New York surprised everyone, winning the title with the lowest winning percentage of all time, with an 82–79 record to edge out second-place St. Louis, 81–81. The Cardinals suffered a crucial blow when Bob Gibson injured his leg, was lost for over a month to the team, and could win only 12 games. Tom Seaver with a 19–10 log copped the Cy Young award, while last year's winner Steve Carlton slipped to 13–20.

San Francisco's Ron Bryant was the league's only 20-game winner as he posted a 24–12 mark and a 3.53 ERA, but only eight complete games in 35 starts. This was now the age of the relief pitcher, despite what Nolan Ryan, Gaylord Perry or a few other pitchers did. Bryant's career is a strange one, as he voluntarily retired in the 1975 season after ten games and a 0–1 record. From 1969 through 1971 he was 16–21 for the Giants, then he turned in a 14–7, 2.90 ERA performance for 1972 before his big season in 1973. Things looked bright for the 26-year-old right-hander heading into the 1974 season. But he suffered a side injury and was only 3–15 with a 5.60 ERA. He never fully recovered and he was out of baseball in 1975 at the age of only 28—another potentially good career lost. His final mark was a so-so 57–56.

Seaver fell one win short of the charmed circle but otherwise was brilliant as he had a league-high 18 complete games and the lowest ERA (2.08). This completed the first phase of his career, during which he won 135 games over seven years. Next season various injuries would limit him to an 11–11 year, but he would rebound to have seven straight winning seasons, including two 20-game years and another Cy Young Award.

Carlton took a tremendous drop as he lost 20 games and saw his ERA go up to 3.90. He still led the league with 40 starts, tied Seaver for most complete games and hurled the most innings (293). He fanned 223, but surrendered the strikeout title to Seaver at 251. Carlton would rebound and post nine straight winning seasons, four of them 20 or better, and win three more Cy Young Awards.

Ferguson Jenkins failed to win 20 games for the first time in seven years, as he was 14–16 with 3.89 ERA and only seven complete games in his last season with the Cubs until the end of his career. He was off to Texas, then the Red Sox, and back to Texas, where he enjoyed some more winning seasons.

Montreal's Mike Marshall had 31 saves and won 14 games as he appeared in a record 92 games. Philadelphia had the most complete games at 49, while Pittsburgh and Montreal had the fewest at 26.

Pitcher/Team	G	GS	CG	W	L	Pct	ERA	SO	W	IP
Ron Bryant, SF	41	38	8	24*	12	.667	3.53	143	115	270

Jack Billingham (19–10) of Cincinnati had the most shutouts at seven, while LA's Tommy John had the best percentage at .696, based on a 16–7 record.

Cincinnati was favored to win easily over New York but instead lost in five games. New York was considered no match for Oakland, but carried them to seven games, leading at one point three games to two.

Willie Mays retired after 21 seasons, and Hank Aaron finished the season with 713 home runs, one behind the Babe's vaunted record.

1974

AMERICAN LEAGUE: ONE MORE TIME

The designated hitter continued to prove a boon to pitchers, as there were nine to join the charmed 20-win circle this year. Baltimore won the East, paced by Mike Cuellar's 22 wins. This was despite a 7–12 log from Jim Palmer, who developed a sore arm and was limited to 26 starts.

In the west Oakland won again, with Catfish Hunter gaining 25 wins. Texas was a surprise second-place finisher, mainly because they had acquired

Ferguson Jenkins from Chicago. He won 25 games, but finished second to Hunter in the Cy Young voting. Perhaps the best performance was turned in by Nolan Ryan, who won 22 games for last-place California.

After a three-year absence, Cuellar returned to the charmed circle with his fourth and final 20-win season as he notched a 22–10 record. Cuellar also led the loop with a .688 winning percentage. Cuellar had one more winning season the next year at 14–12 before he faded to 4–13 in 1976. In two games with California the following year he was 0–1 when he called it a career. He finished with a 185–130, .587 winning percentage, but has had no calls from the Hall. This is not bad, though, for a pitcher who won 143 games after he reached age 32.

Luis Tiant continued his fine pitching for the Red Sox as he logged the largest win (22) total of his career as well as his most complete games (25). Tiant had a 2.92 ERA and worked the most innings of his career (311) as he led the league with seven shutouts. He would slip to 18 wins the next season, but return to win 20 in 1976.

Gaylord Perry won 21 games for the Indians (who again finished below .500), giving him 64 wins in three seasons. Perry turned in other fine numbers, as he had 28 complete games, hurled 322 innings and posted a fine 2.52 ERA. However, as good as those numbers were, someone else was better in each category.

With 25 wins, Hunter had his career-best season as he shared the lead in victories with Jenkins, but won the ERA title with 2.49. In posting his fourth consecutive 20-plus-win season, Hunter logged 23 complete games and pitched 318 innings, the first of two years he would reach that level. Oakland didn't know it at the time, but this would be Hunter's final season as an "A." Next year would find him in New York Yankees' pinstripe.

Jenkins' first season in Texas was the biggest of his career as he posted a 25–12 mark with a 2.83 ERA, also the best of his life. He led the league with 29 complete games, but his 328 innings were second. Despite all these fine marks, he came in second for the Cy Young to Hunter. Jenkins won 17 but lost 18 the next season. He then went to Boston, where he should have been great, but had two mediocre seasons, 12–11 and 10–10, before returning to Texas and winning 46 games in three years. He finished out his career in 1982–83 with the Cubs at 20–24 for the final two years. His overall mark is 284–226, which eventually earned him a spot in the Hall of Fame.

Going into this season, Jim Kaat had been pitching in the majors since 1959 and had won 193 games, all but four with Minnesota. The only time he had won 20 before was when he led the league with 25 wins back in 1966. So, at age 36 he stunned the baseball world by posting a 2.92 ERA en route to a 21–13 year for the also-ran White Sox. This was the first of two successive 20-win seasons he would give the Pale Hose.

Wilbur Wood got his fourth straight 20 win season with exactly that number, but almost got his second straight 20-loss year, as he dropped 19 decisions.

Wood started a league-high 42 games and pitched 320 innings, the fourth year in a row he was over 300. Wood logged 22 complete games and, based on his 3.60 ERA, it seems he could have won a few more games. This was his last big winning season as he was 16–20 in 1975, then suffered a broken knee cap in 1976, which inhibited his effectiveness. He finished with a 21–21 log for the 1976–78 years.

Steve Busby is another example of a pitcher who looked like a world-beater, but came down with shoulder problems and was through before his time. In his first full season in 1973 Busby was 16–15, but was just warming up. He was 22–14 in 1974 and followed that with an 18–12 year. At age 27 it looked like the Royals had found the ace pitcher they needed to make a run for the division title. But Busby suffered a separated shoulder and his career was basically over. He tried pitching up through 1980, but was only 11–12 as he could appear in only 53 games, 36 as a starter, two fewer than he made this year.

Ryan had another great year as he won 22, the highest total of his career. He was first with 333 innings and 367 strikeouts. He also had 26 complete games while posting a 2.89 ERA. Again, any of half a dozen teams in the league would have given him a good shot at 30. Even though they were losers more times than winners, Ryan always enjoyed playing for California and Texas. When he retired he had 324 wins, but he also had 292 losses. Many believe that given decent support, he could have won 400 games. Let the reader speculate.

Chicago's Terry Forster led the league with 24 saves, while Boston led the league with 71 complete games and Minnesota and Milwaukee tied for last with 43.

Pitcher/Team	G	GS	CG	W	L	Pct	ERA	SO	W	IP
Catfish Hunter, Oak	41	41*	23	25*	12	.676	2.49*	143	46	318
Ferg Jenkins, Tex	41	41*	29*	25*	12	.676	2.83	225	45	328
Mike Cuellar, Balt	38	38	20	22	10	.688*	3.11	106	86	269
Luis Tiant, Bos	38	38	25	22	13	.629	2.92	176	82	311
Steve Busby, KC	38	38	20	22	14	.611	3.39	198	92	292
Nolan Ryan, Ca	42	41	26	22	16	.579	2.89	367*	202*	333*
Gaylord Perry, Cleve	37	37	28	21	13	.618	2.52	216	99	322
Jim Kaat, Chgo	42	38	15	21	13	.616	2.92	142	63	277
Wilbur Wood, Chgo	42	42*	22	20	19	.513	3.60	169	80	320

Tiant led with seven shutouts. Oakland again took Baltimore's measure, this time three games to one. In the World Series it was the same story, as Oakland won in five games, with Rollie Fingers winning one and saving two.

NATIONAL LEAGUE: THE MIGHTY RECORD FALLS

The big news in the National League was that Hank Aaron broke the Babe's home run record and finished the season with 733. He would go to the American

League after this year and play two more seasons, hitting an additional 22 to finish with 755.

In the East Pittsburgh edged out St. Louis, making it three times in five seasons the Cardinals had been bridesmaid. No team in the East had a 20-game winner; the highest number was 17 by Jim Lonborg for Philadelphia.

Los Angeles made it back to the top after several years' absence as Andy Messersmith won 20 and Don Sutton added 19. However, the real pitching news was their reliever, Mike Marshall, who won 15, saved 21 and set a record that still stands by appearing in 106 games. He became the first relief specialist to win the Cy Young Award.

Messersmith shared the lead in wins with Phil Niekro, as each won 20. This was his second 20-win season, but one of the two finest of his career. He posted a 2.59 ERA as he logged 292 innings while making 39 starts. After this season he and Dave McNally would challenge baseball's reserve clause, and the players won. If they played the 1975 season without a contract, then they could become free agents. The rest is history.

Niekro won 20 games for the second time in his career and shared the lead for most victories for the first time. His 2.38 ERA was the best of his career. This year he led with 18 complete games and 302 innings pitched. Niekro had six shutouts, but was second to the Mets' Jon Matlack (13–15) with seven. He would win 21 games in 1979, and between 1974 and 1980 Niekro won 123 while losing 115 despite having some excellent ERAs along the way.

Cincinnati was second as Jack Billingham again won 19. Pittsburgh led with 51 complete games and Chicago was last with 23.

Pitcher/Team	G	GS	CG	W	L	Pct	ERA	SO	W	IP
A Messersmith, LA	39	39	13	20*	6	.769	2.59	221	94	292
Phil Niekro, Atl	41	39	18*	20*	13	.606	2.38	195	88	302*

Atlanta's Buzz Capra led with a 2.28 ERA. LA's Tommy John had the top winning percentage at .813, as he was 13–3 despite missing almost half the season. Steve Carlton led in strikeouts with 240. Lou Brock broke Maury Wills single-season record of 104 stolen bases by swiping 118.

Sutton won two games as Los Angeles took Pittsburgh in four games. However, in the World Series, the Dodgers could get only one win from Sutton, as Messersmith lost twice.

1975

AMERICAN LEAGUE: A SURPRISE WINNER WITH TWO ROOKIE FINDS

The Baltimore Orioles and the New York Yankees were expected to battle it out for the title, but they finished second and third respectively. The latter were slowed by injuries to key players, while the former started slowly. Boston came up with two rookies who would star for many years. Fred Lynn played a flawless center field and became the first man ever to win both rookie of the year and MVP. Jim Rice also hit over .300, 22 home runs and had 102 RBIs.

As a result of these two finds, the Red Sox won the pennant. They had 19 wins from Rick Wise, 18 from Luis Tiant and 17 from Bill Lee. The Orioles had two 20-game winners, and the Yankees' Catfish Hunter, who had been made a free agent after a salary dispute with Oakland, tied Jim Palmer for the most victories with 23. Palmer edged out Hunter for the Cy Young Award.

Oakland took the West Division title for the fifth straight year as Vida Blue won 22. Jim Kaat won 20 for the lowly White Sox. The Sox also had Goose Gossage, who led the league with 28 saves. Wilbur Wood failed for the first time in five years to win 20, as he won 16 and lost 20, but led with starts at 43. Undoubtedly, a better team could have at least reversed his record.

Palmer returned to the charmed circle as he led the league with 23 wins, the first of three straight seasons he would lead, and the first of four straight 20-plus-win years. Along the way Palmer also won the Cy Young in both 1975 and 1976. These four seasons were even more productive than the 1970–73 era, as Palmer fully recovered from a sore arm and racked up 86 wins, versus 83 for the former era. His 2.09 ERA and ten shutouts were the best in the league as well as his career. Palmer was the mainstay of the Baltimore staff, despite repeated run-ins with manager Earl Weaver. They had a love-hate relationship.

Mike Torrez had first pitched for St. Louis in the majors in three games in 1967 and his career would last through 1984. Between those years there were good seasons, bad seasons and fair ones.

However, through all those years he only had one 20-win season and it was this year, his lone season in Baltimore, as he was 20–9 to grab the league's best winning percentage at .690. Counting full and part seasons he had winning marks 11 times and losing records seven times. While he had five other seasons of between 15 and 17 wins, he also had years of 9–12, 9–16 and 10 17. His final record is 185–160.

Hunter had his last 20-win season as he posted a league-high 23 for the Yankees and a 2.58 ERA. He led with 30 complete games and 328 innings. His seven shutouts were second to Palmer. Hunter never won 20 again, although he did post a 17–15 mark in 1976. He played out his career with the Yankees and finished in 1979 at only 33 with a 2–9 mark, saying he preferred his farm in North Carolina. When he retired he owned a 224–166, .574 career record, which eventually got him elected to the Hall of Fame.

Vida Blue had his final 20-win year as he was 22–11 with a 3.01 ERA. Blue would still be effective as he won 18 the next year, but when he slumped to 14–19 in 1977 his days at Oakland were ended. He then spent three seasons at San Francisco, winning 46 games, with the best being the first at 18. Then there were two years at Kansas City, 13–12 and 0–5, before a final 10–10 year with

San Francisco. His final career mark is 209–161, similar to Don Drysdale, but no call from the Hall as of this date.

Kaat posted his last 20-win season for the Pale Sox and certainly could have won more with a better team behind him. In two full seasons Kaat won 41 games for the White Sox. The next year would find him in Philadelphia. He would spend the rest of his career there, in St. Louis, and with the Yankees, pitching mostly in relief. He left the game with a 283–237 record.

Nolan Ryan didn't win 20 nor lead in strikeouts. An elbow injury limited him to 28 starts. He would return the next season stronger than ever.

Baltimore and the Yankees tied for team lead in complete games with 70 each, while Chicago was last with 34.

Pitcher/Team	G	GS	CG	W	L	Pct	ERA	SO	W	IP
Catfish Hunter, NY	39	39	30*	23*	14	.622	2.58	177	83	328*
Jim Palmer, Balt	39	38	25	23*	11	.676	2.09*	193	80	323
Vida Blue, Oak	39	38	13	22	11	.667	3.01	189	99	278
Mike Torrez, Balt	36	36	16	20	9	.690	3.06	119	133*	271
Jim Kaat, Chgo	43	41	12	20	14	.588	3.11	142	77	304

Boston's Roger Moret (14–3) had the league's top winning percentage at .824. Boston took Oakland in three straight to head into the fall classic looking for their first World Series Title since 1917. They are still looking, as Cincinnati defeated them in seven games, with five of them decided by one run. Tiant won two games for Boston, while the rest of the staff pitched ineffectively.

NATIONAL LEAGUE: THE RETURN OF THE BIG RED MACHINE

For the fourth time in six years Cincinnati captured the Western Division title, then went on to defeat their Eastern rival Pittsburgh and claim their third pennant. The final victory margin was 20 games, as they did it on power, with five hitters driving in at least 74 runs and four hitting over .300. They had six pitchers to win between 10 and 15, with three achieving the latter.

Randy Jones won 20 for fourth-place San Diego, who probably would have finished last without him.

Meanwhile, in the East Pittsburgh rolled to their fifth title in six years, but would be stopped in the playoffs by Cincinnati. Tom Seaver beat out Jones for the Cy Young Award as his 22 wins helped put New York in third place. Philadelphia placed second on the power hitting of Mike Schmidt and Greg Luzinski.

Seaver was the lone 20-game winner in the Eastern Division as he led the league with 22 wins while posting a 2.38 ERA in 280 innings and leading with 243 strikeouts. This was his fourth and final 20-win season for the Mets. He won 14 for New York the next year and then prior to mid-season 1977 he was traded to Cincinnati, where he would have his final 20-win year.

Jones broke in with San Diego in 1973 and was 7–6. Then came an 8–22, 4.46 ERA 1974 season. No one expected what would happen the next two years, as Jones blossomed into one of the league's top pitchers. In 1975 he was 20–12 for a weak San Diego club. He logged 18 complete games, pitched 285 innings and had the best ERA at 2.24. He would win 22 the next year and then be laid low by that old pitcher's bugaboo—a sore arm.

Two pitchers played without a contract to test the free agency that they had sought in the off-season. Dave McNally pitched in 12 games for Montreal and was 3–6 before retiring from baseball. The other pitcher was Andy Messersmith who had another big year for Los Angeles as he won 19 games, started a league-high 40, pitched the most complete games (19) while leading with 322 innings. He also had a 2.29 ERA with the most shutouts (seven). He was a free agent at the end of the year and signed with Atlanta, but it did him little good.

Messersmith developed a sore arm and pitched through 1979, but never regained his form as he was 18–22 for those four years. Ironically, the two pitchers who sued for free agency and won never benefited. However, the rest of the players saw a gold mine open up to them and the structure of the game was changed forever. Was it good or bad? You decide!

Cincinnati again relied heavily on the bullpen as they had a league low of 22 complete games. Rawly Eastwick led the loop with 22 saves and teammate Will McEnaney added 15 for the Reds. Los Angeles had the most complete games at 51.

Pitcher/Team	G	GS	CG	W	L	Pct	ERA	SO	W	IP
Tom Seaver, NY	36	36	15	22*	9	.710	2.38	243*	88	280
Randy Jones, San Dg	37	36	18	20	14	.588	2.24*	103	56	285

St Louis' Al Hrabosky (13–3) led in winning percentage (.813) and tied for the lead in saves at 22.

Cincinnati again dispatched Pittsburgh, this time in three games, then in a hard-fought Series defeated Boston in seven games. Eastwick was the standout, winning two games and saving a third, while Pete Rose led all hitters with a .370 mark.

1976

AMERICAN LEAGUE: A RETURN TO THE TOP

The players had been locked out in spring training because of a dispute over pitchers Dave McNally and Andy Messersmith, who played without contracts in 1975 and were declared free agents. Bowie Kuhn stepped in and ended the lockout and baseball's 100th season began.

The Yankees, after a 12-year absence, captured the Eastern title quite handily without a 20-game winner. Ed Figueroa gave them 19 and Catfish Hunter and Dock Ellis each had 17. However, they had the premier relief pitcher in Sparky Lyle, who led with 23 saves.

Baltimore had their usual two 20-game winners but finished second, while Boston was third with Luis Tiant winning 21. The biggest pitching news was 21-year-old Mark "The Bird" Fydrich, who was 19–9, with a league-low 2.34 ERA and a leading 24 complete games for fifth-place Detroit. Unfortunately, he injured his arm, won ten more games and was out of baseball by the time he was 26.

Jim Palmer, with 22 wins, won his third Cy Young Award and second in a row. His wins, 40 starts and 315 innings were the most in the league. His 23 complete games and six shutouts were second best in the league. This was the second of two successive 20-plus-win seasons.

The other 20-game winner on Baltimore's staff is an interesting subject. Wayne Garland had a 7–11 record for parts of three seasons with Baltimore when he burst through with a 20–7, 2.68 ERA season. With the advent of free agency, he signed a ten-year contract with Cleveland at what was then an unheard of sum of $200,000 per year. It turned out to be a bust both for him and Cleveland, as he never produced another winning season. His first year he was 13–19 with a 3.59 ERA. Then Garland injured his arm and appeared in 61 games over the next four seasons, fashioning a composite 28–48 to give him a final career mark of 55–66. When we remove his one winning season, he was 35–59. Ironically, the first three involved with free agencies were busts.

Luis Tiant had his final 20-win season with a 21–12 mark for the Red Sox. Tiant posted two more winning seasons for the Red Sox before moving to the Yankees, where he was 13–8 and 8–9 for 1979–80. Then he pitched in 15 games during 1981–82 for Pittsburgh and California, was 4–7 and retired with a final mark of 229–172, but no call from the Hall.

Nolan Ryan had another tough-luck season with California as he won 17 but lost 18 despite a 3.36 ERA, as California had the lowest batting average and fewest runs scored of any team in the league. Ryan added another strikeout crown with 327, led with seven shutouts and hurled 284 innings while pitching 21 complete games. Reviewing Ryan's record, we find he could probably have won 20 or more at least another five times, and maybe 30 a couple. He just couldn't get the necessary support.

Kansas City captured the Western title but lost to the Yankees in five games. California had the most complete games with 63 while Minnesota had the fewest at 29. In terms of 20-game winners, the effects of the DH was dissipating, as the number had declined from introduction with a high of 12 down to three this season.

Fidrich's case is really a tragic story. Here was a 22-year-old kid who loved the game, and the fans loved him. Whenever he pitched, they came out in droves. He filled ballparks. In his rookie year he won 19 and completed 24 games in an era when you weren't supposed to do that, and posted a 2.34 ERA. Then he suffered an arm injury and never fully recovered. He made several futile attempts, but after 27 games and a 10–10 record over four years he was forced to call it quits at age 26 in 1980. What a great potential was lost.

Pitcher/Team	G	GS	CG	W	L	Pct	ERA	SO	W	IP
Jim Palmer, Balt	40	40*	23	22*	13	.629	2.51	159	84	315*
Luis Tiant, Bos	38	38	19	21	12	.636	3.06	131	64	279
Wayne Garland, Clev	38	25	14	20	7	.741	2.68	113	64	232

Palmer won the Cy Young and tied Vida Blue for the most shutouts at six, while Minnesota's Bill Campbell (17–5) had the best winning percentage, .773.

New York was looking for its first World Series title since 1962 but lost in four straight to Cincinnati. The Yankees posted a 5.45 team ERA, being outscored 22–8.

NATIONAL LEAGUE: A NEW POWER RISES, BUT THE BIG RED MACHINE STILL ROARS

For the next several years the Philadelphia Phillies would be one of the most dominant teams in the league. They served notice early in the season, when Mike Schmidt hit four home runs in a slugfest won by the Phillies over Chicago. At season's end they held a nine-game bulge over Pittsburgh, and were led by Steve Carlton's return to the 20-win circle.

Jerry Koosman won 21 for the Mets to help them to third, but their long-time ace Tom Seaver slipped to 14 wins. In the West Cincinnati continued to dominate on their hitting and relief pitching as seven pitchers won between 11 and 15 games, with Rawly Eastwick again leading the league with 26 saves.

Los Angeles got 21 wins from Don Sutton and had five other pitchers in double figures, but finished ten games off the pace. No other Western division team played .500 ball. J. R. Richard chalked up 20 wins for Houston. Randy Jones paced the league with 22 while toiling for weak-sister San Diego.

This was the best year for Carlton since his banner season in 1972 as he won 20 for the third time and led the league with a .741 winning percentage. Over the 1976–1980 period, Carlton won 101 games, three times over 20, and won three Cy Young Awards. He was en route to his seventh 20-win season in 1981, but the baseball strike shut him down.

This was Sutton's 11th season in the majors, all with the Dodgers, but produced his only 20-win year. He broke into the majors in 1966 and was just 34–42 his first three years, despite posting ERAs below 3.00 in two of the seasons. From 1969 through 1978, Sutton never won fewer than 14 and had only one losing year while winning 171 games. His peak period was 1972–76, during which time he was 93–51.

After spending his first fifteen seasons with the Dodgers, Sutton then bounced around with Houston, Milwaukee, Oakland and California before returning to Los Angeles for his final year, 1988. When Sutton retired he had a 324–256 record for 23 seasons. His career was not built on several 20-win seasons, but on steady pitching season after season. Sutton had said he worked most years on a five-man rotation, but that if he had been on a four-man rotation he probably would have had more 20-win seasons, but he might not have lasted 23 years. As of the date of this book he has been ignored by the Hall, although it is still early. Winning over 300 games once meant automatic selection, but that seems to be changing.

From 1971 to 1974 Richard had pitched in 39 games while posting an 11–6 mark for Houston. Finally in 1975 he was made a starter and responded with a 12–10, but 4.39 ERA. Then in 1976 he finally delivered on the promise that had always been there, as he won 20, had a 2.75 ERA and fanned 214 men. He won 18 games each of the next three seasons and had ERAs less than 3.00 in two of them, leading with 2.71 in 1979. Along the way he picked up two strikeout crowns, fanning 303 in 1978 and 313 in 1979. He was 10–4 with a 1.89 ERA, and 119 strikeouts in 114 innings in 1980 when he suffered a stroke. He later recovered, but not sufficiently to ever pitch in the majors. Thus, tragically, a potentially brilliant career was lost. Richard finished with a 107–71 career mark.

Following on the heels of his first 20-win season, Jones led the loop with 22 victories, the most innings (315) and topped the league with 25 complete games while posting a 2.74 ERA. As previously stated, an arm injury would sideline him and he would pitch through 1982, but never have a winning season again.

Koosman enjoyed his first of two 20-win seasons as he was 21–10 for the Mets with a 2.70 ERA and 17 complete games. In most seasons he stood in the shadow of Tom Seaver, but this year it was reversed. Koosman spent 12 of his 19 seasons with the Mets and won 140 games there. Following this year he was 8–20 and 3–15 before heading for Minnesota where he had his next and last 20-win season.

New York topped the league with 53 complete games and Montreal had the fewest with 26. This also marked the first season since the introduction of the DH that the National League had more 20-game winners, as they bested the junior circuit 5–3.

Pitcher/Team	G	GS	CG	W	L	Pct	ERA	SO	W	IP
Randy Jones, San Dg	40	40*	25*	22*	14	.611	2.74	93	50	315*
Jerry Koosman, NY	34	32	17	21	10	.677	2.70	200	66	247
Don Sutton, LA	35	34	15	21	10	.677	3.06	161	82	268
Steve Carlton, Phil	36	35	13	20	7	.741	3.13	195	72	253
J R Richard, Ho	39	39	14	20	15	.571	2.75	214	151*	291

St. Louis' John Denny (11–9) took the ERA title with 2.52, while Seaver was strikeout king with 235. Los Angeles' Rick Rhoden (12–3) had the top winning percentage, .800. Jones won the Cy Young Award, with Koosman second. Cincinnati dumped Philadelphia three straight, then got revenge for their

1939 defeat at the hands of the Yankees by sweeping them in four straight. Johnny Bench batted .633 with two home runs and six RBIs, while Will McE-naney saved two games, as they became the first National League team to win back-to-back World Series titles in 54 years.

Hank Aaron retired with a major league record 755 home runs and 2,297 RBIs. Walter Alston stepped down as manager of the Dodgers after 23 seasons.

1977

AMERICAN LEAGUE: TIME TO BUY
A PENNANT AND NEW CLUBS

Further expansion was inevitable. The American League added Toronto to their Eastern Division and Seattle to the West. Toronto lost 107 games in its maiden season while finishing last, and Seattle finished sixth in a seven-team division while losing 98 games.

With free agency now a way of life, the rich clubs began trying to buy pennants, and none was more avid than George Steinbrenner's New York Yankees. They acquired Reggie Jackson and pitcher Don Gullet from Cincinnati. Jackson supplied power with 32 home runs and 110 RBIs. The latter was best on the team and the former was second to Craig Nettles' 37.

The pitching staff had no 20-game winners, but six pitchers to win between 11 and 16, as they won by 2½ games over Baltimore. The Yankees' chore was made a little more difficult when Catfish Hunter missed half a season and had to settle for a 9–9 mark.

Meanwhile, Jim Palmer won 20 again for Baltimore, as they had their usual assortment of power and pitching depth. Kansas City again surfaced to the top as Dennis Leonard won 20 games, while Dave Goltz did the same for Minnesota. Boston's Bill Campbell was the relief ace with 31 saves. Baltimore led the league with 65 complete games and Seattle tied the league low with 18.

For Palmer this was becoming old hat as he won 20 games for the third year in a row and the seventh in eight seasons. He tied Goltz and Leonard for most wins, while leading with 22 complete games, most starts (39) and most innings (319). Palmer still had one more 20-win season under his belt. His 2.91 ERA marked the ninth time in his career that his ERA had been below 3.00.

This was Leonard's first of three 20-win seasons. After an 0–4 start in September 1974, Leonard righted himself, became a starter in 1975 and posted 15–7 and 17–10 marks the next two seasons before his first 20-win year. From the time he became a starter until he retired in 1986, he had only one losing season, which was his last. However, injuries greatly hampered him after 1981, forcing him to miss almost half of 1982, two-thirds of 1983, all of 1984 and all but two games of 1985. He tried a comeback in 1986, but was only 8–13 and then retired. His final mark of 144–106 could have been perhaps double that, or at least another 100 victories based on past performances.

Goltz pitched in the majors from 1972 through 1983 and was barely over .500 at 113–109. If we remove his 1977 season, he was only 93–98 for his career. Most seasons he was at .500 or a couple of games above, at least through 1979. From 1980 to the end of his career he was only 17–30. His best season next to this year was 1978 when he posted a 15–10 mark. In 1977 Goltz also hurled 19 complete games while logging 303 innings, both personal career highs.

It was another year of plus and minus for Nolan Ryan as he won 19, but lost 16 even though he led the league with 22 complete games, had a 2.77 ERA, pitched 299 innings and had the most strikeouts at 341. Without Ryan California would have battled Oakland and Seattle for the last two spots in the division. He continued to be plagued by lack of proper support.

Pitcher/Team	G	GS	CG	W	L	Pct	ERA	SO	W	IP
Jim Palmer, Balt	39	39*	22*	20*	11	.645	2.91	193	90	319*
Dave Goltz, Mn	39	39*	19	20*	11	.645	3.36	186	91	303
Dennis Leonard, KC	38	37	21	20*	12	.625	3.04	244	79	293

California's Frank Tanana (15–9) had the best ERA, 2.54, and led with seven shutouts, which was more than seven teams had. Sparky Lyle, with 26 saves, won the Cy Young award. New York took Kansas City's measure in five games as Lyle won twice. Rod Carew flirted with .400, but ended at .388 to win the batting crown.

In the World Series, Jackson hit five home runs, had eight RBIs and batted .450. Mike Torrez won two games and the Yanks took the title in six.

NATIONAL LEAGUE: STILL WINNING, BUT NO BRASS RING

The Philadelphia Phillies won their second straight division title but this time lost to the Dodgers in the playoffs. Again they had big seasons from Mike Schimdt and Greg Luzinski, but it was their pitching where they excelled, as Steve Carlton won 23 and Larry Christenson added 19, while relievers Gene Garber and Ron Reed combined for 15 wins and 34 saves.

John Candeleria's 20 victories helped Pittsburgh to second, five games back, while Bob Forsch won 20 for St. Louis and Rick Reuschel the same for Chicago.

In the West, Tommy John, with 20, paced Los Angeles to a ten-game bulge over Cincinnati. The Reds had fine hitting again, as George Foster batted .320, hit a league-high 52 home runs and 149 RBIs, but their pitching let them down. Only Tom Seaver, acquired from New York early in the season, helped. He was a composite 21–6, with a 2.59 ERA.

Carlton had his second successive 20-plus-win season as he led the league with 23 for the second time and also won his second Cy Young Award. His 2.64 ERA was half a run per game lower than the prior year, while his 283 innings hurled were the most he had since 1974.

Candelaria pitched in the majors for 19 seasons from 1975 through 1993. For the first 14 he never had a losing season, with the first ten spent with Pittsburgh. In 1981 he suffered an arm injury but recovered to pitch winning ball. Then after 1988 he journeyed to several ball clubs and was only 13–20 for those years. When he retired he had a 177–122 career mark.

In his lone 20-win season, Candelaria led with a .800 winning percentage and the league's top ERA (2.34). He posted only six complete games in 33 starts, but this was the era of the starter pitching six or seven innings, then the set-up man followed by the closer. The days of 20 or more complete games by a pitcher were rapidly drawing to a close. To illustrate, from 1976 to 1980 he had 38 no-decisions and from 1982 through 1988 another 39 for a total of 77 out of 323 starts, or almost one-fourth.

Forsch picked 1977 for his lone 20-win season. Forsch pitched in the majors for 16 seasons, the first 14¾ with St. Louis where he won 163 of his 168 career victories. The closest Forsch ever came to 20 wins was 15 in 1975 and again in 1982. He had winning marks in 11 of his seasons and was a dependable starter. He may not have been the caliber of Tom Seaver or Bob Gibson, but he was reliable and steady. A good third man on the staff, many seasons he was forced into the first-man role due to the weak pitching staff of the St. Louis team in the 70s. Forsch pitched two no-hitters while with St. Louis and retired with a 168–138 mark.

Reuschel pitched for 19 years in the big leagues, starting in 1972 and finishing in 1991. He missed all of the 1982, most of the 1983 and all of 1984 seasons due to back injuries. The 1977 season was also his only 20-win year in a career that saw most of his service with Chicago. Reuschel would slip to 14–15 in 1978, but rebound to win 18 in 1979. During the strike-shortened season of 1981, he was traded to the Yankees but came back to the Cubs following his injuries. He spent 1985–86 and part of 1987 with the Pirates with mixed success as he was 14–8, 9–16 and 8–6. He finished out his career with the Giants with a 44–30 mark. However, he had his second-biggest season in 1988 for San Francisco as he won 19 games at age 39. After that he tailed off dramatically and finally retired after 1991. His final career mark was 214–191; barring the loss of 2½ seasons, he probably would have won at least 250 games.

John had been in the majors since 1963 and the highest number of games he had won was 16 for the Dodgers in 1973. In 1974 he seemed headed for a great season as he was 13–3, 2.59 ERA, when he tore a ligament and was out of baseball until 1976. Dr. Jobe did a ligament transplant (the first in history) and literally gave John a new arm. He asked for Sandy Koufax's arm, but got Mrs. Koufax's instead. He couldn't even throw a medium ball, but had great control. After a 10–10, 3.09 ERA 1976 season when he won the comeback player of the year award, he won his first 20-game season in 1977 at age 34.

Here he was winning 20 games and pitching at an age when many are out of the game or getting ready to call it quits. Tommy John would fool them all and pitch until 1989 when he was 46, finishing that final season with a dismal 2–7. However, along the way he twice more won 20 or better, and when he retired he had a career 288–231 record. From 1977 through 1980 he was 80–35, averaging 20 wins per year. After the 1980 season John was 204–149 and although he would be 38 entering the 1981 season he had dreams of 300 wins. Thus he pitched until 1989, but fell short. He was only 84–82, which took some of the luster off his career mark.

The unbelievable happened in 1977: the Mets traded Seaver to Cincinnati. He had been the darling of the Mets since he first put on their uniform, way back in 1967 and now he was gone, although he would return for one brief season in 1983. When traded he was 7–3 with a 3.00 ERA. For Cincinnati he was 14–3, 2.35 ERA, which gave him his final 20-win season at 21–6, 2.59 ERA, 19 complete games and the league's most shutouts (seven).

Seaver won 16 each of the next two years, but a shoulder injury limited him to a 10–8 mark in 26 starts in 1980. He had fully recovered in 1981 and was a brilliant 14–2, 2.55 ERA, but the strike cut short his chance for a sixth 20-win season, and a fourth Cy Young award was lost by three points to Fernando Valenzuela. After losing seasons in 1982 and 1983 with Cincinnati and the Mets, he went to the American League to finish out his career. He was 15–11, 16–11 for Chicago his first two years. Then he split his final season between the White Sox and the Red Sox, finishing at 7–13 to ring down the curtain on his career.

Rollie Fingers won the save title with 35 while toiling for San Diego, who set a new low in complete games with 6. Houston set a new low for most complete games with 37. The game had certainly changed from the early part of this century.

Pitcher/Team	G	GS	CG	W	L	Pct	ERA	SO	W	IP
Steve Carlton, Phil	36	36	17	23*	10	.697	2.64	198	89	283
Tom Seaver, Cinn	33	33	19	21	6	.778	2.59	196	66	261
J Candeleria, Pgh	33	33	6	20	5	.800*	2.34*	133	50	231
Bob Forsch, STL	35	35	8	20	7	.741	3.48	95	69	217
Tommy John, LA	31	31	11	20	7	.741	2.78	123	50	220
Rick Reuschel, Chgo	39	37	8	20	10	.667	2.76	166	74	252

Phil Niekro, working for last-place Atlanta, led in defeats with 20, games started (43), complete games (20), innings pitched (330) and strikeouts (262). He won 16 games, and undoubtedly could have won several more with a better club. Lou Brock broke Ty Cobb's career stolen base record of 896.

Los Angeles disposed of Philadelphia in four games but could not contain the Yankees. They lost the Series in six games.

1978

AMERICAN LEAGUE: CHOKE, CHOKE, CHOKE

For the first half of the season, Boston seemed unbeatable with the powerful lineup and pitching that they possessed. But in the second half the Yankees stormed at the Sox to eventually defeat them in a one-game playoff. Ron Guidry had a career-best year as he was 25–3, 1.74, both best in the league. He won the Cy Young and finished second to Jim Rice in the MVP balloting in a hotly contested vote.

Dennis Eckersley won 20 for Boston, while Mike Caldwell was a 22-game winner at Milwaukee. Jim Palmer got his usual 20 for Baltimore, which won 90 games, making four teams to achieve that level. Only two teams in the East were below .500: Cleveland, 69–90, and Toronto, 59–102.

Kansas City won for the third straight season as Dennis Leonard notched 21 wins. No other team had a 20-game winner in the division. New York's Goose Gossage led with 27 saves, while Baltimore had the most complete games, 65, and Seattle and Oakland the fewest at 26. The DH certainly did make a difference in the two leagues, at least when it came to complete games.

Guidry didn't win his first major league game until he was 27 in 1977, but after that he was fantastic, as he won 154 games over the next nine years while losing just 68. Following that, several injuries greatly slowed him down and forced his retirement. He was only 16–23 for those last three injury-filled seasons.

In 1978 Guidry was unbelievable. He was 25–3 with a 1.74 ERA, while posting the top winning percentage (.893) and leading with nine shutouts. He single-handedly pitched the Yankees into the World Series. Guidry won the Cy Young easily, and it took a superhuman season by Jim Rice to deprive him of the MVP, as he came in second. Guidry would pitch winning ball for the next four years, but no 20-win seasons. He would return to that level twice more, starting in 1982.

Ed Figueroa had his best year at 20–9 with a 2.99 ERA. In most seasons he would have had a chance for the Cy Young, but this was his teammate's year. Figueroa had broken in with a 2–8 mark with California in 1974, then won 16 for them the next season before joining the Yankees for the 1976 year. His first year he won 19 and then 16, and now with his first 20-win season it looked like the Yankees would have a strong right-hander to compliment Guidry—Shades of Ford and Terry, Raschi, Reynolds and Lopat or Gomez and Ruffing.

However, it was not to be. Figueroa suffered an elbow injury from which he never fully recovered. He was only 7–9 for 1979 and the first half of 1980 when traded to Texas, where he finished 0–7. He pitched in two games for Oakland the next year, but couldn't answer the bell after that and retired with an 80–67 log.

Eckersley is a pitcher with two careers. From 1975 through 1986 he was a starting pitcher with moderate success, as he won ten or more games in nine of the seasons with a composite 151–128. From 1987 to 1996 he has become one of the premier closers in the game with a 41–37 mark, but more importantly 349 saves. However, back in 1978 he was in the midst of his heyday as a starting pitcher and was the ace of the Red Sox staff. He posted his only 20-win season with a 20–8, 2.99 ERA mark, also a season under other circumstances that could be considered for the Cy Young Award. Eckersley pitched for the Red Sox through mid–1984 and gave them winning ball every year but two. He then was 10–8 and 11–7 for the Cubs before a 6–11 mark finished him as a starter and with the Cubs in 1986. He went to Oakland where he immediately became a relief ace and in his second season saved an incredible 45 games.

Caldwell is also a pitcher with two careers, but both were primarily as a starter, although there was some relief work involved. From 1971 to 1976 he pitched for San Diego and San Francisco and had a 35–50 mark, with just one winning season. In 1977 he pitched for Cincinnati in 15 games and had no record. Then he joined Milwaukee and it looked like no improvement was forthcoming, as he finished out the year at 5–8. However, in 1978 he had his career-best year as he was 22–9, a league-high 23 complete games and a 2.37 ERA. While he never won 20 again, he did give Milwaukee five more winning seasons (69–50) before calling it quits with a 6–13 record in 1984, which made his final record 137–130.

Palmer, with 21 wins, had his fourth straight 20-win season, eighth in nine years, but also his final one. He topped the league with 296 innings and had 19 complete games with a fine 2.46 ERA. Palmer suffered his fourth career injury, an elbow this time, and was reduced to a 10–6 mark for 1979. He came back with 16–10 in 1980 and a 15–5 in 1982 before a shoulder injury limited him to 14 games and a 5–4 mark in 1983. After appearing in five games with a 0–3 record in 1984, Palmer retired. His final career mark was 268–152, 2.68 ERA and a .638 winning percentage, which is fifth-best among pitchers with over 250 career wins. His dream of 300 wins faded, which can be traced to five injuries that cost him at least 75 wins. The remarkable part is that he was able to come back from these career-threatening injuries to post some big seasons. It is too bad he lost all that time, because his victory totals could rank in the top ten.

Leonard won 20 or more for the second straight year, as he had his career high of 21 wins. He was a real workhorse, starting a league-high 40 games and working 295 innings while pitching 20 complete games. Leonard would slip to 14 wins next year, but bounce back for his final 20-win season in 1980.

Nolan Ryan had a leg and thigh injury for the year, but still led with 260 strikeouts, his sixth time out of 11 seasons he would lead.

Pitcher/Team	G	GS	GC	W	L	Pct	ERA	SO	W	IP
Ron Guidry, NY	35	35	16	25*	3	.893*	1.74*	248	72	274

Pitcher/Team	G	GS	GC	W	L	Pct	ERA	SO	W	IP
Mike Caldwell, Milw	37	34	23*	22	9	.710	2.37	131	54	293
Jim Palmer, Balt	38	38	19	21	12	.636	2.46	138	97	296*
Dennis Leonard, KC	40	40*	20	21	17	.553	3.33	183	78	295
Den Eckersley, Bos	35	35	16	20	8	.714	2.99	162	71	268

Kansas City fell for the third straight time to the Yankees, this time in four games, as Leonard lost twice. The Yankees met their old rivals, the Dodgers, and once again took them, this time four games to two. Reggie Jackson again was a big hitting star with two home runs, eight RBIs and a .391 average. However, teammate Denny Doyle led all hitters with a .438 mark.

NATIONAL LEAGUE: SAME WINNERS, SAME RESULT—BUT A RECORD TIED

Philadelphia won again in the East, although it was a little tougher this time, as their margin was only one and half games over Pittsburgh. Neither team sported a 20-game winner, as Steve Carlton was high for the Phillies with 16. The only 20-game winner in the East was Montreal's Ross Grimsley.

The Dodgers, after a tough fight from Cincinnati, edged them without the aid of a 20-game winner, though they had four between 15 and 19. Cincinnati's failure can be traced to Johnny Bench's off year from an injury and Tom Seaver's fall to just 16–14.

Gaylord Perry won the Cy Young Award, becoming the first pitcher to win one in each league, as he won 21 for a mediocre San Diego team. Phil Niekro had 19 wins for last-place Atlanta.

Rollie Fingers paced the loop again with 37 saves. Houston led with 48 complete games, while San Diego and New York tied at 21 for last.

Grimsley had his only 20-win season as he posted 19 complete games, 263 innings and a 3.05 ERA. The ERA and complete games were career-high marks, while only his 296 innings with Baltimore topped this year. Grimsley was in the majors from 1971–82 with Cincinnati, Baltimore, Cleveland and Montreal. His career record was 124–99. His next-best season was an 18–13 mark for Baltimore in 1974.

Perry had a fine 21–6 record with a .778 (league-best) winning percentage and a 2.72 ERA. The only negative to Perry's season was his five complete games in 37 starts, but remember, this was the era of the closer. From 1966 to 1977, Perry never completed fewer than 13 games, seven times exceeding 20. What a change was taking place.

Niekro pitched in a tough-luck season as he had a fine 2.88 ERA, led with 22 complete games and 334 innings pitched. Unfortunately, the Braves were dead last and all he could get for his efforts was a 19–18 record. With better support he could have won at least 25 games, if not more.

Pitcher/Team	G	GS	CG	W	L	Pct	ERA	SO	W	IP
Gay Perry, San Dg	37	37	5	21*	6	.778*	2.72	154	66	261
Ross Grimsley, Mont	36	36	19	20	11	.645	3.05	84	67	263

San Francisco's Bob Knepper led in shutouts with eight, while New York's Craig Swan had the best ERA, 2.43. Pete Rose had another super year, reaching 3,000 hits, and trying an assault on Joe DiMaggio's 56-game hitting streak. He fell short, but did tie Willie Keeler's National League record of 44.

Once again Los Angeles defeated Philadelphia, this time three games to one. However, in the World Series, the Yankees turned the tables on the Dodgers, defeating them four games to two.

1979

AMERICAN LEAGUE: THE COWBOY RIDES HIGH, BUT NOT A CHAMPION

Ever since former cowboy movie star Gene Autry acquired the California franchise in the early 1960s, he had been trying for a World Series winner. Finally, his California club won their division, edging out Kansas City by three games. Unfortunately, Baltimore defeated them in four games, and the old cowboy is still waiting for his first shot at the fall classic.

The only 20-game winner in the West came from Minnesota, where Jerry Koosman won 20 games. In the East, the Yankees suffered injuries and the death of star catcher Thurman Munson. They fell to fourth place despite winning 89 games, one more than California. Tommy John gave them 21 and Ron Guidry added 18.

However, it was Baltimore back on top, as Mike Flanagan showed the way with 23 wins. Jim Palmer had elbow problems, was limited to 22 starts and won 10 games.

Mike Marshall surfaced with Minnesota and led the loop with 32 saves, although the best relief pitcher was probably Jim Kern of Texas. Kern was 13–5, with 29 saves, 1.57 ERA and 136 strikeouts in 143 innings during 71 games.

Flanagan spent all but the last one and one-third season of his 14-year career with Baltimore. He was 146–114 during that time and finished at 9–10 for Toronto. The 1977–80 period was Flanagan's best as he was 73–47, with 1979 being the top when he won 23 and the Cy Young Award. Flanagan had 16 complete games, hurled 266 innings, posted a 3.05 ERA and led with five shutouts. His next closest to 20 wins was the prior year when he won 19.

Following 37 wins in two years at Los Angeles, John joined the Yankees and promptly won 21 games the first season. He logged 276 innings, with a fine 2.76 ERA and 17 complete games. It was a year that would normally qualify a pitcher for the Cy Young, but this was Flanagan's season. John would post one more 20-win year next season.

In his first season in Minnesota, Koosman won 20 games. This was his second and final time in the charmed circle. Koosman won 16 the next season, but then slumped to 3–9 and midway through 1981 he was traded to the White Sox. He had two successive 11–7 seasons there before landing with the Phillies and finishing out his career at 14–15 and 6–4 in 1984–85. Although he had 222 career wins, he has never been a serious candidate for the Hall. His 209 losses are undoubtedly a major factor, as are several poor seasons. One can argue, remove the poor years and he had a fine career. Conversely, the same argument can be made about his good years. Nolan Ryan again led in strikeouts, but this time it was only 223. Milwaukee was first with 61 complete games and Detroit was last with 25. Six of the seven teams in the East were over .500, with Toronto last at 53–109. Four of the seven Western clubs were over .500, with Oakland last at 54–108.

Pitcher/Team	G	GS	CG	W	L	Pct	ERA	SO	W	IP
Mike Flanagan, Balt	39	38	16	23*	9	.719	3.08	150	70	266
Tommy John, NY	37	36	17	21	9	.700	2.97	111	65	276
Jerry Koosman, Mn	37	36	10	20	13	.606	3.38	157	83	264

Guidry was ERA leader at 2.78, while Dennis Leonard had the most shutouts (six), Dennis Martinez the most starts (39), complete games (18) and innings pitched (292). Flanagan copped the Cy Young award.

Baltimore had a lead of three games to one over Pittsburgh and was looking for revenge for 1971 when lighting struck. They scored only two runs in the last three games to go down to defeat.

NATIONAL LEAGUE: HISTORY REPEATS ITSELF

Everyone conceded the Eastern division title to Philadelphia, especially because they acquired Pete Rose and he had a banner year, batting .331. But injuries, off-seasons by several players and a mediocre pitching staff confined them to fourth place. Only Steve Carlton with 18 wins could be counted on consistently.

Meanwhile, Pittsburgh relied on power and a pitching staff that had no winner over 14 games, but six pitchers between 10 and 14, to take the title by two games over surprising Montreal. St. Louis finished a strong third, helped tremendously by Keith Hernandez's .344 batting title, which helped him share the MVP with Pittsburgh's Willie Stargell. This was the first and only time two men shared the crown.

In the West Cincinnati wrested the title from Los Angeles and finished two games ahead of surprising Houston, who had one of the league's two 20-game winners in Joe Niekro. The other was Joe's brother Phil, who turned the trick for last-place Atlanta. Chicago's Bruce Sutter won the Cy Young Award as he had 37 saves. Houston was tops with 55 complete games and Chicago last with 20.

Joe Niekro pitched most of his career in the shadow of his brother, although he posted a 221–204 record over 22 seasons. However, this year he bettered his brother as he led the league with a 21–11, 3.00 ERA record. Joe pitched for the Cubs, Detroit, Atlanta, Houston, the Yankees and Minnesota during his career. When he pitched for Atlanta in 1973–74, Joe was used primarily in relief and posted only a 5–6 record. Prior to joining Houston in 1975 the highest number of games he won was 14 for Chicago in 1968. His first three years in Houston, Joe was used mostly in relief, compiling a 23–20 record. However, starting in 1978 he became a starter and won 103 games for the 1978–84 period, sans the 1981 strike season. He never had a losing season during that stretch and the lowest number of games he won was 14, twice exceeding 20. He was 144–116 for Houston, making him 77–88 for all other teams.

Brother Phil also won 21 but lost 20 as he led the league with 44 starts, 23 complete games and 342 innings pitched. His Atlanta team finished last, and once again his record could have been much better given a decent team. Had he played for Houston, he probably would have won 25 or more and they might have won the division title. As we have already seen, this was the plight of his career. He is now in the Hall, just elected in 1997. With 318 wins, one would think he would be easily elected but it took until now to do so. I believe when the writers looked at those 274 defeats, it scared them. They should remember the caliber of many of the teams for which he pitched.

It will be interesting to see the posture taken when they vote on Nolan Ryan, who retired with a 324–292 record. Will they overlook his 292 losses or chalk that up to the caliber of the teams he played for? What is good for one should apply to the other. Perhaps in Ryan's situation they will be held in awe by his 5,387 strikeouts and seven no-hitters, both major league records that will probably never be broken.

Pitcher/Team	G	GS	CG	W	L	Pct	ERA	SO	W	IP
Joe Niekro, Ho	38	38	11	21*	11	.656	3.00	119	107	264
Phil Niekro, Atl	44	44*	23*	21*	20*	.512	3.30	208	113*	342*

Niekro, Tom Seaver (16–6) and Montreal's Steve Rogers (13–12) shared the shutout lead with five, while Houston's J. R. Richard (18–15) had the best ERA, 2.71, and the most strikeouts, 313. Lou Brock retired from the Cardinals with over 3,000 hits and a career-record 938 stolen bases.

Pittsburgh swept Cincinnati as Stargell hit two home runs and had six RBIs. In the Series, no Pittsburgh pitcher won over one game, but reliever Kent Tekulve saved three.

9

1980–1989

— 1980 —

American League: Finally We Go to the Dance

Kansas City won the Western Division title three straight years only to lose in the playoffs each year, twice to the Yankees. The 1980 season proved to be different, as not only did they win by a 14-game margin over Oakland, they swept the Yankees in three games to finally gain entry to the fall classic. George Brett had a super year, batting .390 to win the MVP, while Dennis Leonard won 20 to pace the mound corps.

Oakland was second, with 22-game winner Mike Norris and three other starters who won between 14 and 19. Billy Martin made little use of his bullpen, getting 94 complete games, with three pitchers exceeding 20.

The East was again the strong division, as the Yankees unveiled power and 22-game winner Tommy John to take 103 wins to Baltimore's 100. Baltimore had 25 from Steve Stone and 20 more from Scott McGregor. Kansas City's Dan Quisenberry won 12 games and saved another 33, high in the loop. The fewest complete games were by California with 22.

John had his final big season as he won a career-high 22 games, while pitching a league-high six shutouts among his 16 complete games. This completed John's four seasons during which he won 80 games, and while he pitched nine more years, the most he ever won again was 14. He finally retired after 1989 with 26 years in the majors, but didn't cover four decades because of the time he started and ended.

If you remove Stone's 1980 season, he is only 82–86 for his career. Stone pitched 11 years in the big leagues and other than 1980 never won more than 15 games in any year. However, 1980 was his year as he won a league-high 25 games, had the best winning percentage (.781) and won the Cy Young Award. The next season he suffered an elbow injury that ended his career. He then went on to become a successful baseball announcer.

McGregor pitched his entire career with Baltimore and posted a 138–108 career mark. He first pitched for them in late 1976 and was 0–1 in three games.

Once he became a regular in 1978 he never had a losing season until 1986, when he was 11–15. A shoulder injury the next year made him only 2–7. He could pitch in only four games in 1988 and was 0–3 when he was forced to retire prematurely. Had the injuries not overtaken him, McGregor probably would have won 200 or more. The 1980 campaign was his best year as he posted a 20–8 mark. His next best was 18–7 in 1983. When we remove his last three years, McGregor's career mark is an impressive 125–83, supporting our thesis that he could have been a 200-game winner barring injury.

Leonard had his last big season, winning 20 games. Injuries would overtake him in 1982 and prematurely end his career. Leonard was a real workhorse, starting 38 times and logging 280 innings. From 1975 through 1981 he pitched at least 202 innings every year. The 202 mark was in the strike-shortened 1981 season. After that injuries diminished his abilities and pitching time.

Norris was in the majors from 1975 through 1983, all with Oakland, and had only a 57–59 career record, but in 1980 he almost won the Cy Young as he was 22–9, 2.54 ERA and 24 complete games. Prior to this season he had been only 12–25 and afterwards 23–25. His career was prematurely ended by a combination of drugs and shoulder problems. Did the drugs bring on the shoulder problem? We will never know, but at 28 a potentially fine career was snuffed out.

Pitcher/Team	G	GS	CG	W	L	Pct	ERA	SO	W	IP
Steve Stone, Balt	37	37	9	25*	7	.781*	3.23	149	101	251
Tommy John, NY	36	36	16	22	9	.710	3.43	78	56	265
Mike Norris, Oak	33	33	24	22	9	.710	2.54	180	83	284
Scott McGregor, Bal	36	36	12	20	8	.714	3.32	119	58	252
Dennis Leonard, KC	38	38*	9	20	11	.645	3.79	155	80	280

Oakland's Rick Langford (19–12) led in complete games (28) and innings pitched (290), while Chicago's Britt Burns (15–13) had the best ERA, 2.64. John also led in shutouts with eight, Cleveland's Len Barker (19–12) led in strikeouts with 187, while Stone won the Cy Young award.

Kansas City had their revenge on New York with three straight wins, as George Brett hit two home runs and had four RBIs.

Kansas City lost the Series four games to two as Quisenberry lost twice and had a 5.23 ERA. Amos Otis batted .478 with seven RBIs, Willie Aikens hit .400 with four home runs and eight RBIs, and George Brett hit .375. However, primarily their pitching let them down.

National League: Finally
They Catch the Brass Ring

The Philadelphia Phillies had been to only two World Series, 1915 and 1950, and had won one game. In a hard-fought battle, they edged Montreal by one game as Steve Carlton won his third Cy Young Award with a 24–9 record.

Mike Schmidt was MVP with 48 home runs and 121 RBIs, and Pete Rose provided team leadership.

No other pitcher in the East won 20 games, although Pittsburgh's Jim Bibby had 19. Joe Niekro pitched Houston to a one-game win over Los Angeles by winning 20 games. He was the only 20-game winner in the West. Bruce Sutter again led with saves, this time 28. Complete game totals continued to fall, with St. Louis the leader at 34 and Chicago the fewest at 13.

For the fifth time in his career, Carlton won 20 or more games as he led the league with 24 wins and also earned his third Cy Young Award. His 24 wins, 304 innings pitched and 286 strikeouts were not only league highs, but his best marks since his super season of 1972. His 2.34 ERA was also his best since that date. With this season behind him, Carlton was 51 wins short of his coveted 300 win goal.

Niekro won 20 games for the second straight year. Although it would be his last 20-win season, Niekro continued pitching winning ball for Houston. After a 9–9 record in the strike-shortened 1981 season, Niekro won 48 games in 1982–84 before tailing off in his last four years. As he finished up with the Yankees and then Minnesota, Niekro was only 28–37 for 1985–88.

On a sad note, J. R. Richard suffered a major stroke and his baseball career was prematurely ended at age 30. He did recover, but could never pitch in the majors again. Richard was 10–4 with 1.89 ERA and 119 strikeouts in 114 innings when he succumbed. What a tragedy!

Pitcher/Team	G	GS	CG	W	L	Pct	ERA	SO	W	IP
Steve Carlton, Phil	38	38*	13	24*	9	.727	2.34	286*	90	304*
Joe Niekro, Ho	37	36	11	20	12	.625	3.55	127	79	256

Bibby had the top percentage at .760 off his 19–6 record, Los Angeles' Jerry Reuss (18–6) the most shutouts with six, and teammate Don Sutton (13–5) the best ERA, 2.21.

Philadelphia hadn't been in a World Series since 1950. Houston had never been, and is still waiting. The playoffs went five games with Philadelphia finally prevailing. Tug McGraw was credited with two saves.

In the World Series, Carlton won twice, while McGraw had one win and two saves. Schmidt was the big hitting star with two home runs, seven RBIs and a .381 average.

1981

AMERICAN LEAGUE: BASEBALL DISHONORED BY STRIKE

The players struck and about 50 games were lost from the schedule for each team. The basic issue was that the owners wanted compensation for any player lost as a free agent. The owners wanted the 16th player on a club as replacement for a player lost in free agency. The players said no. The owners said yes. There was a strike, and the real losers were the fans and the people who work at the parks.

When the season did start the decision was to have the first-half winners play the second-half winner in each division, and that winner play to see who went to the World Series. New York defeated Milwaukee to eventually face Oakland, who had defeated Kansas City.

Needless to say, there were no 20-game winners, as Pete Vukovich, Dennis Martinez, Jack Morris and Steve McCatty tied for the lead with 14 wins each. Dennis Leonard had the most starts (26) and innings pitched (202), Rick Langford the most complete games (18), McCatty the best ERA, 2.32, and most shutouts (4), while Len Barker led with 127 strikeouts.

Several pitchers lost chances to win 20 games because of the strike. The highest number of games Vukovich ever won was 18 the next year, but this season, with a 14–4 mark and based on the games his team lost, he could have won 21 or 22. Martinez began pitching in 1976, and through the 1995 season had 231 victories with 16 the most, a number he reached four times. The 1981 season was his chance for 20 or more, and based on his 14–5 mark, he could have won 21–23.

Scott McGregor already had one 20-win season the prior year and with 13–5 could have had a second. Morris and McCatty both had 14–7 marks and each had the chance for 21–22 wins. McCatty never won over 14 in the big leagues, while Morris reached 20 three times and was the winningest pitcher in baseball during the 1980s.

In one respect we can feel sorry for the lost opportunities, but on the other hand the players didn't have to strike. From the fans' perspective, if they have a disagreement, they should continue negotiating—not destroy the game by striking. Everyone suffers from a strike: the players, the owners, the fans and those whose livelihood is tied to the ball games through sales of concessions, souvenirs and memorabilia.

Rollie Fingers was the save leader with 28 and Oakland the complete game leader with 60, while Seattle was last with 10. In the World Series, New York lost to Los Angeles in four games, as journeyman pitcher George Frazier, who appeared in only 16 games in the regular season and was 0–1, lost three games in the fall classic.

NATIONAL LEAGUE: THE BEST TEAM STAYED HOME

Among the many problems created by the baseball strike was the split season. It boded well for some teams, but the two teams with the best records in their respective divisions didn't have a chance to play for the World Series entry.

Cincinnati, with the best record in baseball, finished second in each half, while St. Louis with the best record in the East was second in each half. As a result neither team made it to the playoffs. Due to the strike, for the first time ever neither league produced a 20-game winner. There had been an occasional season when one league did not have a 20-game winner, but this was the first time neither had one.

Tom Seaver had the most wins (14–2) and best percentage (.875), Fernando Valenzuela had the most complete games (11), most innings pitched (192), most strikeouts (180) and most shutouts (8), while Nolan Ryan had the best ERA (1.69). Valenzuela edged out Seaver for the Cy Young award. Ryan also pitched an unprecedented fifth no-hitter.

The baseball strike cost some pitchers a chance for a 20-win season. Steve Carlton had a 13–4, 2.42 ERA mark and had he not lost 14–15 starts he undoubtedly would have broken the 20-win barrier. Assuming he continued at the same pace, his win total would have been 21–23. This would have given Carlton seven 20-win seasons and put him in an elite class shared by only nine other pitchers.

Valenzuela, although he won the Cy Young and had a fine season, could have been even better if the strike hadn't taken place. Based on his performance in the shortened season, Valenzuela could have won 20 or 21, which would have put him twice in the charmed circle.

The last big loser was Seaver, who with a 14–2 mark and 2.55 ERA could have conceivably surpassed Valenzuela and won his fourth Cy Young, tying him with Carlton and Greg Maddux as the only pitchers to win the coveted award four times. Assuming another 14 starts, and at his pace, it is possible that Seaver could have won 22–25 games. If so, then he might have captured the Cy Young.

However, just as with the American League, the players made the choice to strike knowing what it would do to their individual achievements. One other note: this was Nolan Ryan's second year back in the National League and he had the makings of a fine season when the strike intervened. He was 11–5, 1.69 ERA, 140 strikeouts in 149 innings.

Los Angeles defeated Houston for the right to represent the West, while Montreal took Philadelphia's measure as Steve Rogers won two games and Carlton lost two. Then, with Burt Hooton winning two games and Bill Gullickson losing two, Los Angeles edged Montreal to go to the Series.

The Dodgers defeated New York four games to two in the fall classic. Steve Garvey batted .417 and led all hitters with 10 hits. Pedro Guerrero had two home runs and seven RBIs.

1982

AMERICAN LEAGUE: DOGFIGHTS
ALL THE WAY AS NEW KINGS RULE

Races in both divisions went down to the wire. In the East Milwaukee, with a powerful batting attack, won on the final day over Baltimore by one game, with Boston in third, six back. No team in the league had a 20-game winner for the second consecutive season. Milwaukee's Pete Vukovich was tops in the East with 18. Dave Stieb won 17 for last-place Toronto.

The West saw California win over Kansas City by three games and Chicago by six. The latter boasted the winningest pitcher in the league in Lamarr Hoyt with 19 victories. Vukovich (18–6) and Jim Palmer (15–5) had the best winning percentage (.750), Toronto's Jim Clancy (16–14) had the most starts (40), teammate Stieb had the most complete games (19), shutouts (5) and innings pitched (288), Cleveland's Rick Sutcliffe the best ERA (2.96) and Seattle's Floyd Bannister the most strikeouts at 209.

For the second successive year there was no 20-game winner, although this was a full season. With the increasing use of relief pitchers, it was becoming more difficult to win 20 games because pitchers were pulled quicker, thus getting fewer opportunities to win. The number of no-decisions by starters increased while the number of decisions for relief pitchers was on the rise.

The drug culture didn't exclude sports, including baseball, and several players' careers would be adversely affected. Hoyt had posted back-to-back 9–3 marks for Chicago in 1980–81, mostly in relief. In 1982 he became a starter, although he did make seven relief appearances, and his 19 wins were the league's best. The next year Hoyt again led, this time with 24. However, after that he was 13–18 and spent his last two seasons (1985–86) with San Diego. Following a 16–8 year he was 8–11 and the drugs did him in. He was suspended, and at age 31 his career was ended with a 98–68 mark. His was a record that could have and should have been much better—probably at least 200 victories.

Dave Stieb pitched in the majors from 1979 through 1993, all but the last year with Toronto. During that time he was 175–135, but never won over 18 games. This year he was 17–14 for last-place Toronto. In his early years, Toronto did not have strong teams, negatively affecting Stieb's final record. Three times he won 17 and once 18. Through 1990 Stieb had 166 victories and at age 32 seemed set for several more good seasons, but then the injury jinx hit.

In 1991 Stieb suffered a shoulder separation, followed by back problems that limited his pitching time, and he was only 4–3. Hoping that those problems were behind him, he returned in 1992. But this time Stieb developed elbow problems, again saw limited duty, and was only 4–6. After 14 seasons in a Toronto uniform he went to the White Sox, but because of the injuries of the past two seasons he couldn't perform anymore, was 1–3 and then retired. Injuries undoubtedly took several seasons off his career and cost him perhaps 50–75 victories.

Jack Morris pitched in the majors from 1977 through 1995 and pitched for Detroit (through 1990), Minnesota (1991), Toronto (1992–93) and Cleveland (1994–95). During his career he was 254–186. Although he was 40 when he retired early in 1995, had he not suffered two elbow injuries (1989 and 1993) he might have pitched a couple more years and maybe won 300. During the 1980s Morris won 162 games, with his only losing season being 1989 when he was injured.

In 1982 Morris was 17–16 and, other than the strike-shortened 1981 season and the 1989 injury, the fewest number of wins he had during the 1980s was in 1988 when he won 15. Twice during the period he won 20 or more, and he would be a 21-game winner for Toronto in 1992, then suffer a second elbow injury in 1993. While not known for his low ERAs, he had the reputation for giving up the fewest unearned runs. It seems that when teammates put him in harm's way, he just got tougher.

Vukovich beat out Jim Palmer for the Cy Young award. Dan Quisenberry led in saves with 35, while Kansas City was last with 16 complete games and Detroit first with 45.

California looked poised to go to their first World Series ever as they won the first two games at home, but then traveled to Milwaukee and lost the next three. However, in the World Series, Milwaukee would lose in seven games to St. Louis.

NATIONAL LEAGUE: GETTING EVEN

St. Louis and Cincinnati both felt they had something to get even about. They were short-changed in the 1981 season as neither had a chance to go to the playoffs when they each had the best record in their division.

Cincinnati finished last in the West, as they had lost George Foster, Ken Griffey and Dave Collins because of tight salary policy. Atlanta picked up the torch, edging out Los Angeles by one game and San Francisco by two as ageless Phil Niekro put together a 17–4 season. Dale Murphy led their hitting attack.

In the East, St. Louis parlayed defense, speed and tight pitching to a three-game margin over Philadelphia, which had the league's only 20–game winner in Steve Carlton, who won his fourth Cy Young Award with his last big season. St. Louis had relief ace Bruce Sutter, who saved a league-high 38 games. Philadelphia led with 38 complete games while Chicago was last with nine.

Carlton posted his sixth and last 20-plus win season as he also won his fourth Cy Young Award, an unprecedented event at that time. His record has since been tied by Greg Maddux and could now be broken. This was Carlton's last super season as he posted a 23–11, 3.06 ERA mark, with 19 complete games in 38 starts, 296 innings, six shutouts and 286 strikeouts. All were the league's best save the ERA. It was the fourth time he led in wins, innings pitched and strikeouts, the third time in complete games and his only time to lead in shutouts.

After this year Carlton would win in double digits only two more years (1983–84) although he pitched into the 1988 season. Injuries and Father Time would catch up with him, as the latter does with all athletes if they stay around long enough. When the season ended, Carlton was 15 wins shy of his 300-win goal.

A couple of 19-game winners deserve mention. Steve Rogers spent his entire 13-year career (1973–85) with Montreal and finished with a 158–152 record, but a 3.17 ERA. In his first several years Montreal had some pretty weak teams, and Rogers paid the price as he was 43–56 for his first four seasons, although three of the years his ERA was 3.29 or less.

Starting in 1977 and through 1983, Rogers was 107–79, an indication of what he could have done with better clubs behind him. Montreal didn't have a winning season until 1979. The 1982 season was his tops as he went 19–8 with the league's best ERA, 2.40. He followed this with a 17–12 mark, but then finished his last two years at 6–15 and 2–4.

Fernando Valenzuela broke in fantastically with the Dodgers in late 1980 and became a starter in 1981. Whether he was ever as good as his press notices is still in doubt. Through this date he is still pitching. This year he was 19–13 with a 2.87 ERA and fanned 199 men. From 1981 through 1987, Valenzuela had only one losing season, 12–17 in 1984, even though his ERA was 3.03.

He came with much fanfare and ballyhoo and packed ballparks whenever he pitched in the early days of his career. The real question is, Did he live up to his potential? Only once did he win 20 games and that was 1986 when he was 21–11 to lead in wins but lose out in the Cy Young voting in a close race to Mike Scott. Through 1987 he was 113–82 and at only age 27. Since that time he has been only 45–51, with a couple of trips to the minors and missing all of 1993 and most of 1992. Whether he underachieved or was never as great as he was touted will always be debatable, but he was a tremendous drawing card in the early and mid–80s and did give the Dodgers some stout pitching during those years.

Pitcher/Team	G	GS	CG	W	L	Pct	ERA	SO	W	IP
Steve Carlton, Phil	38	38*	19*	23*	11	.676	3.10	286*	86	296*

Carlton also led in shutouts with six, while Niekro had the top winning percentage at .810.

St. Louis made quick work of Atlanta, taking them in three games. In the Series, which St. Louis won in seven games, Joaquin Andujar won twice while Sutter had two saves. Offensively, Keith Hernandez had eight RBIs.

1983

AMERICAN LEAGUE: THE
20-GAME WINNERS RETURN

After two seasons with no 20-game winners, the league saw four in 1983. Jack Morris got his first, as he helped put Detroit in second place, six games behind Baltimore. Teammate Dan Petry added 19, as the Tigers almost made it two in the charmed circle. Ron Guidry won 21 for the Yankees, who were one game behind Detroit. The East continued its superiority as fifth-place Milwaukee (87–75) had a better record than second-place Kansas City (79–83) in the West. Rick Sutcliffe had 17 wins for last-place Cleveland.

Chicago handily won the West by 20 games as LaMarr Hoyt topped all hurlers with 24 wins and teammate Rich Dotson added 22. The Pale Hose also led the league in runs scored as they put together a powerful hitting team.

Morris, in posting his first 20-win season, led the league with 294 innings while also posting 20 complete games, the only time in his career he achieved that goal. Morris was in the midst of the longest consistent winning stretch of his career. From 1982 to 1987 Morris never won fewer than 16 games, twice winning 20 or better, and posting 111 victories for the period.

Guidry posted his first 20-plus-win season since 1978 as he was 21–9 with a league-high 21 complete games in 31 starts. There are a lot of raps on Billy Martin, but two facts did square away. First, the team he came to manage always did better the first year he was there. They may tail off later, perhaps because his welcome wears thin. Secondly, Guidry had his best years when Martin was managing the Yankees. When he was 25–3 in 1978, Martin was the opening manager, although Lemon finished. This year Martin managed all the way, and in 1985 when Guidry won 22, Martin replaced Yogi Berra as manager after only 16 games. Call it coincidence, fate, luck or whatever, but the fact remains that the three best seasons of Guidry's career, Martin was the manager.

Hoyt followed his 19-win season with the biggest year of his career, as he led the league with 24 wins and captured the Cy Young Award. With 43 wins, Hoyt had now led the league two straight seasons, but darker days were ahead. He would slump to 13–18 next year but rebound in San Diego to 16–8 before his season was stunted at 8–11 in 1986 because of his drug problem, ending his baseball career.

Dotson is one of those pitchers who had one super season in an otherwise lackluster career. His final record was 111–113, but if we remove his 1983 22–7 season then we find Dotson with an 89–106 for a 12-year career, most of which was spent with Chicago. In only four other seasons did he post a winning mark, including a 2–0 record as a rookie in 1979.

Dan Quisenberry had 45 saves to again lead the league, while New York had the most complete games at 45 and Kansas City the fewest at 19.

Pitcher/Team	G	GS	CG	W	L	Pct	ERA	SO	W	IP
LaMarr Hoyt, Chgo	36	36	11	24*	10	.706	3.66	148	31	261
Rich Dotson, Chgo	35	35	8	22	7	.759*	3.23	137	106*	240
Ron Guidry, NY	31	31	21*	21	9	.700	3.42	156	60	250
Jack Morris, Det	37	37	20	20	13	.606	3.34	232*	83	294*

Baltimore's Mike Boddicker led with five shutouts and Petry started the most games with 38. Baltimore defeated Chicago in four games to qualify for the World Series. Baltimore pitching was superb, holding Philadelphia to nine runs in five games and having a team ERA of 1.60 as they took them four games to one.

NATIONAL LEAGUE: NO REPEAT WINNER

St. Louis looked to repeat, but injuries and off-seasons by several key players, plus the trade of Keith Hernandez to New York, doomed St. Louis to a sub-.500 season. Bob Forsch and Joaquin Andujar went from 30–19 to 16–28, while Bruce Sutter slipped to a 4.23 ERA.

Philadelphia regained the division title as John Denny won a league-high 19 games and had the top winning percentage at .760. In the West, Los Angeles won by three games over Atlanta and six over Houston.

Steve Carlton led the league in strikeouts with 275. Mario Soto, pitching for last place Cincinnati, won 17 games and had the most complete games (18), and Denny was the ERA leader at 2.37, making him an easy Cy Young winner.

It continued to get harder for a pitcher to win 20 games as the manner in which starting pitchers were handled was rapidly changing. Not many managers concerned themselves with pitchers having large totals of complete games, although some individual pitchers still prided themselves on these accomplishments. On the other side, there were many pitchers who started looking toward the bullpen in the sixth or seventh inning. Often standard procedure was for the starter to go six or seven, bring in the setup man for one or two innings, and then the closer. Are these always legitimate saves? It's a great argument or discussion for the hot stove league.

Denny had a great year as he won the Cy Young with a 2.37 ERA to go with his 19–6, which also was the league's best winning percentage (.760). To illustrate our point about the complete games, despite his great ERA Denny had only seven complete games. He made 36 starts, but had 11 no-decisions. Another factor in why pitchers find it more difficult to win 20 games is that they are taken out of far too many games early, and the decision goes to another pitcher.

There were ten pitchers with ten or more no-decisions. Charles Hudson was 8–8 in 26 starts; Ferguson Jenkins was 6–9 in 29 starts; Tom Seaver 9–14 in 34 starts; Fernando Valenzuela 15–10 in 35 starts; Pascual Perez 15–8 in 33 starts; Craig McMurtry 15–9 in 35 starts; Phil Niekro 11–10 in 33 starts; Bob Knepper 6–13 in 29 starts; Tim Lollar 7–12 in 30 starts; and Mark Davis 6–4 in 20 starts. Admittedly, not all these pitchers would have won 20 games, but Valenzuela, Perez, and McMurtry would have had the chance. During an earlier era, in 35 starts a pitcher might have four or five no-decisions. Now, to win 20 games a pitcher has to start at least 35 if not 40 games.

One more interesting sidelight: Jesse Orosco led the New York Mets in wins with a 13–7 record, all in relief, as he made 62 appearances and had 17 saves. How the game had changed!

Steve Garvey's consecutive game streak ended at 1,207 when he was injured, thus setting a new National League record. Philadelphia got even with Los Angeles for their losses in the late 1970s, defeating them in four games as Carlton won twice and Jerry Reuss lost twice for LA. The World Series was a different story, as they lost in five games with Charlie Hudson (8–8) taking two losses.

Steve Carlton reached the 300-win club with a 15–16, 3.11 ERA record for 37 starts as he also posted the league high with 284 innings. Carlton had one more winning season in his arm before his downhill slide during the final four years of his career.

1984

AMERICAN LEAGUE: A TIGER ROARS

It had been 16 seasons since Detroit was in the fall classic, but with a hard-hitting crew and deep pitching staff the Tigers won 104 games and beat out Toronto by 15 games. They didn't have a 20-game winner, but Jack Morris, Dan Petry and Milt Wilcox won 54, and Alurelio Lopez and Willie Hernandez were 19–4 in relief and saved 46 games. It was the first time ever the number one and two people in Cy Young voting were relief pitchers, with Hernandez beating out Dan Quisenberry.

In the West, Kansas City overcame injuries to win over California and Minnesota by three games, as Quisenberry set a new record with 44 saves. Milwaukee had the fewest complete games with 13 and Baltimore the most with 48, as the latter had the league's only 20-game winner.

The 1984 season produced only one 20-game winner. It was Mike Boddicker in his only 20-win season, with a 20–11, 2.79 ERA (the league's best) and 16 complete games. Boddicker had pitched in ten games with a 1–0 mark for Baltimore in 1980–82. In 1983 he became a starter and was 16–8, then followed with his 20-win season for the best two years back-to-back of his career. His ERAs for the two years were 2.77 and 2.79. It looked like Baltimore had another Jim Palmer, but it wasn't to be.

Boddicker remained with Baltimore through mid-season 1988, but had only one winning year, 1986 at 14–12. His ERAs for those years were 4.08, 4.71, 4.18 and 3.86 while posting a 42–53. When he was traded to the Red Sox, he returned to the form of the mid-80s as he finished out the year with 7–3, 2.63 ERA. Then came seasons of 15–11 and 17–8 with ERAs in the low threes. After that he was 12–12 with Kansas City in 1991, and then the injury plague took over. Over the next two seasons, Boddicker had knee, back and leg problems, was a combined 4–9 and finally retired at the end of the 1993 season with a final mark of 134–116, which was far less than the early promise had shown.

After 20 years in Atlanta, Phil Niekro joined the Yankees and gave them a 16–8 season. He followed that with a 16–12 year, giving him 32 wins for his only two years at New York. Although Niekro had won 82 games over the past six years, he had only 32 complete games, after having posted 67 in the three prior seasons. Here was another example of how times had changed.

The Red Sox unveiled a 21-year-old rookie, Roger Clemens, who would soon take the league by storm. In 21 games he was 9–4. We would have to wait a couple of seasons as a shoulder ailment limited him to 15 games and a 7–5 record in 1985.

When we speak of complete games, we look at Wilcox, who was 17–8 in 33 starts with no complete games and pitched only 194 innings. Once it was virtually unheard of that a pitcher would start 33 games and pitch fewer than 200 innings, let alone not complete any of them.

A couple of final comments. Tom Seaver had also come over to the American League and in his first season with the White Sox he was 15–11. He followed this with a 16–11 year in 1985. Lamarr Hoyt, last season's big winner, was this year's big loser at 13–18.

Pitcher/Team	G	GS	CG	W	L	Pct	ERA	SO	W	IP
Mike Boddicker, Balt	34	34	16	20*	11	.645	2.79*	128	81	261

The sixth- and seventh-place teams in the West produced the complete game leader and strikeout king as Texas' (seventh) Charlie Hough had 17 complete games and Seattle's Mark Langston had 204 strikeouts. California's Geoff Zahn and Boston's Bob Ojeda led with five shutouts.

Detroit easily handled Kansas City, defeating them three games to none. In the World Series, Morris had two complete game wins and Hernandez saved the other two, as Detroit won in five games. Alex Trammel hit two home runs, had six RBIs and batted .450, while teammate Kirk Gibson hit two home runs, had seven RBIs and hit .333.

NATIONAL LEAGUE: A LONG TIME COMING, AND THEY ALMOST MAKE IT

The final two division winners were strangers to the playoffs and World

Series. San Diego had never been in either and the Chicago Cubs, baseball's oldest continuous franchise, hadn't been in either, since the days of the old eight-team format, when they last played in the 1945 fall classic.

Chicago had a fine hitting attack, but needed a stopper. They acquired Dennis Eckersley from Boston, who won ten games for them, but the real difference was getting Rick Sutcliffe from Cleveland. He had been 4–5 with the Indians, but was 16–1 with the Cubs for a composite 20–6 and the Cy Young Award, while teammate Ryne Sandberg won the MVP. St. Louis had the other 20-game winner in the division, Joaquin Andujar.

Rick Sutcliffe has had his moments of glory and shame during his major league career, which covered 1979–1994. He did pitch in one game in 1976 and two in 1978, but his first full season was 1979. Sutcliffe broke into the league in great fashion by winning 17 games and being named rookie of the year. He quickly faded and was 3–9 and 2–2 the next two seasons, and the Dodgers gave up on him. Then he went to Cleveland where he was 14–8 and 17–11 his first two years.

When he started out 4–5 and 5.17 ERA in 1984, the Indians packed him off to the Chicago Cubs, where he was an unbelievable 16–1 in 20 starts with a 2.69 ERA. His .914 was the best winning percentage in the league, and his overall 20–6 made him a 20-game winner for the only time in his career. This record earned him the Cy Young award.

However, it seems he couldn't stand prosperity, as he suffered a shoulder injury and was 8–8 the next year and 5–14 in 1986 before bouncing back with a league-high 18 wins in 1987. He was then 13–14 and 16–11 before running into more injury problems. From 1990 to 1994 he had shoulder problems twice, a leg injury and a knee injury that greatly reduced his effectiveness and pitching time. His only full season was 1992, when he was 16–15 for Baltimore.

What could Sutcliffe's record have been like if there had not been so many injuries and lack of consistency? I don't know if we have the answer, except to point to his record of 171 wins with all the problems he had, and try to speculate what it could have been.

Andujar spent 12 seasons in the majors and his best three were in St. Louis. He broke in with Houston in 1976, lasted to mid–1981 and was 42–48 for the team. He joined St. Louis after the strike and was 6–1 for the balance of the year. Then he was 15–10 in their pennant-winning season, followed by a disastrous 6–16. He posted his first of two 20-win seasons in 1984 and led the league with four shutouts.

He followed that with a 21-win season, but after that he had nothing but problems. He left St. Louis after the 1985 season and a bad experience in the World Series, joined Oakland and was 12–7, but had a serious leg injury that hampered his performances. The next two years he had shoulder and knee problems and was only 3–5 with Oakland in 1987 and 2–5 with Houston in his final year.

Andujar walked to the beat of a different drummer. At times he was accused of being a "hot dog" or "showboat" by some of his actions on the field. For example, often when he struck out a batter he would "shoot" him, using his hand as a mock gun. Needless to say, this didn't sit well with opposing players; even some of his teammates didn't approve. Andujar threw and batted right-handed, but against certain pitchers and only if there were men on base he batted left-handed. His final career mark was 127–118, and removing his two 20-plus-win seasons he was only 86–92, a less than adequate record.

This was Carlton's last winning season as he was 13–7, with just one complete game in 33 starts. He had 13 no-decisions and finished the season with a 313–207 career mark.

A new pitcher arrived who would soon become the premier right-hander in the league and that was Dwight Gooden. As a rookie he was 17–9, 2.60 ERA and 276 strikeouts in 218 innings. He was being called a right-handed Lefty Grove, another Bob Feller, or, because he was black, another Satchel Paige, Bob Gibson or Ferguson Jenkins. For the next few years he pitched like them, and the ballparks were full whenever and wherever he hurled. By the end of the 1990 season, he had 119 wins and wouldn't be 26 until November 16.

As a pitcher's best years are supposed to be from age 28 to 32, although that theory has been disproved on many occasions, Gooden should have many great years ahead of him. A Hall of Fame spot, 300–350 career wins or even a new National League record, maybe even 400—these were not mere possibilities, but what people considered as events certain to happen. Then came disaster in the form of injuries and drugs, and a great career started sliding away. We will return to this item later.

Mario Soto was 18–7 for fifth-place Cincinnati and had a league-high 13 complete games. The prior season he had won 17 when Cincinnati finished last. Soto did much of his pitching when Cincinnati had losing teams, then when they started to win he came down with shoulder problems and was only 11–19 for his last three seasons (1986–88), after an 89–73 start for some lackluster Cincinnati teams. It was another career cut down before its time.

In a distinctly weaker division, San Diego, the only team over .500, won by 12 games over Atlanta, as no pitcher won over 15 for them, and none in the division won over 18. The Cardinals' Bruce Sutter was the top fireman, setting a new record in saves with 45. Los Angeles led the league with 39 complete games and San Francisco was last with 9.

Pitcher/Team	G	GS	CG	W	L	Pct	ERA	SO	W	IP
Rick Sutcliffe, Chgo	35	35	9	20*	6	.769	3.65	213	85	244
Joaquin Andujar, STL	36	36	12	20*	14	.588	3.34	147	70	261*

Los Angeles' Alejandro Pena (12–6) had the best ERA, 2.48, while Sutcliffe as a National Leaguer had the top percentage, .941. Andujar, Pena and Orel Hershiser tied for the most shutouts with four each. New York rookie Dwight Gooden (17–9) led with 276 strikeouts, while Cincinnati's Mario Soto had the lowest complete game total ever to lead for a full season, with 13.

It looked like the Cubs were finally going to make it back to a World Series when they won the first two, but then the team went to San Diego and lost the last three. The long-suffering Cubs fans continued to wait. In the Series, it was no contest as San Diego won the second game for their only win. They were outscored and outpitched as they went down to defeat.

1985

AMERICAN LEAGUE: TWO HARD-FOUGHT BATTLES AND THREE MILESTONES REACHED

Each division featured a down-to-the-wire battle for the title, while milestones were reached by Rod Carew with his 3,000th hit, and Phil Niekro and Tom Seaver each achieving his 300th career win.

Toronto won its first-ever division title, edging New York by 1½ games, although the latter had the league's top winner in Ron Guidry, who lost the Cy Young award to Kansas City's Bret Saberhagen. The Yankees also had the MVP in Don Mattingly.

In the West, Kansas City edged California by one game as Saberhagen won 20. The playoffs were expanded to seven games and Toronto won the first two, but Kansas City came back to win four of the next five.

Dan Quisenberry again led all relievers, this time with 37 saves. Minnesota topped the league with 41 complete games, while Oakland had the fewest with ten. How the mighty had fallen.

Ron Guidry had his last big season as he posted a league-high 22 wins and the best winning percentage at .786. After this year, Guidry would pitch three more seasons but post only a 16–23 record as a series of ailments and injuries took their toll and forced his retirement.

Bert Blyleven split the 1985 season with Cleveland (last in their division) and Minnesota (77–85), had a 17–16 mark and led the league with 24 complete games, five shutouts, 37 starts, 284 innings pitched and 206 strikeouts. This season in many ways was typical for Blyleven, as he suffered with inept ball clubs for much of his career. Despite all this, he still won 287 games, and had he not suffered an elbow injury that limited him to four appearances in 1982, he probably would have won 300 games.

If baseball ever had a Jekyll-Hyde character as a pitcher, Saberhagen has to be in the top five for the title. From 1984 (his rookie season) through 1994, Saberhagen never put together two successive winning seasons. The closest he came was 1993–94 when he was 7–7 and then 14–4 in the strike-aborted season. For the rest of his career he has alternated winning years with losing years, with the former in the odd and the latter in the even years. This, his first of two 20-win seasons, won for him the Cy Young award for the first of two times, as he would repeat in 1989. He spent the first eight seasons with Kansas City and had a composite 110–78. With the New York Mets in three seasons (1992–94), he was 24–17. His 1995 season was split between New York and Colorado, and he posted a 7–6 mark. For his career he is 141–100, and at age 36, if he can maintain some consistency, could still surpass the 200-win mark.

Another pitcher from whom more would be heard was Frank Viola. While pitching for second-division Minnesota, he was 18–14 following an 18–12 season. Over 1984–88 he won 93 games, highlighted by his Cy Young 24–7 season in 1988. Through 1995 he is 175–147.

Pitcher/Team	G	GS	CG	W	L	Pct	ERA	SO	W	IP
Ron Guidry, NY	34	33	11	22*	6	.786*	3.27	143	42	259
Bret Saberhagen, KC	32	32	10	20	6	.769	2.87	156	38	235

Toronto's Dave Stieb (14–13) had the top ERA, 2.48. There was a two-day work stoppage for both leagues, quickly settled, and only one game was lost by some teams, with others not losing any.

Kansas City went into the Series as underdogs against their cross-state rivals, the St. Louis Cardinals. They won the Series in seven games with a highly disputed victory in game six. In one of the worst calls in baseball history, Kansas City was given a reprieve, won the game and instead of losing in six games, took the title in seven.

NATIONAL LEAGUE: WHITEY BALL
AND AN EXTREMELY BAD CALL

St. Louis was picked to finish last, but Whitey Herzog fielded a team strong on speed, defense and pitching, and at the end the Redbirds edged out the Mets by three games. John Tudor and Joaquin Andujar each won 21 to pace the Redbird express. Runner-up New York had the Cy Young winner in Dwight Gooden (24–4).

In the West, Los Angeles beat out Cincinnati as Orel Hershiser was 19–3 and Fernando Valenzuela won 17. Second-place Cincinnati had the division's only 20-game winner in Tom Browning.

Tudor, in 12 seasons, only eight of which could be considered full years, won 117 while losing just 72. From 1982 to 1988 and again in 1990 (his last year), he won at least ten games per season. His only losing mark was in his rookie season at Boston when he was 1–2 in six games. Tudor pitched for the Red Sox through 1983 and was 39–32, not bad for a left-hander pitching half of his games in Fenway Park. He had one season with Pittsburgh (1984) and was 12–11 with a 3.27 ERA for a team that was last. In the off season he was traded to St. Louis and had his career year as he was 21–8, 1.93 ERA and 10 shutouts. In almost any other year he would have won the Cy Young Award, but not this time with Gooden in the league. Tudor pitched for St. Louis through mid–1988 and was traded to the Dodgers as they were making a stretch drive. He was out most of 1989 with an elbow problem, but following reconstructive surgery by Dr. Jobe he rejoined St. Louis for his final year and went 12–4 in 1990. Perhaps if Tudor had not suffered a knee injury in 1987 and lost a full season in 1989, he might have stayed around longer and won many more games. His record with St. Louis for slightly less than five seasons was 62–26, with a .705 winning percentage.

Andujar had his biggest season as he won 21 games. Early in the year it looked like he would win 26–28, as at one point he sported a 13–3 mark with an ERA considerably below 3.00. Then in the second half he stumbled and finished at 21–12, 3.40 ERA. In the World Series he became embroiled in a rhubarb in the final game and the Cardinal management decided they didn't want him back for 1986, despite his having posted 41 wins in two seasons. He went to Oakland, but injuries curtailed his pitching and by the end of 1988 he was out of baseball.

When it came to pitching honors this year, they belonged to Gooden. He had a fantastic season at 24–4, .857 winning percentage. Gooden led the league with 24 wins, the most complete games (16), the most innings (277) and led with 268 strikeouts while posting an unbelievable 1.53 ERA. The sportswriters were looking for new superlatives with which to describe his endeavors on the field. While he continued to pitch outstanding ball and have some very good records, he never again approached this season or won 20 games. The closest was 19 in 1990.

There were only two honors Gooden didn't have. The shutout title was won by Tudor. Despite Gooden's .857 winning percentage, he ranked second to Orel Hershiser and his 19–3 record, .864 winning percentage and 2.08 ERA. We will be talking more about Mr. Hershiser again.

Browning appeared in three games and was 1–0 in 1984, but this would be considered his rookie season. He won 20 games and was second in the voting for rookie of the year. Through 1995 Browning has never duplicated his rookie year success, although he has a fine career-winning mark of 123–88. But at age 36, with the injury history of the past several seasons, it is debatable how much more effective pitching he can do.

Browning has had only one losing season for Cincinnati and that was in 1987. From 1985 through 1991 Browning won 106 games, with his second best an 18–5 mark in 1988. Then starting in 1992 he had a series of injuries. He had knee problems in 1992 and was 6–5, then a broken finger in 1993 when he was 7–7. In 1994 a broken arm limited him to a 3–1 mark. These were all bad breaks for a good pitcher who was on his way toward 200 career wins.

Pittsburgh had the worst record in baseball at 57–104 and Jose DeLeon was 2–19 for the Bucs. Montreal's Jeff Reardon led the league with 41 saves, as complete games continued to fall.

St. Louis led the league with 37 complete games, while Atlanta had the fewest with nine.

Pitcher/Team	G	GS	CG	W	L	Pct	ERA	SO	W	IP
Dwight Gooden, NY	35	35	16*	24*	4	.857	1.53*	268*	69	277*
John Tudor, STL	36	36	14	21	8	.724	1.93	169	49	275
Joaquin Andujar, STL	38	38	10	21	12	.636	3.40	112	82	270
Tom Browning, Cinn	38	38	6	20	9	.690	3.55	155	70	261

Several milestones were reached during the season. Nolan Ryan got his 4,000th strikeout, and Pete Rose his 4,000th hit. The Cardinals lost the first two play-off games to Los Angeles but won the next four, the last two in the ninth inning on dramatic home runs by Ozzie Smith and Jack Clark.

At the start of this season Steve Carlton had a 313–207, .602 winning percentage, which would have placed him tenth on the all-time list of pitchers with over 300 career wins. However, a combination of pride and the need for money, as a former business manager had made bad investments for him and then absconded with some funds, forced Carlton to continue pitching.

Injuring his shoulder at age 40, the first injury of his career, certainly didn't bode well for the future. Carlton pitched for several teams through 1988 and was a composite 16–37, which greatly tarnished his record. This writer for one believes he would have done better to retire after 1984, but then I didn't have to deal with his financial problems, and if he could get $2,000,000 per year, who can blame him?

Entering the World Series, the Redbirds were favorites and it seemed they would make the prognosticators correct. They led three games to two and carried a 1–0 lead into the bottom of the ninth in game six. Then fate in the form of umpire Don Denkinger struck, when he called Jose Ortega safe at first. Replays and a picture spread later in *Sports Illustrated* definitely proved he was out.

With one of the worst calls ever made, Kansas City got a reprieve, scored two runs and instead of losing the Series in six games, picked up the title in seven.

1986

AMERICAN LEAGUE: EACH STILL LOOKING FOR A CHAMPIONSHIP

Both division winners, Boston and California, parlayed strong teams to a final five-game-plus margin. Boston was looking for the chance to win its first World Series since 1918, while Gene Autry's Angels were trying to get into their first Series ever. Neither achieved their objective, although Boston made it to the fall classic.

Boston was led by a strong hitting attack, backed by MVP and Cy Young winner Roger Clemens (24–4). Jack Morris was a 20-game winner for Detroit, but some of the most effective pitching came from a sub-.500 team, Milwau-kee, where Teddy Higuera won 20 games with a 2.79 ERA.

The Western Division boasted no 20-game winners, as California's Bobby Witt came the closest with 18, while second-place Texas' Charlie Hough (17–10) lost his chance when he broke a finger and was out for over a month. The West also had a pitcher to turn in creditable numbers for a second-division team when Bert Blyleven won 17 games for sixth-place Minnesota.

Clemens had a season quite similar to Dwight Gooden's in 1985 as he was 24–4, .857 winning percentage and 2.48 ERA, all of which were the best for their category in the league. Clemens won the first of his three Cy Young Awards and had the first of his three 20-plus win seasons. From 1986 through 1992, Clemens won 136 while losing 63 to make himself the best pitcher in the league, if not in the majors.

What American League hitters couldn't do, injuries and strikes did, that was slow him down. In 1993 he suffered his first losing season (11–14) as he was sidelined with a groin injury. Then he came back to 9–7, 2.85 ERA in the strike abbreviated 1994 season, and despite injuries was 10–5 in 1995. With a 182–98 career mark, at age 34 as he enters the 1996 season, Clemens can still post a very high total of wins barring any future injuries. His chances for 300 may be faltering, but 250–275 are still in reach. Again, if he stays healthy and pitches into his 40s, 300 is a possibility.

With a 21–8 record, Morris had his second 20-win season and probably would have won the Cy Young had Clemens either not been in the league or not had the season he did. Morris would have one more 20-plus-win season and one more opportunity to win the Cy Young, but he would lose that season to relief ace Dennis Eckersley.

This was Higuera's second season in the majors and the biggest year of his career as he won 20, lost 11, and posted a 2.79 ERA for next-to-last-place Mil-waukee. Higuera had four fine seasons from 1985 to 1988, winning 69 while losing just 38. Then the injury jinx hit him and since that time he has been only 25–26. Many of the seasons he saw limited action, and in 1992 he missed the entire year. His problems have been back and shoulder injuries, and a very promising career was stunted.

Dave Righetti set a new save record at 46 as he did his best to put New York into the play-offs, but Ron Guidry falling to 9–12 kept them second. Minnesota had the most complete games with 39 and New York the fewest at 13.

Pitcher/Team	G	GS	CG	W	L	Pct	ERA	SO	W	IP
Roger Clemens, Bos	33	33	10	24*	4	.857*	2.48*	238	67	254
Jack Morris, Det	35	35	15	21	8	.724	3.27	223	82	267
Teddy Higuera, Milw	34	34	15	20	11	.645	2.79	207	74	246

Morris led with six shutouts, while Blyleven again led in complete games, this time 16, and Seattle's Mark Langston was strikeout king at 245. It looked like California would make it to the World Series when they took three of the first four games in the play-offs, but Boston stormed back to take the last three.

The Series was just the reverse as they won the first two, then went up three games to two only to lose in seven games, when Bill Buckner let a third-out groundball go through his legs in the tenth inning of game six. That allowed New York to win the game instead of Boston, which would have given them the title. Their cry is getting like the old Brooklyn Dodgers: "Wait till next year!"

NATIONAL LEAGUE: A COUPLE OF RUNAWAYS

St. Louis was picked to repeat, but their big slugger Jack Clark got injured, several players had off-seasons, 21-game winner Andujar was traded and Danny Cox and John Tudor, 39–17 in 1985, were 25–20 in 1986. The Mets stormed out of the gate and were never seriously challenged. They won 108 games to win by 22 over Philadelphia.

In the West Houston won handily over Cincinnati, while Los Angeles slipped to sixth place due to key injuries to many players. Their only consolation was they had the league's big winner in Fernando Valenzuela. St. Louis had the top reliever in Todd Worrell, with 36. Los Angeles set a new low for most complete games at 35, while Chicago had the fewest at 11.

Valenzuela finally hit it big as he was 21–11 for a next-to-last-place Los Angeles team. Valenzuela led with 21 victories and also had 20 complete games to lead the league. In fact, he had more complete games than nine other teams in the league, and more than the rest of the Dodger staff combined. After this season Valenzuela would post a 14–14 record, but then injuries would plague him. He would bounce to the minors and come back to the majors, but he was never the same pitcher.

Mike Krukow's career covered the years 1976–89 and he had a 124–117 record. This was by far his best season as the next highest number of victories he ever had was 13 with Philadelphia in 1982. Krukow broke in with Chicago and appeared in two games with no record in 1976. Then from 1977 through 1981 he was 45–50 before being traded to the Phillies. After one season there he came to San Francisco where he spent the rest of his career. After this season he was only 16–13 for the final three years, as shoulder injuries limited his work, especially in 1988–89.

Pitcher/Team	G	GS	CG	W	L	Pct	ERA	SO	W	IP
F Valenzuela, LA	34	34	20*	21*	11	.656	3.14	242	85	269
M Krukow, SF	34	34	10	20	9	.690	3.05	178	55	245

Houston's Mike Scott (18–10) tied for the lead in shutouts with teammate Bob Knepper (17–12) at five, but also led in ERA, 2.22, strikeouts with 306 and innings pitched with 275. These stats gave him the Cy Young award. New York's Bob Ojeda (18–5) had the top winning percentage, .783. Pete Rose retired at the end of the season as the all-time hit leader with 4,256, which is 66 more than the legendary Ty Cobb. Rose also batted approximately 2,600 more times and had a career .303 to Cobb's all-time high .366 or .367, depending upon which baseball authority you accept.

New York won the play-offs in six games with reliever Jesse Orosco winning three games. Then fate smiled on the Mets in the World Series. When they were down three games to two and certain defeat in the tenth inning of game six, Bill Buckner booted a grounder that enabled the Mets to win and then take game seven for the championship. Orosco had no wins but two saves in the Series. Meanwhile, their ace Dwight Gooden was 0–3 in the play-offs and Series.

1987

AMERICAN LEAGUE: THE NAME
OF THE GAME IS LONG BALL

Home runs were hit in record numbers, and the previous year's winners fell precipitously in the standings. Oakland's Mark McGwire set a rookie record when he hit 49 home runs and led the league. Oakland also had one of the league's two 20-game winners in Dave Stewart. The other was Roger Clemens, who won his second straight Cy Young award.

Detroit possessed a powerful attack and won the Eastern Division with the best record in baseball. The next three teams, Toronto, Milwaukee and New York all had better records than the Western Division winner, Minnesota. Toronto's Tom Henke was the save leader with 34, while Boston had the most complete games at 47 and Minnesota the fewest with 16.

Although Boston finished below .500, Clemens continued his mastery as he was 20–9, 2.97 ERA, with the league's most complete games at 18, while he fanned 256 in 282 innings. This was his second straight 20-win season and his second consecutive Cy Young Award. He would do each one another time by 1991. He was certainly laying the groundwork for consideration by the Hall of Fame.

Stewart had pitched in one game for the Dodgers back in 1978 and then didn't return to the majors until 1981, when he was 4–3 with the Dodgers. From then until early 1986 he played for the Dodgers, Texas and Philadelphia with only a 30–35 record to show for his efforts. In 1986, his first year in Oakland, he was 9–5. No one expected what would happen next.

In 1987 Stewart won 20 games, the first of four straight seasons in which he would win 20 or more. While his career certainly wasn't as eventful as Eddie Plank's, there was a similarity. He was always the bridesmaid. Despite winning 20 or more four straight seasons, Stewart never copped the Cy Young Award. It seems someone else was always having a little bit better year that season, or someone was having their career-best year.

However, for the 1987–90 period, no pitcher won more games, not even Clemens. Stewart captured 84 wins to Clemen's 82 for that time frame. When he retired early in 1995 he had a 165–122 mark that might have been better if all those early years hadn't been wasted bouncing from team to team, used mostly in relief.

Pitcher/Team	G	GS	CG	W	L	Pct	ERA	SO	W	IP
Roger Clemens, Bos	36	36	18*	20*	9	.690*	2.97	256	83	282
Dave Stewart, Oak	37	37	8	20*	13	.606	3.68	205	105	261

Clemens led with seven shutouts, Toronto's Jimmy Key had the best ERA, 2.76, and Mark Langston again was the strikeout leader with 262 as he fell one short of 20 wins. Charlie Hough had another good year for last-place Texas, winning 18 games.

After losing the first game in the play-offs to Detroit, Minnesota upset them by winning the next four. Then in the World Series, they defeated St. Louis four games to three, as each team won all their home games, and since Minnesota had the home field edge, they won the Series. During the regular season Minnesota was 56–25 at home, best in baseball, but only 29–52 on the road.

NATIONAL LEAGUE: JACK IS BACK AS THE GIANTS RISE FROM THE ASHES

The Cardinals were built on speed, defense, and pitching, but in 1985 the key was their power hitter, Jack Clark. He was injured, missed 75 percent of 1986 and the Redbirds faded. A healthy Jack Clark in 1987 carried them to the pennant, although he was injured in September and missed the last month. This was to tell in the Series, as Clark could not play.

St. Louis and New York battled it out again, with New York losing by three games and Montreal one game behind them. St. Louis had no pitcher to win over 11 games, as eight pitchers won at least eight games each.

The Mets were hurt when Dwight Gooden was suspended for almost two months because of drug involvement, but he still found time to win 15 games. No pitcher won 20, as Chicago's Rick Sutcliffe was tops with 18. Rick Rueschel with Chicago and San Francisco had the most complete games at 12 (a new low), while Nolan Ryan led with 270 strikeouts and the league's best ERA, 2.76. Rueschel and Los Angeles' Bob Welch each had four shutouts.

Gooden's situation begins his era of tragedy. Although he would win 18 in 1988 and 19 in 1990, the drug problem would continue to plague him. The situation would get progressively worse until he was suspended in 1994 and missed the entire 1995 season. A career that once looked like a sure Hall of Famer was going south. Gooden had a shoulder problem in 1991 that limited him to 27 games, then in 1993 his drug use increased. From 1992 through 1994 he was only 25–32, followed by the suspension for the 1995 season.

Sutcliffe had his second-highest winning season as he garnered 18 wins but lost the Cy Young to reliever Steve Bedrosian. Orel Hershiser had another fine ERA (3.06), but playing for a weak Los Angeles team he could only go 16–16. Certainly with another team he would have posted 20 or more victories.

Another pitcher who could have benefited from a better hitting team was Nolan Ryan. He had the best ERA (2.76) in the league, led with 270 strikeouts, but had a horrible 8–16 record. This is just another example of the support that Ryan received throughout his career. In 34 starts, he could garner only eight wins despite having the league's best ERA. He also failed to complete any of his 34 starts.

Steve Bedrosian led with 40 saves and the Cy Young award. Los Angeles set a low mark for highest number of complete games at 29, while Cincinnati was last with seven.

The play-offs lasted seven games with St. Louis shutting out the Giants in the last two to win the right to represent the National League in the World Series. However, it was frustration time again as each team won on their home field, but St. Louis had only three home games; thus they lost the Series. They were also without the services of Clark, who in just 419 at bats had 35 home runs and 106 RBIs, while drawing a league-high 136 walks in 131 games.

1988

AMERICAN LEAGUE: THE START OF ANOTHER DYNASTY

At season's end only two games separated fourth-place Toronto from first-place Boston. Sandwiched between were Detroit and Milwaukee, one game back of the leaders. Boston won out on their strong hitting and two 18-game winners in Bruce Hurst and Roger Clemens, who tied for the lead in complete games, while leading in shutouts (eight), and strikeouts (291).

In the West Oakland unveiled rookie Jose Canseco, who hit 42 home runs to go with Mark McGwire's 32. Add Dave Stewart's 21 wins and 17 from Bob Welch and Oakland had a 13-game bulge over Minnesota. This was to be the first of three straight titles for Oakland. The West possessed all three 20-game winners, as Frank Viola won the Cy Young Award while winning 24 games for Minnesota and Mark Gubicza won 20 for Kansas City.

Stewart had his second straight 20-win season as he posted a 21–12 mark while leading with 37 starts, 14 complete games and 276 innings. This is the first of three straight seasons that Stewart would lead in starts, and he would also be the leader in innings pitched during two of the next three years.

Viola had broke in with Minnesota in 1982. After two poor seasons in which his ERA was almost five and one-half runs per game, he posted only an

11–25 mark. Then in 1984 he got his pitches under control and won 69 games over the next four seasons. In 1988 he put it all together as he led with 24 wins and had a 2.64 ERA as he won the Cy Young award. Viola would later win 20 games for the New York Mets.

This was Gubzica's fifth season in the majors, all spent with Kansas City. Up to this point he had two winning and two losing years. With a 20–8, 2.70 ERA season at age 25 the future looked bright for the young right hander. He won 15 in 1989, but then developed shoulder trouble that plagued him from 1990 through 1996, producing only one winning season and limiting his activity. He was a combined 47–66 for the period. Through 1996 he owns a 131–133 career mark.

Clemens turned in an 18–12 mark, but based on his other stats could have been the recipient of a few breaks and won 20 games for the third straight season, which also would have made him a stronger contender for the Cy Young Award.

Dennis Eckersley, now with Oakland, and a converted starter who once won 20 games, was the save leader at 45. Texas led with 41 complete games, while Chicago had the fewest at 11.

Pitcher/Team	G	GS	CG	W	L	Pct	ERA	SO	W	IP
Frank Viola, Mn	35	35	7	24*	7	.774*	2.64	193	54	255
Dave Stewart, Oak	37	37*	14*	21	12	.636	3.23	192	110	276*
Mark Gubicza, KC	35	35	8	20	8	.714	2.70	183	83	270

Minnesota's Allen Anderson had the top ERA at 2.45. Baltimore set a major league record when it lost its first 21 games and finished last with a 54–107 record, shades of the old St. Louis Browns. Oakland swept Boston in four games as Bruce Hurst lost twice for the BoSox.

In the Series, Oakland, winners of the most games in the majors and possessors of a potent attack, went down to defeat in five games, scoring only 11 runs as McGwire and Canseco had two hits between them, both home runs.

NATIONAL LEAGUE: AN UNEXPECTED WINNER

St. Louis was never a factor this year as their pitching fell off, and Jack Clark had left for the New York Yankees after a salary dispute during the off-season. New York returned to the top by winning 100 games and finishing 15 in front of Pittsburgh. The Mets' pitching was awesome, led by David Cone (20–3), Dwight Gooden (18–9) and Ron Darling (17–9). Randy Meyers and Roger McDowell won 12 and saved 42 for the Mets.

In the West Orel Hershiser won 23 games to put the Dodgers in first place and give himself the Cy Young award. His victories were matched by Danny Jackson for second-place Cincinnati. The Reds had the top save artist in John Franco with 39. Los Angeles led with 32 complete games and Pittsburgh was last with 12.

This was Cone's second season in the big leagues, and it was a gangbuster year as he led in win percentage at .870 based on his 20–3 season. Cone had pitched in 11 games with no record for Kansas City in 1986, then came to New York and was 5–6 his first year. While Cone has not repeated his 20-win seasons, he has pitched winning ball every year but one. The strike-shortened seasons of 1994 and 1995 probably cost him 20 wins each year as he was 16–5 and 18–8 for the two seasons. Cone was 33 entering the 1996 year; thus, with a 129–78 career mark, he could well exceed 200 wins by a wide margin, barring no serious injuries.

Throughout this book we have seen pitchers that had one or two super seasons in their career and were less than .500 pitchers the rest of the time. This is the story of Danny Jackson. His career record is 109–121, and if we remove this year and his 1994 season (14–6), he is 72–107. Jackson spent his first five years with Kansas City and was 37–49 coming into this year, when he had his career-best season.

After this year Jackson had shoulder problems and then abdominal muscle strains over the next three years, and was only 21–35 for the 1989–92 period. He landed with the Phillies and was 12–11 and the aforementioned 14–6 for 1993–94. Then with St. Louis in 1995, cancer struck and he had an ankle injury, sidelining him for the season after a 3–10 record. In 1996 he was limited to four games and a 1–1 record. At 35, he could still give a decent account if he can overcome some of his past illnesses and injuries.

Although he didn't win 20, Gooden had another good year as he was 18–9, 3.19 ERA. Meanwhile, Rick Rueschel almost made 20 as he posted an 19–11 mark for a San Francisco team barely over .500. Nolan Ryan led all pitchers with 228 strikeouts.

Pitcher/Team	G	GS	CG	W	L	Pct	ERA	SO	W	IP
Orel Hershiser, LA	35	34	15*	23*	8	.742	2.26	176	73	267*
Danny Jackson, Cinn	35	35	15*	23*	8	.742	2.73	161	71	261
David Cone, NY	35	28	8	20	3	.870*	2.22*	213	60	231

Hershiser set a new major league record when he pitched 59 consecutive scoreless innings starting on August 30. He finished the season with six consecutive shutouts as he led the league with eight. In a hard-fought seven-game match, Los Angeles prevailed over the favored Mets, as league MVP Kirk Gibson hit two home runs and drove in six runs, although he batted only .154.

Going into the Series Oakland was favored, especially when Gibson got injured and could bat only once. But what a time at bat it was! In Hollywood fashion he slugged a two-out, two-run pinch-hit homer in the bottom of the ninth off relief ace Dennis Eckersley to give the Dodgers the win in game one. They would win in five games as Hershiser won twice.

1989

AMERICAN LEAGUE: A SEASON OF UPS AND DOWNS

The 1989 season was noted for teams having a series of ups and downs. The Toronto Blue Jays started off 12–24, fired their manager, then regrouped to take the East Division title, while Detroit, second the previous year, fell to last place with the worst record in baseball, 59–103.

In the West, Oakland survived a broken wrist by Jose Canseco to win it all as Dave Stewart won 20 games or more for the third straight year. They also had two near misses, as Mike Moore and Storm Davis each won 19 and Bob Welch 17. Bret Saberhagen was the league's big winner and also copped the Cy Young Award as he won 23 and Kansas City finished second.

Stewart had his best year to date as he was 21–9, but again no brass ring. He tied for the lead in starts with 36 and pitched 258 innings. However, the Cy Young Award went to Saberhagen, and deservedly so. Stewart seemed to have the misfortune always to run into someone having just a little bit better season.

Since winning 20 games and the Cy Young Award back in 1985, Saberhagen had two losing seasons in three as he was 7–12, 18–10 and 14–16 over the past three years. However, he made up for it in 1989 as this was his premier season. He had a 23–6, .793 winnings percentage, 12 complete games, 262 innings and a 2.16 ERA. All these marks were the best in the league. He almost pitched his team into contention for the World Series.

The league almost had two other 20-game winners, but Davis and Moore each came up one win short. Each had his individual best season. Of the top four Oakland pitchers, Moore enjoyed the best ERA, 2.61. Nolan Ryan celebrated his return to the American League by fanning 301 batters to lead in that category for the tenth time in his career. It also marked the sixth time he exceeded 300 strikeouts.

Texas' Jeb Russell led with 38 saves. California topped the complete games with 32 and Chicago had the fewest, nine.

Pitcher/Team	G	GS	CG	W	L	Pct	ERA	SO	W	IP
B Saberhagen, KC	36	35	12*	23*	6	.783*	2.16*	193	43	262*
Dave Stewart, Oak	36	36*	8	21	9	.700	3.32	155	69	258

Saberhagen also led with four shutouts and the only major pitching category he didn't lead, strikeouts, was grabbed by Nolan Ryan with 301. In the play-offs Oakland won the first two games at home, lost the opener in Toronto and then won the last two, as Stewart won two games and Dennis Eckersley saved three. Ricky Henderson, with two home runs, five RBIs and a .400 average, and Carney Lansford with four RBIs and a .455 average, were the hitting stars.

Stewart and Moore each won two games in the Series as Oakland swept the Giants, outscoring them 32 to 14 and batting .301 to San Francisco's .209.

NATIONAL LEAGUE: DRAMA ON AND OFF THE FIELD

The National League was replete with drama and newsmaking events. Bart Giamatti became baseball commissioner on April 1, 1989 and on August 23rd suspended Pete Rose from baseball for life for gambling and betting on games. This has kept Pete out of the Hall of Fame. Nine days later, Giamatti suffered a heart attack and died. Meanwhile, Bill White became the first black to hold a significantly high administrative position in baseball when he was named president of the National League.

On the field, the Chicago Cubs made another try for a pennant and World Series trip as they beat out New York and St. Louis for the East title. Strong pitching led by 19-game winner Greg Maddux was the key.

In the West San Francisco won a hard-fought race from San Diego and Houston, who had the league's only 20-game winner in Mike Scott. San Diego's Mark Davis led with 44 saves, and a 1.85 ERA, enough to earn him the Cy Young award. Atlanta, although losing 97 games, saw a pitching ace develop: Tommy Glavine was 14–8 for the tailenders.

Pitcher/Team	G	GS	CG	W	L	Pct	ERA	SO	W	IP
Mike Scott, Ho	33	32	9	20*	10	.667	3.10	172	62	229

Los Angeles' Tim Belcher (15–12) set a new record for leading in complete games with only ten, and also had the most shutouts with eight, while San Francisco's Scott Garrelts (14–5) had the best ERA, 2.28. The Dodgers' Orel Hershiser (15–15, despite a 2.31 ERA) led with 257 innings pitched and the Cardinals Jose DeLeon (16–11) had the most strikeouts at 201. Remember a few years ago, he was 2–19.

Scott didn't know it at the time, but this would be his last big year, as injuries would befall him and end his career in two years. Scott had pitched for the Mets from 1979 to 1982 with little success as he was only 14–27. On joining Houston in 1983 he became a winner and had only one losing season (1984, 5–11) through this year.

Scott had won the Cy Young Award in 1986 when he was 18–10 with the league's best ERA, 2.23, and most strikeouts (306). This season his numbers were good, but not as impressive, although he managed to win 20 games for the only time in his career. His peak period was 1985–89, as he won 86 games for Houston in that stretch. Following this year he had a letdown and was only 9–13 in 1990, then he had a shoulder injury in 1991 that ended his career. His final mark was 124–108.

San Francisco killed Chicago's hope for a World Series trip by taking the play-offs in five games as Steve Bedrosian saved three. Will Clark, with 13 hits in five games for a .650 average, had eight RBIs and Matt Williams, a .300 hitter with nine RBIs, led the offensive attack as the Giants outscored Chicago 30–22.

In the World Series, the Giants' bats went to sleep as Clark hit .250, with no RBIs and Williams hit only .125 and one RBI. They went down to defeat in four games, with Garrelts losing twice and posting a 9.62 ERA. However, the biggest news was an earthquake that hit just before game three in San Francisco. Fifty people died, and the Series was delayed ten days. When restarted, it was somewhat anticlimactic.

10

1990–1996

──────────── **1990** ────────────

AMERICAN LEAGUE: LOCKOUT,
NO-HITTERS AND A DYNASTY ENDS

The owners locked out the players for the first 32 days of spring training, and when the season started no-hitters became rampant. On day three California's Mike Witt and Mark Langston combined for a no-hit game, while Nolan Ryan pitched his sixth and became the oldest to ever pitch one at age 43. The Yankees' Andy Hawkins threw a no-hitter, but lost 4–0.

Boston grabbed the Eastern Division crown by two games over Toronto as Roger Clemens won 20 or more for the third time in five seasons, while Wade Boggs had the lowest average of his career (.302). Clemens might have won the Cy Young Award, but was sidelined much of September with a shoulder injury.

In the West Oakland continued their mastery as they won by nine games over Chicago, although the White Sox won 94 games. Oakland was paced by Bob Welch with a 27–6 mark, the Cy Young winner, while teammate Dave Stewart won 20 or more for the fourth consecutive season. The A's had four players to hit 20 or more home runs, with Mark McGwire (39, 108 RBIs) and Jose Canseco (37, 101 RBIs) leading the way.

With 21 victories, this gave Clemens 100 wins over the 1986–90 period, and with a few breaks he probably could have had a dozen more. This season a shoulder injury caused him to miss several starts, as he started only 31 times but still had 21 wins. His 1.93 ERA was the best and he had 209 strikeouts in just 228 innings. Certainly a Cy Young performance, but the award went to 27-game winner Welch.

In one respect, Welch fits in the category of pitchers who had one great year and never repeated, except in his case he has won 211 games and has had eight other years in which he won at least 13 games. In 17 seasons he has had only five losing seasons, three in the past four years. Welch pitched for the Los Angeles Dodgers from 1978 through 1987 and had a 115–86 record. Since that time he has toiled for Oakland and produced a 96–60 mark.

287

This was his career-best year as he easily led the league in wins with his 27–6 mark. His .818 winning percentage was the league's best and he had a fine 2.95 ERA. These numbers were creditable enough to win the Cy Young Award. If there be a rap on Welch's year, it was that he completed only two of 35 starts. However, when you have an Eckersley, who saved 45 games, that is the way the game is played today anyway. What is wrong with taking advantage of the bullpen? The days of pitchers completing 25–30 games are over. Maybe they will return, maybe they won't. For now, we must accept the game the way it is played.

The highest number of games Welch won in any other season was 17, which he did for Oakland in 1978 and 1979. His highest victory total as a Dodger was 16 in 1982. After this year, things did not go well for Welch as he had only one more winning season: 1992 with an 11–7 record, when he also had an elbow injury. His composite for 1991–94 was 35–37. Welch decided to retire at the end of the 1994 season.

Stewart had the biggest season of his career, winning 22 games, but once again was shut out from the Cy Young Award, as this year he ran afoul of Welch's best career season. Stewart had his career-best ERA, 2.56, led with 11 complete games, the most starts (36) and highest innings pitched (267). He also shared with Clemens the shutout lead at four. Stewart did have the consolation of winning 20 or more four seasons in a row.

There were several pitchers to win 17 or 18 and perhaps at another time, with another pitching philosophy, some of them may have won 20. Mike Boddicker was 17–8 in 34 starts; Dave Stieb was 18–6 in 33 starts; Scott Sanderson 17–11 in 34 starts; Bobby Witt, 17–10 in 32 starts; Chuck Finley was 18–9 in 32 starts; and Erik Hansen, 18–9 in 33 starts. This season wasn't much different from past ones in regard to pitchers close to the charmed circle.

However, one must remember that pitchers' chances are greatly diminished when they are taken out of games in the sixth or seventh inning. No-decisions have increased. The starting pitcher's role has changed. Most managers ask for six good innings and then are ready to go to the bullpen. There are exceptions for a few pitchers, but not many.

Nolan Ryan led in strikeouts for the 11th time as he fanned 232 batters. This is the last season that Ryan would lead in that department. Chicago's Bobby Thigpen set a major league record with 57 saves, while Toronto tied the record for the fewest complete games with six, and Texas led with the fewest ever at 25.

Pitcher/Team	G	GS	CG	W	L	Pct	ERA	SO	W	IP
Bob Welch, Oak	35	35	2	27*	6	.818*	2.95	127	77	238
Dave Stewart, Oak	36	36*	11*	22	11	.667	2.56	166	83	267*
Roger Clemens, Bos	31	31	7	21	6	.778	1.93*	209	54	228

Ryan won his 300th career game during the season. Yankee owner George Steinbrenner agreed to resign as general manager of the team because of his involvement with gamblers. The suspension lasted one season and he was back.

Oakland disposed of Boston in four straight, as Stewart won twice and Eckersley saved two. Boston scored only four runs, one in each game. Oakland's dreams of another dynasty a la the 1970s came tumbling down when Cincinnati defeated them four straight and pinned two of the losses on Stewart.

NATIONAL LEAGUE: LOCKOUT, NO-HITTERS, JAIL AND THE FIRST OF THREE STRAIGHT

Baseball spring training was shortened by 32 days because of the owners' lockout, and when it began the season saw a record nine no-hitters between the two leagues. On an even darker note, Pete Rose was fined $50,000 and sentenced to federal prison for five months for income tax evasion.

On the baseball field Pittsburgh won the first of three straight Eastern Division titles by a four-game margin over New York ten over Montreal. Chicago, last year's first-place winner, finished below .500 and 20 games out, while third-place St. Louis fell to last, marking the first time in 72 years they had finished that low, longer than any team in baseball.

Doug Drabek paced the Pirates with a 22–6 mark that earned him the Cy Young award, while Bobby Bonilla, Barry Bonds and Andy Van Slyke paced the offense. Frank Viola won 20 games for the Mets, making him a rarity among pitchers, as he won 20 in each league.

Cincinnati won by five over Los Angeles, although no pitcher won over 15 and no hitter had over 86 RBIs. A clutch team performance put it all together. Ramon Martinez was a 20-game winner for the Dodgers. Tommy Glavine, one year away from stardom, was 10–12 for last-place Atlanta.

This was Drabek's fifth year in the majors, all with Pittsburgh. Up to this time his best year was 1988 when he was 15–7, 3.08 ERA. This year was all Drabek's as he led with 22 wins and a .786 winning percentage as he lost only six games. Drabek also turned in a fine 2.78 ERA for his 231 innings of work.

After this year Drabek had a couple of 15-win seasons for the Pirates. Then, feeling a financial crunch, Pittsburgh began moving the big money earners off their payroll, and Drabek was Houston-bound. Here he was expected to win big as Houston was putting together a team to go all the way, but thus far it hasn't happened. His first year was a disaster as he was 9–18, 3.79. He recovered nicely in 1994 at 12–6, 2.64. His 1995 mark was 10–9. He was one of the main reasons Houston failed to win the divisional title in 1996 as he was just 7–9. To date he owns a 137–112 career record.

Viola had his second 20-win season as he was 20–12 for the Mets and almost helped pitch them to a division title. He led with 250 innings while posting a 2.67 ERA. This was Viola's last big season year to date. After a 13–15 record with New York in 1991, Viola moved on to Boston and was 13–12, 11–8, before an elbow injury limited him to six games and a 1–1 record in 1994.

Martinez broke in with the Dodgers in 1988 and for the first two seasons was just 7–7. Then in 1990 he came into his own as he posted a 20–6 mark, with a league-best 12 complete games and a 2.92 ERA. In a different year he might have won the Cy Young, but this was Drabek's season. Since this year, Martinez has not always had the best of everything going for him. He followed this up with a 17–13 record in 1991, but then ran into an elbow problem the next season and had to settle for 8–11 and 10–12 marks over the 1992–93 period. He seemed to recover and was going pretty strong in 1994, when the strike ended his season at 12–7. For 1995 he was 17–7, giving him a career mark of 91–63.

This was Dwight Gooden's last big year as he was 19–7, but had only two complete games in 33 starts. A few years ago, Gooden would have had maybe 15–18 complete games, but even with a pitcher like him the manager goes to the bullpen. There weren't any other pitchers close to the 20-win mark.

New York's John Franco was save leader with 33, while Los Angeles had the most complete games with 29 and St. Louis the fewest with eight.

Pitcher/Team	G	GS	CG	W	L	Pct	ERA	SO	W	IP
Doug Drabek, Pgh	33	33	9	22*	6	.786*	2.76	131	56	231
Ramon Martinez, LA	33	33	12*	20	6	.769	2.92	223	67	234
Frank Viola, NY	35	35	7	20	12	.625	2.67	182	60	250*

Houston's Danny Darwin (11–4), starting and relieving, was the ERA leader at 2.21, while San Diego's Bruce Hurst (11–9) and Los Angeles' Mike Morgan (11–15) led in shutouts with four each. The whiff king was New York's David Cone (14–10) with 233.

Cincinnati won the play-offs in six games as Randy Myers had three saves, while Paul O'Neill led the hitters with a .471 mark. Entering the World Series, Oakland was heavily favored, but were swept by the red hot Reds in four straight, making them losers two years out of three. Cincinnati gained a modicum of revenge for their defeat by Oakland in the 1972 Series.

1991

AMERICAN LEAGUE: FROM LAST TO FIRST

Toronto played leapfrog with Boston as the two changed places for the season, and Toronto finished seven games ahead. Although no pitcher won over 16, the Blue Jays had two at 15 and one at the 16 level. Boston's Roger Clemens won the Cy Young although he failed to win 20 games, finishing with an 18–10 mark. Bill Gullickson, Detroit, was the division's only 20-game winner.

The real news was in the Western Division, where Minnesota went from last place to first place, as Scott Erickson won 20 games and longtime Detroit ace Jack Morris added 18. Detroit's Cecil Fielder became the first player since

Jimmy Foxx to lead the league two consecutive seasons in both home runs (tied with Jose Canseco) and RBIs. Oakland slipped to 84–78 as Mark McGwire slumped to .201, but the real fall was a collapse in the pitching, as Bob Welch and Dave Stewart, 49–17 in 1990, slumped to 23–24, sealing the A's doom.

Gullickson had been pitching in the major leagues since 1979 when he appeared in one game in a Montreal uniform. Prior to this season his best year was 1983 when he was 17–12 for Montreal. Gullickson played with Montreal through 1985 and posted a 72–61 mark. He pitched all of 1986 and most of 1987 for Cincinnati and was 15–12 and 10–11 during his two years. He finished in 1987 at 4–2 with the Yankees.

Then Gullickson spent 1988–89 playing baseball in Japan. His first year back he was only 10–14 with Houston. On joining Detroit he won 20 games for the first time as he tied for the league lead in wins and starts (35). He continued pitching for Detroit, won 14 in 1992 and 13 in 1993, then was only 4–5 in 1994 when he retired at season's end. His final career record is 162–138.

This was only Erickson's second season in the majors, as he had pitched in 19 games for Minnesota in 1990 and was 8–4, 2.87, thus showing a lot of promise for the future. That potential materialized in 1991 as Erickson won 20 games and posted a 3.16 ERA. His .714 was the best winning percentage in the league. It looked like Minnesota had found itself a number-one pitcher on whom they could depend for many years.

In 1992 Erickson was a so-so 13–12 with a 3.40 ERA. Then the bottom dropped out the next two years as he was 8–19, 5.19 ERA and 8–11, 5.44 ERA for 1993 and 1994. In 1995 he was 13–10 with Minnesota and Baltimore, as the Twins traded him about one-third through the season. Which is the real Erickson—1990–91 or 1993–95? He carried a 70–64 career record entering the 1996 season and gave Baltimore a 13–12 season. The jury is still out.

The Cy Young went to Clemens, even though he didn't win 20. He led with a 2.62 ERA, 241 strikeouts and 271 innings pitched. Comparing his ERA and performance to the two 20-game winners, it is pretty obvious that he deserved the award. With a couple of breaks Clemens could have been in the charmed circle. This was the sixth straight year in which he won at least 17 games. He would extend it to seven next year before falling on hard times.

For Morris, his 18 wins marked the 11th time in his career that he had won at least 15 games in a season. He would increase that next year when he posted 21 victories. After 1992 it was downhill for Morris, and he retired in early 1995.

An up-and-coming pitcher was Jack McDowell, who won 17 games and led with 15 complete games. More would be heard from him over the next few seasons. McDowell broke in with the White Sox in 1987 and was 3–0 in four games. An elbow injury in 1987 almost ended his career as he was 5–10 and missed the entire 1989 season, but he came back to win 14 in 1990 and then 17 this year.

Mike Moore posted a 17–8 record as he played Jekyll and Hyde for the past three years. He was 19–7 in 1989, 13–15 in 1990 and 17–8 this season. He would break that string when he was 17–12 in 1992.

Mark Langston had his biggest season with a 19–8 record. Through the 1994 season, Langston has compiled a 151–134 record for 11 seasons of pitching, not always with winning clubs. Teammate Chuck Finley posted his second consecutive 18–9 record. Both of these are outstanding achievements, as California was only 44–64 without these two hurlers. With another club, both probably would have won 20 games.

California finished last in the West with an 81–81 record and reliever Bryan Harvey led the league with 46 saves. Chicago had the most complete games at 28, as Jack McDowell (17–10) had over half of them at 15, which led the league and was more than six entire clubs. New York set a major league record with fewest complete games ever, at three.

Pitcher/Team	G	GS	CG	W	L	Pct	ERA	SO	W	IP
Scott Erickson, Mn	32	32	5	20*	8	.714*	3.16	108	71	204
Bill Gullickson, Det	35	35*	4	20*	9	.690	3.90	91	44	226

Clemens was ERA leader (2.62), strikeout king (241) and had the most innings pitched (271). Although Nolan Ryan didn't lead in strikeouts, he got his seventh no-hitter, a major league record.

Minnesota handily defeated Toronto four games to one as Morris won two games and Rick Aguilera saved three. Kirby Puckett was the hitting star with two home runs, six RBIs and a .429 average.

The Series lasted seven games with Morris winning two, including the final 1–0 victory. Aguilera won one and saved two.

NATIONAL LEAGUE: FROM LAST TO FIRST AND ALMOST ALL THE WAY

Atlanta duplicated Minnesota's feat by going from last place to first place in successive seasons. St. Louis almost did the same in the East, as they finished second to Pittsburgh, who won the title for the second consecutive year. Once again they were led by their big three of Andy Van Slyke, Barry Bonds and Bobby Bonilla on the offense, and this time by 20-game winner John Smiley on the mound.

In the West, Tommy Glavine led the spectacular climb to first place with his first of three consecutive 20-win seasons, as the Braves edged out Los Angeles by one game. Lee Smith set a new National League record with 47 saves as he helped put the Cardinals in second place. Although St. Louis had only nine complete games, they weren't last, as that honor was shared by Houston and Cincinnati with seven each. Atlanta led with 18, a new low record for most complete games.

To date, 1991 has been Smiley's biggest year. His 20–8 mark tied him for most wins and also he had the best winning percentage, .714. Smiley played for

Pittsburgh through this year, and then as the club was on an austerity program he was let go and played 1992 with Minnesota, where he had his second-best season at 16–9. The 1993–94 years were downers for Smiley at Cincinnati. He had elbow problems and a 3–9 mark the first year and only 11–10 the next, but in 1995 he came back with a 12–5 record.

Smiley's road hasn't always been an easy one. After a 5–5, 5.76 ERA season in 1987, he righted himself and was 13–11 and 12–8 the next two years. Then came the injury bugaboo: he broke his hand and was 9–10 in 1990. Following this came his career year, and it looked like a bright future, but Pittsburgh didn't want to spend the bucks so he was gone. Heading into 1996, he stands at 102–76 and in a hitters' year he responded with a 13–14, 3.64 ERA season. What does the future hold for this potentially big-winning left-hander?

Glavine has spent his entire career with Atlanta and owned a 124–82 record heading into the 1996 season. Glavine broke in during the 1987 season and was 2–4, 5.58 ERA. The next year was a disaster at 7–17, 4.57 ERA. He seemed to get it all together and was 14–8 in 1989, but then misfortune befell him and he was only 10–12 in 1990, although Atlanta was also last.

Finally came 1991 and Glavine became the premier left-hander in the league. His 20 wins tied for the lead and marked the first of three straight years he would win 20 or more. Glavine led the league with nine complete games (unbelievable) and posted a 2.55 ERA. Over the next three seasons Glavine won 62 games while losing just 25. He might have had five straight 20-plus win seasons except for the strikes in 1994–95.

In 1994 Glavine was 13–6, and if not for some 45 games taken from the schedule, he might have rung up 20 wins. In 1995 he was 16–7 and lost about four starts, thus there was a slight chance he could have made it that season also.

Barring injury Glavine has an excellent chance of 250–275 wins and a shot for the Hall of Fame. He has three 20-win seasons, one Cy Young Award, and assuming he can continue at the pace of 1991–95 with no serious injury, he ought to make it into the Hall. With the manner in which starters are handled today, it becomes very difficult for a pitcher to win 300 games during his career. Glavine pitching another eight seasons and averaging 15 wins would put him in the 250–275 range.

The only pitchers today with a chance at 300 wins are Roger Clemens, Greg Maddux and Dwight Gooden. Two of the three have major handicaps. Clemens has had a history of shoulder troubles and will be 35 during the 1997 season. Gooden has had his drug problems and it is questionable how effective he can be. Only Maddux, who at this point seems unstoppable, looks like a good chance to make it as he will be 31 at the start of the 1997 year.

Speaking of Maddux, he turned in a 15–11 mark with the most starts (37) and innings pitched (263) for a subpar Chicago Cub team. In a couple of seasons he would join the Atlanta Braves, and with Glavine would form the most dynamite duo since Sandy Koufax and Don Drysdale.

Pitcher/Team	G	GS	CG	W	L	Pct	ERA	SO	W	IP
John Smiley, Pgh	32	32	2	20*	8	.714*	3.08	129	44	208
Tommy Glavine, Atl	34	34	9*	20*	11	.645	2.55	192	69	247

Montreal's Dennis Martinez (14–11) pitched a perfect game, led in ERA (2.39), tied for complete games at nine, and led in shutouts with five. The nine complete games marked a low for leading the league. The Mets' David Cone (14–14), who tied the National League single-game record for strikeouts (19) on the final day of the season, led the league with 241.

Houston unveiled a promising player in Jeff Bagwell, who batted .294, had 15 home runs and 82 RBIs. More would be heard from him very shortly.

The Pirates and Braves battled through seven games before the Braves finally won, four games to three. At one juncture they were down three games to two, but successive shutouts by Steve Avery (18–6) and John Smoltz (14–13) put them in the World Series. Avery and Smoltz each won two games, while Alejandero Pena saved three. Glavine lost his two decisions.

The Braves almost made it all the way, as they carried a lead of three games to two to Minnesota, but lost in 11 innings, 4–3, in game six. Then they lost the finale, a 1–0 heartbreaker, in ten innings. However, Atlanta was building a team that would be a dominant force for several years in the league, especially their pitching staff.

1992

AMERICAN LEAGUE: A WINNER
OUTSIDE THE UNITED STATES

Toronto once again won the Eastern Division title with a very potent attack and bolstered their pitching by adding Jack Morris, who won 21 games. They edged out Milwaukee by four games as Robin Yount got his 3,000th hit, and Baltimore by seven, although young Mike Mussina was maturing as a pitcher and posted a fine 18–5 mark. Boston was last with a 73–89 record, but Roger Clemens still won 18 games, with a league-leading 2.41 ERA and five shutouts.

In the West Oakland climbed back into the number-one slot without a 20-game winner, but a big season from Mark McGwire with 42 home runs and 104 RBIs. Minnesota was second, even though they picked up John Smiley (16–9) from Pittsburgh, as Scott Erickson slumped to 13–12. Chicago rode the bat of Frank Thomas (44 doubles, 24 home runs, 108 runs, 115 RBIs, a league-high 122 walks and a .323 average) and the arm of Jack McDowell (20–10) to third place. Kevin Brown won 21 games for a sub-.500 Texas club. George Brett also joined the 3,000-hit club.

Kevin Appier was 15–8 for a 72–90 Kansas City team, and Dave Fleming was 17–10 for last-place Seattle (64–98). Oakland's Dennis Eckersley led all relievers with 51 saves, a 1.91 ERA, and a 7–1 mark to capture the Cy Young award. California had the most complete games at 28 and Oakland the fewest with eight.

Morris had his last big season as he posted 21 wins. This made it three times he had been a 20-game winner, and the 12th time in his career that he had won at least 15 games in a season. Morris had elbow problems in 1993 and was only 7–12. He spent the strike-shortened 1994 season at Cleveland and while he had a winning record, 10–6, his ERA was 5.60. Early in the 1995 campaign, he retired.

McDowell won the first of two successive 20-win seasons as he posted a 20–10 record with a 3.18 ERA and a league-high 13 complete games. McDowell worked 261 innings in his 34 starts. Over the three-year period (1991–93), McDowell won 59 games for the White Sox. After a disappointing 1994 at 10–9, he would spend 1995 with the Yankees. At age 31 entering the 1997 season, McDowell should have several more potentially good years in front of him.

Brown is a paradox in study. Like many other pitchers he has had only one really big or standout season to date. His entire career has been spent with Texas and prior to 1992 he was 35–32, with his most recent season being 9–12. When he posted a 21–11 season with the most innings at 265, he shocked much of the baseball world. Brown followed that with a 15–12 record, but then had a disappointing 7–9 in 1994 and 10–9 in 1995. Heading into 1996 he was 88–73. Was 1992 a fluke, or will Brown have a repeat? Only time will tell.

Boston finished last, but it wasn't Clemens' fault as he posted a 18–11 record with the most shutouts (five) and the best ERA, 2.41. These 18 wins gave Clemens 136 for the past seven seasons. This is another year that a break here or there would have given him 20-plus victories. It is possible that Clemens could have made seven straight 20-plus-win seasons instead of three. After this year, injuries plagued him through 1995 and he had 192 victories entering 1997. Barring injury or a total collapse, Clemens stands a chance at 300 wins. It won't be easy, but if he can stay healthy and get the good support he once had, the dream could come true. We all know it is much harder with today's pitching philosophy to win 300 career games, but it still can be done. Clemens also looks like a solid candidate for the Hall of Fame.

Several other pitchers deserve honorable mention. Juan Guzman looked like a cinch to win 20, but suffered a broken jaw and had to settle for a 16–5 mark. Jamie Navarro posted a 17–11 record for Milwaukee, and Mussina came of age at Baltimore with his 18–5, 2.41 ERA mark. He had the top winning percentage (.783).

Charles Nagy was 17–10 with Cleveland and Mike Moore 17–12 at Oakland. Dave Fleming, pitching for a Seattle team that had the worst record in the league, was 17–10. His teammate Randy Johnson was only 12–14, but led with 141 strikeouts in 210 innings; however, he also walked 144 men. When he gets his walks under control, we will see a change in his record.

Pitcher/Team	G	GS	CG	W	L	Pct	ERA	SO	W	IP
Jack Morris, Tor	34	34	8	21*	6	.778	4.04	132	80	241
Kevin Brown, Tx	35	35	11	21*	11	.656	3.32	173	76	266*
Jack McDowell, Chgo	34	34	13*	20	10	.667	3.18	178	75	261

Morris was the first Toronto pitcher to win 20 games. Toronto would not be denied, as they won in six games with Jose Guzman (16–5) winning two games, while Tom Henke, who had 34 saves during the season, saved three.

Toronto took the Series in six games to become the first non-U.S. team to be world champs. Jimmy Key (13–13) won two games as did Duane Ward, and Henke saved two. Last year's World Series MVP, Jack Morris, lost twice. Toronto batted only .230 in the Series and was outscored 20–17, but still won four of the six games.

NATIONAL LEAGUE: SO CLOSE YET SO FAR

Fay Vincent, baseball commissioner, was forced to resign because the owners really wanted a puppet for commissioner, or one with less authority. They gave as reasons his handling of the George Steinbrenner situation, the Steve Howe suspension, the attempted move of St. Louis and Chicago to the Western Division, and his refusal to deal himself out of the players-owners negotiations.

On the field, Pittsburgh won a third straight division title, with Doug Drabek the leading winner at 15. Their offense was led by Barry Bonds and Andy Van Slyke, as Bobby Bonilla had signed with the Mets for $5.9 million a year. That was topped by the longterm contract of Ryne Sandberg with the Cubs that averaged $7 million per season.

Chicago had the Cy Young winner in Greg Maddux (20–11), who would take four straight titles and become baseball's best pitcher during that time.

In the West, Atlanta repeated as Tommy Glavine again got 20 wins and Terry Pendleton gave them an MVP season. Houston's Jeff Bagwell hit 18 home runs and had 96 RBIs, but real stardom was just around the corner. Los Angeles came up with a rookie find in Eric Karros, who had 20 home runs and 88 RBIs, but they still finished last.

Maddux had broken in with Chicago in 1986, and in his first two seasons he was 8–18 with an ERA around 5.55. Then in 1988 he was 18–8 and had finally arrived as a pitcher. He was 19–12 as Chicago won the division in 1989. The next two seasons he won 15 games each year, even though the Cubs were below .500. He was 75–64 heading into 1992, and that record could have been improved by 15 or 20 wins given better teams around him.

In 1992 Maddux put it all together as he tied for the lead in wins at 20, had a 2.18 ERA and the most innings pitched, 268. This was the first of two straight 20-win seasons, and the first of four consecutive Cy Young Awards, a major league record. Only Steve Carlton and Maddux have won the award four times, and at Maddux's age he has a chance to win it again.

Except for the strike-shortened seasons of 1993–94, Maddux would have four straight 20-win years. Starting with 1992, one wonders how he lost 11 games given his 2.18 ERA. Then one remembers he was pitching for the Cubs. With a better team, he probably would have had 25. However, the next two years bring that point in to bear. In 1993 he was 20–10 with the best ERA (2.36) when he played for Atlanta. Sometimes it happens that the breaks go against you.

Then in 1994 he was 16–6 with a 1.56 ERA. This season was much like Bob Gibson's 1968, when he was 22–9 with a 1.12 ERA. One wonders how they ever lost. Going back to the 1994 season, with 45 games and 9–10 starts off the schedule, we can see that Maddux probably would have won 22–23. In 1995 he almost won 20 in the shortened season as he was 19–2. Things broke right this time.

At age 31 entering 1997, with 165 wins, he has a chance for 300 career wins, again barring injury or total collapse. At this point the latter does not seem probable. Maddux also is an excellent candidate for the Hall of Fame. With Glavine the two form a dynamic duo. Their combined record for three years is 106–37, .741 winning percentage. At that pace, Atlanta will continue to be tough to beat.

Other pitchers who deserve honorable mention include Bob Tewskbury, who was 16–5, with the league's best ERA at 2.16 for St. Louis. Mike Morgan was 16–8, 2.55 ERA for Chicago.

On the downside, Dwight Gooden posted his first losing year, 10–13, and started his downward slide. Teammate Bret Saberhagen, two-time Cy Young winner, had a finger injury and was only 3–5. Another former Cy Young winner, Orel Hershiser, was 10–15 for last-place Los Angeles.

There are several factors that contribute to the decline of the 20-game winner. First is the pitching philosophy. The manager expects his starter to go six or seven innings, then brings in a setup man for one or two innings and then the closer. What happens then is the setup man may blow a lead, causing the starter to lose a victory. Secondly, a pitcher will be removed late in the game when he is pitching well and has a lead. His relief fails, and there goes another chance for a victory.

Lastly, the number of games a pitcher starts has declined. The days of pitchers starting 40 games are gone. Most managers use a five-man rotation instead of four. Thus most starters get 30–32 starts, and a few maybe 35. With the number of starts reduced, the number of no-decisions increases, and the pitcher has to win a very large percentage of the remaining games to qualify for 20 wins.

Tewskbury is an excellent example of this. He made only 32 starts (five-man rotation). He had a great ERA, but 11 no-decisions. His record was great, 16–5, but with 11 no-decisions there went his chances for 20 wins. If he had been on a four-man rotation, he would have had another eight starts. But then the argument is, would he have been as effective. I believe the reader can see that the number of 20-game winners will continue to dwindle as long as we are using the present method of handling starting pitchers.

Lee Smith again was the top reliever with 43, while Philadelphia had the most complete games at 27 and Houston the fewest with five.

Pitcher/Team	G	GS	CG	W	L	Pct	ERA	SO	W	IP
Tommy Glavine, Atl	33	33	7	20*	8	.714*	2.76	129	70	225
Greg Maddux, Chgo	35	35*	9	20*	11	.645	2.18*	199	70	268*

Philadelphia's Terry Mullholland (13–11) had the most complete games with 12. Atlanta's John Smoltz led in strikeouts with 215, one more than David Cone, who in August was traded to Toronto and undoubtedly would have won the title if he had stayed in the league.

Atlanta stormed to a lead of three games to one over Pittsburgh, then lost 7–1 and 13–4 to make it necessary for game seven. Pittsburgh and Doug Drabek carried a 2–0 lead into the bottom of the ninth, when Atlanta erupted for three runs and the title. This extended Pittsburgh's frustration to three years, as each time they won their division but lost in the playoffs. This was their last hurrah, as the team would be a sub-.500 club for the next few seasons.

Smoltz got two wins for Atlanta, giving him four wins in two years, while Glavine lost twice, giving him four defeats for the two playoffs. Meanwhile, Drabek lost three games for Pittsburgh.

In the Series, Atlanta couldn't come back against Toronto, and they lost in six games. It was a pitchers' Series as Atlanta scored 20 runs and Toronto only 17, and four games were decided by one run, all won by Toronto.

—— 1993 ——

AMERICAN LEAGUE: TWO IN
A ROW MAKES A BELIEVER

Many thought Toronto's win was a fluke, so they set out to prove the world wrong. They started by riding the bats of John Olerud (109 runs, 54 doubles, 24 home runs, 107 RBIs, league high .363), Paul Molitor (122 runs, 37 doubles, 22 home runs, 111 RBIs, .332 average) and Joe Carter (92 runs, 33 doubles, 33 home runs, 121 RBIs, .254 average) to take the East Division title. They also had Roberto Alomar and Tony Fernandez as .300 hitters, while Alomar also had 109 runs and Devon White 116.

Toronto didn't have a 20-game winner, but got 19 from Pat Hentgen and 45 saves (league high) from Duane Ward. At various times they had to hold off the challenges of New York, Baltimore and Detroit, who finished in that order.

Baltimore's Mike Mussina (14–6) lost a chance for 20 wins when he was sidelined almost two months with a shoulder separation. Roger Clemens had his first poor season, finishing at 11–14, 4.46 ERA, while going down with a groin injury that kept him out for over a month.

In the West Chicago had an easier time of it as Frank Thomas again put up big numbers (106 runs, 36 doubles, 41 home runs, 128 RBIs, .317 average), while Jack McDowell took the Cy Young award with his 22–10 mark. Alex Fernandez was a big help at 18–9, while Roberto Hernandez saved 38.

McDowell had the best season of his career as he posted a league high of 22 wins and was the only 20-game winner in the league. McDowell led with four shutouts and a 3.37 ERA in 257 innings as he copped the Cy Young award. McDowell slipped to 10–9 in the strike season and then was off to the Yankees for 1995.

Cal Eldred of Milwaukee (69–93 and in last place) had the most starts at 36, most innings with 258 and was 16–16. The scarcity of 20-game winners is reflected by those who came close, but no cigar. Toronto's Hentgen had 19 in just 32 starts. Jimmy Key had his best year in New York at 18–6 with 10 no-decisions. Mussina might have made it but for a shoulder injury. Chicago's Fernandez had 18–9 in 34 starts, Texas' Kenny Rogers was 16–10 in 33 starts, and the aforementioned Appier had an 18–8 with eight no-decisions. California was only 71–91, but Mark Langston was 16–11 and Chuck Finley, 16–14. Both could have won 20 with a better team.

Randy Johnson had his biggest season to date as he fanned 308 men in 255 innings to take his second straight strikeout title. What was even more encouraging was that his control improved, as his walks dropped from 144 to 95 even though he pitched 45 more innings. Johnson was 19–8, 3.24 ERA with seven no-decisions. Seattle was just two games over .500; thus a break here or there would have made Johnson a 20-game winner.

George Brett, Robin Yount and Nolan Ryan, all sure Hall of Famers, retired at the end of the season. California led with 26 complete games while Minnesota had the fewest with five.

Pitcher/Team	G	GS	CG	W	L	Pct	ERA	SO	W	IP
Jack McDowell, Chgo	34	34	10	22*	10	.688	3.37	158	69	257

McDowell led with four shutouts, while Kansas City's Kevin Appier (15–8) had the lowest ERA, 2.56. California's Chuck Finley (16–14) had the most complete games, 13. Hitting was dominant, as only two teams had ERAs below 4.00. Boston was 3.77 and Chicago 3.70. Dave Winfield collected his 3,000th hit.

Devon White had 12 hits while Dave Stewart (12–8) ran his playoff record to 8–0 with two wins. Jose Guzman (14–3) had two wins while Ward had two saves as Toronto won the playoffs from Chicago in six games. Neither McDowell or Fernandez won a game, each losing two.

The World Series was a slugfest as Toronto won in six games, scoring 45 runs, while Philadelphia had 36. Molitor was the leading hitter with 10 runs, 12 hits, and eight RBIs with a .500 average. But it was Joe Carter who hit a two-out three-run homer to turn defeat into victory in game six and give the Blue Jays the title. Without the home run there would have been a game seven, and who knows what might have happened. Ward won one game and saved two more.

NATIONAL LEAGUE: PITCHING RICH VERSUS ROUGH AND TUMBLE WHILE THE LEAGUE EXPANDS

The National League expanded its boundaries to include Florida and Colorado. Baseball was enthusiastically accepted in both states, with Colorado becoming the first National League team to draw 4,000,000 people.

The Philadelphia Phillies were a motley crew of ballplayers who hit their way to the Eastern Division title. The spark plug was center fielder Lenny Dykstra, who finished second in the MVP voting to Barry Bonds. He became the first leadoff batter to lead in at bats, runs, hits and walks in the same season. The Phillies had 16-game winners in Tommy Green (16–4) and Curt Schilling (16–7).

Montreal finished three games back and St. Louis ten back, as the latter was helped by Bob Tewksbury's career-high 17 wins and Lee Smith's 43 saves. They also had big offensive years from Greg Jeffries, Todd Ziele and Mark Whitten; the latter had four home runs and 12 RBIs in a game in September.

Atlanta, which already had the best pitching in the league, improved even further when they signed Greg Maddux, who won 20 games for the second year in a row and his second consecutive Cy Young award. Tommy Glavine led the staff with 22 wins.

John Burkett and Bill Swift gave San Francisco two 20-game winners as they finished with 103 wins, one behind Atlanta's 104. The Giants had big years from MVP Bonds, Matt Williams and Will Clark. Andy Benes won 15 games for last-place San Diego, loser of 101 games. Randy Myers (Chicago) set a new National League record with 53 saves. Philadelphia led with 24 complete games while Florida had the fewest with four.

By now it was becoming second nature to Glavine to win 20 games as he hit his career high with 22, tying Burkett for the league lead, the second time Glavine had led or shared in this category. This marked Glavine's third straight 20-win season and he also tied teammate Maddux for the most starts at 36. Glavine's streak was stopped in 1994, not by the National League hitters, but by the baseball strike.

Maddux grabbed his second of four consecutive Cy Young Awards with his 20-10 mark. This also marked his second straight 20-win season and like his partner, Glavine, only the baseball strikes kept him from winning 20 or more four years in a row. This season he was even more devastating as he had the best ERA (2.36), the most complete games (eight), and the most innings hurled (267). When reviewing his record and the Atlanta team behind him, one wonders how he lost ten games. Glavine, with a 3.20 ERA, lost only six.

At age 28–32, pitchers are supposed to hit their peak. Burkett did so as he was 22–7 to tie Glavine for the most victories. But he didn't stay there; he went in reverse with a 6–8 mark in 1994. But 1993, he was superb. His 22 wins came within one victory of putting them in the hunt for the World Series.

Burkett had pitched winning ball since becoming a regular starter for the Giants in 1990. He was 14–7, 12–11 and 13–9 over the next three seasons. His 1993 year was considered a maturing process as a pitcher. The Giants thought that with the team they had and a pitcher like Burkett they would be contenders for many years and he would give them many more splendid seasons. Like many before him, and undoubtedly there will be after, it didn't happen, as already evidenced by the total collapse in 1994. In 1995 Burkett was 14–14, giving him a career mark of 81–56 through 1995. The question is what Burkett will show for the 1996 season. For Florida he was 6–10, 4.32 ERA and for Texas 5–2, 4.06 ERA.

Swift is a different story. His career has been one of ups and downs, Jekyll and Hyde. While his career mark entering 1995 is a winning record, 78–62, one must remember that much is built on his 1993, 21–8 mark. This season he was simply superb, as he posted a fine 2.62 ERA. Based on his prior history, no one expected the type of year he had.

Swift broke in with Seattle in 1985 and was 6–10. There followed a 2–9 in 1986, the minors in 1987 and then 8–12 in 1988. Thus after three seasons he was 16–31, not much to write home about. For the next three seasons he was basically a relief pitcher and posted a 14–9 record. The Giants acquired him for 1992 and he was 10–4, but he then suffered a shoulder injury that curtailed his year.

Entering 1993, what could the Giants expect? They might see a 2–9 or an 8–12 Swift—the bull pen Swift. Or would they have to contend with an injured pitcher? He performed magnificently and it looked like he was over the hump, but then the bottom fell out in the strike season of 1994 and he was only 8–7; he came back a bit for a 9–3 in 1995. Maybe he is just another pitcher in the long line of those that had one good year and never repeated.

There are a few pitchers we need to mention—some on the bright side and others on the low side. Bob Tewksbury gave St. Louis another fine year at 17–10, and by walking only 20 men made it 40 walks issued in two years covering 447 innings. A couple examples of why 20-game winners are dwindling, although there were four this year: Greene was 16–4 with 10 no-decisions; Schilling was 16–7 with 11 no-decisions.

Avery had 18–6 with 11 no-decisions. He also had a fine 2.94 ERA. Mark Portugal was 18–4, 2.77 ERA for Houston with 11 no-decisions. Pete Harnisch for Houston was 16–9, 2.78 ERA with eight no-decisions. Andy Benes won 15 games for San Diego (61–101). On the dark side, Dwight Gooden had his second straight losing year, 12–15, and a shoulder injury. Bret Saberhagen was 7–7 and had an elbow injury.

The New York Mets (59–103) looked like the Mets of the 1960s and had some frustrating records. Frank Tanana was 7–15 and then got shipped to the Yankees. Pete Schourek was 5–12, 5.96 ERA. But the capper had to be Anthony Young at 1–16; entering 1995, he had a career 9–41 mark.

Pitcher/Team	G	GS	CG	W	L	Pct	ERA	SO	W	IP
Tommy Glavine, Atl	36	36*	4	22*	6	.786	3.20	120	90	239
John Burkett, SF	34	34	2	22*	7	.759	3.65	145	40	232
Bill Swift, SF	34	34	1	21	8	.724	2.82	157	55	233
Greg Maddux, Atl	36	36*	8*	20	10	.667	2.36*	197	52	267*

Houston's Portugal (18–4) had the league's top percentage, .818, while teammate Harnish (16–9) led with four shutouts. The strikeout king was Cincinnati's Jose Rijo (14–9) with 227. The expansion teams each finished sixth as Florida won 64 games and Colorado 67. The Mets were last in the East with 59–103, while San Diego was the basement holder with a 61–101 mark in the West.

Atlanta's hopes for a third straight trip to the Series were dashed as Mitch Williams won two and saved two, although Philadelphia was outscored 33–23. Fred McGriff was the hitting star for Atlanta with 10 hits and a .435 average.

The Series was a real old-fashioned slugfest as Toronto outscored Philadelphia 45–36 in taking four of six games. The turning point was game four, with Toronto up two games to one. Philadelphia was ahead 14–9 when Toronto erupted for six runs in the eighth to win the game, 15–14. Philadelphia won the next day, but instead of being up three games to two, it was just the reverse. Then came game six, when Philadelphia led 6–5 in the bottom of the ninth only to have Joe Carter hit a three-run homer to end it all and make Toronto champion for the second straight season.

Hitting stars were many, but pitching was bad as the Phillies had a 7.57 team ERA, and Williams lost two games.

1994

AMERICAN LEAGUE: THE SEASON
THAT COULD HAVE BEEN

For the second time in 13 years almost a third of the baseball schedule was wiped out by a strike, when the ballplayers walked off the field effective August 12, 1994. No pitcher won 20 games, but several were on course to achieve that goal, some headed for their biggest seasons.

New York won the Eastern Division title as Jimmie Key with 17–4 won the Cy Young Award. Second-place Baltimore had two potential 20-game winners in Mike Mussina (16–5) and Ben McDonald (14–7).

In the West Chicago won as Frank Thomas put up a big year in 113 games (106 runs, 34 doubles, 38 home runs, 101 RBIs and a .353 average). Cleveland was next, just a game off the pace. Kansas City was four back as David Cone (16–5) lost a chance for 20 wins, as did Seattle's Randy Johnson, who also lost a chance for a third straight season with over 300 strikeouts.

In the three-division setup, Texas won the West with a sub-.500 record, but was getting big years from Will Clark and Juan Gonzales. Fans were excited about the upcoming playoffs, even if the team didn't play .500 ball.

Perhaps the biggest loser was Ken Griffey, Jr., who had 41 home runs and was only a few games off the pace set by Roger Maris. Runs were being scored at a tremendous rate, à la 1930. The only team with an ERA below 4.00 was Chicago with 3.96.

New York's Paul O'Neill won the batting crown with a .359 mark, while teammate Wade Boggs had a .342 season to dispel rumors he was over the hill as a high-average hitter. Cal Ripken continued his pursuit of Lou Gehrig's 2,130 consecutive game streak, and assuming baseball resumed in 1995, he would break the record in early September.

Needless to say, there was no World Series.

In strikes there are never winners, only losers. The owners lost fortunes because the games weren't played. The players lost salaries and career stats, which for those with an eye toward the Hall or certain records is extremely important.

The concessionaires and souvenir sellers lost their income and their daily support. To many this is their main livelihood, and with the strike they had to go on welfare or draw unemployment if they couldn't locate other work. They didn't have the bank accounts of the owners or ballplayers. However, the greatest losers were the fans who for over 100 years have supported their teams, through good and bad times. For them to be treated like this was wrong. They got their revenge, as attendance was down over 20 percent in 1995. Hopefully it will come back, but the owners and players alike owe a lot to the fans—the fans don't owe the owners and players.

As a result of the strike, several pitchers lost chances for big seasons. One might argue that it's their own fault, but let's not get into that issue. Jimmy Key of New York was 17–4, a cinch for 20-plus wins. Baltimore had Mussina with 16–5 and McDonald at 14–7, both given good chances of winning 20. Kansas City's David Cone was 16–5, while Randy Johnson was 13–6. In Johnson's situation it also cost him a chance for a second straight 300-strikeout season, the first pitcher since Nolan Ryan to achieve that. He finished with 204 in 172 innings.

NATIONAL LEAGUE: OH, WHAT A SHAME!

Because the owners and players couldn't agree on a fair settlement, baseball fans everywhere were deprived of one of the classic seasons in the history of the game. The league, like the American, had been divided into three divisions. Montreal took first place in the East from Atlanta, who was in the driver's seat for the wild card, a la football.

Cincinnati was a game better than Houston in the Central, while Los Angeles was the only team over .500 in the West. However, here the attention was on rookie Raul Mondesi, who was over .300 and giving the Dodgers a chance to have the rookie of the year three years in a row, following Eric Karros and Mike Piazza, who was putting up another fine season.

Matt Williams was on a pace to tie or break Roger Maris' record of 61 home runs when the strike hit, as he had 43 with 96 RBIs. Teammate Barry Bonds had 37 home runs. Many had superlative seasons. One of the finest was from Jeff Bagwell who had 104 runs, 32 doubles, 39 home runs, 116 RBIs, and a .368 average in 110 games before he broke his wrist for the second straight season. Bagwell was selected the MVP.

San Diego's Tony Gwynn lost his chance to be baseball's first .400 hitter since Ted Williams as he finished at .394. Many other players had fine seasons cut short by the strike, but the real losers were the fans, and those who work at the stadiums for their livelihood.

Gregg Maddux (16–6, 1.56 ERA) won his third straight Cy Young award, the first pitcher to do so, but lost a chance for his third straight 20-win season, while teammate Tom Glavine (13–6) lost a chance for his fourth straight of 20 victories or more. Other hurlers who lost a chance for 20 wins were Ken Hill (16–5) and Danny Jackson (14–6).

While it certainly was a hitter's paradise, there were some fine moments and years for certain hurlers. Only five teams finished below 4.00 ERA, with Atlanta the best at 3.57.

1995

AMERICAN LEAGUE: FINALLY
AGAIN AND FOR THE FIRST TIME

The season wasn't interrupted by a strike, but 18 games were lost as the season was started late due to the use of replacement players in spring training and then the late start for the regulars. When it got started, it proved to be a whale of a season in hitting, pitching and team performances.

For the first time ever a wild card play-off system like that of other major sports was used. The Cleveland Indians, after a 41-year absence, finally made it back to the World Series. The last time they were there they lost in four straight after setting the American League season wins at 111 (remember, that was 154-game schedule).

This season the Indians did win two games in the Series, but lost. During the regular season they won 100 games, losing only 44. Extended to a full season they would have had 111 wins, tying the American League record, but in comparison to the 154-game schedule, they would have to win 117 to make it equal.

Seattle, long the doormat of the West, got into its first play-off, mainly on the pitching of Randy Johnson, known as "The Tall Unit," and the hitting of Edgar Martinez (.356. 29 HR, 113 RBIs), Tino Martinez (.293, 31 HR, 111 RBIs) and Jay Buhner (.262, 40 HR, 120 RBIs). Ken Griffey, Jr. was injured for much of the season and only hit .258 with 17 home runs and 42 RBIs.

Boston was the winner in the East with New York the wild card. Cleveland had easily captured the Central and Seattle won the West in a one game play-off with California. In August, California had an 11-game bulge, but two nine-game losing streaks placed them second. They came back to win their last five games to tie for first, but lost the play-off. Their collapse must go alongside the 1951 Dodgers, the 1964 Phillies and the 1978 Red Sox.

No pitcher won 20 games, but had the season included 162 games, there were seven who potentially might have been there.

Mike Mussina of Baltimore led the league with 19 wins. The 27-year-old Mussina has been with Baltimore since 1991 and has compiled a 71–30, .703 record. The strike has short-circuited Mussina from the 20-win circle each of the past two seasons. In 1993 a shoulder injury forced him to miss over a month, but he was still 14–6, following a 18–5 mark in 1992.

Johnson was an unbelievable 18–2, 2.46 ERA with 294 strikeouts in 215 innings. He too has lost a chance for 20 wins two straight seasons due to strikes, as well as a chance for three consecutive 300-strikeout years. This season he could have won 20, but had ten no-decisions. After an erratic career start, he is now 99–64 and at 32 should have several more strong seasons ahead of him.

David Cone split his year with Toronto and New York and finished at 18–8. This is the second straight season that he has lost a chance for 20 wins because of a baseball strike. Cone will be 33 when the season starts and with 129 career wins, barring injury or a sudden collapse, should win 20 couple more times and break the career 200-win level.

Kenny Rogers of Texas had his biggest season as he was 17–7 with seven no-decisions. At age 31, he seems poised to have some big years for the Rangers. Entering 1996 he was 70–54.

Three pitchers who each won 16 and would have had to win all of their remaining decisions were Tim Wakefield (16–8), Orel Hershiser (16–6) and Charles Nagy (16–6). Wakefield had burst on the scene in 1992 with Pittsburgh and was 8–1, and then won two games in the play-offs. Then the bottom fell out and for the next two years he was of little value. He started off like he was going to win 25 or more as he was 14–1, with a ten-game winning streak. Then he slowed down and finished at 16–8, 2.95 ERA—still very good, especially for someone considered washed up in spring training. He had only been 6–9 during 1993–94. Wakefield will turn 30 late in the 1996 campaign and, barring any relapse, should have some productive years ahead.

Hershiser had spent his entire career with Los Angeles, where he was 134–102. He was coming off a 6–6 season for the Dodgers, but the Indians took a chance on him and he responded with a 16–6 mark. Hershiser seems fully recovered from the shoulder problems of the early 1990s and while he won't blow any hitters away, he will give the team solid, dependable starts. At 38 he still has some pitching in that arm and can help tutor younger members.

Nagy has spent his entire career with Cleveland and entering 1995 was only 41–43, but he seemed to reach his potential as he was 16–6. Nagy won't turn 29 until May of 1996 and as these are supposed to be the prime-cut years for a pitcher, potentially he could give the Indians some big seasons.

Cal Ripken broke Lou Gehrig's consecutive game streak of 2,130 in September. Johnson was easily the Cy Young winner. Let's hope in future years that 162 games can be played and nobody has to review the season on a "what-if," "could have" or "maybe" basis. There are no winners in a baseball dispute, only losers.

NATIONAL LEAGUE: AT LONG LAST, A CHAMPIONSHIP

The Atlanta Braves ran away and hid from the rest of the Eastern Division as they won by 21 games. The Braves had a fine hitting attack led by Fred McGriff (.280, 27 HR, 93 RBIs), Chipper Jones (.265, 23 HR, 86 RBIs), David Justice (.253, 24 HR, 78 RBIs) and Ryan Klesko (.310, 23 HR, 70 RBIs), but it was their pitching that dominated the league.

They were led by four-time Cy Young winner Greg Maddux (19–2, 1.63 ERA), Tommy Glavine (16–7, 3.08 ERA), John Smoltz (12–7, 3.18 ERA) and reliever Mark Wohlers (7–3, 2.09 ERA, 25 saves). Maddux became only the second pitcher to win four Cy Young Awards. Steve Carlton is the other, but Maddux won four years in a row.

Cincinnati had a relatively easy time in the Central, although Houston's chances would have been much better if 1994 MVP Jeff Bagwell hadn't got off to a slow start. He was well below .200 at one point. Then when he got hot, he broke his wrist for the third year in a row. In 114 games Bagwell finished at .290 with 21 home runs and 87 RBIs. The other factor that hurt was that their pitching staff didn't perform up to its expectations.

The only interesting race was in the West where the Dodgers edged Colorado by one game, but they got in as the wild card. Thus in only their third season as a formal franchise, they made the play-offs. Los Angeles did it on a combination of pitching and power. On the mound they had Ramon Martinez (17–7, 3.66 ERA), Hideo Nomo (13–6, 2.54 ERA, 236 strikeouts in 191 innings) and Ismael Valdes (13–11, 3.08 ERA). Nomo was the first Japanese to play in the United States and was rookie of the year as he led in strikeouts.

The Dodgers' hitting attack was led by Mike Piazza (.346, 32 HR, 93 RBIs), Eric Karros (.298, 32 HR, 105 RBIs) and Raul Mondesi (.285, 26 HR,

88 RBIs). Karros, Piazza and Mondesi had each been rookie of the year for 1992–94 respectively. This year would have been even bigger for Piazza, but an injury kept him out for almost one month.

Again the strike intervened, but this time at the start of the season. The labor dispute was not settled until late in March, thus delaying the regulars starting their spring training. The replacement players went home and the regulars had three weeks of training. The season began with 18 games cut from the schedule.

Once again there were no 20-game winners, but given a full season, four might have made the grade.

First for consideration was Maddux, who at 19–2 would have undoubtedly won 20 or more. Even in an abbreviated season he could have won 20, as he had seven no-decisions. This was the second consecutive year he missed 20 games due to a shortened year. Maddux already has won 20 twice, but missing those two seasons could jeopardize his chance of winning 20 or more six times, as only 19 pitchers have done in their careers. Maddux turned 31 during the 1997 season and with 165 victories has a chance to win 300 games. Perhaps he still may have six or more 20-win seasons. If he continues to pitch the way he has in 1992–95 (when he won four straight Cy Young Awards), he probably will make it.

Teammate Glavine also lost a chance at 20 wins, although his case is a little more iffy. He had 16 wins and would have had to win his last four starts or at least four of five. Glavine has three 20-win seasons under his belt and was also 31 entering the 1997 season. With 139 career wins, he seems to have a good chance to hit at least the 250 mark. Prior to the two abbreviated seasons, he had won 62 over the 1991–93 period. For both he and Maddux the answer lies in longevity, durability and consistency. If both can pitch until they are 40 and maintain the quality of their performances then they can both probably reach these goals.

Entering 1995, Pete Schourek was only 23–26. He broke in with the Mets in 1991 and was 16–24 before coming to the Reds and posting a 7–2 mark in 1994. This season he really developed and was 18–7, 3.22 ERA. With a shortened season he lost his chance for a 20-win year. However, at only 27 he should have several more good years ahead of him.

The final pitcher who lost a chance for 20 wins was Ramon Martinez, who finished at 17–7. Martinez has had one 20-win season and this was his second at 17 wins. He will be only 28 when the season begins. Thus, precluding any disaster or accident, Martinez should return to the charmed circle. He entered 1996 with a 91–63 career mark.

One concern is the lack of settlement in the labor dispute between the owners and the players. Potentially another strike could happen, and if it did, irreparable damage to the game could occur. In 1995 attendance was down 17 percent, but increased dramatically in 1996. Interleague play in 1997 should return the fans to the game. However, if there is another major work stoppage, it could drive fans away at an even greater rate than in 1994. Let's hope they all can work out their differences.

1996

AMERICAN LEAGUE: THE YEAR OF THE BOOMING BAT

The 1996 season wasn't very kind to pitchers, especially in the American League. Home runs were hit at a record pace as the teams averaged about 11 runs per game. Detroit set an American League record with a 6.42 ERA, and for almost the first half of the season the ERA was in excess of seven.

The Yankees won the Eastern Division, while Cleveland again took the Central and Texas won its first title ever when it captured the Western crown, leaving Baltimore as the "wild card" team.

While the emphasis certainly was on hitting, there were some pitching bright spots. The Yankees' Andy Pettitte led all pitchers with a 21-8 mark and a 3.87 ERA. This was only Pettitte's second season in the majors and at 24, he should have many promising years in front of him.

Toronto's Pat Hentgen was the league's only other 20-game winner, joining the circle for the first time as he finished at 20-10, 3.22 ERA, winning his 20th on the final day of the season. He won the Cy Young Award (1996). Hentgen won't turn 28 until November, 1996; thus he should just becoming into the prime years of his career. He will enter the 1997 season with a career 67-43 record.

Baltimore's Mike Mussina was a bridesmaid once again as he chalked up 19 wins, just missing joining the charmed circle. Mussina had four chances for his 20th victory, but in those last four starts he could only muster a 0-2 record with two no-decisions. Mussina has been a bridesmaid several times, but never the bride. He has twice won 19, 18 once, 16 and 14. His career mark is 90-41 through 1996. Strikes have twice deprived him of 20-plus-win seasons and this year he fell just a little short.

With 22 players hitting over 30 home runs, led by Mark McGwire's 52, and several teams setting individual home run records, including a new major league record of 257 by Baltimore, it was a tough season for pitchers. However, there were still some noteworthy achievements. Charles Nagy posted a fine 17-5, 3.41 ERA for Cleveland and only ten no-decisions kept him from 20 wins.

Ken Hill of Texas turned in a 16-10, 3.36 ERA season and had nine no-decisions. He keeps coming close, but no cigar. Two of the most frustrating seasons belonged to Boston's Roger Clemens and California's Jim Abbott. Clemens was only 10-13, but had a highly respectable 3.63 ERA and led the league in strikeouts with 257. His ERA compares quite favorably with some of the big winners in the league. Most notably, Mussina, who had a very high 4.81 ERA, but still was 19-11. Teammates Tim Wakefield (14-13, 5.14 ERA) and Tom Gordon (12-9, 5.59 ERA) fared much better.

In late September Clemens tied his own major league record for single-game strikeouts by fanning 20 batters. With some breaks Clemens could have won 20 games. It was just one of those disappointing years.

Abbott's situation was of a different nature as he posted the worst record in baseball at 2-18, 7.48 ERA. However, this is a small hill to climb compared to the one he already had mounted. Remember, Abbott was born without a right hand. He overcame this handicap to make it to the majors and, including this horrible season, has a career 80-100 record.

Pitcher/Team	G	GS	CG	W	L	Pct	ERA	SO	W	IP
Pettitte, NY	35	34	2	21*	8	.724	3.87	162	72	221
Hentgen, Toronto	35	35	10	20	10	.667	3.22	177	94	265*

All in all, it was a satisfying season, especially after a strike-shortened 1994 and a delayed 1995. Let's get back to playing baseball.

NATIONAL LEAGUE: NEW WINNERS AT THE TOP

While baseballs rocketed out of the park at an alarming rate, it wasn't quite the carnage or onslaught as seen in the American League. Perhaps the lack of a DH makes up for that, or perhaps there is a slightly better caliber of pitching in the senior circuit.

Atlanta, with baseball's best pitching staff, won the Eastern title, while St. Louis ended a nine-year hiatus and captured the Central crown and San Diego, with a three-game sweep of Los Angeles on the final weekend, edged them by one game.

Only one pitcher made it to the charmed circle and that was Atlanta's John Smoltz, who won 20 games for the first time. He did it in a big way by posting a 24-8, 2.94 ERA season and led the majors with 276 strikeouts. At one point in the season, it looked like Smoltz might win 30 games—or come very close.

He lost his first decision and then won 14 in a row before hitting a slump and going just 7-7 in his next 14 decisions. However, down the stretch he regrouped and finished with three straight victories to become the winningest pitcher in a single season in Atlanta's history. He easily won the Cy Young Award, which gives the Atlanta team five of the last six Cy Young Winners dating back to 1991.

Greg Maddux, he of the golden arm, didn't win 20, but was only 15-11, despite a fine 2.72 ERA. Two stretches during which he didn't win a game for several weeks eliminated his chances for a 20-plus-win year. Teammate Tommy Glavine also had a very fine ERA at 2.98, but had to settle for a 15-10 season.

Glavine, like Maddux, had the misfortune to be taken out of several close games and see the victory go to a relief hurler. Glavine had 11 no-decisions and Maddux nine for the season, whereas Smoltz had only three.

The pitcher with the best ERA in baseball was Florida's Kevin Brown with a 1.89 and a final 17-11 record. With any decent support he could have won 23-25 games and seriously challenged Smoltz for the Cy Young Award. Another interesting story is St. Louis' Andy Benes, who started 1-7 but won 17 of his final decisions and was the league's second-biggest winner at 18-10.

Benes' younger brother, Alan, posted a 13-10 record in his rookie season to give the duo 31 wins, most by a pair of brothers since the Perrys won 38 for Cleveland in 1974. St. Louis fans are hoping the Beneses will be another set of Dean brothers, but minus the career-ending injuries.

Pitcher/Team	G	GS	CG	W	L	Pct	ERA	SO	W	IP
Smoltz, Atlanta	35	35	6	24	8	.750	2.94	276	55	253

Down three games to one Atlanta came back to defeat St. Louis in seven games. New York then defeated Atlanta in six games after losing the first two.

Appendix A
Ranking of Pitchers by Number of 20-Win Seasons

The first listing below is for those elite nine pitchers who in the 20th century have won 20 or more games in at least seven different seasons. Warren Spahn and Christy Mathewson achieved the goal 13 times, while Walter Johnson made it 12 times. No other pitcher made it in double digits. Although Cy Young won 20 or more 16 times, ten of them were in the 19th century. Thus he is not in this group, but he is in the group with six 20-win seasons since this is a reference for those who had their 20-win seasons in the 20th century.

The pitchers are listed in order by the highest average number of wins per season. I have indicated the number of seasons each pitcher won 20 or more, total wins in those seasons and average wins per year. In parenthesis after each pitcher's name are the years he played in the big leagues. Following his number of average wins per season are indicated the years he achieved the charmed circle. If two pitchers have the same average wins per season, they are listed alphabetically. The same format is followed for all the categories.

Seven or More 20-Win Seasons

Pitcher	Times Achieved	Total Wins	Average Per Season
Pete Alexander (1911–30)	9	241	26.77 (1911, 13–17, 20, 23, 27)
Christy Mathewson (1900–16)	13	347	26.69 (1901, 03–14)
Walter Johnson (1907–27)	12	308	25.67 (1910–19, 24–25)
Lefty Grove (1925–41)	8	192	24 (1927–33, 35)
Eddie Plank (1901–17)	8	187	23.38 (1902–05, 07, 11–12, 15)
Ferguson Jenkins (1965–83)	7	152	21.71 (1967–72, 74)
Bob Lemon (1946–58)	7	151	21.57 (1948–50, 52–54, 56)
Warren Spahn (1942, 46–64)	13	276	21.23 (1947, 49–51, 53–54, 56–61, 63)
Jim Palmer (1965–84)	8	169	21.13 (1970–73, 75–78)

Six-Time Winners

Pitcher	Total Wins	Average Per Season
Joe McGinnity (1899–1908)	162	27 (1901–06)
Cy Young (1890–1911)	161	26.83 (1901–04, 07–08)
Jack Chesbro (1899–1909)	154	25.67 (1901–06)
Mordecai Brown (1903–16)	148	24.67 (1906–11)
Bob Feller (1936–41, 45–56)	144	24 (1939–41, 46–47, 51)
Juan Marichal (1960–75)	140	23.33 (1963–66, 68–69)
Robin Roberts (1947–65)	138	23 (1950–55)
Steve Carlton (1965–88)	137	22.83 (1971–72, 76–77, 80, 82)
Wes Ferrell (1927–41)	136	22.67 (1929–32, 35–36)
Vic Willis (1898–1910)	136	22.67 (1901–02, 06–09)

Five-Time Winners

Pitcher	Total Wins	Average Per Season
Carl Mays (1915–29)	116	23.2 (1917–18, 20–21, 24)
Carl Hubbell (1928–43)	115	23 (1933–37)
Stan Coveleski (1912, 16–28)	113	22.6 (1918–21, 25)
Burleigh Grimes (1916–34)	113	22.6 (1920–21, 23–24, 28)
George Mullin (1902–15)	112	22.4 (1905–07, 09–10)
Jim "Catfish" Hunter (1965–79)	111	22.2 (1971–75)
Gaylord Perry (1962–83)	110	22 (1966, 70, 72, 74, 78)
Tom Seaver (1967–86)	109	21.8 (1969, 71–72, 75, 77)
Early Wynn (1939, 41–44, 46–63)	108	21.6 (1951–52, 54, 56, 59)
Hippo Vaughn (1908, 10–21)	107	21.4 (1914–15, 17–19)
Bob Gibson (1959–1975)	106	21.2 (1965–66, 68–70)

Four-Time Winners

Pitcher	Total Wins	Average Per Season
Ed Walsh (1904–17)	118	29.5 (1907–08, 11–12)
Dizzy Dean (1930, 32–41, 47)	102	25.5 (1933–36)
Hal Newhouser (1939–55)	101	25.25 (1944–46, 48)
Rube Waddell (1897, 99–1910)	97	24.25 (1902–05)
Red Faber (1914–33)	93	23.25 (1915, 20–22)
Lefty Gomez (1930–43)	92	23 (1931–32, 34, 37)
Addie Joss (1902–10)	92	23 (1905–08)
Urban Shocker (1916–28)	91	22.75 (1920–23)
Wilbur Wood (1961–78)	90	22.5 (1971–74)
Wilbur Cooper (1912–26)	89	22.25 (1920–22, 24)
Mike Cuellar (1959, 64–77)	89	22.25 (1969–71, 74)
Deacon Phillippe (1899–1911)	89	22.25 (1901–03, 05)

Pitcher	Total Wins	Average Per Season
Paul Derringer (1931–45)	88	22 (1935, 38–40)
Eppa Rixey (1912–17, 19–33)	88	22 (1916, 22–23, 25)
Dave McNally (1962–75)	87	21.75 (1968–71)
Johnny Sain (1942, 46–55)	85	21.25 (1946–48, 50)
Bob Shawkey (1913–27)	84	21 (1916, 19–20, 22)
Dave Stewart (1978, 81–95)	84	21 (1987–90)
Jack Taylor (1898–1907)	84	21 (1902–04, 06)
Luis Tiant (1964–82)	84	21 (1968, 73–74, 76)
Red Ruffing (1924–42, 45–47)	82	20.5 (1936–39)

Three-Time Winners

Pitcher	Total Wins	Average Per Season
Jack Coombs (1906–18, 20)	80	26.67 (1911–13)
Eddie Cicotte (1905, 08–20)	78	26 (1917, 19–20)
Sandy Koufax (1955–66)	78	26 (1963, 65–66)
Denny McLain (1963–72)	75	25 (1966, 68–69)
George Uhle (1919–34, 36)	75	25 (1922–23, 26)
Claude Hendrix (1911–20)	73	24.33 (1912, 14, 18)
Rube Marquard (1908–25)	73	24.33 (1911–13)
Dazzy Vance (1915, 18, 22–35)	72	24 (1924–25, 28)
Bucky Walters (1934–50)	72	24 (1939–40, 44)
General Crowder (1926–36)	71	23.67 (1928, 32–33)
Russ Ford (1909–15)	69	23 (1910–11, 14)
Ron Guidry (1975–88)	68	22.67 (1978, 83, 85)
Howie Camnitz (1904, 06–15)	67	22.33 ((1909, 11–12)
Larry Cheney (1911–19)	67	22.33 (1912–14)
George Earnshaw (1928–36)	67	22.33 (1929–31)
Noodles Hahn (1899–1906)	67	22.33 (1901–03)
Sam Leever (1898–1910)	67	22.33 (1903, 05–06)
Don Newcombe (1949–51, 54–60)	67	22.33 (1951, 55–56)
Vida Blue (1969 86)	66	22 (1971, 73, 75)
Tommy Bridges (1930–46)	66	22 (1934–36)
Hooks Dauss (1912–26)	66	22 (1915, 19, 23)
Jim Kaat (1959–83)	66	22 (1966, 71, 75)
Roger Clemens (1984–96)	65	21.67 (1986–87, 90)
Mort Cooper (1938–49)	65	21.67 (1942–44)
Harry Coveleski (1907–10, 14–18)	65	21.67 (1914–16)
Bill Dineen (1898–1909)	65	21.67 (1902–04)
Ted Lyons (1923–42, 46)	65	21.67 (1925, 27, 30)
Nick Altrock (1898, 1902–09, 12–19, 24)	64	21.33 (1904–06)
Jesse Haines (1918, 20–37)	64	21.33 (1923, 27–28)
Phil Niekro (1964–87)	64	21.33 (1969, 74, 79)
Frank Owen (1901, 03–09)	64	21.33 (1904–06)
Lon Warneke (1930–43, 45)	64	21.33 (1932, 34–35)
Vean Gregg (1911–18, 25)	63	21 (1911–13)

Three-Time Winners *(continued)*

Pitcher	Total Wins	Average Per Season
Tommy John (1963–74,76–88)	63	21 (1977, 79–80)
Vic Raschi (1946–55)	63	21 (1949–51)
Jesse Tannehill (1894, 97–1911)	63	21 (1902, 04–05)
Pete Donohue (1921–32)	62	20.67 (1923, 25, 26)
Tommy Glavine (1987–96)	62	20.67 (1991–93)
Jack Morris (1977–94)	62	20.67 (1983, 86, 92)
Dennis Leonard (1974–86)	61	20.33 (1977–78, 80)
Bobo Newsom (1929–30, 32, 34–48, 52–53)	61	20.33 (1938–40)
Mel Stottlemyre (1964–74)	61	20.33 (1965, 68–69)
Jack Weimer (1903–09)	60	20 (1903–04, 06)

Two-Time Winners

Pitcher	Total Wins	Average Per Season
Joe Wood (1908–15, 17, 19–20)	57	28.5 (1911–12)
Jim Bagby, Sr. (1912, 16–23)	54	27 (1917, 20)
Tom Seaton (1912–17)	52	26 (1913–14)
Bill Donovan (1898–1912, 15–16, 18)	50	25 (1901, 07)
Togie Pittinger (1900–07)	50	25 (1902, 05)
Whitey Ford (1950, 53–67)	49	24.5 (1961, 63)
Dick Rudolph (1910–11, 13–20, 22–23, 27)	49	24.5 (1914–15)
Don Drysdale (1956–69)	48	24 (1962, 65)
Cy Falkenberg (1903, 05–15, 17)	48	24 (1913–14)
Ed Killian (1903–10)	48	24 (1905, 07)
Jeff Pfeffer (1911, 13–24)	48	24 (1914, 16)
Ed Rommel (1920–32)	48	24 (1922, 25)
Frank Smith (1904–12, 14–15)	48	24 (1907, 09)
Jeff Tesreau (1912–18)	48	24 (1913–14)
Mickey Lolich (1963–79)	47	23.5 (1971–72)
Al Orth (1895–1909)	47	23.5 (1901, 06)
Babe Ruth (1914–21, 30, 33)	47	23.5 (1916–17)
Dizzy Trout (1939–52, 57)	47	23.5 (1943–44)
Dave Ferriss (1945–50)	46	23 (1945–46)
Jack Harper (1899–1906)	46	23 (1901, 04)
Mel Parnell (1947–56)	46	23 (1949, 53)
Jess Barnes (1915–27)	45	22.5 (1919–20)
Waite Hoyt (1918–38)	45	22.5 (1927–28)
Jack Powell (1897–1912)	45	22.5 (1902–03)
Ed Reulbach (1905–17)	45	22.5 (1908, 15)
Fred Toney (1911–13, 15–23)	45	22.5 (1917, 20)
Lefty Williams (1913–20)	45	22.5 (1919–20)

Pitcher	Total Wins	Average Per Season
Chief Bender (1903–17, 25)	44	22 (1910, 13)
Larry Jansen (1947–54, 56)	44	22 (1947, 51)
Sad Sam Jones (1914–35)	44	22 (1921, 23)
Frank Lary (1954–65)	44	22 (1956, 61)
Herb Pennock (1912–17, 19–34)	44	22 (1921, 23)
Jim Perry (1959–75)	44	22 (1969–70)
Jim Scott (1909–17)	44	22 (1913, 15)
George Suggs (1908–15)	44	22 (1910, 14)
Frank Viola (1982–95)	44	22 (1988, 90)
Babe Adams (1906–07, 09–26)	43	21.5 (1911, 13)
Joe H. Coleman (1965–79)	43	21.5 (1971, 73)
Red Donahue (1893, 95–1906)	43	21.5 (1901–02)
Jim Maloney (1960–71)	43	21.5 (1963, 65)
Orval Overall (1905–10, 13)	43	21.5 (1907, 09)
Nolan Ryan (1966, 68–93)	43	21.5 (1973–74)
Bret Saberhagen (1984–95)	43	21.5 (1985, 89)
Hooks Wiltse (1904–15)	43	21.5 (1908–09)
Mike Garcia (1948–61)	42	21 (1951–52)
Mel Harder (1928–47)	42	21 (1934–35)
Tex Hughson (1941–44, 46–49)	42	21 (1942, 46)
Joey Jay (1953–66)	42	21 (1961–62)
Randy Jones (1973–82)	42	21 (1975–76)
Bill Lee (1934–47)	42	21 (1935, 38)
Pat Malone (1928–37)	42	21 (1929–30)
Al Mamaux (1913–24)	42	21 (1915–16)
Erskine Mayer (1912–19)	42	21 (1914–15)
Jack McDowell (1987–96)	42	21 (1992–93)
Rip Sewell (1932, 38–49)	42	21 (1943–44)
Joaquin Andujar (1976–88)	41	20.5 (1984–85)
Johnny Antonelli (1948–61)	41	20.5 (1954, 56)
Lew Burdette (1950–67)	41	20.5 (1958–59)
Jerry Koosman (1967–85)	41	20.5 (1976, 79)
Art Nehf (1915–29)	41	20.5 (1920–21)
Kid Nichols (1890–1901, 04–06)	41	20.5 (1901, 04)
Joe Niekro (1967–88)	41	20.5 (1979–80)
Camilo Pascual (1954–71)	41	20.5 (1962–63)
Howie Pollet (1941–43, 46–56)	41	20.5 (1946, 49)
Dean Chance (1961–71)	40	20 (1964, 67)
Spud Chandler (1937–47)	40	20 (1942, 46)
Ray Kremer (1924–33)	40	20 (1926, 30)
Greg Maddux (1986–96)	40	20 (1992–93)
Andy Messersmith (1968–79)	40	20 (1971, 74)
Claude Osteen (1957, 59–75)	40	20 (1969, 72)
Gene Packard (1912–19)	40	20 (1914–15)
Roy Patterson (1901–07)	40	20 (1901–02)
Bill Pierce (1945, 48–64)	40	20 (1956–57)
Bill Singer (1964–77)	40	20 (1969, 73)

One-Time Winners

Pitcher	Total Wins	Pitcher	Total Wins
Dolf Luque (1914–15, 18–35)	27 (1923)	Bob Purkey (1954–66)	23 (1962)
Bob Welch (1978–94)	27 (1990)	Hal Schumacher (1931–42, 46)	23 (1934)
Doc White (1901–13)	27 (1907)	Ralph Terry (1956–67)	23 (1962)
Joe Bush (1912–28)	26 (1922)	Red Ames (1903–19)	22 (1905)
Bill James (1913–15, 19)	26 (1914)	Ewell Blackwell (1942, 46–55)	22 (1947)
Jack Quinn (1909–15, 18–33)	26 (1914)	John Burkett (1987, 90–96)	22 (1993)
Charlie Root (1923, 26–41)	26 (1927)	Steve Busby (1972–80)	22 (1974)
Larry Benton (1923–35)	25 (1928)	Mike Caldwell (1971–84)	22 (1978)
George McConnell (1909, 12–16)	25 (1915)	Nick Cullop (1913–17, 22)	22 (1915)
Johnny Morrison (1920–30)	25 (1923)	Dave Davenport (1914–19)	22 (1915)
Steve Stone (1971–81)	25 (1980)	Curt Davis (1934–46)	22 (1939)
Ron Bryant (1967, 69–75)	24 (1973)	Richard Dotson (1979–90)	22 (1983)
Tony Cloninger (1961–72)	24 (1965)	Doug Drabek (1986–96)	22 (1990)
Dwight Gooden (1984–94, 96)	24 (1985)	Sammy Ellis (1962, 64–69)	22 (1965)
Clark Griffith (1891–1914)	24 (1901)	Dick Ellsworth (1958, 60–71)	22 (1963)
Bob Groom (1909–18)	24 (1912)	Bob Friend (1951–66)	22 (1958)
LaMarr Hoyt (1979–86)	24 (1983)	Kirby Higbe (1937–43, 46–50)	22 (1941)
Larry Jackson (1955–68)	24 (1964)	Carmen Hill (1915–16, 18–19, 22, 26–30)	22 (1927)
George Pipgras (1923–24, 27–35)	24 (1928)	Thornton Lee (1933–48)	22 (1941)
Schoolboy Rowe (1933–43, 46–49)	24 (1934)	Jim Lonborg (1965–79)	22 (1967)
Jack Sanford (1956–67)	24 (1962)	Mike McCormick (1956–71)	22 (1967)
Bobby Shantz (1949–64)	24 (1952)	Earl Moore (1901–14)	22 (1910)
John Smoltz (1988–96)	24 (1996)	Mike Norris (1975–83)	22 (1980)
Ed Summers (1908–12)	24 (1908)	Bob Porterfield (1948–59)	22 (1953)
Frank Allen (1912–17)	23 (1915)	Bob Rhoads (1902–09)	22 (1906)
Red Barrett (1937–40, 43–49)	23 (1945)	Preacher Roe (1938, 44–54)	22 (1951)
Mike Flanagan (1975–92)	23 (1979)	Nap Rucker (1907–16)	22 (1911)
Bob Harmon (1909–16, 18)	23 (1911)	Reb Russell (1913–19)	22 (1913)
Orel Hershiser (1983–96)	23 (1988)	Henry Schmidt (1903)	22 (1903)
Danny Jackson (1983–96)	23 (1988)	Tully Sparks (1897, 99, 1901–10)	22 (1907)
Ellis Kinder (1946–57)	23 (1949)	Monte Weaver (1931–39)	22 (1932)
Nick Maddox (1907–10)	23 (1908)	Earl Whitehill (1923–39)	22 (1933)
Sal Maglie (1945, 50–58)	23 (1951)	Ed Willet (1906–15)	22 (1909)
George McQuillan (1907–18)	23 (1908)	Earl Wilson (1959–60, 62–70)	22 (1967)
Roscoe Miller (1901–04)	23 (1901)	Clyde Wright (1966–75)	22 (1970)

Pitcher	Total Wins	Pitcher	Total Wins
Whit Wyatt (1929–45)	22 (1941)	Hugh Bedient (1912–15)	20 (1912)
Hank Wyse (1942–47, 50–51)	22 (1945)	Bert Blyleven (1970–92)	20 (1973)
Stan Bahnsen (1966, 68–82)	21 (1972)	Mike Boddicker (1980–93)	20 (1984)
Johnny Beazley (1941–42, 46–49)	21 (1942)	Dave Boswell (1964–71)	20 (1969)
Bill Bernard (1899–1907)	21 (1904)	Harry Brecheen (1940, 43–53)	20 (1948)
Tiny Bonham (1940–49)	21 (1942)	Tom Browning (1984–95)	20 (1985)
Hank Borowy (1942–51)	21 (1945)	Jim Bunning (1955–71)	20 (1957)
Jim Bouton (1962–70, 78)	21 (1963)	Guy Bush (1923–38, 45)	20 (1933)
Ralph Branca (1944–54, 56)	21 (1947)	Ray Caldwell (1910–21)	20 (1920)
Ernie Broglio (1959–66)	21 (1961)	John Candeleria (1975–93)	20 (1977)
Kevin Brown (1986, 88–96)	21 (1992)	Ben Cantwell (1927–37)	20 (1933)
Doc Crandall (1908–16, 18)	21 (1915)	Watty Clark (1924, 27–37)	20 (1932)
Jim Grant (1958–71)	21 (1965)	Andy Coakley (1902–11)	20 (1905)
Ken Holtzman (1965–79)	21 (1973)	Jim Colborn (1969–78)	20 (1973)
Sam Jones (1951–64)	21 (1959)	King Cole (1909–12, 14–15)	20 (1910)
Vern Kennedy (1934–45)	21 (1936)	Ray Collins (1909–15)	20 (1914)
Dickie Kerr (1919–21, 25)	21 (1920)	David Cone (1986–96)	20 (1988)
Ed Lopat (1944–55)	21 (1951)	Murray Dickson (1939–40, 42–43, 46–59)	20 (1951)
Scott Perry (1915–21)	21 (1918)	Larry Dierker (1964–77)	20 (1969)
Andy Pettitte (1995–96)	21 (1996)	Bill Doak (1912–24, 27, 29)	20 (1920)
Elmer Riddle (1939–45, 47–49)	21 (1943)	Pat Dobson (1967–77)	20 (1971)
Dutch Ruether (1917–27)	21 (1922)	Dick Donovan (1950–52, 54–65)	20 (1962)
Slim Sallee (1908–21)	21 (1919)	Al Downing (1961–77)	20 (1971)
Al Schulz (1912–16)	21 (1915)	Jimmy Dygert (1905–10)	20 (1907)
Ferdie Schupp (1913–22)	21 (1917)	Dennis Eckersley (1975–96)	20 (1978)
Bill Sherdel (1918–32)	21 (1928)	Howard Ehmke (1915–17, 19–30)	20 (1923)
Willie Sudhoff (1897–1906)	21 (1903)	Hod Eller (1917–21)	20 (1919)
Don Sutton (1966–88)	21 (1976)	Scott Erickson (1990–96)	20 (1991)
Bill Swift (1985–86, 88–96)	21 (1993)	Carl Erskine (1948–59)	20 (1953)
Dummy Taylor (1900–08)	21 (1904)	Bob Ewing (1902–12)	20 (1905)
John Tudor (1979–90)	21 (1985)	Lou Fette (1937–40, 45)	20 (1937)
Bob Turley (1951, 53–63)	21 (1958)	Ed Figueroa (1974–81)	20 (1978)
Fernando Valenzuela (1980–96)	21 (1986)	Freddie Fitzsimmons (1925–43)	20 (1928)
Bill Voiselle (1942–50)	21 (1944)	Patsy Flaherty (1899–1900, 03–05, 07–11)	20 (1904)
Johnny Allen (1932–44)	20 (1936)	Bob Forsch (1974–89)	20 (1977)
Steve Barber (1960–74)	20 (1963)	Rube Foster (1913–17)	20 (1915)
Gene Bearden (1947–53)	20 (1948)	Chick Fraser (1896–1909)	20 (1901)
		Wayne Garland (1973–81)	20 (1976)
		Ned Garver (1948–61)	20 (1951)

One-Time Winners *(continued)*

Pitcher	Total Wins	Pitcher	Total Wins
Dave Goltz (1972–83)	20 (1977)	Bill Monboquette (1958–68)	20 (1963)
Sam Gray (1924–33)	20 (1928)	Buck O'Brien (1911–13)	20 (1912)
Bob Grim (1954–62)	20 (1954)	Joe Oeschger (1914–25)	20 (1921)
Ross Grimsley (1971–80)	20 (1978)	Claude Passeau (1954–71)	20 (1940)
Mark Gubzica (1984–96)	20 (1988)	Gary Peters (1959–72)	20 (1964)
Bill Gullickson (1979–87, 90–94)	20 (1991)	Fritz Peterson (1966–76)	20 (1970)
Harvey Haddix (1952–63)	20 (1953)	Jack Pfiester (1903–04, 06–11)	20 (1906)
Luke Hamlin (1933–34, 37–42, 44)	20 (1939)	Rick Reuschel (1972–91)	20 (1977)
Billy Hands (1965–75)	20 (1969)	Allie Reynolds (1942–54)	20 (1952)
Pat Hentgen (1991–96)	20 (1996)	Flint Rheem (1924–28, 30–36)	20 (1926)
Ray Herbert (1950–51, 53–66)	20 (1962)	J. R. Richard (1971–80)	20 (1976)
Otto Hess (1902, 04–08, 12–15)	20 (1906)	Ray Sadecki (1960–77)	20 (1964)
Teddy Higuera (1985–94)	20 (1986)	Pete Schneider (1914–19)	20 (1917
Billy Hoeft (1952–66)	20 (1956)	Herb Score (1955–62)	20 (1956)
Tom Hughes (1900–13)	20 (1903)	Mike Scott (1979–91)	20 (1989)
Alex Kellner (1948–59)	20 (1949)	Joe Shaute (1922–34)	20 (1924)
Elmer Knetzer (1909–17)	20 (1914)	Chris Short (1959–73)	20 (1966)
Mike Krukow (1976–89)	20 (1986)	John Smiley (1986–95)	20 (1991)
Vernon Law (1950–51, 54–67)	20 (1960)	Allen Sothoron (1914–15, 17–22, 24–26)	20 (1918)
Lefty Leifield (1905–13, 18–20)	20 (1907)	Paul Splittorff (1970–84)	20 (1973)
Dutch Leonard (1933–36, 38–53)	20 (1939)	Lefty Stewart (1921, 27–35)	20 (1930)
Ramon Martinez (1988–96)	20 (1990)	Rick Sutcliffe (1976, 78–94)	20 (1984)
Sam McDowell (1961–75)	20 (1970)	Sloppy Thurston (1923–27, 30–33)	20 (1924)
Scott McGregor (1976–88)	20 (1980)	Mike Torrez (1967–84)	20 (1975)
Lee Meadows (1915–29)	20 (1926)	Virgil Trucks (1941–43, 45–58)	20 (1953)
Cliff Melton (1937–44)	20 (1937)	Jim Turner (1937–45)	20 (1937)
Jim Merritt (1965–75)	20 (1970)	Rube Walberg (1923–37)	20 (1931)
		Bob Wicker (1901–06)	20 (1903)
		Roger Wolff (1941–47)	20 (1945)
		Irv Young (1905–08, 10–11)	20 (1905)

20-Game Winners
by Category and Total Wins

Category	Number of Pitchers	20-Win Total
Seven or more seasons	9	85
Six seasons	10	60
Five seasons	11	55
Four seasons	21	84
Three seasons	43	129
Two seasons	74	148
One season	204	204
Total	372	765

Appendix B
20-Game Winners Listed Alphabetically

    This section contains all the pitchers in the 20th century who had a least one season of 20 or more victories. The pitcher's career win-loss record, winning percentage, and career ERA are listed. For the reader's convenience, I have included a column indicating how many times each pitcher was in the charmed circle; thus you can readily check that hurler's standing in his group.

	Won	Lost	Percentage	ERA	20-Win Seasons
Babe Adams	194	140	.581	2.76	2
Pete Alexander	373	208	.642	2.56	9
Frank Allen	50	67	.427	2.93	1
Johnny Allen	142	75	.654	3.75	1
Nick Altrock	83	75	.525	2.67	3
Red Ames	183	167	.523	2.63	1
Joaquin Andujar	127	118	.518	3.58	2
Johnny Antonelli	126	110	.534	3.34	2
Jim Bagby, Sr.	127	88	.591	3.11	2
Stan Bahsen	146	149	.495	3.61	1
Steve Barber	121	106	.533	3.36	1
Jess Barnes	152	149	.505	3.21	2
Red Barrett	69	69	.500	3.53	1
Gene Bearden	45	38	.542	3.96	1
Johnny Beazley	31	12	.721	3.01	1
Hugh Bedient	59	53	.527	3.09	1
Chief Bender	212	128	.624	2.46	2
Larry Benton	127	128	.496	4.03	1
Bill Bernhard	116	82	.586	3.04	1
Ewell Blackwell	82	78	.512	3.30	1

	Won	Lost	Percentage	ERA	20-Win Seasons
Vida Blue	209	161	.565	3.26	3
Bert Blyleven	287	250	.534	3.31	1
Mike Boddicker	134	116	.536	3.80	1
Tiny Bonham	103	72	.589	3.06	1
Hank Borowy	108	82	.568	3.51	1
Dave Boswell	68	56	.548	3.52	1
Jim Bouton	62	63	.496	3.58	1
Ralph Branca	88	68	.564	3.79	1
Harry Brecheen	133	92	.591	2.92	1
Tommy Bridges	194	138	.584	3.57	3
Ernie Broglio	77	74	.510	3.75	1
Kevin Brown	105	84	.556	3.51	1
Mordecai Brown	239	130	.648	2.06	6
Tom Browning	123	90	.577	3.94	1
Ron Bryant	57	56	.504	4.02	1
Jim Bunning	224	184	.549	3.27	1
Lew Burdette	203	144	.585	3.66	2
John Burkett	92	68	.575	3.93	1
Steve Busby	70	54	.565	3.72	1
Guy Bush	176	136	.564	3.85	1
Joe Bush	195	183	.516	3.51	1
Mike Caldwell	137	130	.513	3.81	1
Ray Caldwell	133	120	.526	3.22	1
Howie Camnitz	133	106	.556	2.75	3
John Candeleria	177	122	.592	3.33	1
Ben Cantwell	76	108	.413	3.91	1
Steve Carlton	329	244	.574	3.22	6
Dean Chance	128	115	.527	2.92	2
Spud Chandler	109	43	.717	2.84	2
Larry Cheney	116	100	.537	2.70	3
Jack Chesbro	198	132	.600	2.68	6
Eddie Cicotte	208	149	.583	2.38	3
Watty Clark	111	97	.534	3.66	1
Roger Clemens	192	111	.634	3.05	3
Tony Cloninger	113	97	.538	4.07	1
Andy Coakley	58	60	.492	2.36	1
Jim Colborn	83	88	.485	3.80	1

	Won	Lost	Percentage	ERA	20-Win Seasons
King Cole	56	27	.675	3.11	1
Joe H. Coleman	142	135	.513	3.69	2
Ray Collins	84	62	.575	2.51	1
David Cone	135	80	.628	3.16	1
Jack Coombs	158	110	.590	2.78	3
Mort Cooper	128	75	.631	2.96	3
Wilbur Cooper	216	178	.548	2.89	4
Harry Coveleski	81	55	.596	2.39	3
Stan Coveleski	215	142	.602	2.89	5
Doc Crandall	102	62	.622	2.92	1
General Crowder	167	115	.592	4.12	3
Mike Cuellar	185	130	.587	3.14	4
Nick Cullop	57	55	.509	2.73	1
Hooks Dauss	222	182	.550	3.30	3
Dave Davenport	73	83	.468	2.93	1
Curt Davis	158	131	.547	3.42	1
Dizzy Dean	150	83	.644	3.04	4
Paul Derringer	223	212	.513	3.46	4
Murray Dickson	172	181	.487	3.66	1
Larry Dierker	139	123	.531	3.30	1
Bill Dineen	171	179	.489	3.01	3
Bill Doak	169	157	.518	2.98	1
Pat Dobson	122	129	.486	3.54	1
Red Donahue	166	175	.485	3.61	2
Pete Donohue	134	118	.532	3.87	3
Bill Donovan	186	139	.572	2.69	2
Dick Donovan	122	99	.552	3.66	1
Richard Dotson	111	113	.496	4.23	1
Al Downing	123	107	.535	3.22	1
Doug Drabek	137	112	.550	3.43	1
Don Drysdale	209	166	.557	2.95	2
Jimmy Dygert	57	49	.538	2.65	1
George Earnshaw	127	93	.577	4.38	3
Dennis Eckersley	192	165	.538	3.49	1
Howard Ehmke	166	166	.500	3.75	1
Hod Eller	60	40	.600	2.62	1
Sammy Ellis	63	58	.521	4.15	1

	Won	Lost	Percentage	ERA	20-Win Seasons
Dick Ellsworth	115	137	.456	3.71	1
Scott Erickson	83	76	.522	4.23	1
Carl Erskine	122	78	.610	3.99	1
Bob Ewing	124	118	.512	2.49	1
Red Faber	254	213	.544	3.15	4
Cy Falkenberg	130	123	.514	2.68	2
Bob Feller	266	162	.621	3.25	6
Wes Ferrell	193	128	.601	4.04	6
Dave Ferriss	65	30	.684	3.64	2
Lou Fette	41	40	.506	3.15	1
Ed Figueroa	80	67	.544	3.51	1
Freddie Fitzsimmons	217	146	.598	3.51	1
Patsy Flaherty	67	84	.444	3.10	1
Mike Flanagan	155	124	.556	3.88	1
Russ Ford	99	71	.582	2.59	3
Whitey Ford	236	106	.690	2.74	2
Bob Forsch	168	136	.553	3.76	1
Rube Foster	58	34	.630	2.36	1
Chick Fraser	175	212	.452	3.68	1
Bob Friend	197	230	.461	3.58	1
Mike Garcia	142	97	.594	3.26	2
Wayne Garland	55	66	.455	3.89	1
Ned Garver	129	157	.451	3.73	1
Bob Gibson	251	174	.591	2.91	5
Tommy Glavine	139	92	.602	3.45	3
Dave Goltz	113	109	.509	3.69	1
Lefty Gomez	189	102	.649	3.34	4
Dwight Gooden	168	92	.646	3.26	1
Jim Grant	145	119	.549	3.63	1
Sam Gray	111	115	.491	4.18	1
Vean Gregg	92	63	.594	2.70	3
Clark Griffith	237	146	.619	3.31	1
Bob Grim	61	41	.598	3.62	1
Burleigh Grimes	270	212	.560	3.53	5
Ross Grimsley	124	99	.556	3.81	1
Bob Groom	119	150	.442	3.10	1
Lefty Grove	300	141	.680	3.06	8

	Won	Lost	Percentage	ERA	20-Win Seasons
Mark Gubzica	132	135	.494	3.93	1
Ron Guidry	170	91	.651	3.29	3
Bill Gullickson	162	136	.544	3.93	1
Harvey Haddix	136	113	.546	3.63	1
Noodles Hahn	130	93	.583	2.55	3
Jesse Haines	210	158	.571	3.64	3
Luke Hamlin	73	76	.490	3.77	1
Billy Hands	111	110	.502	3.35	1
Mel Harder	223	186	.545	3.80	2
Bob Harmon	107	133	.446	3.33	1
Jack Harper	80	64	.556	3.58	2
Claude Hendrix	144	116	.554	2.65	3
Pat Hentgen	67	43	.609	3.92	1
Ray Herbert	104	107	.493	4.01	1
Orel Hershiser	165	117	.585	3.19	1
Otto Hess	70	90	.438	2.98	1
Kirby Higbe	118	101	.539	3.68	1
Teddy Higuera	94	64	.595	3.61	1
Carmen Hill	49	33	.598	3.44	1
Billy Hoeft	97	101	.490	3.94	1
Ken Holtzman	174	150	.537	3.49	1
LaMarr Hoyt	98	68	.590	3.99	1
Waite Hoyt	237	182	.566	3.59	2
Carl Hubbell	253	154	.622	2.98	5
Tom Hughes	131	175	.428	3.10	1
Tex Hughson	96	54	.640	2.95	2
Jim Hunter	224	166	.574	3.26	5
Danny Jackson	110	122	.474	3.89	1
Larry Jackson	194	183	.515	3.40	1
Bill James	37	21	.638	2.28	1
Larry Jansen	122	89	.578	3.58	2
Joey Jay	99	91	.521	3.77	2
Ferguson Jenkins	284	226	.557	3.34	7
Tommy John	286	224	.561	3.31	3
Walter Johnson	417	279	.599	2.17	12
Randy Jones	100	123	.448	3.42	2
Sad Sam Jones	229	217	.513	3.84	2

	Won	Lost	Percentage	ERA	20-Win Seasons
Sam Jones	102	101	.502	3.59	1
Addie Joss	160	97	.623	1.89	4
Jim Kaat	283	237	.544	3.45	3
Alex Kellner	101	112	.474	4.41	1
Vern Kennedy	104	132	.441	4.68	1
Dickie Kerr	63	34	.609	3.83	1
Ed Killian	102	78	.567	2.38	2
Ellis Kinder	102	71	.590	3.43	1
Elmer Knetzer	69	69	.500	3.15	1
Jerry Koosman	222	209	.515	3.36	2
Sandy Koufax	165	87	.655	2.76	3
Ray Kremer	143	85	.627	3.76	2
Mike Krukow	124	117	.515	3.90	1
Frank Lary	128	116	.525	3.49	2
Vernon Law	162	147	.524	3.76	1
Bill Lee	169	157	.518	3.54	2
Thornton Lee	117	124	.485	3.56	1
Sam Leever	195	100	.661	2.47	3
Lefty Leifield	124	97	.561	2.47	1
Bob Lemon	207	128	.618	3.23	7
Dennis Leonard	144	108	.576	3.69	3
Dutch Leonard	191	181	.513	3.25	1
Mickey Lolich	217	191	.532	3.44	2
Jim Lonborg	157	137	.534	3.86	1
Ed Lopat	166	112	.597	3.21	1
Dolf Luque	194	179	.520	3.24	1
Ted Lyons	260	230	.531	3.67	3
George McConnell	41	51	.446	2.60	1
Mike McCormick	134	128	.511	3.73	1
Jack McDowell	119	77	.607	3.78	2
Sam McDowell	141	134	.513	3.17	1
Joe McGinnity	246	142	.634	2.66	5
Scott McGregor	138	108	.561	3.99	1
Denny McLain	131	91	.590	3.39	3
Dave McNally	184	119	.607	3.24	4
George McQuillan	85	89	.489	2.38	1

	Won	Lost	Percentage	ERA	20-Win Seasons
Nick Maddox	43	20	.683	2.23	1
Greg Maddux	165	104	.613	2.88	2
Sal Maglie	119	62	.657	3.15	1
Pat Malone	134	92	.593	3.74	2
Jim Maloney	134	84	.615	3.19	2
Al Mamaux	76	67	.531	2.89	2
Juan Marichal	243	142	.631	2.89	6
Rube Marquard	201	177	.532	3.07	3
Ramon Martinez	106	69	.606	3.46	1
Christy Mathewson	373	187	.660	2.13	13
Erskine Mayer	91	70	.565	2.96	2
Carl Mays	207	126	.622	2.92	5
Lee Meadows	188	180	.511	3.38	1
Cliff Melton	86	80	.518	3.42	1
Jim Merritt	81	86	.485	3.65	1
Andy Messersmith	130	99	.568	2.86	2
Roscoe Miller	39	45	.464	3.45	1
Bill Monboquette	114	112	.504	3.69	1
Earl Moore	162	154	.513	2.78	1
Jack Morris	254	186	.577	3.90	3
Johnny Morrison	103	80	.563	3.64	1
George Mullin	228	196	.538	2.82	5
Art Nehf	184	120	.605	3.20	2
Don Newcombe	149	90	.623	3.56	3
Hal Newhouser	207	150	.580	3.06	4
Bobo Newsom	211	222	.487	3.98	3
Kid Nichols	362	207	.636	2.95	2
Joe Niekro	221	204	.520	3.59	2
Phil Niekro	318	274	.537	3.35	3
Mike Norris	57	59	.491	3.91	1
Buck O'Brien	29	25	.537	2.63	1
Joe Oeschger	82	116	.414	3.81	1
Al Orth	204	189	.519	3.37	2
Claude Osteen	196	195	.501	3.30	2
Orval Overall	108	71	.603	2.24	2
Frank Owen	82	67	.550	2.55	3
Gene Packard	85	69	.552	3.01	2

	Won	Lost	Percentage	ERA	20-Win Seasons
Jim Palmer	268	152	.638	2.86	8
Mel Parnell	123	75	.621	3.50	2
Camilo Pascual	174	170	.506	3.63	2
Claude Passeau	162	150	.519	3.32	1
Roy Patterson	81	73	.526	2.75	1
Herb Pennock	240	162	.597	3.60	2
Gaylord Perry	314	265	.542	3.10	5
Jim Perry	215	174	.553	3.44	2
Scott Perry	40	68	.370	3.07	1
Gary Peters	124	103	.546	3.25	1
Fritz Peterson	133	131	.504	3.30	1
Andy Pettitte	33	17	.640	4.00	1
Jeff Pfeffer	158	112	.585	2.77	2
Jack Pfiester	71	44	.617	2.04	1
Deacon Phillippe	188	109	.633	2.58	3
Billy Pierce	211	169	.555	3.27	2
George Pipgras	102	73	.583	4.09	1
Togie Pittinger	115	112	.507	3.10	2
Eddie Plank	326	193	.628	2.35	8
Howie Pollet	131	116	.530	3.51	2
Bob Porterfield	87	97	.473	3.79	1
Jack Powell	245	253	.492	2.97	2
Bob Purkey	129	115	.529	3.79	1
Jack Quinn	247	218	.531	3.29	1
Vic Raschi	132	66	.667	3.72	3
Ed Reulbach	182	106	.632	2.28	2
Rick Reuschel	214	191	.528	3.37	1
Allie Reynolds	182	107	.630	3.30	1
Flint Rheem	105	97	.520	4.20	1
Bob Rhoads	97	82	.542	2.61	1
J. R. Richard	107	71	.601	3.15	1
Elmer Riddle	65	52	.556	3.40	1
Eppa Rixey	266	251	.515	3.15	4
Robin Roberts	286	245	.539	3.40	6
Preacher Roe	127	84	.602	3.43	1
Eddie Rommel	171	119	.590	3.54	2
Charlie Root	201	160	.557	3.59	1

	Won	Lost	Percentage	ERA	20-Win Seasons
Schoolboy Rowe	158	101	.610	3.88	1
Nap Rucker	134	134	.500	2.42	1
Dick Rudolph	122	108	.530	2.66	2
Dutch Ruether	137	95	.591	3.50	1
Red Ruffing	273	225	.548	3.80	4
Reb Russell	81	59	.579	2.34	1
Babe Ruth	94	46	.671	2.28	2
Nolan Ryan	324	292	.526	3.19	2
Bret Saberhagen	141	100	.585	3.26	2
Ray Sadecki	135	131	.508	3.78	1
Johnny Sain	139	116	.545	3.49	4
Slim Sallee	174	143	.549	2.56	1
Jack Sanford	137	101	.576	3.69	1
Henry Schmidt	22	13	.629	3.83	1
Pete Schneider	59	86	.407	2.66	1
Al Schulz	47	62	.431	3.32	1
Hal Schumacher	158	121	.566	3.36	1
Ferdie Schupp	61	39	.610	3.32	1
Herb Score	55	46	.545	3.36	1
Jim Scott	107	113	.486	2.30	2
Mike Scott	124	108	.534	3.54	1
Tom Seaton	93	65	.589	3.14	2
Tom Seaver	311	205	.603	2.86	5
Rip Sewell	143	97	.596	3.48	2
Bobby Shantz	119	99	.546	3.38	1
Joe Shaute	99	109	.476	4.15	1
Bob Shawkey	196	150	.566	3.09	4
Bill Sherdel	165	146	.531	3.72	1
Urban Shocker	187	117	.615	3.15	4
Chris Short	135	132	.506	3.43	1
Bill Singer	118	127	.482	3.39	2
John Smiley	115	90	.561	3.67	1
Frank Smith	139	111	.556	2.58	2
John Smoltz	114	90	.559	3.40	1
Allen Sothoron	91	100	.476	3.31	1
Warren Spahn	363	245	.597	3.08	13
Tully Sparks	121	137	.469	2.79	1

	Won	Lost	Percentage	ERA	20-Win Seasons
Paul Splittorff	166	143	.537	3.81	1
Dave Stewart	168	129	.566	3.95	4
Lefty Stewart	101	98	.508	4.19	1
Steve Stone	107	93	.535	3.96	1
Mel Stottlemyre	164	139	.541	2.97	3
Willie Sudhoff	103	135	.433	3.57	1
George Suggs	99	91	.521	3.11	2
Ed Summers	68	45	.602	2.42	1
Rick Sutcliffe	117	92	.560	3.83	1
Don Sutton	324	256	.559	3.26	1
Bill Swift	79	63	.556	3.65	1
Jesse Tannenhill	197	116	.629	2.79	3
Dummy Taylor	117	106	.525	2.75	1
Jack Taylor	152	139	.522	2.67	4
Ralph Terry	107	99	.519	3.62	1
Jeff Tesreau	115	72	.615	2.43	2
Sloppy Thurston	89	86	.508	4.24	1
Luis Tiant	229	172	.571	3.30	4
Fred Toney	139	102	.577	2.69	2
Mike Torrez	185	160	.536	3.96	1
Dizzy Trout	170	161	.514	3.23	2
Virgil Trucks	177	135	.567	3.38	1
John Tudor	105	68	.607	3.19	1
Bob Turley	101	85	.543	3.65	1
Jim Turner	69	60	.535	3.22	1
George Uhle	200	166	.546	3.99	3
Fernando Valenzuela	171	141	.548	3.54	1
Dazzy Vance	197	140	.585	3.24	3
Hippo Vaughn	178	137	.565	2.48	5
Frank Viola	176	150	.540	3.72	2
Bill Voiselle	74	84	.468	3.83	1
Rube Waddell	193	143	.564	2.16	4
Rube Walberg	155	141	.514	4.16	1
Ed Walsh	195	126	.607	1.82	4
Bucky Walters	198	160	.553	3.30	3
Lon Warneke	192	121	.613	3.18	3
Monte Weaver	71	50	.587	4.36	1

	Won	Lost	Percentage	ERA	20-Win Seasons
Jack Weimer	97	69	.584	2.23	3
Bob Welch	211	146	.591	3.47	1
Doc White	189	156	.548	2.39	1
Earl Whitehill	218	185	.541	4.36	1
Bob Wicker	64	52	.552	2.73	1
Ed Willett	102	99	.507	3.08	1
Lefty Williams	82	48	.631	3.13	2
Vic Willis	247	204	.548	2.63	5
Earl Wilson	121	109	.526	3.69	1
Hooks Wiltse	139	90	.607	2.47	2
Roger Wolff	52	69	.430	3.41	1
Joe Wood	116	57	.671	2.03	2
Wilbur Wood	164	156	.512	3.24	4
Clyde Wright	100	111	.474	3.50	1
Whit Wyatt	106	95	.527	3.79	1
Early Wynn	300	244	.551	3.54	5
Hank Wyse	79	70	.530	3.52	1
Cy Young	511	315	.619	2.63	6
Irv Young	63	95	.399	3.11	1

Appendix C
Team-by-Team Analysis of 20-Game Winners in the 20th Century

American League

To complete this study, I did an analysis of each team and the number of 20-game winners who played for each franchise. The history of some of the teams gets somewhat complicated, but I have tried to sort out the proper genealogy for each club.

The Philadelphia Athletics played in the American League from 1901 to 1954 and then were transplanted to Kansas City as the Athletics, where they remained through the 1967 season. At that time they moved to Oakland and have been there ever since.

Meanwhile, Kansas City did not have a team in 1968, but fielded one in 1969. They became known as the Royals and are still in existence.

The St. Louis Browns played from 1901 to 1953, then transferred to Baltimore for the start of the 1954 season and have played there ever since under the name of the Baltimore Orioles.

The Washington Senators were in the American League from 1901 to 1960, when the franchise was moved to Minneapolis as the Minnesota Twins. However, another franchise under the name of the Washington Senators played ball in D.C. from 1961 through 1971; therefore, we have considered this as one entity for our purposes. Since the 1972 season, they have played in Dallas as the Texas Rangers.

The last franchise that has a different history involved two teams. Seattle opened with a ball club in 1969 that lasted only one season; they were moved to Milwaukee the next year. This was to make up for the loss of the Braves in the National League that had moved to Atlanta. The franchise in Milwaukee became the Brewers.

Seattle had to wait another seven years for the next expansion. They became the Seattle Mariners in 1977 and have remained so through the current season.

A sidelight to the analysis; when we review Washington, they have had 21 20-game winners for 71 seasons, but on removing Walter Johnson they had only nine as he accounted for 12 during his career. No other team had a single pitcher make such an impact on a franchise's longterm statistics.

I have ranked each team in order by the average of 20-game winners per season. I have listed the years each team played, the number of seasons, the total of 20-game winners and the average per season for 20-game winners.

Franchise	Seasons	20-Game Winners	Average Per Season
Philadelphia (1901–54)	54	35	.65
Cleveland (1901–96)	96	57	.59
New York (1901–96)	96	56	.58
Baltimore (1954–96)	43	23	.53
Chicago (1901–96)	96	51	.53
Oakland (1968–96)	29	14	.48
Detroit (1901–96)	96	44	.46
Boston (1901–96)	96	44	.46
Minnesota (1961–96)	36	13	.36
Kansas City Royals (1969–96)	28	8	.29
Washington (1901–71)	71	21	.30
St. Louis (1901–53)	53	13	.25
California (1961–96)	36	6	.17
Milwaukee (1970–96)	27	3	.11
Toronto (1977–96)	20	2	.10
Texas (1972–96)	25	2	.08
Seattle (1969, 1977–96)	21	0	.00
Kansas City A's (1955–67)	13	0	.00

National League

The National League genealogy of teams is not as complicated as the American as only one franchise made two moves. The Boston Braves played in Boston through 1952 and then were the Milwaukee Braves through 1965. In 1966 the franchise moved to Atlanta and has been there as the Braves since that date.

The New York Giants played in the Big Apple through 1957. In 1958 they moved to the West Coast and became the San Francisco Giants.

The Giants' arch rival, the Brooklyn Dodgers, played in Flatbush through 1957, then the following year moved to the West Coast and became known as the Los Angeles Dodgers.

All other franchises have either been in place since 1901 or when established during expansion, have never moved.

Nine of the 12 20-game winners in Milwaukee were achieved by one pitcher, Warren Spahn.

Franchise	Seasons	20-Game Winners	Average Per Season
Milwaukee Braves (1953–65)	13	12	.92
New York Giants (1901–57)	57	47	.81
Chicago (1901–96)	96	51	.53
Pittsburgh (1901–96)	96	43	.45
Brooklyn Dodgers (1901–57)	57	24	.42
Cincinnati (1901–96)	96	38	.40
St. Louis (1901–96)	96	37	.39
Boston Braves (1901–52)	52	20	.39
Los Angeles Dodgers (1958–96)	39	14	.38
San Francisco Giants (1958–96)	39	14	.38
Philadelphia (1901–96)	96	28	.29
Atlanta Braves (1966–96)	31	8	.26
New York Mets (1962–96)	35	8	.23
Houston Astros (1962–96)	35	5	.14
San Diego (1969–96)	28	3	.11
Montreal (1969–96)	28	1	.04
Colorado (1993–96)	4	0	.00
Florida (1993–96)	4	0	.00

Federal League

The Federal League operated for only two seasons, 1914 and 1915. After the 1915 season Judge Kenesaw M. Landis was able to get a peace agreement among all owners and the Federal League was disbanded after just two years in existence.

Seven cities domiciled a team for two years, while Indianapolis and Newark split a franchise for the 1914–15 seasons. There were 17 20-game winners in the two years and because there were only two years, I will just list the number of 20-game winners by team.

Team	Number of 20-Game Winners
Kansas City	3
St. Louis	3
Baltimore	2
Buffalo	2
Chicago	2
Pittsburgh	2
Brooklyn	1
Indianapolis	1
Newark	1

Index